Social Studies for Our Times

Social Studies for Our Times

Richard E. Gross
Rosemary Messick
June R. Chapin
Jack Sutherland

John Wiley & Sons
New York / Santa Barbara / Chichester / Brisbane / Toronto

Library of Congress Cataloging in Publication Data
Main entry under title:

Social studies for our times.

  Includes index.
  1. Social sciences—Study and teaching (Elementary)—United States. 2. Social sciences—Study and teaching (Secondary)—United States. 3. Civics—Study and teaching (Elementary)—United States. 4. Civics—Study and teaching (Secondary)—United States.
I. Gross, Richard E.
H62.S7247184   300'.7   78-2733
ISBN 0-471-02340-X

Printed in the United States of America

10 9 8 7 6 5 4 3 2 1

Contents

Preface

We enter an era when the public as well as our own students have lost patience with social education programs that are not delivering what they promised. While authorities in the field can justly point to causal factors far beyond our classrooms, in the years ahead we can expect increasing demands for proof of both the efficacy and the timeliness of our instruction. Indeed, these are difficult times for teachers. Already we have more responsibilities than can be met satisfactorily. Now, however, lay and parental groups may seek major goals in new directions such as legal and/or ethical studies. A renewed concern for citizenship education also arises. Within the same neighborhood, some parents may desire the implementation of a back-to-basics philosophy in the schools while other parents favor an open education or, possibly, classrooms featuring highly individualized instruction. In addition, other new trends such as multicultural education, moral education, and career education further confuse teachers as to what approaches and content are most appropriate for their students. There seems only to be agreement that the social education program of almost every school should be improved.

We want to help beginners as well as experienced teachers to select vital subject matter, to offer practical advice on organization and instructional techniques, and to contribute to an understanding of current practices and tendencies. In doing this, we draw on a considerable variety of personal experiences at different levels of education. We are also grateful to the many teachers, colleagues, and former students for the insights they have given. In particular, we thank Emily Girault for her aid in conceptualizing this volume as well as for the chapter on the Family.

The social studies seek individual and social efficacy. Drawing heavily on the social sciences our curricular aim is to attain a reciprocal balance between essential knowledge and wisdom, prime skills and competencies, and worthy attitudes and values. We have responded to the challenge of mounting and implementing such a sociocivic education. We trust that those reading and using this book will find here key ideas, guidelines, and processes that will enable our colleagues—young and old—to evolve and successfully offer a meritorious and critically needed *Social Studies for Our Times*.

Richard E. Gross
Rosemary Messick
June R. Chapin
Jack Sutherland

Social Studies for Our Times

SECTION 1

The Challenge: Social Studies Education

An overview of the social studies is presented in this section. In Chapter 1 the justification for the social studies as a vital part of the school curriculum is explored. Ways of perceiving the social studies are elaborated in Chapter 2. Chapter 3 discusses the processes and questions involved in organizing a social studies program. The curriculum planning cycle is completed in Chapter 4 with a presentation of the possibilities and constraints of evaluating programs and student progress in social studies.

What will his future be like?

CHAPTER 1

The Place and Importance of Social Education

Introduction: Our Credo

The social studies should provide a fundamental core of learnings for all children and youth throughout their years of elementary and secondary schooling. Indeed, the social studies are central in the proper general education of our young people, focusing as it does on humankind, on our institutions, and our relationships with nature and with one another.

For the new society established on the American continent 200 years ago, education became a prime need—particularly sociocivic education. Thomas Jefferson echoed the spirit of the times, advising that if the people were not able to understand and direct our social system and its government, the remedy was not to take the power from the free citizenry but "to inform them by education" for, as he said, "I know no safe depository for the powers of society but the people themselves." If we consider the three traditional roles of education that have been common to the foundation of public schools—literacy, moral and character formation, and citizenship—the social studies make prime contributions toward each goal and are central in two. The social studies are basic in social education, in preparing functioning citizens with requisite knowledge, skills, and attitudes that enable each to grow personally in living well with others, and in contributing to the ongoing culture.

The broad context of social studies is presented in this section. Chapter 1 defines the place and importance of social education. Chapter 2 presents the various curricular and instructional models around which social studies may be organized. Chapter 3 elaborates how to organize a social studies program. Chapter 4 carries the program planning process full cycle to consider how evaluation may be conducted in the social studies.

The Evolution of the Social Studies

In this, our Bicentennial era, the demands for a program of sociocivic education that helps youngsters truly learn what it means to be an American citizen in the modern world are far more imperative than when the concept of the social studies was launched about 75 years ago. The term "social studies" originally tended to encompass topical studies related to understanding and living in society that were not parts of the usual history, geography, or political economy offerings. Unfortunately around 1900, as is still true in many foreign countries, the social studies were often designated as subjects for the non-college-bound pupils. Gradually, however, the import of the emerging field came to be understood by many educators — such as John Dewey, W. H. Kilpatrick, and Harold Rugg. Additionally, academicians — such as the historians Charles Beard and J. H. Robinson — came to recognize the potential of centering multidisciplinary courses, units, and lessons in social issues that cut across subject matter boundaries and therefore enabled the teacher to draw on several relevant disciplines. Textbooks and course guides began to reflect these ideas, and the social studies were on their way.

The NEA Commission on the Reorganization of Secondary Education made a significant contribution toward furthering the social studies through its 1918 report. Subsequently, such true social studies offerings as Community Civics and Problems of Democracy became increasingly common. Many secondary school teachers naturally continued to offer separate disciplinary-centered courses but these became increasingly enriched through the use of a broad field approach where, for example, a history course included more important matter from areas such as geography and economics. Meanwhile, at the elementary school level, curriculum planners, textbook publishers, and progressively oriented teachers began to design programs and units focusing on basic human activities or key social processes such as the search for security, the evolution of transportation and communication, and studies of the family in different cultures and of other social institutions. These frequently featured a relatively contemporary emphasis and these units often included elements outside of the social studies, such as music and art. Gradually, such units began to replace traditional compartmentalized history and geography offerings in numerous forward-looking schools. Such programs went well beyond the frequently cited definition of the social studies offered in the 1930s by Edgar Wesley, one of the founders of the field, as "the social sciences simplified for pedagogical purposes."

The concept of the social studies fit well with the ideas and practices of progressive education. But, unfortunately, many teachers never became convinced of the importance of the field. Many others were unprepared to move from conventional, subject-centered courses to the newer topical or issue-oriented offerings. Numerous teachers had little or no background in the contributing social sciences and often parents and pressure groups came to react against having children explore problem areas. They seemed to prefer the traditional courses they themselves had once studied. Subsequently the agonies of the Depression years and then World War II greatly limited educational innovation — although both cataclysms underscored the need for social studies understandings from propaganda analysis and poverty units to studies of displaced persons and of war and peace. Immediately thereafter, the reactionary years of the McCarthy era were anything but conducive to the development of the social studies. In spite of the emerging demands growing from the impact on American life of the Korean and Vietnamese wars, and increasing, worldwide problems and disaffection, the elementary school particularly seemed to want to shy away from these harsh realities.

Following the appearance of the Soviet Sputnik, substantial federal funds became available for curriculum development. Eventually over 50 social studies projects were launched in the 1960s to enable the schools to offer more fitting programs. *Our Working World, Man – A Course of Study,* the Taba program, Social Science Lab Units, and numerous other offerings became available for the elementary teacher.

The foregoing programs in recent years have been part of what is labeled the "New Social Studies." These were highly publicized in the last decade in thousands of teacher institutes as leaders once again attempted to move social studies instruction from the mere imparting of subject matter. The New Social Studies aims to lead boys and girls to find excitement and motivation in the processes of social education via exploration, inquiry, and discovery. They are also concerned with using timely content that students perceive as being relevant; but the major emphasis is on helping pupils develop the competencies and attitudes essential for citizens in a free society – citizens who will wish and be able to maintain and extend the fundamental values of our way of life. In spite of this, however, today thousands of schools and teachers still continue to overlook the prime potential of the social studies in enabling children and youth to learn how to live in society.

Toward a Viable Program of Social Education

We should not be arguing over how much geography or history to offer, or where to place economics or government studies, or about the articulation between sociology and anthropology, nor be trying to turn out little psychologists or social scientists. These never-resolved issues have plagued the program since its inception. No curriculum, even one totally sociocivic oriented, could possibly encompass all that just the social sciences have to offer. Yet the social studies demand much more.

While we need to be concerned about the fundamental ideas and concepts accruing from history and the social sciences, we recognize two other elements central in enabling social studies education to attain its ends.

First, using the term "society" in a broad – and even international – sense, we have to identify clearly what it is about our society that needs to be understood, cherished, passed on, and extended or enlarged. Then we should examine how these elements may conflict, be impaired, are malfunctioning, or need reshaping or revitalization. We thus arrive at principles and questions about them, value-problems, and personal and social issues. At this point we are in an improved position to select the vital core of the social studies. But we are still not ready to choose a scope and sequence of learnings.

Second, we need to identify the competencies, the skills, and the subskills that will enable the citizen in a modern, democratic society to function as he or she must if the social system is to flourish and if the individual is to live fruitfully and not just exist. We will now have better identified the "should" and the "how" elements so often neglected in the past, along with the hitherto predominant "what" aspects of social education.

At this point we are then ready to try and balance social imperatives, individual needs and competences, and the ideas, procedures, and skills accruing from the academic disciplines into a social education program.

Such a program can be thematic, topical, or problem centered. It can be organized in a great variety of ways on a daily, weekly, or term basis. It will employ a large variety of strategies and related media and sources. Being broadfield, it will naturally bridge across into other curricular areas. The social studies —learning to live in society—then naturally become the center of social education in the school.

This is not something accomplished two or three hours a week, something to attend to when there is time, current events, or social vignettes to fill in when the "basics" can be put aside for a while or mere disjointed activites to embellish the school day. No, social education is the vital *raison d'être* for schooling, and above all it should be the heart of elementary education in a free society.

In the elementary school the roots are set; personalities are stabilized; it is natural to cooperate with families, neighborhood groups, and institutions; the eager, young learner has an inner desire to understand society and the enveloping environment; a teacher is not designated as an economics or history instructor. In such a setting the mentor should find it natural to introduce such topics as Our Harbor; How Our Parents Make Their Livings; Families Around the World; How People Express Their Religious Beliefs; or Why We Have Rules for Living Together—all common illustrations of topics that can provide rich cores for a major emphasis on learning to live in so-ciety and for learnings in the other basic areas as well.

Limitations in Current Programs

Yet in far too many schools such learnings are not experienced. Beyond the factors already indicated, how can this be explained?

We have been seriously handicapped by our failure to establish a minimum set of national goals that clearly indicate the centrality of the social studies in the general education of children and youth.[1] We social studies educators have never mounted a true social studies program throughout all the grades—one that is well planned, sequenced, timely, issue centered, and skill oriented—in short, a decision-making curriculum of sociocivic learnings and experiences. A material contribution to this key weakness has been our failure to produce and to employ teachers who can accomplish such a curriculum.

Particularly tragic here is the decline of the social studies from the organizational center of the elementary school program. (Of course, in many places social studies have never attained this position.) Unfortunately, current back-to-basic trends, elementary school testing programs, and a seemingly growing agreement on the part of many elementary school teachers all contribute to a threatening attitude that the social studies are relatively unimportant; thus, what should be the heart of the elementary school program often receives scant attention at best and, as in Washington,

---

[1] See Richard E. Gross and Dwight Allen, "Time for a National Effort to Develop the Social Studies Curriculum," *Phi Delta Kappan*, May 1963, pp. 360–366.

D.C., several years ago, is in danger of outright elimination.[2]

Studies of the preparation and credentialing of teachers reveal very minimal backgrounds in history and the social sciences on the part of many teachers—even at the secondary level—who are responsible for social studies learnings. It is understandable why an elementary teacher with only two or three college history courses and possibly not even a single course in geography or American government is reluctant to plunge into social studies in any depth. University teacher training programs and state licensing requirements are to be faulted for their shortsightedness in allowing such provisions.

We also seem to have failed to convince administrators of the unique needs and functions of the social studies. The continuing assignment of inadequately prepared personnel to instruct in our field is one of the greatest causes of its ineffectiveness. Informative institutes need to be created to bring the New Social Studies into the ken of school administrators. Teachers who understand the importance of social studies should give their administrator a key book or article on the field that they have found particularly inspiring or helpful. Such individuals should see to it that *Social Education,* the excellent journal of the National Council for the Social Studies, is circulated among the staff. They should also press for faculty discussions of substance on the place and role of social studies in their school. The principal should be invited to observe rewarding class sessions and urged to feature the

social studies at a PTA meeting. Only through such actions will we develop necessary understanding and support for the fact that the social studies are fundamental too.

We have neglected to inform and coopt essential parental and public support. We have also failed to reach key agencies and organizations in our communities. Thoroughly knowledgeable lay leaders and groups can be of tremendous aid in furthering our efforts. If we are not convincing advocates for the social studies, these individuals and groups can be serious stumbling blocks. Under such circumstances we become vulnerable to outside pressures and too often have to bow to controls and censorship that limit the right of the pupils to learn.

Social studies have to do with actual conditions of living, with problems boys and girls face at home, find in the community, and experiences on TV. A large part of the social education program should feature controversial elements of immediate life. Individuals and institutions from parents and business men to local agencies and organizations should be interviewed, used as guest speakers, be visited, and ultimately cooperated with in mutually valuable community projects.

The school has been highly isolated for too long. Independent and small group studies that move into the real world of the community, state, and region are long overdue. Fortunately, today parents and pupils are breaking down the castle walls and filling in the moats. The concept of the school as an island has been years in dying but it has helped maintain a remote social studies program where students have little chance to apply or act on their studies and conclusions.

The last suggestion leads us to urge the importance of social studies programs and activities that reinforce the individual's sense of responsibility and the social

---

[2] For detailed information on current offerings and trends see Richard E. Gross, "The Status of the Social Studies in the Public Schools of the United States: Facts and Impressions of a National Survey," *SOCIAL EDUCATION*, March 1977. pp. 194–200, 205.

concerns of boys and girls. We also wish to challenge the lack of commitment and relativism that has come to characterize too much of our existence in and out of school. Claiming objectivity we have allowed apathy and indecision to take hold in our schoolrooms where the boys and girls wonder if we stand for anything and if anything is worth standing for. We have the opinion that there are principles we must extend; there are sanctions we must live by. Integrity, justice, and compassion are only three examples; we maintain that these and other such basic qualities need to be carefully built back into our programs. Our failure to maintain ethical, value-oriented emphases in the social studies where youth may come to understand why they hold certain beliefs inviolate, how to work to extend them, as well as gain the strength to stick by them when need be, may, indeed, be our greatest challenge in creating a viable curriculum for social education that will serve well the coming generation and the future of our nation. If we celebrate a Tricentennial, it will depend heavily on what is or what is not accomplished by our schools in enabling young people to truly learn how they must live in society.

Our Rationale for the Social Studies

A rationale is not just a list of objectives nor is it a full-blown philosophy of education. It is a statement concerning the role of education and it usually includes a conception of what constitutes a good citizen and a good society. A rationale, of course, is closely related to the values of the society and reflects the beliefs of its authors as well. We have already indicated certain prime aspects of our rationale; but the import of knowing where one is trying to go and why leads us now

to specify and reemphasize these prime concerns as guidelines for planning and instruction.

A rationale can be thought of as a set of principles to which the school and the community are willing to commit themselves and also to which they will allocate resources necessary for implementation. We should recognize that an American rationale developed for the social studies in the late 1970s is not going to be appropriate for all times and all places. For a powerful, global leader in an era of multiple social problems on both the national and international scene, a different rationale is indicated than one that would serve a small or somewhat isolated country in a period of relatively limited social crisis. Other factors, such as technological developments that affect a society, may also necessitate related changes in what must be done in the schools. Also, although some national commonalities are in order, because of special circumstances certain elements of a rationale for the social studies may not be appropriate for a particular school with its own peculiar set of problems and challenges. Therefore, it should always be recognized that while a rationale should be as clearly defined as possible, in the real world its implementation may take different forms in different schools and that there may even be variations for special groups or circumstances within a given school.

What then are the major purposes of social studies education? We have identified two major goals. One purpose of the social studies is *to prepare students to be well-functioning citizens in a democratic society.* The social studies program should enable students to participate effectively in societal activities as individuals and as members of groups. This means that far more attention must be given to involve students in the activities of their schools and communities than is now the case. It is only if schools provide experiences in social participation that many pupils will be likely to be adequately and responsibly active in social participation as adults. Of course, the goal of preparing students for such sociocivic roles in a free society is a goal that is not just unique to the field of the social studies. This purpose has always been an important component in other subject areas as well. But, nevertheless, the social studies field has always regarded the goal of effective citizenship as prime in its own educational realm.

The second purpose of the social studies is *to help students make the most rational decisions possible about public as well as private issues under consideration.* To be able to make effective decisions, the social studies program should provide students with the ability to understand and utilize data, concepts, generalizations, and the modes of investigation drawn from the various social sciences such as anthropology, economics, geography, history, political science, psychology, and sociology.

The emphasis, however, should not be just learning the major ideas in a disciplinary field. There must be an equal concern for the teaching of skills. These include the traditional skills such as reading, listening, speaking, viewing, writing, and time-space orientation skills as well as the newer inquiry or thinking competencies as those found in recognizing a problem, developing hypotheses, data collection and analysis, and testing a hypothesis.[3]

We also think that the social studies should be more concerned with helping students make the most rational decisions that they can in their own personal lives.

[3] These latter skills are largely "newer" because they have not been emphasized adequately in the past; actually in terms of the modern era they were suggested as a regular and fundamental part of every child's experience in 1910 when John Dewey underscored these essentials in his volume *How We Think,* Boston, D. C. Heath, 1910.

In effect, this assumes that a social studies program will enable pupils to develop and to employ a personal set of values that will help pupils participate in the societal decision-making process as well as in their individual lives.

Major Components of the Rationale

The two goals we have identified for the social studies involve four major components: (1) the knowledge area of the social sciences, (2) the skills needed to find and use or apply the knowledge component, (3) the development and clarification of a personal set of values, and (4) sociocivic participation in the society. In practice, all of these components are woven together. There is substantial overlap between knowledge, skills, values, and social participation. Skills, for example, are intimately interrelated to understanding and attitudes; these competencies depend on knowledge and they have values attached to them. But, in practice, to make sure that students can effectively master these elements, it is necessary to focus on a given component and to devise suitable learning experiences that will help pupils attain the basic social studies goals.

The four fundamental components we have identified for the social studies assume that individuals in our society have the opportunities to learn, to make decisions, and then to act on their conclusions. In effect, the rationale presented here with its two basic goals and four social studies elements implies the existence of a just society in which individuals are treated as humane persons capable of making fair and wise decisions. It further emphasizes that one of the most important values in American society has been the widely shared belief in the ideal of equality—however, this concept may have been violated in actual practice. The basic idea in a free society is that each person should have egalitarian rights and related responsibilities. Politically our nation rests on the premise that "all men are created equal." This conception about equal opportunity of the individual to both develop and contribute has also been translated into the economic realm. Here it is held that every person should have equal opportunities to grow and to achieve success and the good things in life. This belief also predicates such fundamental rights as freedom of association, equal educational opportunities, and existence of an open, plural society with options for individuals and groups to be different. The social studies rationale presented here is undergirded by such basic American values. It, in turn, must contribute to their furtherance and broader application.

Characteristics of an Optimum Social Studies Program

The two major goals of social studies—to prepare students to be citizens in a democratic society and to help them make the most rational decisions they can about civic and social issues—may sound rather lofty and somewhat far removed from the realities of the school and its environment. The implications of these purposes and their correlaries may not be as clear or as specific as we desire. Thus, we now outline some of the major principles that result from these goals as guidelines for optimum social studies curriculum and instruction.

Instead of a typical and traditional statement of objectives for the social studies, we have delineated the essentials of a superior program in this field.

Teachers and others who use these guidelines should be helped to find direction toward purposeful program development and effective social studies instruction. These statements are not intended to be objectives that can be transferred directly to courses of study. Instead, these are characteristics to be used as prime references in formulating specific teaching aims and activities developed at the local level through grade-by-grade selection and development of themes and teaching units.[4] Individually developed programs will naturally reflect in addition the attention given to factors that are unique within each local setting. The following 20 guidelines may also be used in reviewing and evaluating established social studies offerings and programs. Again, such assessment should take into consideration the particular and specific aims that have been developed by an individual teacher, school, or district. But we have here a general "measuring stick" that should prove useful to curriculum planners, community review groups, and administrators, as well as to teachers concerned with developing an optimum program of social education.

A social studies program is effective if it:

1. Is based on the moral, intellectual, emotional, and physical needs of individuals and on the needs of the society of which they are members.
2. Uses the best available information about learning and its relation to the development of children and youth, especially in that it reaches and challenges the capabilities of each individual.
3. Features, in the United States, the essences of the American way at life, providing individuals with continuing opportunities for democratic living.

---

[4] Actual steps and format for such planning in the development of scope and sequence are presented in the next chapter.

4. Provides a series of experiences that help individuals understand and appreciate that the rights and privileges of our free society entail attendant responsibilities and duties.
5. Emphasizes the importance of spiritual values and provides for the acquisition of those ethical components rooted in our human experience and long cherished in American culture.
6. Promotes particularly the dignity of humankind and the ideal in our free society that people of all races, creeds, ethnic groups, and of both sexes shall have equal opportunities to excel.
7. Gives prime attention to persistent and current societal problems and utilizes contributions from the behavioral sciences, as well as knowledge of the past, in helping learners formulate suggested resolutions for those problems.
8. Stimulates creative as well as reasoned action based on an objective study of controversial issues where individuals and groups use problem-resolution techniques and develop related skills for effective thinking and wise decision making.
9. Emphasizes the fact that democracy is a process through which ideas and institutions are submitted to public discussion and debate and it places value on the contributions of varied Americans to the development of democratic traditions.
10. Brings into balance the concepts and approaches of history and the social sciences, emphasizing the interrelatedness of social, political, economic and environmental forces in the United States and in the world.
11. Develops understanding and appreciation of other peoples and ways of life and of the reciprocal contributions to civilization made by varying individuals and groups of our own nation and from other countries and cultures.
12. Illustrates how science and technology have helped make peoples of the world increasingly interdependent and have also contributed to numerous social, economic, and political problems such as environmental pollution or the control of the seas that are international in scope

and that can only be resolved on a global basis.
13. Builds an awareness of basic human needs and the development of skills and attitudes that enable individuals to contribute positively towards good human relations in family, school, and communities.
14. Is process oriented, giving adequate attention to the development of varied learning skills and operational competencies that are required for effective citizenship in a democratic state.
15. Utilizes and interrelates other subjects and curricular areas in order to further its purposes.
16. Includes and reflects the continuing evaluation of individual's achievements and progress in terms of behavior, understandings, competencies, values, and attitudes.
17. Is flexible enough to meet the individual differences of students and teachers in varying local environments, yet maintains a continuity of purpose and content that gives direction to the program at all levels.
18. Is developmental from kindergarten through the twelfth grade, reenforcing and expanding knowledge, skills, and attitudes at each level, and encourages an appropriate variety of approaches and emphases at different educational levels.
19. Permits ongoing revision to incorporate new research findings and to meet the emerging demands of our changing society and of the individuals therein.
20. Is taught by persons who have the breadth and depth of preparation that will enable them to instruct effectively the wide range of topics that comprise the social studies.

Challenges to the Teacher of the Social Studies

The ideal situation mirrored in the foregoing 20 characteristics can be attained only through the leadership of capable and professionally oriented teachers. From Plato to contemporary educational theorists, we have been reminded regularly that the teacher is the key catalyst in the educative process. Teachers must be prepared to make learning in the social studies the vital and important adventure that it can be. This calls for teachers with rich backgrounds in the social sciences and related humanities and sciences; with full knowledge of how children and youth grow, develop, and learn; and for teachers who are also skilled in organizing experiences for learning and in using appropriate methods and materials of instruction. The major aim of this book is to help develop such mentors for the area of social education.

Recent and current developments in education and in the milieu of the school place both new challenges and increased responsibilities on the instructor. Growing parental and community interest in schooling, for example, now provides wider options and resources at the same time that it demands better communication and cooperation between the school and those individuals and organizations in the locality who were formerly less directly involved in education. Thus, on top of the skills of explanation and placation, competencies in carrying out joint enterprises, as well as in maintaining good personal relationships with adults, become a much greater need for teachers today.

Most teachers are meeting increasingly sophisticated and often even more mature children than they have had to deal with in the past. These are young persons with ever more complex lives and with contacts and concerns frequently stretching far beyond the confines of school or neighborhood. These pupils need to be dealt with in an ever more guidance-oriented manner. Often this must include a shockproof mien that

frankly admits controversy, deep ethical and issue-oriented topics, and that must face problems formerly not even mentioned in classroom settings.

This situation is complicated in numerous instances by increasingly reluctant learners. This becomes particularly true when we are working with middle-school and adolescent pupils. Here are youngsters looking toward expanding personal adventures in an ever more exciting and involving world—a world with them and right ahead of them in which, unfortunately, the school seems to play an ever less important part.[5]

A free-wheeling, very open society emerges where old value patterns are being shattered. Conflicting attitudes and practices abound. What does this ask of the teacher? We think it calls for mentors who can lead children and youth particularly in the exploration of problem areas and of related value questions. These instructors need to recognize and provide for certain of the options and variations that exist but at the same time they must help provide some of the stability and security that all youngsters need and that society expects the school to provide.

One of the best ways the teacher can exemplify worthy standards is to model them personally and to maintain classroom environments that reflect the qualities we wish to promote. A major challenge is to decide which "public" we represent. How "different" can we be then from the policies or seeming lack of them found at home, in the peer group, or in the community? Additionally, how can we counter clearly virulent influences prevalent in the communicative media such as violence or promiscuity presented on TV or in a magazine in a nonjudg-

---

[5] See, for example, Celestino Fernandez, Grace Massey, and Sanford Dornbusch, "High School Students' Perceptions of Social Studies," *The Social Studies*, March/April 1976, pp. 51–57.

mental manner? Several recent investigations have resulted in claims that after the family itself television has replaced the school as the second greatest influence in the shaping of children.

The implications of the foregoing are substantial, to say the least, for teachers and schools. The film and the video tape are media with which it is most difficult to compete. Demanded on the part of the teacher in response are preparation, organization, motivational matter, and approaches that can to some degree rival the color, creativity, and drama that young TV watchers have come to expect.

The teacher, of course, cannot compete as an entertainer; thus, he or she must above all be highly skillful in truly involving students in the learning process. Such motivation can lead pupils willingly into books, social studies laboratory experiences, and other conventional means of education characteristic of the school. But today, unquestionably, much time and effort must be given by the teacher to establishing an optimum environment for learning. Intense self-preparation is indicated. This book seeks to contribute significantly to developing these essential qualities.

Bibliography

American Council of Learned Societies. *The Social Studies and the Social Sciences.* New York: Harcourt, Brace, 1962.

Barr, Robert, James Barth and S. S. Shermis. *Defining the Social Studies.* Washington, D.C.: National Council for the Social Studies, Bulletin 51, 1977.

Brubaker, Dale and Murray Thomas. *Curriculum Patterns in Elementary Social Studies.* Belmont, Calif.: Wadsworth Publishing Company, 1973.

Cox, B. and B. Massialas. *Social Studies in the United States.* New York: Harcourt, Brace, 1967.

Estvan, Frank. *Social Studies in a Changing World.* New York: Harcourt, Brace, 1968.

Fenton, E. *The New Social Studies.* New York: Holt, 1967.

Gross, R. E. and L. D. Zeleny. *Educating Citizens for Democracy.* New York: Oxford University Press, 1958.

Hoffman, A. J. and T. Ryan. *Social Studies and the Child's Expanding Self.* Scranton, Pa.: Intext, 1973.

Jarolimek, John. *Social Studies in Elementary Education.* New York: Macmillan, 1977.

Joyce, Bruce (Ed.). *New Strategies for Social Education.* Chicago: Science Research Associates, 1971.

Kellum, D. *The Social Studies—Myths and Realities.* New York: Sheed & Ward, 1969.

Kenworthy, L. *Social Studies for the '70s.* Boston: Ginn/Blaisdell, 1969.

Krug, M., et al. *The New Social Studies.* Itasca, Ill.: Peacock, 1970.

National Society for the Study of Education. *Social Studies in the Elementary School.* Chicago: 56th Yearbook, Part II, 1957.

Massialas, B. and F. Smith. *New Challenges in the Social Studies.* Belmont, Calif.: Wadsworth, 1965.

Michaelis, John. *Social Studies for Children in a Democracy.* Englewood Cliffs, N.J., Prentice-Hall, 1977.

Shaver, J. and H. Berlak. *Democracy, Pluralism and the Social Studies.* Boston: Houghton-Mifflin, 1968.

Taskforce on Curriculum Guidelines. *Social Studies Curriculum Guidelines.* Washington D.C.: National Council for the Social Studies, 1971.

Womack, J. *Discovering the Structure of the Social Studies.* New York: Benzinger, 1966.

How can social studies contribute to these
children's education?

CHAPTER 2

Curricular and Instructional Models for the Social Studies

Recent Tendencies in the Social Studies

I n Section 1 we have identified our view of the social studies. There are several varying definitions and models for both social studies curriculum and instruction. These variattions are reflected in state guides, district syllabi, course titles and topics, as well as by the units developed and taught in a local school. Over the years theorists have identified several different schools of thought and related practices.[1] These viewpoints are discussed subsequently as we examine each of the models we have identified. Differentiation in some cases will be difficult as a given individual lesson, course, or volume seldom reflects a "pure" or single model. Nevertheless it is of value to consider differing major thrusts and emphases in social education programs.

Looking back over the past several decades, we can observe elements of all of the models we will discuss in the prescriptions, recommended practices, and materials developed by the numerous new social studies projects. Their products, spawned largely between 1960 and 1975 from textbooks and course guides to media kits and comprehensive total programs, evidence both different models and, frequently, the fact that they do not clearly fall within one of the categories established by leaders who are trying to clarify or unify the field.

The projects, as well as the newer materials developed directly by commercial publishers and their authors during the above-mentioned era, resulted in unparalleled innovation and experimentation. This unprecedented ferment in the history of the social studies was, of course, accompanied by extensive change in the entire area of education. During and following a long period—including

[1] Donald W. Oliver, "Categories of Social Science Instruction," *High School Journal*, April 1960, pp. 387–397; J. L. Barth and S. S. Shermis, "Defining the Social Studies: An Exploration of Three Traditions," *Social Education*, November 1970, pp. 743–751; and Dale Brubaker et al., "A Conceptual Framework for Social Studies Curriculum and Instruction," *Social Education*, March 1977, pp. 201–205.

two wars—schooling had remained quite stable, if not stagnant, for many years. The pressures for improvement stemmed from many factors—from the masses of children and youth who now needed to be educated to the technical know-how finally opened to educational application.

The "reform" that became characterized as the "new social studies" grew along with and out of a five-pronged development that affected all aspects of education in the United States. We mention these briefly.

(1) Curricular Renovation
Leaders and theorists in most fields of schooling became very concerned with updating and improving the school program. During this period thousands of curriculum development programs were conducted in local districts and schools and many states launched thorough, large-scale revision efforts. Additionally, numerous academicians and professional organizations became involved. Many of the resulting programs benefited from the substantial flow of federal funds, an important element that had not been available until this era. In this manner a number of elements of current school curicular offerings were born. Although a late entry, the new social studies appeared as a part of this movement. But for those involved the times were often frustrating. New programs demanded teacher education that frequently was not available. The new programs moved in diverse directions and the field of the social studies was further fragmented by the appearance of ever more varied alternatives, many of which had not been properly evaluated. At the same time, teachers were sometimes not clear on criteria for choosing. Some of the projects were disciplinary centered, others were multidisciplinary, and many were specialized topical offerings or reflected the growing interest in the behavioral sciences. The cup of the social studies certainly ran over![2]

(2) Altered Patterns of School and Classroom Organization
During this period a variety of modifications was initiated in an attempt to help make the school program more teachable and learnable. Led by J. Lloyd Trump of the National Association of Secondary School Principals and other key school administrators and university educators, the movement had its greatest impact at the high school level.[3] When we review the altered patterns evolved, it is apparent that these were, in part, attempts to gain some of the intimacy, spontaneity, planning advantages, and cross-disciplinary ties that characterize a good elementary school environment. Such, for example, was the move toward flexible or modular scheduling that freed high school instructors and their students from the self-same, lockstep weekly and daily program that down through the years has constrained any variation in the number, length, and placement of class hours. So too were the growing tendencies toward independent study and individualization and the employment of teacher aids. Related to growing guidance concerns, other schools tried plans such as waiving regular classes for one day a week or eliminated study halls and instituted open-campus arrangements, allowing pupils considerable freedom compared to former arrangements. There were also experiments with the 12-month school year and several plans appeared

---

[2] Two good sources listing the projects are Bob Taylor and T. L. Groom, *Social Studies Education Projects: An Index,* Washington, D.C., A.S.C.D. (NEA), 1971 and the Social Science Education Consortium, *Social Studies Curriculum Materials Data Book,* Boulder, Colo., 1971, with subsequent supplements.

[3] See, for example, J. Lloyd Trump, *Images of the Future,* Washington, D.C.,. NAASP, 1959 or his *Focus on Change,* Chicago, Rand McNally, 1961.

where pupils received several short vacations during the school year rather than the single long summer vacation.

Another innovation was the highly publicized and extensive introduction of a great variety of team teaching arrangements. These were both intra- and interdisciplinary. Team teaching was particularly attractive in the social studies area where instructors with varying specialties could join together and share their expertise with one another's pupils. Because of similar aims and emphases, especially in the junior high schools, cross-disciplinary experiences were often offered between English and social studies. In spite of the virtues, numerous of these trials proved abortive for a variety of reasons and today carry-over seems to have been minimal.[4] Nevertheless, such developments clearly added to the air of creative change that characterized the era.

(3) Changing School Designs and Facilities
Many of the aforementioned developments could only be adequately tried in new or in extensively remodeled school buildings. The years of depression and warfare that had held back school construction now seemed to have been a blessing as the extensive growth in school facilities could now move along modern lines. With the boom in building, rich opportunities were at hand for theorists and architects to make their dreams come true. Across the nation there rapidly appeared a great variety of new schools that looked little like the conventional structures of the past. The new buildings often have movable walls and a variety of different-sized and shaped rooms and furnishings. Some included row on row of monklike carrels for independent study, tape learning, or the use of computer terminals. At the other extreme were vast open-spaced, tentlike instructional areas where many teachers and hundreds of children were sometimes forced to plan together, teach together, and, it was claimed, learn together. Learning laboratories, a new version of the older concept of the laboratory classroom, reappeared; these were equipped and organized in a different fashion from the traditional secondary schoolroom. (Another example of the "moving up" of a worthwhile concept that has long marked elementary school rooms is evidenced.) Resource centers and sublibraries were built. Much of this was found on attractively developed school sites with recently undreamed-of accouterments, from carpeting to air conditioning, that contribute to a well-functioning educational process.

(4) New Instructional Materials and Media
Pouring forth from project centers and publishers came an accompanying stream of new matter and devices that were meant to facilitate both new and old curricula. If a school program, for example, was to be inquiry oriented, it needed complementary materials not traditionally available. Additionally, schools suddenly had millions of dollars in federal funds to spend. These developments were, of course, linked to the technological and electronic revolution that had swept new machines into the world of learning. Our oldest "programmed" learning device, the textbook, was being discussed in the past tense by enthusiastic proponents of the new media. Many publishing houses were bought up by the producers of the machines who some thought might not only replace the printed volume but even the teacher! Videotapes and viewing screens, computerized teletype arrangements, and a host of mechanistic programs were born that, it was anticipated, would guarantee pupil progress. Unfor-

---

[4] Richard E. Gross and Jack Fraenkel, "Team-Teaching: Let's Look Before We Leap," *Social Education*, May 1966, pp. 335–337.

tunately, today the schools have still not come close to intelligently and successfully adapting and using the media made available to us. They still promise tremendous potential toward creativity, motivation, and efficiency, as well as providing for flexibility and individualization in learning.[5]

The honeymoon with TV, language laboratories, programmed learning, and teaching machines proved short and illusory. Nevertheless, discovery-oriented materials, case-study kits, role-playing scenarios, source packets, and simulation booklets all began to be employed as textbook supplements and, in some cases, did supplant typical texts. The developments of this era forced textbook authors and publishers into substantial efforts to redesign American schoolbooks; another basic factor was the paperback revolution of the preceding era. While textbooks remain, their import has been somewhat reduced in the shaping of instruction in our schools.

(5) Reform in Teacher Education

All four of the foregoing factors had impact on both preservice and in-service teacher training efforts. The new curricula and new means clearly indicated the need for revisions in programs and emphases for teacher preparation. New media also opened the door to new knowledge and necessary skills often, up to this time, outside of the ken of typically prepared teachers. Thus thousands of institutes and workshops were organized for experienced mentors while year-long intern-apprenticeships became a feature of initial credentialing. Microteaching and videotaping were instituted at hundreds of colleges and universities. Self-directed or individually paced learning modules were introduced where pro-

spective student teachers were largely expected to prepare themselves. It was a heady time of optimistic reformation that frequently brought colleges of education into closer contact with local schools in what was hoped to develop as actual partnerships in teacher education; but as with many reform movements, a great deal here proved sterile. Overenthusiasm led to some shoddy efforts and lacks in communication, coupled with inadequate evaluation, led to misunderstandings that made it difficult to prove the efficacy of hastily mounted projects. Within this vortex of new directions and emphases, almost an entire new generation of teachers was being shaped. From the flux of this age came the many thousands of teachers who would eventually be responsible for social studies education over the next 35 years.

These new teachers and the five areas of change that helped shape them were and still are in turn affected by the complex matrix of pressures in the milieu of the school. Over the years the surrounding forces have sought increasingly compulsive roles in shaping the curriculum. They can provide the program developer or the teacher with real dilemmas. This is especially true of the conflicting demands that characterize the volatile area of sociocivic education where lay persons and pressure groups are especially concerned and watchful.

As a result, no single document or law, no one course guide or basic textbook can by itself be the greatly dominant factor in shaping the school program. In addition to these, consider such further forces as the traditions of the disciplines, teachers' backgrounds, demands of parents and special interest groups, administrative directives, accrediting standards, school board regulations, and the allocation of funds and the sources of these monies. Add to these the needs of students, community demands, and state,

---

[5] See the special issue of *Phi Delta Kappan* of February 1977 on the question "Will Technology Revolutionize Education?"

national, and international conditions—
all of these also have their influence on
what is taught in the classroom. Therefore, no matter what the official state
framework for education, specifically
stated school aims, or the educational
philosophy of the teacher are, each one is
bound to result in an eclectic application.
A particular theory, approach, or model
may be most apparent at any one juncture of school curriculum or instruction,
but realistically there are considerable
overlaps and amalgamations in conceptions as well as in use. Each offering,
therefore, is modified and infiltrated by
the practical factors of existence—social,
economic, political, and educational.

Varying Models for the Social Studies Program

In spite of what has been stated above,
when an observer enters either an elementary or a high school classroom and
views a social studies lesson, the predominant ideas of the instructor concerning
how to organize and approach the social
studies content is usually evident. Even
classes or offerings with the same titles
may reveal one teacher providing extensive individualized instruction in an independent study format, allowing considerable pupil option on specifics, while the
mentor in the next room has all the
youngsters focusing on the textbook in a
large group situation, reciting and learning identical subject matter. On the other
hand, teachers may provide nearly identical offerings under labels as varied as
"Citizenship" and "Human Understanding," each mirroring the same prototype
of the social studies in spite of supposedly basic differences reflected in the
designated titles.

A broad and eclectic field such as the
social studies would seem to demand a
somewhat flexible model encompassing a
variety of bases and options. Indeed,
unless we look on the social studies as a
unique discipline in and of itself, a single
model that accommodates the elements
involved may prove impossible to construct.[6] However, at least five major
models are in evidence. There are considerable overlaps between these constructs and teachers frequently move
from emphasizing one model to one or
more of the others during the period of
weeks that encompass a given social studies unit. It is also impossible to fully separate curricular models from instructional
models. Often a particular technique to
be employed is indicated by the content
being emphasized. Or, a given program
model may be heavily process oriented
and in this case curriculum and instruction are largely inseparable. We will approach the following five models initially
as curricular models but then in each
case will indicate prime methodology that
tends to accompany each model. We will
conclude the chapter by presenting a
general systems model for teaching that
should be helpful from the standpoint of
planning and instruction and that also is
pertinent, no matter what the curricular
emphasis.

The five models include (A) the disciplinary model, (B) the multidisciplinary
model, (C) the citizenship education
model, (D) the problem-inquiry model,
and (E) the humanistic/personal model.

(A) The Disciplinary Model
This is the traditional model and probably the one most frequently found in the
schools. It views the social studies as comprised of courses, topics, or lessons cen-

---

[6] See, for example, S. P. McCutchen, "A Discipline
For the Social Studies," *Social Education*, February
1963, pp. 61–65, a classic attempt to so define the
content and perimeters of the field.

tered largely on a single-disciplinary base. Emphasis tends to be on factual and conceptual content. While there may be some attention to learning particular skills, current events, and similar civic knowledge not centered directly in the subject matter of history or geography, for example, the prime focus in organizing according to this model is on understandings accruing from one of the social sciences or history. Such facts and concepts and related generalizations are conceived of as helping attain the stated social studies aims or, indeed, in many cases are viewed as the prime aims in themselves. They are commonly viewed also as being fundamental in enabling the teacher to meet the other varied purposes of social education.

Often in this model we find a textbook-centered offering and it may be one that calls for a heavy emphasis on memorization. The teacher is sometimes primarily a giver of questions and a hearer of answers. There is great faith that transfer of these learnings will occur in the sociocivic experiences of the student.

A variation of this model conceives of social studies as an investigatory social science. Equally disciplinary centered, it aims at producing young people who not only grasp the prime understandings of the subject field but who also possess competency with the processes that characterize the research patterns of the discipline. Followers of this variation of the model tend to give considerably more time to providing experiences where the skills of history or one of the social sciences are emphasized. In recent years when theorists have been discussing the "structure" of the discipline approach, they have meant to identify an emphasis that concentrates on both the generalizations and the investigative processes that characterize a given subject.

Another difference besides the emphasis on disciplinary methodology exists

between mentors employing what we may designate as Model A-2 (neutral-investigatory) and those using the foregoing disciplinary Model A-1 (imparting factual) who purposefully select, from the social sciences and history, matter that reinforces their sociocivic objectives. Often these Model A-2 instructors claim to be much more open and objective; frequently they try to be neutral. They desire to avoid teaching answers, giving opinions, or otherwise trying to directly influence pupil attitudes as they believe characterize practitioners of disciplinary Model A-1. They see their roles as instructional catalysts and they attempt to lead their pupils to discover answers, draw their own conclusions, and to apply their learnings as they see fit. This variation of the general model has important and worthy aims; but as explained in Chapter 1 it tends to neglect the important value elements that the public expects the schools to treat, let alone to inculcate. A pupil brought up primarily on Model A-2 might become a young expert in political science or be most efficient in applying the processes of sociology, but he or she might well not only be relatively noninformed but even nonfunctional on policy issues, on deciding wisely why we should follow a specific strategy, or on the societal and ethical bases for proper action.

(B) The Multidisciplinary Model

This model includes those programs that have also been entitled "interdisciplinary" or in some cases "fused." The model reflects more accurately the concept of the social studies and the realities of human experience than does disciplinary Model A. No event or movement in life occur within the neat confines that can be circumscribed by a single subject; nor can these developments be fully comprehended via a single subject. Multidisciplinary Model B has been featured by theorists and publishers since the early years of the social studies. It allows the author, curriculum developer, or teacher to entitle or emphasize an offering with the single-disciplinary designation of "history" or "economics," but it requires cross-disciplinary experiences within that offering. Here it asks that such economic lessons or history units, for example, be broadfield, drawing on the contributions both in fact and concept as well as on the skills and competencies from a number of the social sciences and history. Such input from the sister disciplines are employed when or where they are useful to illustrate a point, to develop richer concepts, or to build needed abilities.

Some theorists who favor this model believe that a particular discipline such as history or anthropology may be the best carrier of social studies learnings and favor a continuing central emphasis from grade to grade on that particular discipline.[7] Others, however, believe that any one of the social sciences or history can provide the core in the social studies curriculum but recognize that none are adequate in themselves. Economic understandings, for example, are enlarged by a geographical base; psychological insights are enriched when considered in their societal setting.

Model B-1 (within field), for there is also a variation of this overall model, has tended to be topical in its scope and sequence. Basic human activities or fundamental social processes, rather than a combination of disciplines, have served as the organizing element in such a curriculum. Thus, units and offerings tend to reflect titles such as "War and Peace," "Communication and Transportation in the United States," "The Chinese Fam-

ily," "Products and Production in Our State," "How Humankind Worships," or "The Progress of Science." Such programs lend themselves to depth studies and to comparative analyses between societies, regions, nations, and periods of time. Teachers using this model incorporate attention in particular to the contemporary and more recent aspects of the selected topics; on the other hand, numerous such courses or lessons may contain a heavy historical element. Unfortunately, teachers trained with majors in single disciplines or with little background in the broadfield of the social sciences have often found it difficult to apply this model.

Model B-2 (beyond field) is a variation that goes beyond the social sciences and history in establishing its perimeters; otherwise it is similar in its multidisciplinary focus. In this case curriculum planners and instructors explain that the topics treated, such as "Technological Inventions," "Aesthetic Expression," "The Search for Shelter," "Our Harbor," or "The Money System," cannot be adequately served by even history and the social sciences. They point out that other curricular areas from music and art to mathematics and home economics must also be drawn upon to attain full understandings. Model B-2 has particular appeal to elementary teachers and serves them well. Because of the broad subject matter exposure in their own preparation, in the variety of subjects for which they are responsible, and since they frequently teach them to a single group of children who are together all or much of the day, this model is easily applied. Units centered in social studies topics but bridging to several other subject matter areas are most natural for elementary teachers. Units like these take time and creativity in planning and organization, but such a six- or eight-week unit on Latin America, for example, can be a

---

[7] The "Our Working World" social studies program, for example, developed by Lawrence Senesh and published by Science Research Associates, is centered in economics but draws on and incorporates learnings from history and the other social sciences.

highly motivated learning experience. Such units are compatible to the inclusion of a great variety of activities, from the maintenance of travel diaries and flag construction to mathematical computations of trip costs and the preparation of representative national cooking recipes.[8] Teachers involved in Model B classes usually employ a variety of small group techniques and projects investigated lend themselves to committee work; at the same time, individual study assignments can also easily be incorporated into the overall organizational strategy.

(C) The Citizenship Education Model

Teachers following this curricular emphasis are particularly concerned with the sociocivic goals of the social studies. They view the social studies as a core of general education; overriding aims are the needs of society and also reflect those of the individual. While such teachers are not attempting to produce little social scientists or even to build comprehensive understandings of the various disciplines, these are drawn on as needed in their classes, units, and lessons. As is true of the other models, approaches and emphases here coincide in part with the other organizational patterns. However, again, no matter the titles involved, such teachers tend to commonly use topical approaches. The offering may be labeled "Geography," but the lessons and units from "Our People and Our Land" to "Men In Space" reflect a broad cultural emphasis, a values orientation, and a concern for human welfare and a well-functioning free society.

Character education and the development of concerned young citizens who can and will act responsibily are central features of Model C. This approach appeals to many public elements in society. The model not only concerns itself with the maintenance and transfer of worthy aspects of our civilization, but it aims to contribute toward social improvement and fuller fruition of our ideals. The extension of the worthy goals of the civilization to more peoples and areas of the globe is also a major concern. Lessons and units frequently feature group study and service projects in the school and community. There is a participatory emphasis including considerable discussion and exchanges of opinions among the pupils, sharing in decision making, and even joint efforts with other classes and cooperation with organizations in the locality. Teachers may include considerable teacher-pupil planning as a part of these class projects. Again, such features tend to promote a contemporary emphasis as pupils tie learning to application and actions related to social, governmental, economic, and other important topics.

Some educational writers have made the mistake of identifying a highly propagandistic or indoctrination approach to the citizenship education model.[9] When this model is properly conceived and carried out, such elements are not employed. The virtues of social values and national goals can be featured and taught without rote indoctrination. The able teacher using this model provides the kind of environment, materials, and learning experiences by which the virtues of the system are exemplified and proved out. If an instructor with a sociocivic orientation is classified as fitting the citizenship education model but employs a highly doctrinnaire, unopen, and propagandistic approach, we should again

---

[8] One of the best sources for ideas and directions to so organize instruction is Lavonne Hanna et al., *Unit Teaching in the Elementary School,* New York, Holt, Rinehart and Winston, 1963; see especially Chapters IV and V.

[9] See, for example, James L. Barth and S. Samuel Shermis, "Defining the Social Studies: An Exploration Of Three Traditions," *Social Education,* November 1970, pp. 743–751.

divide this model into two variations with Model C-1 (civic action) illustrating the general model we have presented here and Model C-2 (indoctrination) applying to the unsatisfactory emphasis discussed immediately above.

(D) The Problem-Inquiry Model

Again, this model for the social studies curriculum shares elements of some of the others. It includes, for example, the strong social concerns held in the citizenship education model and it also features its student action emphasis. In its orientation toward process it draws heavily on the social science disciplinary and multidisciplinary models as it desires to build research and problem-solving competencies on the part of the learners.

The roots of this model go back in part nearly 70 years to John Dewey and his view that most experiences in the classroom should be problem centered and that pupils need to be helped especially to build the skills of scientific thinking.[10] The application of these qualities in class, school, and community have been exemplified in the Senior Problems developed during the 1920s and 1930s in our high schools. Several cycles of activity on behalf of this model have occurred during the ensuing years.[11] And we have just experienced another cycle under the call for inquiry that has been very predominant in the last decade. In recent years elementary school teachers have had greatly increased exposure to this organizing concept because of the revival of interest in induction and discovery that characterized much of the new social studies movement. Many of the projects and publications that grew out of these developments featured aspects of the problems approach. From the films, games, and investigations of the MACOS[12] program to the quasi-archaeological involvement with artifacts reproduced from the excavation of an ancient Greek villa in one of the MATCH[13] kits, numerous pupils in the lower grades have had exciting exposures to elements of this model. Relatively few schools, however, have moved to a fully problem-centered social studies program, in spite of the availability of comprehensive resources from entire sets of inquiry-oriented textbooks for each grade to the rich reservoir of problem and discovery type sources found in the Holt Data Bank.

Teachers using this model employ both past and current content in the study of the selected issues. Unfortunately, the controversial aspects that can emerge may deter some instructors from trying this model; elementary teachers seem to be particularly reticent and it is a sad commentary that they thereby rob their students of the right to learn at the same time that they undermine their own freedom to teach.[14] Again, in this model, emphasis is on means, on completing accurate analyses, and on making wise individual and group decisions. Follow-up activities often move beyond the classroom and into applications in school and com-

---

[10] In John Dewey, *How We Think*, Boston, D. C. Heath, 1910.
[11] See, for example, Richard E. Gross and Raymond Muessig, editors, *Problem-Centered Social Studies Instruction: Approaches to Reflective Teaching*, Washington, D.C., National Council for the Social Studies, Curriculum Bulletin #14, 1971.

---

[12] *Man: A Course of Study* (MACOS) is a middle-grades program offered by Curriculum Development Associates, Washington, D.C.
[13] These multimedia, interdisciplinary class kits were developed by the Boston Children's Museum. They are distributed by American Science and Engineering Co. In addition to the Greek kit, others are offered on medieval people, a Japanese family, the Indians who met the Pilgrims, and so on.
[14] A recent national study reports that only up to 80 percent of the elementary teachers are willing to become involved with their pupils in hot issues; this is, however, a much higher percentage than those reported in several previous studies; see Richard E. Gross, "The Status of the Social Studies in the Public Schools of the United States: Facts and Impressions of a National Survey," *Social Education*, March 1977, p. 199.

munity. If carried out well, this model may successfully join the civic concerns of the previously discussed Model C with the objective orientation and critical thinking skills sought by the proponents of this problem-resolution model.

(E) The Humanistic/Personal Model
Still hazy in its content and boundaries, this is the most recently evolving model for the social studies. Even some of the proponents of its elements have not as yet recognized its possibilities as a central organizing force for the shaping of a new, new social studies. It brings together a wide array of strategists, critics, and curriculum thinkers, many of whom have interests well beyond current conceptions of the field. Its roots go back a goodly number of years to those who believe the school, let alone the social studies, had, above all, a prime personal development and guidance function. As these leaders observed dramatic changes in our family and social structures, these advocates of such emphases saw the school stepping into the gaps and rising challenges of a radically different age. These proponents of what we might also designate a human fruition model eventually found a bevy of new cohorts among the reactors and reformers who dominated professional and popular educational literature during the debacle of the Vietnam conflict and the youth revolt of that era.

This approach is the most eclectic and amorphous of our models, including recommendations stemming from a diverse group of gurus, from Margaret Mead and Erik Erikson to Sydney Simon and Lawrence Kohlberg. This model is highly oriented toward the individual student; thus, it tends to have a loose structure and open channels for the inclusion of creative, original, and immediate pupil-evolved content. In its concern for self-realization, empathy, human dignity, and moral considerations, it features aspects of philosophy, religion, communications, social psychology, aesthetics, and the arts, most of which are not usually thought of as within the domain of the social studies. Within the undelimited confines of this emerging pattern, we can find the value clarifiers and representatives of the sensitivity movement on one hand, and on the other those concerned with youth rights and the law or the savers of our environment. Individuals concerned with global needs as well as futurists are also sympathetic toward aspects of Model E.

At this point, however, it is highly questionable as to whether an inclusive and coherent model can be evolved out of the multiple interests and emphases apparent. Nevertheless, if one is concerned with social education in both its highly personal and individual sense, as well as with its broadest implications for the survival of humankind, these planners of social studies curricula must find ways to incorporate the valuable and important understandings, skills, and attitudes accruing from the aforementioned movements into a timely learning pattern.

A Multi-Dimensional Supramodel

At this juncture it is probably apparent to the reader that few, if any, actual social studies programs or offerings fall into the mold of a pure model. As we have indicated, the typical teacher cannot be accurately described as practicing entirely within one pattern, nor probably should they. Each of the foregoing models holds fundamental contributions to social education; deserving elements from each merit inclusion in any well functioning effort. The challenge is for the classroom teachers in individual school settings to evolve the most appropriate scope and sequence that capitalizes on the various insights and approaches.

The sources of the social studies curriculum are multiple, extending beyond even the models we have identified. Only a multidimensional supramodel will serve to encompass all that should be included. Such a model will recognize and incorporate imperatives that reflect:

1. Essential human activities and processes.
2. Social goals, needs, and problems.
3. Tasks and concerns of children and youth.
4. Fundamental understandings and skills from history and the social sciences.
5. Relevant learnings from other curricular areas.
6. Contemporary developments and issues.

It is our premise that a national framework of such learnings should be developed. Then teachers and schools in varying American communities will shape and select specifics and options that meet the unique demands of their own clientele and situation. Thus, a common strand for learning to live in society will spread across the country that still allows differing states and regions and their particular needs to be accommodated. But social studies essentials from Maine to Hawaii and from Florida to Alaska will have been identified and there will be some hope that the great bulk of American pupils will have been exposed to these essences of sociocivic education.

In the meantime better district syllabi and state guides may provide some such direction. Ultimately, however, the implementation, the education that really counts, will be what is recognized and accepted by classroom teachers as being vital. What they, in one manner or another, incorporate into their curriculum and instruction for children and youth is crucial.[15]

---

[15] A helpful guide for local committees is Raymond H. Muessig, Editor, *Social Studies Curriculum Improvement*, Washington, D.C., National Council for the Social Studies, Bulletin #36, 1965, pp. 117.

Can there be any doubt that teachers need to give considerable effort in this direction? Can there be any question that they should be provided with the adequate time and assistance to properly carry out such responsibilities? If the agreement and selectivity that needs to become a reality is ever to be attained in mounting a comprehensive and timely program of social education, it is imperative that classroom teachers be encouraged and enabled to give much more attention and effort to curricular and instructional planning than has ever been true in the past.

A Systems Model for a Teaching-Learning Situation in the Social Studies Classroom

It is not enough to have established a basic curriculum model for approaching social education. For planning purposes the teacher must also consider class organization for social studies. We recommend that this be conceived in terms of a social system in miniature. Other classes, to be sure, are social systems, the difference being that the subject matter of the social studies lesson is the social system in the largest sense. There are many definitions of the social studies, each examining the subject manner from a different perspective. One of the newer definitions includes the idea that social studies content is social systems, past, present, and future. More properly, these might be referred to as societal or sociocultural systems inasmuch as the social system or subsystem exists along with the political system, the ideological system, the economic system, the ecological system, the cultural system, and others. In this sense, the social system consists of social roles, patterns of interaction, role behavior, role expectation, socioeconomic status, group relations, and the like.

Since the subject matter of the social studies *is* the societal system, it is imperative that the social studies teacher understand the concept of system, the nature of societal systems and subsystems, and to understand the way his or her class operates as a system. As a social system, a class is like any other system—it is a set or combination of interacting parts functioning as a whole. These parts work independently and are identifiable, but they also function interdependently, interacting with other elements. The component parts differ in one system or another, whether the heart and various kinds of blood vessels in the human circulatory system or the circuits, memory banks, and printout mechanism of a computer.

The Nature of Societal Systems

In any societal system there are people and a network of interacting relationships among them. The remaining component parts in a societal system are the following.

1. Stated or professed *goals,* including generalized beliefs. For example, the stated goals of the familial system would be to regulate procreation in order to best assure the preservation of the society.
2. *Resources*—material or immaterial—and arrangements for their allocation. In the economic system, the resources are land, labor, and capital. Land is obviously a material resource; labor of an intellectual kind might be considered immaterial. A capitalistic economic system allocates these resources differently from a communistic economic system.
3. Behaviors of the participants in the system. Any societal system develops *rules of be-*

havior over a period of time. Some of these rules evolve into traditions. The system also develops defined behaviors for different situations; that is, circumstances call for predictable behavior. For example, in the religious system, entry into certain churches on Sunday morning calls for prescribed behaviors: quiet, solemnity usually, kneeling and crossing oneself before entering the pew, responding at given times in specified ways during the service, and the like.

4. *Roles and positions* of the participants. Roles are clearly defined, learned throughout life, and performed more or less automatically by the participants. Most roles are differentiated in one way or another and the role incumbents are assigned positions in the system. Thus, in the social system, there are leader roles, follower roles, agitator roles, apathetic roles, and the like. There are, similarly, youthful roles, mature roles, feminine roles, masculine roles, intellectual roles, and so on. A young man whose behavior is feminine is not playing his role the way society expects him to. A person who occupies the role of a major elected official has a position that is different—and "higher"—than a person whose role is to follow orders and not make decisions for him or her self.
5. The system has *outcomes.* The system's participants success in reaching the professed goals. Families are stable, inheritances are passed on, the society is maintained. Functions are accomplished by the system that may or may not be consistent with the goals, and participants successfully perform these functions. This means, for example, that whereas a stated goal of a democratic political system is to distribute political power equitably and reasonably so that political activities are carried out and allocated, the distribution may in fact be far from equal since only a bare majority of the American people participate actively in the system.

A social studies class also has goals, resources, behaviors, roles, positions, and outcomes. It can be compared to a societal system, a political subsystem, a social subsystem, or whatever. But it is not necessary to select the "right" system and limit the systems analysis to that one. In the medical world, a neurologist might direct his or her attention to the human body's nervous system, a dermatologist to the integumentary system, and an orthopedist to the skeletal system. None of these is the "right" way to look at the human body. Similarly, the social studies class can be analyzed from any or all of the above perspectives mentioned above and from another one as well.

The Instructional System

The construct of a systems model for the social studies class as a teaching-learning environment is little or no different from a model for nearly any other kind of class. The breadth of the field of the social studies, however, means that the model is broader and more inclusive than one for most other instructional fields unless one organizes and instructs in a multi- or interdisciplinary format.

To understand this system, answers are needed to several questions: (1) *What is to be taught (and learned)?* (2) *With what* in the way of resources and (3) *How* is it to be taught and learned? (4) *In what contexts* is the content that is to be learned to be placed and (5) In *what way* are pupils to be deployed? (6) *What organizational plans* are needed? (7) *For what ends,* and (8) *How well* do the students reach these objectives and learn what they've started out to learn?

Although the questions are in sequence, there is no assumption that this is a linear model. Each part of the teaching-learning system is an entity of its own, but each is interdependent with all others. A modification in one part of the system may alter the entire system, and it may affect all other elements. This aspect of systems analysis is a major concept in social studies education, one that is im-

portant for teachers to understand in order for them to help their students. In turn, the students must develop this concept as they process social data to come to grips with the larger societal system. For instance, a modification in the political subsystem that broadens the suffrage has an impact not only in the political system itself but on the social system (newly enfranchised voters view themselves more importantly than the disenfranchised, for example) and on the economic system (as when these new voters may be the balance in electing representatives who change the degree of government involvement in the economy).

Since this construct is not linear, since the process of answering the key questions does not have to progress inalterably from one point to the next, what is it?

A Graphic Representation of the Model

At least a two-dimensional figure is necessary to illustrate the systems model of the teaching-learning situation (Figure 2.1).

Actually a teacher can start any place on the polygon as he or she organizes instruction. Teachers are generally taught to start with the objectives of the lesson, but, in practice, many social studies teachers start with some knowledge or skill, something they think is important to be learned. Second-rate social studies teachers sometimes hear about a good film, and they organize a lesson around that resource. Or a poorly trained teacher will see a demonstration of a simulation game or read about the value of groups and will start at the activities point or the pupil deployment point. These practices, which are not recommended, can lead to satisfactory instruction as long as the teacher thinks about the other elements in the system and re-

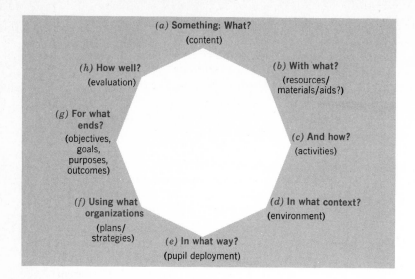

Figure 2.1

members the fundamental principle of systems analysis; a system is a whole, each element is an important contributor to the whole, and the modifications of one element can adversely affect the entire system.

A Lesson Plan Example

Suppose a teacher is "in" to war/peace studies. She is convinced that all her students should know about the background of the Vietnam war so that, as future citizens, they will not allow their country to get involved in such an episode again. She is starting with the *what* in the instructional system. Of course, as a good teacher, she will ultimately include all the elements in the construct and may even change her starting point or modify the content. It would be possible to progress through the basic questions, not in a linear order, but in any one of several sequences, as illustrated by the following:

Why should something about the Vietnam war be taught? For what purpose?

How should the students learn about it? Since there is a good pamphlet available, how about having them read it and discuss it?

But a teacher can't just hand her students a pamphlet and say, "read it, you'll like it." The teacher has to motivate the students, raise questions about the topic, help the students identify the problem, guide them in gathering data, and work with them in the analysis of the data in the solution of the problem. This process requires careful organization.

What strategy should be used? Can these learnings be linked to other subjects or to other elements of the learning day and week? If the teacher is committed to the new social studies and to inquiry learning, then she should soon realize that an expository activity such as reading alone will not be appropriate to the evidential-inferential process. Perhaps the instructor is not really committed to inquiry learning; a didactic or expository strategy may be best in this particular instance.

What pupil deployment should be used? Since the classroom is furnished with movable desks, should the physical arrangement be changed from one in which students are in rows facing the teacher? How does the deployment of students relate to the other elements in the system model — the activities, the strategy, the resources? Watching a film to obtain background information may be handled better in rows.

Buzz groups to identify the problem and subproblems would be better in clusters. Such decisions are also related to the enveloping context of the community and the learning options it holds. From museums to resource visitors, for example, knowledge about Vietnam can be personalized and increased.

What sorts of evaluation should be used that are consistent with the model as a whole and the other elements in the model? Graphically, the mode of operation within the model described above might be shown in the diagram below. Note that it is not a linear operation, moving clockwise along the points of the polygon. Furthermore, a full depiction of the operation might show steps being retraced, new sequences being followed, and the like (Figure 2.2).

As a result of examining all elements in the model and of reassessing the operation of the system as a whole, the teacher may well decide that the *what*— the content—needs to be reexamined. She may decide that the Vietnam war is ancient history to her students and that another case might better illustrate the subject matter of war/peace studies. The teacher may also be aware that she should perhaps work with the students to

see what subject matter excites them, rather than selecting content that interests the teacher.

Another teacher might have started with a clear-cut goal in mind, perhaps to have students develop skill in analyzing propaganda in the mass media. The outcome of this skill is that the students, when given several newspapers covering the same span of time, will be able to identify propaganda, separating fact from opinion, and will be able to identify and explain the seven basic types of propaganda, all in one class period. The goals dictate the teaching aids— newspapers—but a decision still has to be made as to whether the students will work singly, in pairs, or in small groups. The teacher should know that an inquiry strategy is called for. Then a careful progression through the remain elements in the systems model will follow, with a recheck and revision of some of the elements already considered.

A Course-of-Study Example

Let's take another example, this time the case of a social studies teacher who is in the process of organizing, or reorganizing a course. Let's say he is assigned to teach American government at the eighth-grade level because that is either a state requirement or because the course of study adopted by the local school board requires it. He starts, therefore, with the *what*, the broad content area of American government.

He has a list of the materials available in the social studies resource center, which is mostly devoted to history and geography. He has access to the county film library, but he has no budget for field trips, new print materials, or guest speakers. He knows *with what* he is going to teach, as well as what he doesn't have available, which is important to know, too. And *how* is he going to teach Ameri-

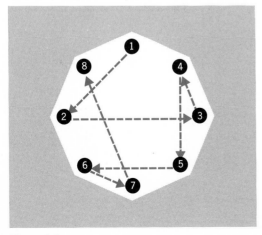

Figure 2.2

can government? That remains to be seen. He's not wedded to any one or two learning activities or teaching techniques and he plans to use the ones that are appropriate for each lesson, episode, or unit.

He can also use a variety of organizational schemes, although he believes that *what manner* a student approaches learning depends on whether it is cognitive, affective or psychomotor. Furthermore, it is important for the instructor to give careful thought to the organization, placing the learner at the center of all consideration. The teacher should also consider the *contexts* of learning from conditions within the school to opportunities in the community and beyond—as an excursion to the state legislature, which may be possible with parental drivers and aid from a local service club. *What way* he deploys the students will be influenced by other considerations, but in a *social* studies class it is important that students' *social* learning not be ignored. Therefore, a variety of pupil learning arrangements should be utilized consonant with a variety of learning activities, resources, and strategies, and because different humans have different learning styles. *What plan* of attack should be used by the teacher? It should be one that is most effective in bringing out the desired kind of learning. The new social studies, for example, emphasizes a strategy of the evidential-inferential processing of social data. This strategy allows for many different types of learning activities, even expository ones if they fit into this mode of inquiry.

The general goal of this teacher is to help develop enlightened self-actuating citizens. *For what* specific *ends* the instruction is directed will be developed with each unit and lesson, citing the terminal

behaviors that are the outcome of the instruction and the means by which they can be verified. Evaluation will be used throughout the model, assessing materials, activities, and organization, as well as the students' progress toward the objectives in order to answer the question, *how well.*

A graphic representation of this teacher in action is shown in Figure 2.3:

Thus, the construct of the social studies classroom as a system works equally well whether for a 20-minute lesson or for a year-long course. It works, also, for a five-day episode, a four-week unit or for a K-12 program of studies. Using it, a teacher can gain a better understanding of the instructional process and maximize the learning of his or her students. Furthermore, teachers find that treating the instructional process as a teaching-learning system is more consistent with the structures and content of the social science disciplines as the study of past, present, and future societal systems.

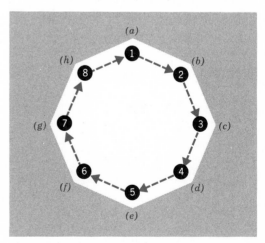

Figure 2.3

Bibliography

Banks, J. and A. Clegg. *Teaching Strategies for the Social Studies.* Reading, Mass.: Addison-Wesley, 1973.

Brubaker, Dale. *Secondary Social Studies for the 70's; Planning for Instruction.* New York: T. Y. Crowell Company, 1973.

Crowder, William. *Persistent-Problems Approach to Elementary Social Studies.* Itasca, Ill.: F. E. Peacock, 1973.

Feldman, M. and E. Seifman. *The Social Studies: Structure, Models & Strategies.* Englewood Cliffs, N.J.: Prentice-Hall, 1969.

Fraser, Dorothy (Ed.). *Social Studies Curriculum Development: Prospects and Problems.* Washington, D.C.: National Council for the Social Studies. 39th Yearbook, 1969.

Goldmark, B. *Social Studies: A Method of Inquiry.* Belmont, Calif.: Wadsworth, 1968.

Gross, R. E. and R. Muessig. *Problem-Centered Social Studies Instruction.* Washington, D.C.: Curriculum Bulletin #14, N.C.S.S., 1971.

Joyce, Bruce et al. *Three Teaching Strategies for the Social Studies.* Chicago: Science Research Associates, 1972.

Lee, John. *Teaching Social Studies in the Elementary School.* Glencoe, Ill.: Free Press, 1974.

Lowe, William. *Structure and the Social Studies.* Ithaca, N.Y.: Cornell University Press, 1969.

Martorella, Peter. *Concept Learning in the Social Studies: Models for Structuring Curriculum.* Scranton, Pa.: Intext Educational Publishers, 1971.

Michaelis, John, *Social Studies Curriculum in a Democracy: Recent Trends and Developments.* Englewood Cliffs, N.J.: Prentice-Hall, 1972.

Michaelis, J. and A. Johnson. *The Social Sciences: Foundations of the Social Studies.* Boston: Allyn and Bacon, 1965.

Morrissett, Irving (Ed.). *Concepts and Structure in the New Social Science Curricula.* New York: Holt, Rinehart and Winston, 1967.

Muessig, Ray (Ed.). *Social Studies Curriculum Improvement.* Washington, D.C.: N.C.S.S. Bulletin #36, 1965.

Ploghoft, M. and A. Schuster. *Social Science Education in the Elementary School.* Columbus, Ohio: Merrill, 1976.

Wehlage, Gary and Eugene Anderson. *Social Studies Curriculum in Perspective: A Conceptual Analysis.* Englewood Cliffs, N.J.: Prentice-Hall, 1972.

Zodikoff, David. *Comprehensive Teaching Models in Social Studies.* Dubuque, Iowa: Kendall/ Hunt, 1973.

How can the social studies program be balanced to best promote individual learning?

CHAPTER 3

Organizing the Social Studies Program

Introduction

Someone once said that planning for social studies was really like planning the whole school day. And it is. To attend to the broad citizenship goals—being responsible as an individual and as a member of the group, learning to value and think critically, acquiring empathy for others and accepting their differences—demands that the total school and class environment be used as a laboratory. Defining a scope and sequence of content and selecting a set of curriculum materials is important. The other considerations that give meaning to social studies are equally important. This section suggests some program check points that can be used for broad social studies planning. As we will see later, these checkpoints can fit a variety of class organization and management patterns.

Social Studies Components

Organizing experiences that encourage and induce elementary school students into the roles of seekers of knowledge about and conscientious actors within the realm of our planet is a big order. When we think about social studies, it is essential to look at what students might do in a program during the course of their elementary schooling. The checklist below is topical. We believe that every topic on the checklist should be observable in a broadly conceived social studies program at some time during the school day or in the course of a week at school. Read the activity descriptions in Chart 3.1. Which action topics do you see exemplified in each?

Chart 3.1   Action Opportunity Checklist for Social Studies Programs

School years		ACTIVITY
Primary	Intermediate	
*	*	Community involvement
*	x	Current affairs
*	x	Group responsibility
x	x	Empathy for others, acceptance of differences
x	x	Skill practice and extension
x	x	Knowledge growth
x	x	Change in nature of tasks

x means at least a daily occurrence.
* means at least a weekly occurrence.

Activity 1: One fourth grade student is blindfolded. He is seated with another student who is helping him do math. No great attention is given the working pair. When the recess time comes, another student comes to take the "blind" classmate outside. After recess the "blind" boy passes on his role to a classmate. Throughout the day, the "blind" students attempt to participate normally in class activities.

A few minutes before dismissal time the whole group participates in a discussion about the day's events. One "blind" boy, Jeb, begins by telling how it felt not to see. "At first it was fun! I made a game of guessing who was talking by listening to their voices. But by recess time I wanted to play dodge ball and couldn't. From there on, it got worse. If I hadn't promised to do this when my name was drawn, I would have taken off this old blindfold!"

Several helpers express themselves. "Helping was o.k. for awhile. It gets to be a drag after awhile. You can't do what you want to."

"He acted like he didn't want us to help him . . ."

"It was creepy! I didn't like always having to hand her stuff at the cafeteria."

At this point Mr. Marcus, the teacher, asks the class to make statements describing what the experiment has taught them about handicapped people. Several comment that the day has made them see how difficult simple things are for handicapped persons. One girl remarks that she learned that anyone can help a blind person if she wants to.

Activity 2: Ms. Bowmer's first graders gather around the sharing rug as they finish hanging up their clothes and storing their lunches. Once the calendar is changed and attendance taken, Ms. Bowmer asks, "Who remembers what our sharing assignment for today was?"

" 'Wild Kingdom'!" nearly everyone shouts.

"Let's see who was a careful viewer. Raise your hand if you remember what last night's show was about. Yes, Martha?"

"About ostriches and how they hatch their eggs."

"Yes. Who can tell us one thing you learned for our Mothers and Babies Chart?"

As children volunteer information Ms. Bowmer fills in chart spaces about the ostrich under headings of: "where born," "how born," "how many," "how fed," "enemies," "defense," independence." This is the fifth animal the class had worked on and answers are quick in coming. To summarize, the children reread their contributions from the chart. Ms. Bowmer knows she can expect at least 20 stories today about tall birds who run fast and lay big eggs.

Activity 3: The fifth-grade Weather Reporter group is meeting to read the weather map in today's local newspaper. They are responsible for reporting to the whole group three minutes of weather news which is part of the twice-weekly News Review. Each combines three days worth of data on a different aspect of the weather, which is transferred in grease pencil to large laminated charts. To participate in this section of News Review, students have to pass a weather-map reading test.

Activity 4: Miss Lieber's mixed primary group is studying "What Makes Our Environment." Several eight-year-olds have chosen to be environmental surveyors. Miss Lieber's aide, Mrs. Meyer, is leading them in a first survey around the school. At designated points the aide stops the group and directs its observations. At the school entrance, "What do you see that is student created here?"

"Mud on the sidewalk."

"Trash all around the barrel."

"What do you see as causes for each thing you observed?"

Students hypothesize item by item.

"Now, let's fill out our observations sheets for station 1, day 1 from what we have just mentioned. You will come back to each station tomorrow by yourselves and record what you see."

You should have detected opportunities for each checklist item in these four glimpses of social studies programs. A given activity often combines several of the checklist items so that separating or dissecting one from another becomes artificial. However, for the purpose of activating your own planning ideas, let us explore further possibilities for each checklist activity type. Can another item be added to the checklist?

Community Involvement

Possibilities for student involvement with the community can be sponsored by both individual teachers and by schoolwide efforts. The scope of these opportunities should be the school and the neigh-borhood. The questions that should guide community studies are: What is our community like? and How can it be organized for the benefit of all who live in our community? All students should have chances to participate throughout their school years in organized ongoing activities such as cafeteria duty, school patrol, library helpers, custodial assistants, cleanup efforts, beautifying school and grounds, recycling centers or senior citizen and shut-in callers. Beyond these everyday kinds of activities, individual teachers should seek ways of involving students in shorter-term community action projects. The issues of energy conservation in homes, and neighborhood renewal are excellent vehicles for more formal study that leads students to achieve tangible evidence of their involvement.

Study of the community is often allowed to stop with a description of services a citizen can expect to be performed with no hint that the idealized descriptions might be discrepant with the student's reality or what to do about changing undesirable conditions. From their earliest years in school, students should be exposed to the stormy, vital process of community allocation of resources and of local decision-making. Parents, PTA members, principals, city councilpeople and city service administrators or resource visitors from a bank or insurance firm can help explain elements of economics or help answer such questions as Where do school supplies come from? Why are there unpatched potholes in the streets? Why doesn't the school have a music teacher this year? How can we get a crossing light?

Current Affairs

Commercial newspapers written for student consumption constitute only a minor resource for the almost endless issues current affairs study can offer; for example, the scope of current affairs should not be bound to what is offered in one of these weekly or biweekly papers. Study of current affairs should take advantage of the constant media input and consider whatever topics or issues young students can comprehend.

Growing up in a television-saturated environment has loosened the time and space limitations on children's thinking. However, television exposure makes for distorted, incomplete understandings because the viewing is usually not complemented by discussion and analysis or background about what was seen. Continued exposure to discussion of issues and events heard about on television is a necessity if students are to become more than passive receptacles of data concerning the world that surrounds them. One purpose of current events is to illustrate how interdependent the life systems of our planet are. Each child must come to see himself/herself as ultimately dependent upon events outside himself and his nuclear family.

How can this awareness be engendered in our social studies programs? First, teachers must become better models. If we are unable, for example, to pull down the wall map and point out where the latest earthquake in Eastern Europe occurred and discuss it in response to children's questions, then we can bet that our students are not likely to have their interest in learning more about what is happening in the world beyond the classroom walls reinforced. Second, we should avoid making current events into a newspaper clipping count or reading comprehension check. The latter is a worthy objective, but not very inspiring of student enthusiasm about current events!

Some strategies that have proven successful involve a schoolwide rotational system where each class has several op-

portunities throughout the year to organize and present news for the whole school over the loudspeaker or closed-circuit television systems. The same procedure can work within one classroom group with students rotating the news coverage from weather to sports to local to national news reporting. Teacher help in how to take notes, how to read from notes and a whole host of communication skills will be necessary to make this project fully rewarding.

Strategies do not necessarily have to replicate the news gathering to news reporting cycle. Primary students can be directed to discuss topics gathered from their home television viewing during sharing periods. These topics need not be restricted to newscasts. Special and regular nature programs are good resources. Intermediate students find interest in choosing one or two topics to follow for a period of time. Sometimes focusing on a given country, or issue for several weeks is worthwhile. This can also be encouraged on an individual or committee basis. This strategy allows students to analyze how the business of newsmaking is conducted as well as to gain an indepth acquaintance with a subject.

One fifth-grade class recently chose to follow the trial of Patty Hearst. The teacher had reservations about the complexity of the trial and lurid press coverage of the case. Nearly every student became an articulate defender of either the state or the defense. These students engaged in some substantive thinking about what this trial portrayed of American society. They learned a great deal about the rights of the accused, how criminal court trials proceed and the names and functions of each courtroom official. The teacher brought the local newspaper to class every morning to share. He found students becoming eager to have a chance to read about other topics as they saw him spending time and discussing the news he found in the paper with them. In this case, his reservations about the students' choice of topic were erased by the kind of continuing participation and growing understanding the students demonstrated.

Group Responsibility

Personal reports of outstanding learning experiences often emphasize the importance of becoming part of a group effort. We must see to it that our segmented society where individuals tend to surround themselves with gadgets that isolate them from others is not duplicated in our schools. Children need a variety of occasions when they can join with others to accomplish a common goal such as writing and presenting a play, solving a playground scheduling problem by arranging to rotate the sport played on the diamond, or baking and selling cupcakes to earn money so everyone can go on a camping trip.

Opportunities for collaboration and cooperation should be promoted in more formal or academic work as well. As a change of pace, allow individuals to help each other pass a skills or knowledge exercise. Some teachers have gotten good results by requiring members of a group to coach each other until the whole group acquires the desired level of knowledge or skill. The smallest group is a dyad. Numerous opportunities exist from sharing and planning to decision making for pupils to discuss and work in pairs. Skills related to human understanding and listening, for example, are promoted by such partnership exchanges.[1]

Empathy — Acceptance of Differences

A child's ability to communicate and relate to others can be stunted or enhanced through his/her school experience. Two elements for enhancing the development of empathy are exposure and modeling. We should work from the premise that differences are natural, factual, and good—a value judgment. Recognizing this fact and accepting this value judgment come gradually. The process is less painful if each child begins with himself/herself. From their earliest sharing times children should be led to consider their own uniqueness and the rights of others to also be unique.

Exposure to different-appearing individuals who perhaps behave differently may lead children to greater awareness. This heightened ability to notice differences may actually be detrimental to a child's ability to relate to people not perceived as similar to her or himself. How to get along with and have a caring feeling for these "others" must be modeled. Real-life conflicts, with which most schools abound, are the best raw material for implementing this aspect of a total social studies program.

This process can be initiated by using commercially prepared materials that explore conflictual situations based on problems of sharing, shunning, and discriminating. After the skills of "walking in another's shoes" have been tried out on topics that are distant from the group's moment, the focus can be turned on local class problems. The modeling is an adjudicating process. How do each of the parties to the dispute feel? Is it possible for sincere people to disagree? What can each side do to build a better situation.[2]

---

[1] See examples in L. Zeleny and R. Gross, "Dyadic Role Playing of Controversial Issues" *Social Education,* December 1960, pp. 354-358, 364.
[2] Suggested steps for promoting skills of problem resolution are found in R. E. Gross, "How to Handle Controversial Issues," *How-To-Do-It Bulletin #14,* Washington, D.C., National Council for the Social Studies, 1971.

Skills Development

Skills in location, comprehension, and organization of knowledge and cooperating competencies should be continuously developed in an integrated manner throughout the student's elementary school career. Many school districts have sequential skills development guidelines that set out year-by-year objectives. Commercial programs often outline the skills that use of their materials develop. We will be examining some of these skills in more detail in a few pages. For now, let us emphasize that each broad skill category mentioned above should be developed incrementally within each level or year of a social studies program.

Knowledge Growth

Are we brave enough to ask students what they are learning about in school that they did not know before? Straightforward questions that require a child to summarize and enumerate can tell us a great deal about the impact our social studies program is having on that child's conscious cognitive pool: "What can you locate on a globe?"

"What have you learned about people that you did not know?" "What have you learned about yourself and your community?" "What do you now know about our country's history?" A true measure of quality in any program is how much students can relate about it. In social studies the child's range of topics and examples should grow wider the longer he or she is in school.

Task Variety

Perhaps this category is redundant when listed with all the previous ones on the checklist. Even so, observing the kinds of activities associated with social studies that students engage in, over a week's period, for example, allows a kind of summary of program quality. Variety should be evidenced in both student intake of information and student production of information and in the arrangement of students according to the task at hand. The sample recording chart shown in Chart 3.2 can be expanded and specified. It can provide a means of checking activity variety in a social studies program by following the kind of tasks several students perform during the period of a week. These pupil experiences should reflect our multiple goals; in our planning we need to regularly check that learning activities adequately reflect attitudinal and competency as well as knowledge aims.

Integration of Subjects

Social studies goals demand integration with other subjects. Nothing can happen in social studies without using language.

Chart 3.2 Sample Recording Chart for Individual Student Tasks

INFORMATION INTAKE	A[a]	SG	LG	INFORMATION OUTPUT	A	SG	LG
Listen				Talk			
Watch movie				List			
Read				Write			
Locate				Draw			
Observe				Role play			
Interview				Make model			
Ask questions				Demonstrate			

[a] A—alone; SG—small group; LG—large group.

This combination of language arts with social studies is a reality. The teaching decision is whether to consciously develop language skills necessary for accomplishing specific social studies activities as an integrated plan. Decisions not to integrate these two areas have led to frustrations for both teachers and students. Students often cannot proceed to get at the social studies content because they have not been helped by specific instruction in how to use the index of books or how to organize and conduct an interview, for example. And teachers often question themselves about what they are actually evaluating when checking test answers or written summaries. Often the grades given represent more of an assessment of the student's language skills than anything else.

A social studies program integrated with language arts can take on various appearances. Most often specific process skills are taught as they are needed as the unit segment below shows.

Some of these skills such as interviewing are traditionally identified as language arts skills. Yet, how much more meaningful the skill becomes when learned because the student has an immediate use for it. Anyone who has ever had to practice letter writing just to learn conventional forms need no further convincing of this point. This kind of subject matter integration makes skill learning more attractive for students. Since language skills are being specifically taught, they should be evaluated as such. This kind of intergration still allows for separation of language arts from social studies for evaluation purposes.

Integration of social studies with other forms of expression such as music, art, dance, and drama is natural and essential when dealing with topics that focus on the formal elements of cultures. Possibilities for the integration of social studies with math and science depend on the topic studied. Map-reading skills naturally lead to using math to figure distances, time changes and travel times. The whole range of environmental topics lend themselves to combining science and social studies. Students need to learn about energy sources and means of energy conversion in order for the human, or problematic, aspects of energy to have meaning. The same is true for studying other resources. Learning about the water cycle must go hand in hand with

Unit Topic: My Family (primary level)

TOPIC	ACTIVITY
1. Nuclear-extended family	Begin individual booklet with page for each family member.
2. Family roles	*Observe filmstrips and record family members and jobs in each family type.
3. Participant observation	*Practice job analysis during lunch hour.
4. Participant observation	Record who does what at home. Share information in class.
5. Charting data	*Practice pictographs using pet collection data of class and individual Baggie collections.
6. Charting data	Compose individual and group pictographs of data about families.
7. Family backgrounds	Discuss how we learn to do things and have certain preferences. Prepare data collection sheet for parent interviews.
8. Interviewing	*Listen to taped interview and fill out data sheet from it.
9. Interviewing	Conduct parent interviews.

The asterisks identify points of specific skills teaching in this unit segment. Notice that care is taken to practice the skills involved in a project before assigning the project.

examining water pollution's effects and studying how it can be diminished.

Time Management

Building daily schedules for a group of students requires that optimal learning conditions be arranged within the following constraints. The constraints to be juggled are students' psychological and physical needs, the building plan for playground, multipurpose room, and mediacenter use, the physical arrangement of your teaching post, and basic school curriculum and organizational policies.

Teachers in most schools fall into scheduling practices that are traditional in that particular school. This usually means a separate subject approach with the "essential" skills coming earlier in the day while the students have more energy and the less essential areas saved for after lunch, as seen in Chart 3.3. Schedule A is typical of this kind of approach. Schedule B is typical of a more fluid, self-contained classroom. Direct instruction in reading and math basics continues on a group rotation basis throughout both morning blocks of time. Some students will be working with math activities while others are engaged in one or another reading task. The teacher does not expect to work directly every day with each child in both reading and math.

Schedule C allows for intergration of subject matter areas according to the theme or topic being studied in social studies or science. The content of each work period would vary in Schedule C. Work for each block of time would be related to the main topic. For instance, the topic of Pacific Island Life would mean that reading and story time would concentrate on stories, films, and all sorts of library sources on islander life-styles, legends, economies, and transportation. Along with regular math skill development would be some exercises in calculating travel distances between islands and produce prices for copra. Songs, games, art, and dance from the islands would be part of the integrated day. Language arts would perhaps include writing pen pal letters to an island class, or doing research for a skit about the islanders' belief concerning The Creation or practicing a Hawaiian poem with hand gestures.

The kind of schedule you build orients how you organize instruction. Scheduling is less flexible in schools where teachers attempt to group students from several classrooms homogeneously for reading or math instruction. Smooth movement of students and materials between teaching posts so that time is not lost becomes very important under this system. Allowing one group to come to a

Chart 3.3   Three Daily Schedules

SCHEDULE A		SCHEDULE B		SCHEDULE C	
8:30	Sharing, reading	8:30	Sharing, reading, and math	8:30	Sharing, planning
9:40	Snack, break	9:40	Snack, break	8:45	First work period
9:50	Math	9:50	Reading and math cont'd.	9:45	Snack, break
10:40	Recess	10:40	P.E.	10:00	Second work period
11:00	Spelling, writing	11:00	Story, work time on sci-	11:00	P.E.
11:40	Lunch		ence, social studies	11:30	Story
12:30	Story	12:00	Lunch	11:45	Lunch
12:45	Science, social studies	12:40	Music, art, work time	12:30	Third work period
1:45	Recess	1:45	Recess	1:30	Recess
2:00	Art, music, P.E.	2:00	Writing, spelling	1:45	Fourth work period

logical stopping point, even though the process may take time beyond the scheduled number of minutes, is perceived as nearly criminal.

Back to the Basics: Another Planning Consideration

There is a growing concern that the schools should move back toward more emphasis on the basics. The "back to the basics" movement is difficult to define since there is no uniformity of agreement among the advocates of basic education as to what it should be. Regardless of these differences, there have probably been three major reasons for more Americans, including some teachers, to favor basic education. One has been the widespread publicity about the decline in SAT scores of entering college students. Second has been the rising costs of the schools and the necessity to cut costs. Third, there have been the concerns, if not fears, about the deteriorating discipline and growing violence in some schools.

Many parents, both minority as well as middle-class white, are disturbed that too many young people do not have a high level of skill in the ability to read, figure, spell, and write. They note that with television many young people are not reading very much. These people feel that the schools should be more structured and more teacher directed.

The back to the basics movement has also included more emphasis on behavior — students should have to work hard and should obey their teachers. In some cases it is felt that students should have to follow a dress code, and conform to accepted American values. This may include teaching about patriotism and citizenship in the schools as well as inculcation of students in the basic American values such as the Protestant ethic.

Specifically, some basic education advocates want increased proficiency in such skills as reading, math, handwriting, and grammar. They often want "new" math deemphasized and more time spent on computational skills. They want students to work harder and to have more homework.

To achieve these goals of basic education, the teacher should have more authority and "be in charge of" the class. The class should not be student centered but teacher directed. Teachers should have high expectations for their students who should learn what the teachers ask. This means more frequent reporting to parents about each student's progress. Report cards, in addition, need to be clear on what has been learned.

How does the back-to-basics movement affect social studies programs? On the elementary level, it is felt that more teachers, responding to the pressure, have been spending more time on their reading and math programs and less on other subjects in the curriculum. Many elementary teachers apparently have been unable to use their social studies programs to increase skills such as reading.

These concerns may lead to a stabilization or decline in the number of elective courses available to secondary students. At all grade levels, there may be less time spent on inquiry and games or role playing. Instead, there may be more support for a traditional textbook with more specific facts, especially about American history and government.

The push for basic education is not going to disappear. This means it may be necessary for schools and teachers to listen carefully to what parents want for their children. In some cases, this may involve setting up basic schools as alternative schools or allowing some classes within a given school, to put more emphasis on the basics. In any case, the back to the basics movement is forcing schools to clarify what is being done in their social studies program. Vagueness is not a good answer to parents and is not helpful in achieving social studies objectives. Planning must take into account the concerns of parents.

Behavioral Objectives

Advocates of the behavioral objectives approach believe that instruction is improved by setting up a clear definition of the desired instructional outcomes. They usually envision the behavioral objectives process as consisting of three major steps: (1) setting up behavioral objectives, (2) devising a wide variety of learning experiences to achieve the objectives, and (3) testing and evaluation to see if the behavioral objectives have really been met.

We should distinguish between behavioral objectives and goals. Goals are statements of broad general purpose and are not concerned with a particular achievement within a specified time period. Behavioral objectives, in contrast, are desired accomplishments that can be measured within a given time. Thus, an objective describes what the learner is to know, will be able to do, or will demonstrate as a consequence of instruction. In some cases, the objective also outlines what the level of acceptable performance is and under what conditions (amount of time and the like) the student is to perform the objective.

Social studies objectives are normally divided into three main categories: (1) knowledge and understanding, (2) attitudes and values, and (3) skills and competencies. In only a few school districts

and among a few teachers would social participation—active citizenship participation in the community—be included as a fourth category.

Translating the broad social studies goals such as effective citizenship or an appreciation of democracy into specific behavioral objectives is not easy. Often the following common errors are found in statements of objectives:

1. Objectives are stated in vague terms—to develop an appreciation of the various racial and ethnic groups in the USA or to learn to work together democratically in and out of the classroom.
2. The objectives refer only to subject matter and not to the mental process(es)—the economic law of supply and demand; the Articles of Confederation, the duties of a police officer.
3. The objectives are stated in terms of non-observable behavior—the student will be inspired to search on his/her own for more information on urban problems or that the student will be creative.

In fact, objectives often contain several faults as well as referring only to trivial points that are both unrelated to individual or societal needs. Examples of the latter are to have students memorize the state capitals or to know the names of the dogs of the explorers of Antarctic.

What are some helpful hints for teachers to write objectives? First, teachers should clarify the time span for their objectives. Are they writing the objectives for the whole academic year, for a teaching unit that will last for six weeks, or for a given day? Of course, the objectives for a given day will be much more specific than the more general objectives for the whole.

Second, writing down the following words or the equivalent helps to focus attention on what the student will do instead of just the role of the teacher.

"The student will . . ."

Then comes the action word or the verb. What will be asked of the student? Will the student write, speak, jump, inspect, compare, recognize, summarize, contrast, select, or organize? There are, of course, many possibilities but some verbs will challenge the students to use higher levels of thinking. Students should not stay at the memory level and it is helpful for teachers to check their verbs to see what they are expecting of their students.

Let us assume that we want the student to *compare*. The objective now reads as follows:

"The student will compare . . ."

What is now missing? Of course, it is the content. What data will the student be asked to process? Let us insert some content. The objective now reads:

"The student will compare the roles of children with those of adults in the Bali culture." (Or any other culture group you may wish to study.)

Is this anything else? Some authorities would now like the criteria or the acceptable level of performance given. Thus, the objective may now read:

"The student will compare the roles of children with those of adults in Bali families giving three roles of the children and three roles for adults."

Some teachers have found other formats to be more useful. Thus, the objective can be written as follows:

"Given a map of a familiar area, the student will demonstrate his/her ability to interpret map symbols by identifying the objects that correspond to the symbols on the map."[3]

---

[3] *Social Science*, Instructional Objectives Exchange, University of California, Los Angeles, Objective 1.

Then the criteria, recognition of seven (of five) symbols is listed separately after the objective. The particular format used is not the important point. What is essential is that the objectives should be as clear as possible on what particular behavior the students are meant to acquire after having gone through one or a series of learning experiences.

The behavioral objectives approach, which is mandated in certain school districts, raises serious issues. One is the work and unwillingness of many teachers to write objectives. Too many teachers found the behavioral objectives approach to be time consuming with little in the way of benefits. It has also led to identifying trival matter because such things are often more easily assessed. Others feel that it cuts off students interests and creativity. On the other hand, advocates of the behavioral approach believe that much of what goes on in education is aimless because of the lack of clear objectives on the part of many teachers. Current public demands for accountability will probably be reflected in continuing efforts to promote such precise statements of aims and related assessment practices.

Teacher-Student Planning

Some teachers have felt that the behavioral objectives approach is incompatible with the teacher-student planning approach. The following case is an illustration of teacher-student planning. Read this illustration with this possible conflict in mind.

A junior high school unit on human relations was begun at the students' own sphere of operations when they selected their special problem and stated it as, "How can we get along better with people?" The study was launched by means of a class discussion of their own experiences in human relationships. They classified these as dealing with people at home, at school, and in the community. As students name their own activities, that might fall under each heading, two members of the class wrote those mentioned on the board.

The following samples from the class contributions were listed:

Things We Do with and for People at Home

Feed baby

Run errands for
     mother and dad

Play games

Have parties

Entertain company

Watch television

Things We Do with and for People at School

Work on school
     paper

Walk to and from
     school

Play on teams

Study lessons

Go to social hours

Go on field trips

See movies

Work on committees

Talk to friends

Help others with lessons

Things We Do with and for People in the Community

Go to church

Go to parties and picnics

Go to shopping
     center

Play ball on teams

Deliver papers

Baby sitting

When the students saw the list on the board, they classified them under the following headings: chores, hobbies, safety, sports, recreation, work, personality, manners, and use of leisure time and chose four areas for special study: hobbies, sports, safety, and personality. On a written ballot each child indicated his or her first and second preference of an area for study. The class officers worked out the study group membership lists from these ballots. Finally a plan and time schedule for study was worked out.[4] Thus a unit of study was launched by application of the principle of motivation, that is, work should begin where the pupil is and lead on from there to reasonable goals of learning.

What behavioral objectives might the teacher have planned for this session? In terms of handling data and personal planning, these objectives would have been appropriate:

1. Students will classify items relating to their daily activities.
2. Students will list several personal arenas of human relationships.
3. Students will select areas of study in human relations.

In terms of knowledge or content no objective really fits this kind of initial joint planning session. And as a unit this example represents an extreme version of student input to instruction. But in order, more teacher-directed units or instructional plans, there is a definite role for teacher-student planning. This point planning should take place at various

---

[4] Ruth Cunningham and Associates, *Understanding Group Behavior of Boys and Girls*, Bureau of Publications, Teachers College, Columbia University, New York, 1951, pp. 245-246.

points during an instructional sequence. Note the superiors in the following sequence of unit activities. Each one denotes the need for continued teacher-student or teacher-whole class planning.

As Chart 3.4 demonstrates, a teacher can aid and abet learning in his/her classes by allowing and encouraging the students to have a voice in what is going to be done in the class. This does not mean that students are going to tell the teacher what to teach or what not to teach. But when students suggest a general pattern of what they like to learn and the order of presentation, the teacher can get an invaluable insight into their interests and, consequently, do a better job of teaching. During the course of the year the teacher can judge the growth of the students by seeing how well they plan their work.

Eventually, the teacher can share numerous aspects of decision making with the pupils. In doing so we promote student commitment to the tasks at the same time that important skills and understandings are being built. "Whats," "wheres," "whos," "whens," "whys," and "hows" can all be included. "What topics should we consider for current affairs this week?" "Where among these places should we visit?" "Who is to serve on which committee?" "When shall we have the test?" "Why is it important that we study this problem?" "How would we best be able to follow-up on our conclusions?" These and numerous other opportunities exist on a daily basis to help students become fully involved in *their* school learning experiences.

The argument in favor of teacher-student planning is that one of the skills

Chart 3.4 Preliminary Plan for Four-Week Problem Unit

	MONDAY	TUESDAY	WEDNESDAY	THURSDAY	FRIDAY
1st week	Problem presensation and discussion	Clarification and definition of problem and subproblems	Teacher-student planning on procedures of problem study[a]	Determination of individual student problems and/or committee assignments[a]	Day in library
2nd week	Continuing research in classroom and library[a]	Committee progress reports[a]	Class discussion	Work in class; teacher-student conferences on individual projects[a]	Guest lecturer
3rd week	Individual and group classroom and library work[a]	Motion picture	Discussion and pre-planning of field trip[a]	Open as needed[a]	Field trip
4th week	Assessment of field trip and lecture[a]	Open as needed[a]	Open as needed; probably final group reports[a]	Review of suggested conclusions and possible action[a]	Final evaluation

[a] Indicates elements requiring student-teacher planning.

that the teacher is trying to teach is the skill of organizing and planning. The best way for students to learn the skill is to practice it rather than to hear it preached to them. Also the goals of teaching then become student goals. Teacher-student planning does not have to be present in every step of the instructional process.

The hallmark of this method is when the teacher finds a middle ground between the one-way instruction of the "I want you to . . ." and the ineffective and empty, "What do you want to do today?" There is more than one way to bring this about. Perhaps the best way is with a teacher who is broad in scholarship, interested in teaching, and eager for the students to learn; the teacher will "spontaneously" get her/his students interested in the planning process. This may take many forms. It may be a complete class organization replete with student planning committees, work committees, reporting to the group with the accent on group dynamics. Or it may be through the teacher's questioning, prodding, encouraging, and urging.

Whatever form it takes, here are a few hints that might make it easier.

1. Do not give up if it does not work the first time. Student planning is a skill that needs to be learned as any other skill. The first attempts will, of course, be halting and awkward but the skills will come only with the practice.
2. Students must be conversant with the subject matter to do any detailed planning. Care in outlining steps a group is to accomplish and the range of choices that can be made are necessary to profitable planning.
3. Make sure that there is some learning of both knowledge and skills at all times. It does little to have, for example, groups list and categorize items that have no meaning beyond the skill of listing and categorizing as a group practice.
4. Be on hand to serve as a group facilitator as well as a resource person. In reality, two kinds of instruction occur simultaneously under teacher-student planning: the subject matter and the planning process.

One of the reasons why teaching is a complicated and sometimes confusing process is that the instructor is teaching two audiences at once: the student as an individual and the students as a group. And so often the former is lost in the latter! So in planning for instruction, the teacher must account for differences in the students in the class. All the personality factors that make the human race so glorious also make teaching more difficult. What motivates some bores others; what challenges one frustrates many; what overwhelms many may encourage a few. And so it goes.

In these days of diagnostic teaching, individualization of instruction becomes increasingly more important. One of the best approaches to individualization is through the unit plan. This type of planning can allow the teacher to plan for and with different individuals in the class. There are many means of learning the same general information and these can be explored so that all the students can be stimulated. Similar unit goals can be reached for differing students by varied learning experiences. This means that there must be activities so that class nonreaders can learn as well as the more precocious ones. When real teacher-student planning occurs, there should be even more attention devoted to setting individual behavioral objectives. Thus, no conflict need exist between teacher-student planning and instruction aimed at achieving behavioral objectives. The more clearly stated the purposes and scope of learning, the more responsibility and self-direction students can assume. Student-teacher sharing in the tailoring of broad goals of instruction to the student's needs and interests can only be a positive, although time-consuming, process.

Teaching Group Skills

Working together does not come naturally for adults. Public enthusiasm during the past 10 years for sensitivity training and group process sessions attests to the lack of facility adults in our society feel about positively relating to others while working toward mutual goals. Even though this is true, teachers often expect young students to perform productively in group settings!

Consider the self-involvement of the typical preschool child. When asked about the workings of the solar system, the child explains that the sun follows him/her! Young children play in the same sandbox, but rarely do they play together. Their contacts are usually to define "mine" from "yours," and almost always there is no "yours." How can teachers assist the development of the young child's relational skills? Following is a list of suggested activities teachers can employ throughout the school day in sequentially developing group cooperation skills.

Sequential Development of Group Skills
1. Form pairs in lines for walks and passage to other places.
2. Use pairs for exercises with balls, special duties, sharing materials.
3. Appoint students to lead routine activities and let them choose a substitute rotating from boy to girl.
4. Plan classroom cleanup tasks with class using pairs to share chores.
5. Discuss daily and weekly schedule with students.
6. Plan center and game scheduling so that students work in groups of two to three

and select others to take places when finished.
7. Use student teams for helping each other in drill work.
8. Structure make-it-together groups of three to four for cooking, art, and drama projects.
9. Assign three to four research tasks of 15 minutes such as looking up a word list in dictionaries.
10. Assign groups of four to five problem-solving tasks of one session such as listing essentials for fifteenth-century ocean explorer's gear.
11. Assign groups of four to six creative tasks to develop and present such as dramatization of fables, favorite stories, historical events.
12. Assign groups of four to six topics to research and present about which they already have some basic information.

Teachers of middle-grade students often attempt committee work at the level described in item 12. When the students have no idea how to proceed, teachers conclude that this group just cannot work together. This may be true. However, it is not the students, but their lack of practice that is at fault. Building cooperative process skills is like building skill in any other area. Tasks must be presented in a simple-to-complex sequence and opportunity to practice under varied circumstances must be arranged.

One further question about group work deserves mention. This is the question of student placement in groups and selection of group leaders. Situations to *avoid* are placing all the poor readers together, allowing strong personalities to always be leaders, appointing group leaders and allowing them to choose group members, and allowing friendship cliques to dictate groupings. Again, a middle way between totally free student choice and teacher-dictated assignment needs to be found.

Long-Range and Unit Planning

Organizing for social studies instruction requires the teacher to consider the year's calendar approximating blocks of time needed for development of social studies topics suggested for students by the school district. In order to do this, these steps are recommended:

1. Read district or county or state social studies curriculum guide for level you are assigned to teach and levels preceding and succeeding yours.
2. *Skim* teacher manuals and student basal texts available for your use noting discrepancies and continuities between texts and curriculum guides.
3. Gather and *skim* resource units from other teachers, district libraries, and the like, for further ideas on instructional materials and activities for suggested social studies topics.
4. Discuss approaches and emphases with other teachers—of the same grade, of the children in the previous year, of the next grade.
5. Plot topics on year's calendar by yourself or with team members.

Once your calendar is initially plotted you are ready for the more detailed planning process. Some social studies activities concerning current affairs and community involvement should be scheduled as ongoing projects not necessarily tied to the social studies time or topic being studied. To implement instruction for the first topic you plotted on your calendar, you should make a broad plan in the following order.

Teacher Steps in Unit Planning

1. Check whether students had unit last year and whether unit interests them.
2. Gather and read student and teacher background sources on topic.
3. Make initial outline of student knowledge, skills and valuing objectives to be gained.
4. Decide how best to organize students for topic study.
5. Sequence activities for unit.
6. Organize evaluation plan for stated objectives.
7. Make visual materials, write student instructions, organize learning environment.

"There are many roads that lead to Rome," a famous unit planner is alleged to have said. Another equally famous unit planner is said to have responded, "Ah yes! Do you mean Roma, Italia; Rome, New York; or Rome, Georgia?" What the first sage had in mind was that, if our objectives are clear to us, we can use almost any materials to get there. The second wise person, however, was indicating the dilemma faced by most teachers. This is that the instructional materials, especially basal textbooks, often dictate the instructional objectives and the routes we take to accomplish them. They do this because of the topics discussed and the way the coverage of the topics is organized. Let us see a case in point.

Mr. Thurston teaches sixth-grade social studies and math in a departmentalized middle school. In social studies he is to develop units on Western Hemisphere geography and cultures. He has decided to do separate units on Canada, the United States, Central America, Andean countries, and eastern South American countries. His broad objective is to develop the understanding that geography and history influence the culture(s) of a region.

In thinking about the Andean unit, he visualized two possibilities for organizing student study (Figure 3.1). Under each of thses examples the pertinent facts about the common daily human activities of government, religion, trade, transportation, production, education, housing, food, clothing, and entertainment could be investigated. However, when Mr. Thurston analyzes the basal textbook and

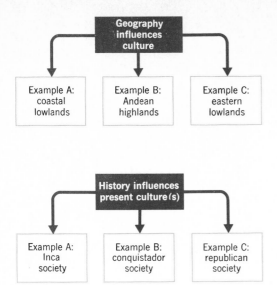

Figure 3.1   Unit topic alternatives.

other materials he has at hand or can acquire, he realizes that there is not enough student material to divide the class into six committees and do fairly independent research. Materials that he can arrange for students highlight the highlands region and the Inca society.

Mr. Thurston can resolve this planning difficulty in several ways. One solution would be to preserve his content categories or outline and assume responsiblity for presenting the material in more of a lecture form. Another resolution would be to follow a more traditional read-and-recite organization from the basal text, thus covering only the Andean highlands Inca period. Yet another solution would be to combine some of his original geographical divisions so that he could use his basal textbook and other materials to best advantage. For example, the influence of history and geography in the Andean Highlands, the Argentine Pampas, the American South, and the Canadian Eastern Seaboard could provide ample comparative samples to fully develop student understandings about

the ways geography and history express themselves in peoples' lives.

If Mr. Thurston feels that cooperative work in committees and development of individual research skills are important enough, he will decide on the third option. This means that he must go "back to the drawing board" and rethink the original categories into which he divided the year's study. He may come up with a long-range plan that looks like this:

☐ Physical geography of the Western Hemisphere.

☐ Political and cultural geography of the Western Hemisphere.

☐ Comparative life-styles of the Western Hemisphere.

In reality, Mr. Thurston may not become aware of the inadequate nature of materials for students until the year gets under way, and he tries to decide how to organize students for study as is indicated in step four of the above teacher steps in unit planning. This does not mean he should muddle through with no change in his original plan. Changes and adjustments in the long-range plan will have to be made as the year progresses. More drastic reorientation of the content, or rerouting of a way to Rome, may have to wait for another year. Such rerouting will always be assisted by the teacher who continously questions him/herself regarding the broad objectives set out at the beginning of the year. Are they being accomplished, or does the actual progress of classroom activities really lead to another Rome?

There is another aspect teachers like Mr. Thurston need to take into consideration. Teachers in departmentalized or team settings have added long-range planning responsibilities. Since they do not have students for an integrated day in which all subject matter comes into play, they cannot know how students are doing in reading and other related skills.

A common complaint among middle-grade teachers is that their students do not know how to write a paragraph or make a summary from an outside reading or use the card file in the library.

Many times students are not at fault. Their teachers have assumed someone else taught them these skills. As an essential part of the long-range planning process teachers of English or language arts and social studies, in particular, need to agree on which skills will be taught by whom and when projects that apply these skills can be initiated.

Typical Unit Sequences

Once lone-range preparations are completed, teachers need to consider the several possibilities available for sequencing the unit activities for optimal student learning and use of time.

Activity Sequence

1. *Introduction:* Makes evident unknowns, problems, questions, and contradictions using one of the following devices:

☐ Arranged environment: explores pictures, realia, and the like, that raise student interest and consciousness.

☐ Fantasizing: asks students to react to problem as though they were in it.

☐ Pretest: assesses student's knowledge using pencil-and-paper test.

☐ Personal assessment: assesses students' knowledge, attitudes, and interests through interviews or inventories.

☐ Case study: presents instance of problem to be studied in unit for analysis.

☐ Local problem: explores awareness through field trip or picture or testimony.

2. Planning. Sets procedures, objectives, requirements for and with students; study of unit.

3. *Study:* Plans and evaluates group and individual progress daily. Instructs groups and individuals as needed. Provides materials and stimuli as needed. Encourages continuing student review and self-assess-

ment.

4. *Culmination:* Plans how to share what was learned. Organizes concluding activities. Assesses individual and group progress toward objectives.

Sometimes diagrams help clarify an idea. Figure 3.2 shows the flow of activity in a unit organized around group work. Committee and individual research is emphasized in the sequence shown in the figure. Under this kind of organization, there would be a continual interplay between total group planning and small group or independent activities. The teacher role is to serve as a large group facilitator and a small group and individual resource person.

A unit activity sequence that follows the group work pattern might look like this unit for middle grades on advertising. Briefly, content objectives for this unit were for students to identify kinds of persuasion in advertising, to state positive and negative objectives of advertising, and to state several effects advertising has on their lives.

1. *Introduction:* Teacher plays guessing game with class responding by filling in gaps in advertising jingles such as:

    "Wow! I would have had a __V-8__."
    "It's the real thing, __Coke is__."

    Class discusses how and why we all know these jingles. Word advertising is introduced and connotations discussed.

2. *Planning:* Teacher asks what are sources of advertising. Product packaging, newspapers, magazines, radio, TV, and billboards. General questions are formulated: Why is there advertising? Who advertises? What does advertising cost? What kind of advertising is best? Most effective? Groups for each source are formed to investigate general questions about advertising.

3. *Study:* Teacher gives TV and radio group recording equipment and billboard group a camera, and distributes beginning collection of relevant sources to other groups. Groups meet to plan work.

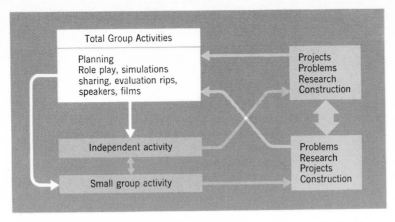

Figure 3.2 Group work unit activity sequence.

Teacher uses ads and dittoed pages to teach idenification of persuasion devices. Speakers from advertising agency and local consumer action group talks to class. Groups continue to develop answers to general questions and find examples of various persuasion devices from their sources. See Chart 3.5. Individuals take test on identifying persuasion devices in ads until they can successfully identify six types. Individuals choose among options: give a presentation on advertising to a group not in class, write a letter to manufacturer about product ad, write "What I Learned about Advertising," or draw or record advertisements on one product showing "good" and "poor" advertising.

4. *Culmination:* Individuals may choose to share project with class. Groups present reports to whole class.

Other types of organization often referred to by teachers are individualization and learning centers, or stations. These categories are not mutually exclusive. For example, learning centers can promote both individual and group work, since group work can require individuals to do independent research that will contribute to a group task. To offer variety and spur motivation, units should be organized to include more than just one means—individualization or group work or learning centers—or engaging students in learning. As an example of this check the integration of individual with group occasions in the following learning center outline. This outline included only station titles and tasks.

Topic: Who Am I? (Primary Grades)

CENTER TITLE	ACTIVITIES
A. What We See	1. Categorize pictures according to people, structure, activities.
	2. Play description guessing game with two or three others.
	3. Draw objects seen on way home, list one quality remembered about each.
	4. Watch filmstrip of life in Andes. Make story about what others see that we do not.
B. The Mirror	1. Draw own face.
	2. Draw someone else's face and compare to yours.
	3. Listen to tape on inherited characteristics.
	4. Fill out family characteristics chart.

C. Getting to Know Me	1. Weigh, measure, record various body parts on personal data cards.
	2. Record personal data on class chart.
	3. Research personal weight and height record at home.
	4. Watch film on child growth and development.
	5. Discuss sequence of child learning.
D. Values	1. Watch film about growing up.
	2. List qualities wanted and rank.
	3. Rank pictures of people according to qualities liked.
	4. Discuss picture rankings.
E. Different People	1. Collect pictures of people different from self.
	2. List how they appear different.
	3. Group pictures according to most and least liked.
	4. Discuss reasons.
F. Friends	1. Categorize pictures of children in problem situations according to "Friend," "Not Friend."
	2. List things a good friend does to show he or she is a friend.
	3. Look at *A Friend Is . . .* book.
	4. Make your own poster about "A Friend Is . . ."
G. Feeling Afraid	1. Listen to "Whistle a Happy Tune" from *The King and I.*
	2. Listen and read *Where the Wild Things Are, Billy Goats Gruff, Hansel and Gretel.*
	3. Discuss why we pretend not to be afraid.
	4. Write story about "My Afraid Time."
H. Trust Walk	1. Take blindfold trust walk with a partner.
	2. Discuss how it felt.
	3. Discuss when and why we need others.
I. Life Line	1. Collect early pictures of self and sequence.
	2. Make time line of your life on paper.
	3. Decorate paper disks describing important life events and string on yarn.

Some of these activities are of necessity individual. Some only can be engaged in by groups. Some could be organized as either individual or group activities according to the teacher's perception of time constraints and pupil needs.

The activity sequence of this approach to unit organization would look like Figure 3.3.

Some topics or units, such as in Figure 3.3, can be organized best by using the learning station or center approach. Usually a station or center type of organization is better suited to topics where every student should have firsthand contact with as many as possible of the unit activities. A more traditional organization, where one group of students researches an aspect of the general topic, is

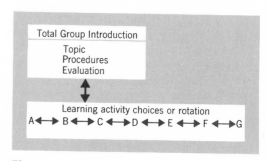

Figure 3.3   Center unit activity sequence.

appropriate when the teacher chooses to emphasize development of group decision making and cooperation skills. The advantage to the group work unit model is that it does not demand the detailed preplanning that the center approach to unit planning does. By the same token,

Chart 3.5

Name Calling
This involves attaching a label or tag to a person in an attempt to put him or her down. He or she may be called a "radical," a "racist," or a "Communist."

Glittering Generality
This describes a person or product in a favorable light and is usually the opposite of name calling. Such hazy terms as "pure," "modern," "honest," and "democratic" are examples.

Transfer
This involves putting together a symbol or idea that a reader likes with another symbol that he or she may not necessarily like. The pretty girl on the billboard probably has nothing to do with the performance of the car, but the linkage could influence the reader to buy.

Testimonial
In this device, the name of a famous movie star is often used to endorse brand "X" soap, thus giving the idea that popularity and success can be traced to the use of the product.

Card Stacking
This involves rigging the facts by concealing certain information or by emphasizing other information. A toothpaste ad might stress the taste and ignore the actual cleansing qualities.

Plain Folks Device
Here the propagandist tries to become "one of us," or the politician rolls up his or her sleeves and decides to just "talk."

Bandwagon Procedure
This is an appeal to the group instinct and urges one to "do it" because everyone else is doing it.

Repetition
A message is repeated so often that people may begin to believe it.

once a center unit is launched, the demands on teacher resourcefulness diminish.

Finding Resources for Long-Range and Unit Planning

Locating, evaluating, and arranging for informative sources and learning experiences are time-consuming tasks. The preparation periods granted during the school day can never allow teachers all the time necessary for this crucial element of instructional planning. Because teachers are so pressed for time, they often fall into read-and-recite classroom routines.

We are fully sympathetic with the problem lack of adequate planning time represents for teachers. We doubt that schools as institutions will change significantly toward granting more "school time" for the top priority business of instructional planning. This is a goal toward that every local staff and teachers' organization should work.

Whether or not there is adequate school time, better instructional planning depends on knowing what kinds of resources to bring to such planning. First and foremost are your local and state directives. Use the help available from district guides and resource centers and county offices of education. In addition, some valuable generic kinds of resources to look for in the district or county or education section of the library are the following.

Objectives and Curriculum

Social Studies k–6: A Guide for Curriculum Revision is the compleat guide for teachers engaged in curriculum revision. Details from scope and sequence charts to classroom arrangement are covered—everything for the long-range planner.
Lloyd Smith and Joan Schreiber
Department of Public Instruction
Des Moines, IO

Profiles of Promise is a set of 45 pamphlets, each describing an innovative K–12 program.
Frances Haley, editor
CRIC/ChESS
855 Broadway
Boulder, CO 80302

Social Studies Curriculum Materials Data Book is an annotated bibliography of what is commercially and experimentally available in social studies materials and practices. Updated annually.
Social Science Education Consortium
855 Broadway
Boulder, CO 80802

Ethnic Studies Curriculum Guidelines provides a rational and comprehensive set of guidelines for integrating ethnic/minority concerns and content throughout the social studies. Evolved by James Banks, Carlos Cortes et al.
National Council for Social Studies
1515 Wilson Boulevard #101
Arlington, VA 22209

Social Studies Behavioral Objectives catalogues behavioral objectives from basic to complex in
Westinghouse Learning Press
770 Lucerne Drive
Sunnyvale, CA 94086

skills, knowledge, and some affective areas.

10X Objectives Exchange— this collection of behavioral objectives serves as a bank from which
P.O. Box 24095
Los Angeles, CA 90024

teachers can lend and borrow objectives. Specify area and level when making request.

EPIEgram is the *Consumer Report* on education products. Most of the evaluations are on
Educational Products Information
  Exchange Institute
463 West Street
New York, NY 10014

hardware; however, the occasional coverage given software merits attention.

Social Studies is one of several specialized wholesalers of all commercial materials for social
School Service Catalogue
P.O. Box 802
Culver City, CA 90230

studies. Publishes handy catalogue annually with periodic topical supplements.

Local Resources

Speakers bureaus of organizations such as:

☐ University or college

☐ Chamber of Commerce

☐ League of Women Voters

☐ Better Business Bureau

☐ Local chapters of ethnic and civil rights groups

☐ Local historians or long-time residents

☐ Local groups concerned with foreign affairs

☐ Local government and business representatives

Places to visit:

☐ Local businesses

☐ Local newspaper plant

☐ Local cemeteries

☐ Local museums

☐ Local libraries

☐ Local ethnic halls and neighborhoods

☐ Churches

☐ Manufacturing plants

☐ City and county services

☐ Transportation and shipping depots

☐ Antique shop and dealers

☐ Family attics and treasure troves

Not included in this list is the wonderful, chaotic world of free and inexpensive materials. Private businesses and public agencies are publishing free and/ or inexpensive pamphlets, filmstrips, and brochures every day that can be marvelously useful to the organized teacher who writes for these materials far enough in advance to have them arrive in time for instructional purposes. Following are catalogues to this category of resource.

Educator's Guide to Free Social Studies Materials
Educators Progress Service
Randolph, WI 53956

Free and Inexpensive Teaching Aids
Bruce Miller
Box 369
Riverside, CA 92502

Free and Inexpensive Learning Materials
George Peabody College for Teachers
Nashville, TE 37203

Chart 3.6 Lesson Plan Outline

A. LESSON PLAN OUTLINE

Unit <u>Who Am I?</u> Date(s) <u>2-16 to 2-19</u>

Objectives	Procedures	Materials	Evaluation
Same as unit: Skills—list, classify, work together. Knowledge— family tree, similarities and differences of humans. Friendship qualities values— shares materials listens to others shows concern discusses differences without hostility	Start centers D,E F. All finish A,B	Centers A,B,C D,E,F. Return Andes f.s.; pick up "Growing" film. Get scale from nurse again. Friend. Is . . . from library	Daily planning before center work on keeping folders in cubby and checking off activities with aide at end of each session

B. LESSON PLAN OUTLINE

Topic <u>Advertising</u> Date(s) <u>10-2</u>

Objectives

Students will explain persuasion devices in own words.

Students will illustrate persuasion devices with ads, own drawings or dramatization.

Materials

Slides of ads from magazines. Dittoed sheets on persuasion devices, old magazines, scissors, paste, paper.

Procedures

1. Ask "How ad get us to buy?" List student ideas on chalkboard.
2. Go through persuasion techniques on ditto.
3. Show slides and identify each one using ditto.
4. Assign partners to make up one brochure illustrating at least five devices. Alternate choice is to dramatize two devices for class to guess tomorrow.

Evaluation

1. Work turned in next day showing five correct identifications.
2. Dramatizations of two devices.
3. Student identification of devices in dramatizations.

Selected Free Materials for Classroom Teachers
Ruth H. Aubrey
Fearon Publications
6 Davis Drive
Belmont, CA 94002

Lesson Planning

Within the framework of the unit, the teacher constructs daily plans. Some days call for more planning and organization than others, depending on the class activities of the day. These plans should be organized around the generalizations related to that day's work that the student needs to learn in order to add to his understanding of the unit. Experienced teachers *may* need only to note a set of page references and pupil or group names in the appropriate time block of their plan books to teach a successful lesson or effectively supervise a period of time. Planning in greater detail is necessary, however, for most teachers to keep a steady grasp on the relationship of the day's activities to the objectives of the unit and the year or course.

To facilitate detailed lesson planning, teachers usually ditto plan outlines and fill them in for the coming week or weeks on the Thursday or Friday of the current week. Here are two favorite plan outlines (Chart 3.6).

Bringing to life the general objectives chosen for the unit requires that the teacher make appropriate matches between the daily topics and activities chosen to present them. Obviously, planning a student panel to discuss the new topic of persuasion techniques is a mismatch of topic, student readiness, and activity.

There are days when direct teacher presentation is essential. Usual occasions for direct teacher presentations are when:

☐ New, unknown concepts are to be presented.

☐ Explanations of new skills are in order.

☐ Review of written work or projects to further illuminate a topic is needed.

☐ Discussion of an issue about which a group of students has partial information appears crucial for further progress to occur.

To be more effective on these occasions detailed planning that focuses on leading questions, specific motivational devices and content points to be made will ensure better student learning.

Every teacher develops his/her own special formula for planning. Just as every principal or supervisor expects to see his/her formula on the plan book. Usually, principals are concerned that plans be detailed enough for a possible substitute to read and be able to carry out. Of course, plans get constantly changed by forces outside a teacher's control such as the firetruck's visit to school or that special assembly another class invites everyone else to attend at the last minute. Even so, there are times when detailed planning can help teachers guide students more directly to achieve learning objectives.

Bringing to life general objectives chosen for the unit requires that the teacher make appropriate matches between the daily topics and activities or strategies used to present them. Try your skill at matching the topics and strategies below:

The pitfall awaiting experienced teachers is reteaching a unit or lesson without rethinking it. The essence of daily lesson planning is not the kind of form used nor the manner in which the form is written nor how well the same lesson went last year. It is the creative match the teacher designs between:

1. Student readiness.
2. The desired knowledge or skill or value.
3. The activities best suited to 1 and 2.

One group of students is never exactly like another. Thus, teacher creativity in lesson planning is a career-long obligation.

Topic

A. Scale on a map ___ ___ ___
B. Reaction to film, *Ishi, Last of His Tribe* ___ ___ ___
C. Concept of rules ___ ___ ___
D. Organizing group investigation ___ ___ ___
E. Celebrating Martin Luther King Day ___ ___ ___
F. Picture of children stealing from a store ___ ___ ___
G. Summarizing reading assignment ___ ___ ___
H. Practicing geographical place names ___ ___ ___.

Activity/Strategy

1. Small group meetings
2. Panel discussion
3. Direct teacher instruction
4. Role play
5. Individual study
6. Large group discussion

Our answers may differ from yours. Check to see why.

A. _3_ If scale is a new concept, the teacher should explain why it is useful, how it is organized, and pose several problems of scale reading so the explanation can be clarified.

B. _6_ or _3_ Depending on the ability of the class to listen to each other 6 or 3 would be better. In general small groups give more people a chance for expression. Teacher-structured questions would be necessary in any case.

C. _3_ _5_ _4_ Choice of 3 or 4 depends on teacher creativity and class time available. Role playing several situations, then inducing the concept ramifications may be more motivating to students. Older students may learn about the concept through assigned independent reading.

D. _1_ _6_ Students will need some task structuring for this, but they should decide among themselves who will do what.

Perhaps each group should report its progress to the large group as a wrapup to the session.

E. _2_ _5_ Students derive more meaning from this type of celebration when they learn to teach others.

F. _4_ _6_ This is a valuing exercise. Possibilities for exploring all sides of the situation must be part of the session.

G. _3_ _5_ _1_ Students who do not know how to summarize need to have direct instruction in this skill. Students who have some control over summarizing will reinforce the skill by sharing their summaries or working out a joint summary with others.

H. _5_ _1_ Some students learn this kind of drill task best by themselves. Others need to have the motivation of a small, competitive group setting.

Bibliography

Chase, W. Linwood and Martha Tyler John. *A Guide for the Elementary Social Studies Teacher*. Boston: Allyn and Bacon, 1972.

Gilliom, M. Eugene (ed.). *Practical Methods for the Social Studies*. Belmont, Cal.: Wadsworth, 1977.

Hanna, Lavone, Gladys Potter, and Neva Hanaman. *Unit Teaching in the Elementary School*, revised edition. New York: Holt, Rinehart and Winston, 1963.

Jarolimek, John. *Social Studies in Elementary Education*. New York: Macmillian, 1977.

Joyce, Bruce et al. *Three Teaching Strategies for the Social Studies*. Chicago: Science Research Associates, 1972.

Lee, John. *Teaching Social Studies in the Elementary School*. Glencoe, Ill.: Free Press, 1974.

Michaelis, John. *Social Studies for Children in a Democracy*. Englewood Cliffs, N. J.: Prentice-Hall, 1977.

Oliner, Pearl. *Teaching Elementary Social Studies*. New York: Harcourt Brace, 1976.

Preston, Ralph and Wayne Herman. *Teaching Social Studies in the Elementary School*. New York: Holt, 1968.

Seif, Elliott. *Teaching Significant Social Studies in the Elementary School*. Chicago: Rand McNally, 1977.

Why is evaluation so important to students?

CHAPTER 4

Evaluation in Social Studies

Evaluating and Planning

Evaluation is not something that happens at the termination of a unit or course. To be effective and fair, evaluation should be part of the planning cycle. To accomplish this, there are three important phases of the planning evaluation cycle. The diagnostic phase of the planning cycle entails finding out where the students are (see Figure 4.1). A favorite device for diagnosing what students know about a topic is the pretest. This can be a pencil-paper test over knowledge that the unit will present. In addition, the pretest can discover how students perform in skill areas such as making an outline or distinguishing fact from opinion. Pretests are predominately the pencil-paper variety with the teacher reading the items and choices for students unable to read independently. This mode functions fairly well for the realm of knowledge, but less well for skills and even less reliably for value areas.

In the realm of knowledge, imagine how many repetitions of that first rough year of the Pilgrims could be avoided

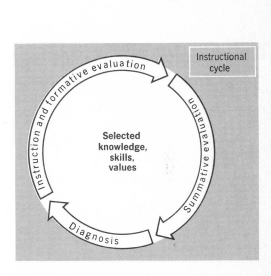

Figure 4.1 Instructional cycle.

each year during November if teachers took time to verify that students already know the basic facts about what has come to be known as the first Thanksgiving. A pretest, of course, emphasizing recall of 1624, Plymouth, and Squanto would probably indicate that students needed further instruction to master these facts.

And, if the principal objective of the annual Thanksgiving unit is that students list the who, where, and when of the first event, further "go-rounds" are merited.

Some cautions about diagnosing student value orientations via pencil-paper instruments are in order. An example follows:

The Pilgrims showed they were thankful by____.
1. Being nice to the Indians.
2. Eating a big meal.
3. Giving thanks to God.

For a student to respond "properly" to this item tells us nothing really about the student's attitude toward thankfulness or sharing or the Pilgrims or the Indians. A related issue is the common requirement of federal and state-funded projects for pencil-paper attitudinal and valuative pre- and posttests on student self-concept. If such devices are administered en masse and more than once, the results become less and less representative of substantice attitudinal change and more and more a "testwise" student response. A less formal general diagnosis may, of course, be attained via oral questioning and from the student's contributions—or lack of them—to a group discussion of a proposed unit or lesson.

The purpose, then of this phase is to assist teachers with further instructional planning. The results of diagnosing may be several: the topic may be discarded, prerequisite skills may have to be taught before the instruction originally intended can proceed, instruction may have to be differentiated to meet individual student interests and needs. The benefit of this phase is that knowledge of where students are greatly increases a teacher's probability of organizing successful learning experiences for students. Diagnosis does not end at this point. Students and their work should be approached diagnostically throughout the learning epi-

sode. Even a final examination of student attainment should be examined analytically in terms of why or why not aims were or were not reached and to what are the next steps indicated.

Formative evaluation is the daily or frequent assessment students and teachers make of the student's progress and the adequacy of the teacher's instructional performance. Younger students require greater and sustained teacher effort on this phase. Questions pursued as part of this phase might be, for example:

☐ Why has this been difficult to learn?

☐ What words do we need further work on?

☐ What problems are you having with this map?

☐ What items do we still need more information about?

☐ What kinds of disagreements are you discovering among the settlers?

☐ What hypotheses are you prepared to change or maintain?

☐ How can we better organize these data?

Briefly then, the purpose of formative evaluation is to probe to what degree unit or instructional objectives are being accomplished. The results assist the teacher in day-to-day planning what to reteach for whom. The benefit is the same as that of the diagnostic phase, greater learning strides for individual students. And, at the same time then, the teacher is enabled to better ensure readiness for success in large-group activities.

Summative evaluation means a rounding up of the results of instruction. This phase of evaluation occurs at termination points of units or courses. It allows the teacher and student to compare what is known now to what was known before instruction, to compare what the student can do now that he/she did not know how to do before. At this point in the instructional sequence, final tests, presentations, and project evaluations are all appropriate. The purpose of summative evaluation is to measure and interpret the students' progress in a global fashion. The results are benchmarks or guideposts to future instructional planning and interpreted data about student learning that can be communicated to parents and students. The benefit is the well-rounded view of student and teacher performance that the planning-evaluation process leading to this phase can provide. It is particularly important that this phase of assessment is balanced, not only in terms of attempting to evaluate growth in skills and attitudinal change as well as of achievement of knowledge, but in the types of instruments used. For them, balance is indicated in terms of what has and has not been emphasized in previous unit evaluation.

Objectives and Evaluation

Without objectives teachers have no systematic way of connecting the instructional activities of the classroom to the significance of student performance and the overall direction of the curriculum. It is our feeling that instructional objectives offer a valuable middle route between evaluation that requires strictly defined behavioral objectives on the one extreme, and on the other extreme, an evaluation that amounts to measuring a student's performance only in terms of how other students taking the same test have scored. We refer in the former case to objectives that specify:

1. The *person* who is to perform the learning behavior.
2. *Specific behavior* required to demonstrate accomplishment of the objective.

3. *Learning outcome* or product by which the accomplishment of the objective can be evaluated.
4. The *conditions* under which the behavior is to be performed.
5. The *criterion* or standard to be used to evaluate accomplishment.[1]

And in the latter case, we refer to standardized tests for social studies that examine only the most general knowledge and skill areas, and allowing for no individual variations. Of 10 standardized tests bear little relation to what knowledge, skills, and values were the focus of the social studies instruction actually conducted.

Instructional objectives, as defined here, are a less stringent version of behavioral objectives. They clarify what is expected of the student without stipulating all the exacting circumstances of the student's behavior.

Example 1:

Behavioral—Given a map of the state, student will use map index to locate five of six given points in 10 minutes.

Instructional—Student will locate points using map index.

Example 2:

Behavioral—Given five descriptions of decisions, students will list the norm, the sanction, and the roles of each in 15 minutes.

Instructional—Students can identify instances of sanction, norm, and role.

In formulating instructional objectives teachers need to consider the levels of cognitive and affective functioning their instructional sequence inspires in students. Handbooks I and II of the *Tax-*

---

[1] Ambrose A. Cleggs Jr., "Developing and Using Behavioral Objectives in Geography," *Focus on Geography: Key Concepts and Teaching Strategies*, Phillip Bacon, ed., 40th Yearbook, Washington, D.C., N.C.S.S., 1970, p. 292.

Taxonomy of Educational Objectives

KNOWING—COGNITIVE	VALUING—AFFECTIVE
1. Knowledge—repeats, lists	1. Receiving—listens, observes
2. Comprehension—gives examples, interprets	2. Responding—participates, complies
3. Application—explains, solves, demonstrates	3. Valuing—initiates
4. Analysis—outlines, categorizes, relates	4. Organization—judges, derives
5. Synthesis—investigates, revises, creates	5. Characterization of values—displays, practices
6. Evaluation—ranks, judges, compares	

onomy of Educational Objectives[2] by Bloom, Krathwohl, and Masia are the classic tools for this facet of instructional planning. According to these educational psychologists, knowing and valuing occur in simple to more complex forms.

Critics have traditionally complained that elementary social studies does not lead students beyond the level of reciting such things as the names of the 50 states and their capitals, the presidents of the United States in order of office, and other information that leads nowhere. However, according to these hierarchies of mental and moral operations, acting on the levels of repeating and listening represents only the threshold of mental operations. Teachers can use these hierarchies to gauge the validity of critics' claims about their instruction. Do instructional objectives and/or unit products direct students primarily to lower-level thinking such as identification, recall, or listing? Or, must students seek information, organize it, and make judgments about it? On the valuing side, are students expected only to hear out another point of view? Or, is instruction structured so that conflicting points of view are analyzed?

A misuse of the Bloom taxonomies would be an attempt to write objectives that reflect every level of the cognitive and affective domains for one unit or instructional sequence. Indeed, Piaget's theory of mental and moral development counsel that younger children have not

yet developed a mental apparatus that can function at the higher congitive levels of evaluation, synthesis and analysis. Nor, can younger children perform value analysis to the degree and kind required of levels four and five on the affective taxonomy. However, the taxonomies of educational objectives provide a means to analyzing existing objectives and writing a greater variety of mental operations into instructional sequences.[3]

In sum, the more care used in formulating instructional objectives, the more direction and structure the evaluation of learning can have.

Realms of Evaluation

Separating "knowing about" from "knowing how to" from "knowing why" is often arbitrary. In reality, we are motivated by our value systems to use knowledge or understandings at the same time we use skills. For purposes of assisting the teacher plan, however, the realms of knowledge, skills, and values are separated. In practice, teachers find themselves repeating certain of the objectives

[2] Bloom, Benjamin (editor) et al., *Taxonomy of Educational Objectives*, Handbook I and II, Chicago, David McKay, 1956, 1964.
[3] Also see Norris M. Sanders, *Classroom Questions—What Kinds?* New York: Harper & Row, 1966 for application of cognitive taxonomy to social studies questions and test construction.

in the skills and values realms in nearly every plan they write. This is as it should be. Acquiring competency in these realms is a long-term process that requires repetition in varied contexts. The same is also true for higher-order thinking skills and concept learning, which are often categorized in the knowledge realm.

Following are some generic ideas for evaluation tasks involving the realms of knowledge and skills.[4] They can help organize planning objectives and evaluation for nearly any topic.

Factual Recall

1. Arrange in order the steps in a process.
2. Match events with periods of time.
3. Supply key words missing in statements of fact essential to the unit.
4. Match vocabulary and definitions.
5. Select from a collection of facts those related in some designated way.
6. Support a generalization with essential facts.
7. Match objects or agencies with their functions, principles with their applications.
8. Support response to true-false items with confirming data.
9. Distinguish between facts that are subject to change and those that will not vary with time.
10. Make statements of fact derived from charts, diagrams, and graphs.
11. Select from a list of facts those that are useful in solving a given problem.
12. Place events or persons on a time line.
13. Support responses to a multiple choice item with data.
14. Alter false items to make them true.

Beyond the Factual

1. Match statements of cause and effect.
2. Distinguish between facts and generalizations in a given list of statements.

3. Supply the generalization to be drawn from a given set of facts.
4. Select the conclusion to be drawn from a chart, diagram, or graph.
5. Support a given generalization with facts.
6. State the generalizations that can be drawn from a field trip or other project.
7. Match a generalization with its supporting data.
8. Select the generalization that may explain why a given situation exists.
9. Draw conclusions from an imaginary dialogue in which an issue is discussed, that is, what person had inaccurate information, what person's comments reveal prejudice, and so on.
10. State the most important ideas learned from the unit of work.
11. State an opinion about why a particular unit of work was chosen for study.
12. Select responses to a multiple-choice item that emphasize why something happened or why a condition exists.
13. Match pictures with the generalizations they represent.

Many of these tasks would require students to use knowledge and skills simultaneously. Performance of these tasks can occur during all phases of an instructional sequence. Using performances during the formative phase for evaluation is legitimate, especially for younger students. Naturally, performance has to be a continuing element of all-important skill assessment.

Evaluating progress in the realm of attitudes and values can be part of an instructional sequence or unit in two ways. First is through the content of instruction. Students can be involved in value issues concerning nearly any topic. Second, instructional sequences can incorporate frequent opportunities for exercises in such areas as cooperation, group decision making, and so on. Thus, some structured means to observe and promote interpersonal attitudes and values is afforded. Chart 4.1 suggests some techniques that can be used. These tech-

---

[4] Adapted from "Evaluating Understandings, Attitudes and Skills and Behaviors in Elementary School Social Studies," *35th Yearbook of National Council for the Social Studies*, Maxine Dunfee, ed. Washington, D.C., N.C.S.S., 1965.

Chart 4.1 Techniques for Evaluating the Valuative Realm

A. STUDENT AS REVEALED BY SELF-REPORTS

Student	*Sample*
1. Answers questions	Why is studying the Indians important?
2. Participants in discussion	I feel that way about the treatment of the Indians because . . .
3. Responses to attitude scale	Conquistadores were right to take gold and silver to Europe
4. Responses to opinion poll	(a) Osgood Semantic Differential: Indians were ugly—beautiful, good—bad, wild—civilized
5. Forces responses	(b) Rank order set of items such as contributions of Spanish—horses, cows, guns, diseases, religion, literacy, and so on to New World
6. Keeps a diary	I didn't do my reading because . . .
7. Responses to multiple-choice items	When I'm in this class—

B. STUDENTS AS INFERRED FROM PROJECTIVE TECHNIQUES

1. Responses to open-ended questions, themes	How I feel about busing
2. Responses to unfinished stories/pictures	
3. Analyses of role playing	
4. Choices of words that describe topic	List several words that tell about the Conquistadores
5. Lists good and bad aspects	List several good effects and bad effects of the Conquistadores presence in the New World

C. STUDENTS AS INFERRED FROM OBSERVED BEHAVIOR

1. Contributions to class discussions	Requires audiotaping or class observer making protocols, or teacher keeping checklist
2. Incident recorded on anecdotal record	Behavior described as recalled by teacher

niques are categorized according to the general means the teacher would use to collect data.

Not every technique is appropriate to every unit. Nor should these techniques, when related to unit topics, be employed as part of the formative phase of evaluation. Pre- and posttesting of attitudes about a topic, during both diagnostic and summative phases, can be revealing. Many techniques, however, are best suited to the summative phase. Students need a basic knowledge and exposure to issues before their responses can assume much significance when a topic outside their daily routines of living is the focal point. In essence, functioning on the higher levels of the cognitive and affective taxonomies becomes fused when students have enough background information and valuing experiences to formulate some reasoned conclusions.

Organizing Evaluation

Evaluation should be a continuous, long-range process. It should go hand in hand with instructional planning. To facilitate this process, teachers must concern themselves with record keeping.

One of the first steps in any new unit is for students to organize a folder for collecting work related to the unit. Older students can often keep their own and maintain individual notebooks. A more sophisticated version of the student work folder is the contract. These recordkeeping devices come in all degrees of complexity. Their intent is to lay out in graphic detail the assignments expected of students. Usually, the contract system is a vehicle for allowing individuals and sometimes groups to proceed at their own pace through a prescribed series of tasks, assuming more responsibility for promptness, thoroughness, and accuracy than otherwise might be the case. What-

ever means used to collect student work, teacher reference to the finished work will be easier if a checklist for each student is stapled on his/her collection of work as shown in Chart 4.2. At any point during instruction, a teacher keeping this kind of record can verify how much an individual student has accomplished and what difficulties the student may be encountering.

Other pencil-paper devices that teachers employ to get some evidence for group work skills are observation and self-evaluation sheets (see Chart 4.3). Teacher observations are quickly blurred by the frequency of events in a classroom. Observation sheets can be designed for whatever items for which the teacher needs data. They can be used over time or as a one-shot sampling. Student self-evaluations are useful for prompting student introspection and providing a point of reference for teacher-student conferences.

Chart 4.2 Sample Checklist of Student Unit Assignments

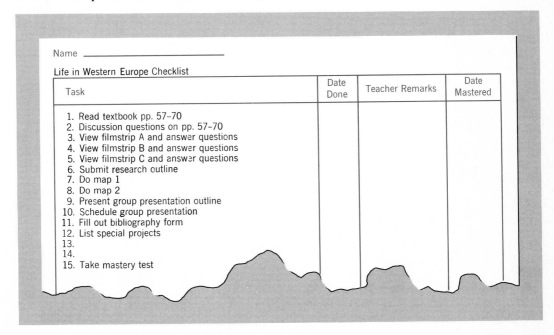

Task	Date Done	Teacher Remarks	Date Mastered
1. Read textbook pp. 57–70			
2. Discussion questions on pp. 57–70			
3. View filmstrip A and answer questions			
4. View filmstrip B and answer questions			
5. View filmstrip C and answer questions			
6. Submit research outline			
7. Do map 1			
8. Do map 2			
9. Present group presentation outline			
10. Schedule group presentation			
11. Fill out bibliography form			
12. List special projects			
13.			
14.			
15. Take mastery test			

Name _____
Life in Western Europe Checklist

Chart 4.3   Sample Group Work Evaluation Forms

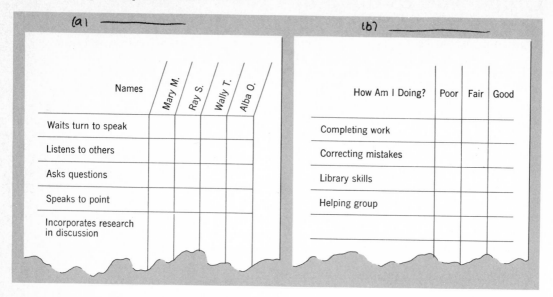

(a)

Names	Mary M.	Ray S.	Wally T.	Alba O.
Waits turn to speak				
Listens to others				
Asks questions				
Speaks to point				
Incorporates research in discussion				

(b)

How Am I Doing?	Poor	Fair	Good
Completing work			
Correcting mistakes			
Library skills			
Helping group			

Tests are the most common pencil-paper devices used to evaluate learning. For younger children these have minimal utility. Questions read by the teacher that can be answered by marking the proper illustration or multiple choice item can be used with some success; but once reading is accomplished, orally dictated quizzes may have more negative than positive aspects. Asking individual students to arrange picture sets in sequence and draw pictures to illustrate concepts or generalizations can also convey a sense of the younger student's understandings. Unfortunately tests that use matching items, true-false statements, short-answer fill-ins, and essay questions are frequently testing reading and writing accomplishment more than social studies knowledge.

Next we suggest some recommendations and cautions about kinds of tests and test items. As students mature through the grades, it is quite necessary that they develop competencies for taking increasingly difficult paper-and-pencil tests. A part of our teaching should be devoted to such instruction. In our world that constantly demands rapidity, we can be certain that objective-type tests will remain with us. The computer and modern technology also assure us that these kinds of tests will be our major form of formal assessment. Such examinations, however, take time and care to prepare properly and, while teacher-constructed objective tests can be speedily graded, they are frequently badly constructed and poorly worded. Additionally, certain of the forms of objective items just do not provide good evaluation; these ought to be used cautiously for particular purposes, if at all.

The best example of a commonly misused objective item is that old favorite — the true-false query. Its use guarantees a 50 percent chance of guessing the right answer. Some teachers try to overcome this detriment by developing a long battery of questions with duplicative items worded in different ways. Others ask students to tell why a "true" item is true or require students in some way to correct the "false" items.

Completion or filling-in-the-blank items tend to be very pedestrian and reinforce rote drill-type learning. Seldom does the incomplete statement kind of item lend itself to the higher levels of questioning and learning.

Matching and arrangement items at times may have a place, but frequently these also seem to be used to measure relatively inconsequential facts. Again, without care and preparation, poor wording and organization lead these to be less than satisfactory items. To keep students from being confused and from spending too much time checking up and down matching columns, usually no matching item should have more than five parts in the first column and possibly a sixth foil in the second column, which discourages arriving at the last match by default. Irrelevant, out-of-category, or practically impossible matches that often give themselves away should also be avoided.

Arrangement-in-order or sequence test items sometimes seem to be set up so as to confuse the pupil rather than assess his or her knowledge of events or chronology. Often it is better to ask children for specific dates in single items; however, where time sense is desired or where the teacher wants to check on cause and effect relationships, the teacher may best assess student compre-hension by developing a three-item query where the students are asked to place the three events in proper order or to designate the development which occurred between the other two.

The multiple-choice item seems to be the best of the objective item types. Again, they do take time and care to properly develop but, if well conceived, they enable the teacher to assess higher level competencies and they also avoid some of the weaknesses of the other kinds of objective items. Normally, four foils are the maximum necessary. The use of a fifth choice sometimes stretches the credibility of the completion terms and may end up with a fully unrealistic option. Four realistic foils, wherein one, however, is clearly correct or the best, are sufficient; in some cases, however, teachers use a fifth and/or a sixth foil as in the following example.

The government of the United States of America is:
1. A national republic
2. A representative democracy
3. A federation
4. All of these
5. None of these

While there is clear evidence that essay-type examinations lend themselves

A Poor Matching Question
Which were major battles of each war?
_____1. American Revolution (a) Yorktown
_____2. War of 1812   (b) Buena Vista
_____3. Mexican War   (c) Gettysburg
_____4. Civil War   (d) Marne
_____5. World War I   (e) New Orleans

An Improved Matching Question
Which battles were "turning points" in each war?
_____1. American Revolution (a) Yorktown
                             (b) Bunker Hill
                             (c) Saratoga
_____2. Civil War   (a) Atlanta
                             (b) Bull Run
                             (c) Gettysburg

Example of Sequence Item
Arrange the following events in order they grew out of one another.
_____A. The Civil War
_____B. The Compromise of 1850
_____C. The Kansas-Nebraska Act

_____A. Southern States leave Union
_____B. Election of Lincoln
_____C. The Civil War

to rather subjective assessment by teachers, they remain a most valuable instrument for student assessment. If the teacher desires to ascertain student ability to organize a topic, to explain a complex development, to reveal their depth of knowledge, to indicate their opinions and their reasoning on a problem-issue or how well they express themselves, certainly the paragraph answer or short essay is a most appropriate instrument.

Poor Essay Question

1. Discuss the French Revolution.

Improved Essay Question

1. (a) Explain the basic and immediate causes of the French Revolution.
   (b) How can the major developments of the Revolution be divided into phases?
   (c) Why did the French Revolution fail?
   (d) What were the long-term results of the Revolution?

In developing essay questions, instructors should have their purposes clearly in mind. They certainly need to avoid very general or broad questions that give testees a little direction and really allow almost anything to be offered in the way of an answer. Ideally the teacher should state for himself/herself or outline what will constitute a minimally satisfactory answer, a good one, and an excellent answer. The teacher can then approach grading in a more objective manner. He or she will also have to decide how and the extent to which spelling, punctuation, and other elements of grammar are to be counted in the evaluation. Those who are teaching reading or writing, as well as social studies, will find essay questions a helpful way of joining and relating assessments in these different areas.

It is important to share test results with pupils as soon as possible. Ideally these tests should be discussed at length with the class and/or individuals. Conferential exchanges over the marking of the essays are most valuable in terms of prompting student growth in skills, as well as in maintaining morale.

Pupils need frequent writing assignments to help prepare them to perform well on essay and short-answer tests. Younger boys and girls can be prepared for the more extensive essay assignment or test by the regular use of short-answer questions that require them to write at least several sentences or a paragraph or two. To introduce pupils to the ability to organize and write the longer essays, a series of related questions can be used, each calling for answers of but a sentence or two. As in the previous example, one question builds on the other and gradually the pupil learns how to put several parts into a more extensive and complete answer. Continuing experience with such assignments and questions is quite valuable in bringing young people to both competency and ease in employing this important element of communication.

In typical tests, skills are frequently overlooked in the emphasis on achievement of knowledge. We have underscored the importance of a skill-centered social studies program, and it is, therefore, imperative that a teacher so inclined gives adequate attention to skill-oriented assessment. Combinations of different types of objective items are often used here and we think it is particularly important to build into such testing programs items that include map use and interpretation, chart and tabular reading, graphing, and picture and cartoon analysis. Such items are particularly valuable in ascertaining pupil competency in inquiry. For numerous examples we suggest use of the valuable booklet developed for the National Council for the Social Studies, entitled *Selected Items for Testing of Study Skills and Critical Thinking*.[5]

---

[5] Bulletin No. 15 by H. T. Morse and G. H. McCune, revised edition, 1971.

Each teacher will need to decide on the kinds of evaluation items and instruments he or she will use. As is true of much in schooling, variation would seem to be in order. Different aims or skills are often best assessed in different ways. A variety of measures throughout the unit are in order, and in the final or comprehensive test, variation may also provide for fairer assessment. We always have differing pupils of varying abilities who have learned different things to different degrees or in varying ways. Good tests, therefore, usually include a variety of both objective and the more subjective essay-type questions; they may also feature sections or options geared to certain pupils and particular assignments.

As suggested previously students should be given tests as instructional devices. They need to be helped to succeed in this aspect of evaluation. How to look for the disqualifiers of "All, always, never, none" in true-false statements should be taught. How to use the process of elimination for matching items should be practiced. Once the "testwise" skill is developed, tests can be used to assess knowledge with more validity.

The reliability of test results of younger students is easy to doubt. Hunger, fatigue, a new mitt to play ball with at recess, worry about losing milk money and a million other things are competing with a test for the attention of the younger student. For this reason it is the better part of wisdom not to rely heavily on tests to evaluate younger students. Pictures drawn, models constructed, verbal responses offered and data manipulations completed as they occur during the formative phase of instruction are the best indicators available of what the student knows. These restraints are less binding for middle-grade students who are reading independently. Even so, unit tests should never be the primary basis for evaluating more advanced elementary school students. Indeed, in a formal sense too many middle school teachers may test too much. Using traditional type tests in usual ways, it is our estimation that less than 20 percent of a student's grades should be determined in that manner.

May we also suggest that much self-evaluation be employed. Students can keep their own records. They should be helped to "mark" or "grade" themselves. For example, red pencils can be distributed and the teacher and class discuss a test, each student marks his or her own paper. Students are much more interested in their own performance than in grading some one else's. At the same time, such self-evaluation becomes a much more direct learning experience for the students involved and assessment becomes much more than testing student attainment.

In summary, evaluation should be understood as part of the instructional planning process. Where this perception prevails, the following characteristics of evaluation should be notable in a classroom:

1. Planning and evaluation is part of every lesson.
2. Students know what objectives they are to derive from the instruction.
3. Students and teacher share assessment of student progress toward objectives.
4. Students have repeated and varied exposure to desired knowledge and skills.
5. Students are evaluated on the same cognitive levels as they were instructed.
6. Students are allowed some latitude about the pacing and selection of their learning.

There is no conventional gauge or instrument to measure some of the most worthwhile activities that go on in a good social studies class. How does one measure intellectual excitement and curiosity? How does one record a student's breakthrough in critical thinking? How does one measure the feeling of purposefulness in a group work session? A substantive change in attitude toward a minority? There are ways. Or, they could be invented. But would the recording of these less tangible elements be worth the trouble? Most teachers would shout, "No! Don't burden us with more bookkeeping." We agree on trivial record keeping. But there is more to evaluation than grade books. Evaluation should serve the planning process. It contributes to motivation. It should be used to provide students with better learning opportunities. It should help students understand their own needs and strengths and weaknesses. It must enable us to answer questions about student progress and efficacy put to the school by parents and community officials. To the degree that organized forms of evaluation assist, rather than hinder, these ends, they should be instituted and followed.

Bibliography

Banks, James A. with Cleggs, Ambrose A. Jr. *Teaching Strategies for the Social Studies: Inquiry, Valuing and Decision Making.* Reading, Mass.: Addison-Wesley, 1973.

Berg, Harry D., ed. *Evaluation in Social Studies.* Thirty-fifth Yearbook of the National Council for the Social Studies. Washington D.C.: NCSS, 1965.

Bloom, Benjamin S., ed. *Taxonomy of Educational Objective: The Classification of Educational Goals, Handbook i. Cognitive Domain.* New York: McKay, 1956.

Fraenkel, Jack R. *Helping Students Think and Value: Strategies for Teaching the Social Studies.* Englewood Cliffs, N.J.: Prentice-Hall, 1973.

Krathwohl, David R. ed. *Taxonomy of Educational Objectives: The Classification of Goals, Handbook ii. Affective Domain.* New York: McKay, 1964.

Popbam, W. James. *Educational Evaluation.* Englewood Cliffs, N.J.: Prentice-Hall, 1975.

Sanders, Norris M. *Classroom Questions — What Kinds?* New York: Harper & Row, 1966.

Servey, Richard. *Social Studies Instruction in the Elementary School.* San Francisco: Chandler, 1967.

Thomas, R. M. and Brubaker, Dale. *Decisions in Teaching Elementary Social Studies.* Belmont, Cal.: Wadsworth, 1971.

Section 2

The Social Studies and the Social Sciences

There is an anecdote attributed both to "Fats" Waller, the colorful pianist-singer-composer of the 1930s and 1940s, and to the legendary jazzman, Louis Armstrong. When asked to define jazz, the reply was, "If you have to ask, you can't ever know." Definitions are not always the most satisfactory means of understanding terms or of comprehending concepts. Social studies (or social study or social science or social sciences) may not be easier to define or describe than is jazz, but a person can go through a series of auditory experiences with jazz and begin to "know" it. The best way to know the social studies (and the social sciences) would be through a series of appropriate experiences. Actually, most readers will already have had a number of these experiences. That doesn't mean they comprehend the social studies. People have also listened to jazz without ever knowing what it was.

Comprehending the social science foundations of the social studies, like any kind of comprehension, is a complicated process, part experiential and part vicarious or verbal. In Chapter 5 we help the reader to "know" social science by first defining and describing it in the context of general knowledge, second by indicating the scope of social science, and third by analyzing the nature of social science. Then we examine the nature of social science by studying its intellectual structure. Finally, we examine the relationship between the scholarly field of social science and the curriculum area, the social studies.

In subsequent chapters we dissect social science further into the component social science disciplines, investigating, first, the classic social science disciplines of history and geography, then the policy sciences of political science and economics, and, last, the behavioral sciences of anthropology, sociology, and psychology. At the conclusion of this section the reader should have a general understanding of the nature of social science and its component disciplines as foundations of the social studies.

Why is it necessary for students to understand
our sociocivic processes?

CHAPTER 5

Social Sciences as Foundations of the Social Studies

Defining and Describing Social Science

Humankind has accumulated much knowledge over the millenia of time, a body of knowledge that is constantly growing. This growth has come virtually in geometric proportions, each addition to the existing knowledge multiplying as it contributes to varied recombinations of knowledge. The expansion of knowledge has become so dramatic that it is not at all inaccurate to refer to it as a "knowledge explosion."

This body of knowledge is conventionally divided into the three well-known subdivisions of natural science, the humanities, and social science. The most common attempt to differentiate among them is that each focuses on a different aspect of phenomena—natural, esthetic and spiritual, or social. Natural science focuses on the natural world of minerals, plants, animals, space, energy; the humanities focus on the esthetic and spiritual experiences and expressions of human beings as found in philosophy, literature, and the arts; and social science examines human beings as social creatures, spatially distributed over time.

Social science is one of a number of ways of looking at life and experience, of organizing our knowledge of life and experience. The social sciences provide "the different perspectives necessary to obtain a rounded picture of human behavior and human societies."[1] So, too, we can say that philosophy or art is one of a number of ways of looking at life and organizing our knowledge. How can we define social science? There are a number of good definitions available:

The study of human beings in society.

The intellectual discipline that studies humankind.

The disciplines studying human relationships.

The scientific study of Homo sapiens as a social being.

Those disciplines that are concerned primarily with the study of society and human relationships in order to clarify the group life of human beings in space and time.

---

[1] Robert S. Browne et al., *The Social Scene: A Contemporary View of the Social Sciences*, Cambridge, Mass., Winthrop Publishers Inc., 1972, p. 2

The National Science Foundation's definition is one of the most complete:

> The social sciences are intellectual disciplines that study man as a social being by means of the scientific method. It is their focus on man as a member of society and on the groups and societies that he forms, that distinguishes the social sciences from the physical and biological sciences.[2]

It is also possible to define social science from specific perspectives. Social science is the study of societal systems and subsystems: the social system of roles and role behavior (i. e., sociology), the cultural system of norms of behavior or customs (anthropology), the political system of social control and power allocation (political science), the economic system of producing, distributing, and consuming goods and services (economics), and the ecosystem of the elements of space-ship earth, which humans need and use (geography). Social science may also be considered as the intellectual analysis of the significant problems where human choices are required: the choices that have influenced subsequent events, decisions about resource allocation, public policy decisions, locational choices, and choices made in social situations.

Up to a point, the terms social studies, social science, and social sciences may be used interchangeably inasmuch as they are all systematic investigations of human societies and social behavior. Differentiation among the terms is necessary, however, if we are to understand the relationship between social studies of the public school system and social science of higher education. Social science

suggests the unitary nature of social knowledge and a concern for avoiding parochial divisions between scholarly specialties, but it also implies social knowledge at an advanced level. Social sciences infers a holding company, a collection of specific disciplines all sharing a common focus on humankind, disciplines such as anthropology, economics, or political science. Social studies is the term more often used to refer to this area of knowledge as taught in elementary and high school, yet some university professors prefer to designate their area of scholarship as the social studies rather than the social sciences in order to demonstrate the humanistic rather than the scientific thrust of their scholarship.

The difference between social science (or social sciences) and social studies is most conspicuous in two aspects. First, social science is generally considered to be the resource from which the content of the social studies is drawn. The scholarly endeavors of university and college social scientists provide the raw material in history, geography, sociology, and the like, for use in social studies classrooms in elementary and secondary schools. Social science also provides the raw material for the study of problems of society, for the exploration of social themes, or any of a number of other ways of organizing the curriculum. Second, social science has as one of its hallmarks its commitment to a "value-free" position. As we shall see a little later, the social scientist attempts to maintain scholarly disinterest by keeping value questions at a distance. The psychologist or anthropologist may be concerned with how values affect human behavior, but his or her approach to them is supposed to be value free. The public school system, on the other hand, is an instrument of society; it is supposed to reflect the values of that society. In the United States, schools are generally thought to have a commitment to the de-

---

[2] National Science Foundation, *Knowledge into Action: Improving the Nation's Use of the Social Sciences*, Washington, D.C., U.S. Government Printing Office, 1969, p. 7.

velopment of effective citizens, citizens who are enlightened supporters of the democratic political system. Schools should at least help students understand their own values, the values of others, and the importance of values to human behavior.

The scholarly research foundations of social *science* and the value commitment of social studies are important differentiating characteristics. They may, however, lead to erroneous assumptions. Social science does not have exclusive claim to the use of inquiry; the public schools can and do use inquiry modes as a part of their instruction although it may be of a different order of magnitude. Nor does the place of values in the social studies mean that young people are indoctrinated into certain value systems by the schools. The commitment, however, to the scientific method is also a value.

If social science is the foundation of the social studies, it is important that we understand what social science *is* and what comprises the social science*s*.

The Scope of Social Science

To grasp fully the meaning of the term social science we must look at its scope, what is included within the arbitrarily established boundaries of the body of knowledge. Some descriptions of the scope of social science list the contributing disciplines: anthropology, economics, geography, history, political science, psychology, and sociology. Such a listing is hardly helpful because it tells us little of what is included in social science, especially if we don't know what geography or psychology are in the first place.

The scope of social science may be considered as comprising four major elements: (1) the nature of societies and cultures, (2) human activities and processes in spatial distribution, and the interaction

of cultural, biotic, and physical elements, (3) basic social systems and institutions as well as the relationships between individuals and institutions and among political, economic, and social institutions, and (4) changes in human relationships, reinterpretations of relationships among present and past events. What is included in each of these four elements?

1. *The nature of societies and cultures.* The social scientist is interested in studying the ways of life and distinctive characteristics of organized groups of people, whether they are tribes, nations, ethnic units, or inhabitants of large culture areas.

2. *Human activities and processes in spatial distribution, and the interaction of cultural, biotic, and physical elements.* Although human beings are fundamentally the same in their erect stance, their marvelously complex and dexterous appendages, their capacity for thought and speech, they do develop different patterns of behavior as they find themselves distributed over the space of the earth. The unique way of life learned by a group of people—what social scientists call culture—is the product of interaction of previously learned behavior, the other elements of life in the environment (both plant and animal), and the physical elements including soil, minerals, and weather. Thus a Netsilik Eskimo has evolved a culture that makes dwellings out of the abundantly available snow, a light source out of the plentiful blubber of sea mammals, and neither alcoholic beverages (there being insufficient plant life for fermentation) nor a word for war. (The Netsilik had no experience with killing people simply because they are different or they covet land.) Human activities and processes differ in many ways along the shore of large bodies of water as compared to arid flat interiors or high mountain valleys, in tropical rainforests or on polar plateaus. Human beings are distributed widely over the space of planet earth, and social scientists wish to determine what factors account for similarities in human activities despite widely varying environments and what accounts

for differences in the behavior of human groups occupying the same space.

3. *Basic social systems and institutions as well as the relationships between individuals and institutions and among political, economic, and social institutions.* Human societies can be examined as systems, comprising interacting and interdependent parts functioning as a whole. Thus all human societies develop economic systems (allocating scarce resources), political systems (providing mechanisms of social control and the management of power), and social systems (involving interaction at the personal and familial level), among other systems. The organized and regularized ways of meeting basic human needs within the systems are institutions, which are not places but patterns of behavior relating to making a living, worship, socializing the young to adult roles, and the like. Even though institutions are found among all human groups, the specific kinds and patterns of behavior will differ. Thus, it may seem "natural" for the institution of the family to be monogamistic among Europeans and Americans, but it is equally "natural" among Saudi Arabians to have a polygamous family institution. Economic institutions and political institutions differ, too; what is good (and "natural") for one nation may not be good (or "natural") for another. Human beings are affected daily by the institutions around them: religion, education, economics, politics; and by the systems of which they are a part: the value system, the socioeconomic status system, and the like. Individuals affect these systems and institutions. The institutions themselves interact; the economic institution does not exist in isolation from the political institution (system) nor does the institution of the family exist apart from the institution of education.

4. *Changes in human relationships, reinterpretations of relationships between present and past events.* Much of the work of social scientists involves comparing humans, individually or collectively. As we have seen, social scientists are interested in comparisons between human societies or groups in a

variety of situations, but they are also interested in the development of human behavior patterns and the changes that take place over periods of time.

The scope of social science is very broad, concerned as it is with so many aspects of human behavior. Perhaps social science as a concept is best understood by grasping what social scientists *do*, and what they do is to conduct investigations into society and human relationships and then communicate their findings. Operationally, we can summarize the scope of social science by indicating the following: (1) social scientists are curious about the nature of societies and cultures, (2) they investigate human activities and processes, (3) they try to understand social systems and institutions, and (4) they probe changes in human relationships. Furthermore, they try to understand the nature of causality in human affairs. While it is true that social scientists try to find answers, it is more important that they be able to ask good questions because without good questions it is impossible to produce accurate answers.

Social Science as a "Who Done It?"

The kinds of questions asked by the social scientist are further aids in understanding what social science is all about. There are four broad questions that are clues to the nature of this field:

1. What's going on?
2. Why do things (social phenomena) behave as they do?
3. Who am I? Who are we? What am I (we) doing here?
4. What do I (we) do next?

All these questions, of course, are to be considered within the context of the scope of social science. These questions, and many more specific ones deriving from them, are directed at Homo sapiens as a social being.

Social science is both social (focusing on man in the generic sense) and science (a body of verified knowledge and a method of deriving and extending this knowledge). As science, it shares with other sciences—earth science, physical science, materials science, computer science—a body of specific facts, terms, concepts, principles, generalizations, and the like, which make up the body of verified knowledge—and the process by which the facts and generalizations were "discovered" and verified. Thus, any science is both product (the knowledge) and process (the methodology or mode of inquiry). Since modern social science gives increasing attention to the methodology (because facts and terms can become outdated and change), it might be more appropriate to refer to the field as social sciencing or social study, terms emphasizing process. Regardless of which term is used, the work of the social scientist is not unlike that of another kind of an investigator, the detective in his or her attempt to probe, "Who done it?" The social scientist, of course, goes far beyond that basic question because he/she wants to know *why* it was done, and may also want to know how this adds to our understanding of the basic characteristics of a society.

The Nature of Social Science

Characteristics of Social Science

There are several important characteristics of social science, most of which are shared by other sciences. First of all, science is a means of answering questions about the unknown and about the known; it provides explanations. People not only wish to "discover" the truth

about phenomena of which we are ignorant, but they wish to have explanations for the commonplace, and they wish to verify "knowledge" and beliefs long held. Second, science rests on empirical foundations: careful observation of phenomena, gathering data in an objective fashion, and precise definitions of terms. Nonscientific ways of "knowing"—hunches, common sense, folklore, consulting oracles—are inadequate means of providing explanations. A third characteristic of science is the public nature of the procedures. Communicating the results of scientific investigation in scholarly journals or at meetings of scientific associations is one way of both spreading knowledge and ensuring the public nature of the procedures. As public knowledge, scientific findings can be checked by other scholars for accuracy, and the research can be replicated—performed again using different subjects but under essentially the same conditions. Many scientists will not engage in secret research, even for their government, because to do so violates this important scientific canon of public procedures.

The three characteristics of science discussed thus far make no distinction between social science or natural science. Both areas of knowledge answer questions about the unknown, are based on empirical foundations, and make their procedures public—each within its own scope. On the two remaining characteristics, social science and natural science diverge from one another. In its goal of providing explanation, understanding, and predictions, science produces generalizations. The natural sciences are concerned with *universalistic* generalizations and the social sciences produce *probabilistic* generalizations. A universalistic generalization is a statement that links facts, provides explanations, and/or suggests causes that are universally true, that is, statements that are always and under all conditions true. A one-pound object dropped from an aircraft is *always* going to succumb to the gravitational pull of this planet and fall to earth. It makes no difference whether it's from a 747 flying at 40,000 feet over the polar ice cap, a helicopter over the Sahara Desert, or a hang glider over Yosemite Valley. Universalistic generalizations can be used to predict consequences with great accuracy. These kinds of generalizations enabled lunar astronauts to explore the moon and to return safely; and the Viking Lander to travel 220 million miles into space, land where directed, and to explore the surface of Mars by remote control from earth. Laws of nature, the term the natural scientist usually applies to universalistic generalizations, are useful in large part because they *can* be used to predict with high accuracy what will happen given a certain combination of events. Natural science generates large numbers of laws: Newton's laws of motion, Boyle's law of gases, and Ohm's law of electrical current, among others.

The social scientist *cannot* predict with absolute certainty. He or she can develop generalizations about human behavior which will link facts, provide explanations, or suggest causes, but these generalizations are accurate only in terms of their probability of happening. They may be quite accurate when related to groups of people, but can be applied to individuals only in terms of tendencies or statistical probabilities. People who vote Republican *tend* to be above average in income and education and *tend* to come from small towns and rural areas. That doesn't mean, however, that a social scientist can predict that a Sam Beecher, a successful small businessman and Congregational church elder from a Maine farming center, will be a Republican. There may be a .90 probability that blacks will vote Democratic, but one can't predict that the next black of voting age

that one meets will vote Democratic any more than one can predict with total accuracy that the next flip of the coin will be heads (or tails). One can only make the statement that the probability of heads is .50 (but so, too, is the probability of tails).

Finally, science is characterized as being ethically neutral and value free. The scientist studies what *is* rather than what he/she thinks *ought to be.* This aspect of science is easier to maintain in natural science than it is in social science. A medical scientist has little difficulty in maintaining his or her neutrality and scientific objectivity in studying disease, but social scientists have more difficulty in freeing themselves from involvement in the social conditions that they may be studying. For years there was little or no question that social scientists should strive to maintain their investigations in a value-free atmosphere, but in recent years this has been brought into question. Should social scientists be disinterested and not valuative if their investigations reveal social evils? Should the social scientist maintain neutrality in learning more about poverty, discrimination, injustice? Many social scientists now think not. The question of neutrality has recently invaded the scientific community of physicists, chemists, geneticists. Can the natural scientist avoid taking responsibility for the consequences of his or her research? Too, as we noted at the outset of this chapter, the matter of values is one of the aspects differentiating the social studies from the social sciences.

These five characteristics help us understand the differences and similarities between the social sciences and the natural sciences. They also help us see the difference between the social sciences (or the natural sciences) and the humanities. The humanities do not necessarily rest on empirical foundations and they are not necessarily concerned with producing universalistic or probabilistic generalizations. Furthermore, the humanities tend, by their very nature, to be valuative or normative rather than rigorously disinterested.

The Structure of Social Science

Knowledge about human society, however, has little meaning or utility unless it is organized. This is equally true whether one looks at social science as an integrated whole or at its component disciplines.

> "Organization of knowledge in the social sciences is essential to any achievement of significance by individuals, groups, or society. Without knowledge, we perish; without organization, knowledge pertaining to any large area of affairs is useless."[3]

One way of organizing knowledge is in terms of the conventional subdivisions we have already discussed: social science, natural science, and the humanities. Each focuses on a different aspect of natural, spiritual, or social phenomena. Yet it is not the focus that differentiates these subdivisions. After all, human beings are the focus of two or the three subdivisions, and they are frequently the object of study by the third. A more distinguishing characteristic of these three branches of knowledge is their structure — the concepts used to define the subject matter and their mode of inquiry, the manner of investigating unknown phenomena and of verifying knowledge that we shall examine in due course.

The structure of the humanities is different in some very fundamental ways from the structure of natural science, and both the humanities and natural science structures differ from the structure of social science. It would be more accurate, in fact, to refer to the structures of the humanities or natural science or social science because the concepts appropriate to astronomy are different from the concepts of chemistry in many respects and the mode of inquiry of physics may be somewhat different from the mode of inquiry of botany. And because the concepts of anthropology are different from the concepts of economics and because the mode of inquiry of geography is different from political science, some scholars prefer the term social sciences. Such a term implies a sort of holding company for a group of related disciplines.

The structure of a discipline is the intellectual framework of that discipline. It is the organization imposed on what otherwise would be a melange of disjointed facts, information, and ideas. Some scholars compare the structure of knowledge to the grammar of a language, and grammar is the implicitly understood patterns of relationships and the organization of the components of a language. Without a grammar it is virtually impossible to put words together in a fashion by which there can be communication. Without a structure (or more correctly structures) of knowledge, there is no organized framework within which we can relate ideas and information.

More specifically, structure is the body of imposed conceptions that define the investigated subject matter and the characteristic modes of inquiry by which the investigation is carried out. To understand the structure of social science (or of anthropology or political science, for example) we must know the most important and most powerful concepts of social science (or anthropology or political science) and its mode of inquiry. Such

---

[3] Charles A. Beard, *The Nature of the Social Sciences*, New York, Scribner's, 1934, pp. 14–15.

a list of concepts provides another way of identifying the scope of social science.

Let us start with the cognitive products relating to concepts, or more specifically to facts and attributes, concepts, generalizations, and constructs. Perhaps the best way to understand these cognitive products is by the use of a model, a cone of abstraction. (Figure 5.1). The layout of the cone suggests that each of the cognitive products, starting at the bottom, builds on the other. Each, however, is more than the sum of the cognitive products below it.

Facts are the building blocks of information that are the foundation of a body of knowledge. We could fill volumes with the facts of social science: George Wahington was the first president of the United States, the Missouri-Mississippi is the longest river in North America, the American extended family consists of father-mother-children-grandparents-and other close relatives, the capital of West Germany is Bonn. Closely related to facts as a building block of knowledge are attributes that are the distinguishing characteristics of properties of things, events, ideas, and the like. Attributes can give concrete information about a "thing" or can define its features, as illustrated by such attributive statements as "A dog has four legs"; "A bird has feathers and flies"; "An orchestra consists of several musicians who play music." In the context of social science we could discuss the attributes of rivers (they contain water), families (groups of people related to one another, usually husband, wife, and children), or capital (a city that is the center of government or other major functions).

Social Science Concepts

Concepts are a higher-level cognitive product than facts and attributes. Experience with facts and attributes can help us develop concepts that provide a part of the framework of a body of knowledge and, more important, our whole conceptual world. Having at our command a body of facts is no guarantee that we will grasp appropriate concepts, however. Seeing a number of trees—facts—will not necessarily enable us to observe and comprehend a forest. Through experience we learn to sort out and label the objects and events that form our conceptual world. The "boxes" into which we sort out these objects and events are at first rather large and undiscriminating, and we may develop some *misconceptions* because the labels we use do not relate to fine points of difference among the objects and events. With more experience and greater intellectual and social maturity, the "boxes" are refined and multiplied. Instead of a single box labeled "car," we add others identified as "truck," "sportscar," "bus," "station wagon," and the like. Later we may refine these to make fine distinctions among the contents of the boxes—"Austin Healey," "Ford," "Chevy," "VW," and on almost endlessly.

A concept is an abstract idea, generalized bodies of attributes associated with the symbol of a class of things. The word or symbol we use for a concept, for example, institutions, is not the concept. The abstract body of meaning that we internalize and associate with the symbol is the concept. A concept, therefore, refers to the category of attributes or events

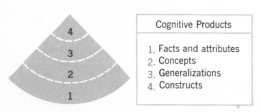

Cognitive Products
1. Facts and attributes
2. Concepts
3. Generalizations
4. Constructs

Figure 5.1

that are common across a variety of objects or experiences.

Concepts have certain qualities. There are concrete or tangible concepts such as soil, mountains, and cities because they refer to a class of things that have concrete existences that can be known directly through the senses. There are also abstract concepts such as socioeconomic classes, customs, and motivation because they cannot be "known" empirically but they can be experienced. Furthermore, concepts can range from the simple (e.g., home) to the complex (e.g., love). Most social science concepts are both abstract and complex.

The most important quality of a concept is its central dimension, the properties or indicators that set it off from other similar concepts. We could list all of the attributes of a dog—that it has four legs, a tail, fur, ears, paws, a certain size—and we still would not have internalized the concept because we couldn't distinguish a dog from a cat or a koala. The dog's bark and its domesticated nature are among its central properties.

Concepts are not taught; they are learned by experience. Definitions of concepts can be memorized, but that does not mean that the concept is internalized and understood. One way a person can be helped to learn concepts is in the form of vicarious experience, that is, through a series of examples of the concept accompanied by a series of nonexamples. The examples may help a person understand the attributes associated with the concept. Nonexamples are also useful in eliminating some characteristics that might otherwise be associated with a concept. For example, to develop the concept of a sailing vessel, we could show someone a series of pictures of sailing vessels, all different sizes and shapes (schooners, brigs, sampans, caravels, etc.). We could show another series of pictures, all of which are nonexamples: subma-

rines, freighters, tankers, passenger liners, motor-powered yachts. We could carry this a step further, refining the concept, and try to develop the concept of galleon by showing different pictures of galleons (Spanish galleons, English galleons, fifteenth-century galleons, sixteenth-century galleons, three-masted ones, four-masted ones, etc.), accompanied by nonexamples of other sailing vessels (sloops, Yankee clippers, ketches, yawls, etc.).

Because concepts are products of experience and because individual experience is unique, concepts tend to be subjective.

> "When someone, for example, tells us that he sees a "house," he is not really communicating his actual experience, but a highly simplified and generalized version of it—an interpretation that reflects the cultural consensus regarding the essential (criterial, identifying) attributes of "house." His actual conscious experience of the event is infinitely more particularistic with respect to size, shape, style, hue, brightness, and presumed cost than the message communicated by his generic use of the term "house." If he actually tried to communicate his detailed cognitive experience, it would not only take him half a day, but he would still also be unable completely to express in words many of its more subtle nuances."[4]

Mature, reasonably well-educated people have at their command a large but limited number of concepts. They have, potentially, an unlimited number of

[4] David P. Ausubel, *Educational Psychology: A Cognitive View,* New York, Holt, Rinehart and Winston, 1968, p. 505.

facts. The number of powerful interdisciplinary social science concepts is rather small, although there are a large number of specific and restricted concepts in the disciplines comprising the broad field of social science.

More meaningful than more definitions and further elaborations is a list of these powerful interdisciplinary social science concepts that can help us intuit the concept of a concept!

1. Habitat—the "natural" setting or environment within which humans carry out their life activities.
2. Culture—the learned behavior distinctive of a group or society.
3. Institutions—the patterned responses to basic human needs such as producing and managing children, making a living.
4. Resources and resource allocation—the raw materials in the habitat that can be converted to human use and the systems by which these are allocated and to whom.
5. Interaction: competition, cooperation, accommodation, assimilation—the particular forms of behavior that emerge as people come in contact with one another.
6. Conflict and conflict management—competition may lead to conflict over human goals or the means of their achievement, but conflict cannot continue indefinitely; there are means of resolving it, or managing it.
7. Power—the authority to make binding decisions, to "control" human behavior.
8. Technology and industrialism—tools plus techniques for using them constitute technology, from a stone hand ax to a sophisticated space station; industrialism includes the total impact on human life of advanced technology.

The above are substantive concepts; they help define the subject matter scope of a discipline. There are three remaining important interdisciplinary concepts of another order.

9. Social change—human societies develop and progress, in accelerating fashion.

10. Choice: values/valuing—although culture shapes much human behavior into automatic responses, people are constantly faced with making all kinds of choices, choices that are made based on some system of values.
11. Multiple causation—events do not just happen, they are caused, and they are caused not by one factor, but a multiplicity of factors.

These 11 core concepts comprise only one of a number of lists of integrating social science concepts. Most of the lists are longer; very few are shorter. Most social scientists agree on the key concepts, but different frames of reference account for the differences in the list.[5]

A list of major concepts such as above may also serve to identify the scope of social science. If we analyze the scope of social science already presented (see pages 77-78) we will note the nature of societies and cultures includes such concepts as culture, institutions, and social change; that human activities and process include interaction, habitat, conflict, and resources; and so on through the rest of the list. Increasingly in the social studies, scope is being stated in lists and categories of concepts.

Why are concepts and the learning of concepts important in social science? They, of course, define the subject matter to be investigated. They also provide the framework within which facts can be energized. An isolated bit of information may help provide a correct answer on

[5] See, for example, Bernard Berelson and Gary A. Steiner, *Human Behavior, An Inventory of Scientific Findings*, New York, Harcourt, Brace and World, 1968; California Commission on Teacher Preparation and Licensing, *Social Science Scope and Content Framework*, Sacramento, CTPL, 1975; California State Department of Education, *Social Sciences Education Framework for California Public Schools*, Sacramento, CSDE, 1975; Roy A. Price et al., *Major Concepts for Social Science*, Syracuse, Syracuse University Press, 1965; Social Science Education Consortium *Newsletter*, vol. II, no. 1, April 1966.

certain types of examinations or it may be useful in winning trivia contests, but it is not apt to be retained and used by most people outside the context of a body of concepts. New information makes sense when related to a firmly grasped set of concepts.

Concepts are vital building blocks in the construction of generalizations, whether they are universalistic or probabilistic. As a statement that links facts, provides explanations, and/or suggests causes, generalizations utilize concepts. In fact, one may define generalizations as statements that show relationships among concepts. With a relatively small number of concepts, a person can develop an almost unlimited number of generalizations, particularly as he/she becomes proficient in the evidence-inference process from which valid generalizations are made. Perhaps the best way to understand the "concept" of generalization is through a series of examples! The following list of 18 generalizations is typical of the type that K-12 pupils should develop from the social studies.

1. Man's comprehension of the present and his wisdom in planning for the future depend upon his understanding of the events of the past that influence the present.
2. Change is a condition of human society; civilizations rise and fall; value systems improve or deteriorate; the tempo of change varies with cultures and periods of history.
3. Through all time and in all regions of the world, man has worked to meet common basic human needs and to satisfy common human desires and aspirations.
4. People of all races, religions, and cultures have contributed to the cultural heritage. Modern society owes a debt to cultural inventors of other places and times.
5. Interdependence is a constant factor in human relationships. The realization of self develops through contact with others. Social groupings of all kinds develop as a means of group cooperation in meeting individual and societal needs.
6. The culture under which an individual is reared and the social groups to which he belongs exert great influence on his ways of perceiving, thinking, feeling, and acting.
7. Democracy is dependent on the process of free inquiry; this process provides for defining the problem, seeking data, using the scientific method in collecting evidence, restating the problem in terms of its interrelationships, arriving at a principle that is applicable, applying the principle in the solution of the problem.
8. The basic substance of a civilization is rooted in its values; the nature of the values is the most persistent and important problem faced by human beings.
9. Man must make choices based on economic knowledge, scientific comparisions, analytic judgment, and his value system concerning how he will use the resources of the world.
10. The work of society is done through organized groups; and group membership involves opportunities, responsibilities, and the development of leadership.
11. Organized group life of all types must act in accordance with established rules of social relationships and a system of social controls.
12. All nations of the modern world are part of a global independent system of economic, social, cultural, and political life.
13. Democracy is based on belief in the integrity of man, the dignity of the individual, equality of opportunity, man's rationality, man's goodness, man's practicality, man's ability to govern himself and to solve his problems co-operatively.
14. Anthropologists hold that physically man is the product of the same biological evolution as the rest of the animal kingdom. Man is in many ways similar to other animals, but a most important difference exists as a result of man's rationality and in the body of knowledge, beliefs, and values that constitute man's culture.
15. All human beings are of one biological species within which occur the variations

called races. The differences between races is negligible.

16. Environment affects man's way of living, and man, in turn, modifies his environment.

17. One of the factors affecting man's mode of life is his natural environment. Weather and climate that cause regional differences in land forms, soils, drainage, and natural vegetation determine the relative density of population in the various regions of the world.

18. Because man must use natural resources to survive, the distribution and use of these resources determine where he lives on the earth's surface and to some extent how well he lives. The level of his technology determines how he produces, exchanges, transports, and consumes his goods.[6]

Some concepts are so vast, complex, and abstract that they are of a different order than the kinds of concepts that we have already identified. Such concepts, sometimes called constructs, are organizations of interrelated generalizations and concepts. They are not simply classes or categories of attributes but theories, philosophies, ideological systems, models, or myths. Examples are Democracy, Idealism, Imperialism, Marxism, and Christendom. These are the highest cognitive products, the understanding of which would be among the ultimate goals of social studies teachers.

The Modes of Inquiry of Social Science

But concepts and related cognitive products are only half of the structure of social science. The other is the inquiry process, which includes the process of coming to know. Social science inquiry is

[6] *Building Curriculum in Social Studies for the Public Schools of California*, Bulletin of the California State Department of Education, Vol. XXVI, No. 4, May 1957, pp. 46–47. Used by permission.

a form of "Who done it?" in the general area of human behavior and social interaction. It begins with the broad questions:

What's going on?

Why do things behave as they do?

These kinds of questions are not the exclusive province of the social scientist, however. They, and others, are the kinds of questions that the lay citizen asks about everyday social behavior and about societies, and they are the kinds of questions that the child asks at the frontier of his or her knowledge. Thus, the basic elements of inquiry are much the same for the child in school as they are for the professional social scientist.

Although the inquiry process varies somewhat with the specific social science discipline, there are two main elements in common: evidence and inferences. The fledgling social scientist in school and the professional historian or anthropologist must consider (a) What kind of data shall be used? (b) How shall the data be treated? (c) What conclusions can be drawn from the data? (d) How shall it be communicated? The answers to these questions is in large part a matter of asking specific questions: What's the nature of society X? How does it compare with society B (or with other societies)? What factors account for the development of the unique characteristics of society Y? What social process is most influential in a culture? How do the various social institutions—economic, political, religious—interrelate with one another? How is humankind affected by the physical, biotic, and cultural environment? What accounts for changes in human relationships over time? How does the past influence the present and vice versa? How do the characteristics of group A compare with group B? What factors account for certain types of behavior (bravery, criminality, striving for success, alienation)?

The inquiry process starts with making observations of social phenomena, present or past, out of which we develop hypotheses, define our terms, and gather our data or evidence. Having gathered our evidence, we subject it to analysis, a cross-examination process that is concerned with determining the validity of the evidence and, if it passes the test, of drawing inferences in the form of supporting or rejecting our hypothesis. Depending on the nature of our inquiry, we will communicate the inference by different means, orally or in writing, with (or without) charts, tables, pictures, and so on.

Our process of evidence gathering and inference making may involve experiment, as when a psychologist uses rats in a maze to test a hypothesis about reward and punishment. It may involve fieldwork, as when an anthropologist lives with a preliterate tribe and studies its culture. It may involve a series of case studies, as when a team of political scientists study decision making in a particular political unit. It may involve a survey, as when an economist collects information about economic output or when a sociologist attempts to determine people's opinions about mandatory school busing. It may involve unearthing and examining documents that will tell us more about past personages and events. In each instance, the particular social scientist will have to decide that data to use, how it shall be treated, what conclusions can be drawn from it, and how the conclusions are to be communicated.

Regardless of what particular scholarly method of inquiry is used, all scientists gather and analyze evidence and draw inferences from it. Let's take a simple example. Simple observation will reveal that some automobiles carry bumper stickers. Although some of them are commercial, plugging some product or tourist attraction, most of them convey socially important messages. Casual observation might lead one to the hypothesis that certain types of vehicles are more likely to carry noncommercial bumper stickers than others and that there are even differences in the kinds of message according to the kind of automobile. One such hypothesis might be that VW beetles are more likely to carry "liberal" bumper stickers ("Save the Whales") than any other make of automobile or that pick-up trucks and campers are more likely to carry "conservative" bumper stickers ("America — Love It or Leave It," "Register Communists, Not Guns") than passenger autos. Since an hypothesis is only an educated guess that is worthy of investigation and is testable, we don't know whether they are true or false until we gather the data and draw inferences from it in the form of conclusions. How would you set about to prove or disprove these hypotheses? What kind of data would you gather? How would you communicate the inferences made?

One does not need to be a university social scientist to conduct a survey testing the above hypothesis. Elementary students as well as high school students can do research and are able to carry out investigations. Examples of some types of investigations are the following: A science experiment relative to social studies might be a study of different diets using hamsters as the subjects. There could be an experimental group on a diet of coke and potato chips and a control group fed a balanced diet. To test the hypothesis of whether people learn by mistakes, or by observing other people's behavior, students could carry out a psychological experiment using a paper maze and repetitive trials, noting the time the subject takes to complete the maze and the number of errors. Students could do field work to answer questions such as: What happens at school during lunch? What are the customs and activities? A careful record of observations would be kept and generalizations drawn from the evidence. Still another type of student research would be case studies, perhaps an investigation of the student council and how it makes decisions, or a study of a young child (a sibling, cousin, or neighbor). Or, of course, students could conduct a survey, such as the bumper sticker example, or a questionnaire on what TV programs are watched, which are preferred, and the like. An excellent and valuable learning activity could be historical research in which students reconstruct the past by writing a family history using oral interviews, birth certificates, photos, letters, and the like.

The inquiry portion of social science structure goes by many names: the evidence-inference process, research, systematic investigation, or mode(s) of inquiry. The basic process is fundamentally the same regardless of which name is used. Furthermore, young people can become proficient in it at their level of sophistication and in so doing are engaged in basically the same process as the social scientist in his or her advanced research. In a later chapter we will examine the use of inquiry in the schools.

Where We've Been and Where We're Going

By now you have an introductory knowledge of the social science foundation of the social studies. Unlike Fats Waller or Louis Armstrong, we say that you *have* to ask in order to know. But we also recognize the importance of having experiences in order to know. Asking questions is basic to inquiry, if only to help us ask better questions.

A foundation is a support system. It may be a base as in most homes or it may be a base plus a core from which walls are suspended as in some new office buildings. Perhaps the social science foundations of the social studies are more like a geodesic dome in which the support system and the exterior are merged into one.

Social science is one of a number of ways of viewing life and experience. It is the systematic study of humankind and the groups and societies formed by humans in interaction with one another. The nature of social science includes its characteristics and its scope and, most importantly, its structure.

We have not examined the facts, principles, and other detailed information of social science. There is not time nor space to do this, nor is it the purpose of this book to do so. Furthermore, facts are easily forgotten and some may become outdated. The structure of a discipline can be more easily retained by a learner than unrelated facts; it functions as the framework around which facts and specific information are organized and to which new information can be added.

We are now ready to take this introductory knowledge and expand it to include some new knowledge about the nature of each of the social science disciplines. To continue our analogy of architectural structure, we can say that within the bare walls and roof (or within our geodesic dome) we are ready to divide the interior into compartments—the specific social science disciplines. A knowledge of the disciplines is important to round out our knowledge of social science as the foundation of the social studies. It is also important because one of the major aspects of the new social studies in the past two decades has been the attention given to the disciplines. Examples of this disciplinary thrust are to be found in elementary projects at the

University of Georgia (anthropology), the University of Colorado (economics), and the Education Development Center's MACOS (anthropology), among others.

We will examine seven social science disciplines grouped into categories: the classic disciplines of history and geography, the policy sciences of economics and political science, and the behavioral sciences of anthropology, sociology, and psychology.

Bibliography

Ausubel, D. P. *Educational Psychology: A Cognitive View.* New York: Holt, Rinehart and Winston, 1968.

California State Department of Education. *Social Sciences Education Framework for California Public Schools.* Sacramento: California State Department of Education, 1975.

Hebert, Louis J. and William Murphy (eds.). *Structure in the Social Studies.* Social Studies Reading Number 3. Washington, D.C.: The National Council for the Social Studies, 1968.

Homans, George C. *The Nature of Social Science.* New York: Harcourt, Brace, and World, 1967.

Martorella, Phillip H. *Concept Learning in the Social Studies: Models for Structuring Curriculum.* New York: Intext, 1971.

Morrissett, Irving (ed.). *Concepts and Structure in the New Social Science Curriculum.* West Lafayette, Ind.: Social Science Education Consortium, 1966.

Price, Roy A. et al. *Major Concepts for Social Science.* Syracuse: Syracuse University, 1965.

Senn, Peter R. "Social Science Described" in part 1 of *Social Science and Its Methods.* Boston: Holbrook Press, 1971.

Tanck, Martin. "Teaching Concepts, Generalizations, and Constructs" in Dorothy McClure Fraser (ed.). *Social Studies Curriculum Development: Prospects and Problems.* 39th Yearbook of the National Council for the Social Studies. Washington, D.C.: The Council, 1969.

The following books are general in nature and not only have pertinent portions on the social science foundations of the social studies but have sections or chapters on most of the social science disciplines treated in the subsequent chapters of section II.

Abcarian, Gilbert and Monte Palmer. *Society in Conflict: An Introduction to Social Science.* San Francisco: Canfield Press, 1974.

Browne, Robert S. et al. *The Social Scene.* Cambridge, Mass.: Winthrop Publishers, 1971.

Feldman, Martin and Eli Seifman (eds.). *The Social Studies: Structure, Models, and Strategies.* Englewood Cliffs, N.J.: Prentice-Hall, 1969.

Mendoza, Manuel G. and Vince Napoli. *Systems of Man: An Introduction to Social Science.* Lexington, Mass.: D. C. Heath, 1977.

Pirtle, Wayne G. and John J. Grant. *The Social Sciences: An Integrated Approach.* New York: Random House, 1972.

Why is it important to make history meaningful to students?

CHAPTER 6

The Classic Disciplines: History and Geography

As American schools became secular and dropped their emphasis on religious instruction, the development of citizenship moved in to fill the void. Curriculum began to expand beyond the three R's, and among the first additions to it were those subjects designed to develop a spirit of nationalism. History, particularly the study of the heroes of a growing nation, was expected to be the prime means of developing good citizenship. But a young nation had to learn about the country and a trading nation had to know about the rest of the world, and this of course meant the study of geography.

We call history and geography the classic disciplines because they were the first subjects systematically studied and they have continued to be the heart of the social studies program up to the present day. History and, to a lesser degree, geography, have both declined in importance as the other social sciences have become more prominent in the social studies program, but it would be difficult, indeed, to imagine a social studies program without both of them. They also may be considered classic because they provide two essential

dimensions for the study of humankind—a time dimension and a space dimension. All social phenomena exist in time and in space. The other social sciences are essentially concerned about social conditions that are "timeless" and that exist in a general setting. History provides an important perspective by which we may understand the place of events in terms of their development over time. Geography provides another kind of perspective, the habitat that influences culture and in turn is shaped by humankind. The physical, biotic, and cultural setting in which human interaction takes place must be investigated if a comprehensive understanding of the human condition is to take place. The eighteenth-century German geographer, Johann von Herder, put it in another way, typical of his era

"The stage and book of God's household—history the book and geography the stage . . . Whoever studies one without the other understands neither, and whoever despises both should live like the mole, not on, but under the earth."

Both of these disciplines straddle the other two major areas of knowledge: history may be allied with the humanities, particularly in the area of literature, and geography has common elements with natural science, particularly meteorology, geology, astronomy, and biology, but also chemistry and physics.

History and the Social Studies

History used to be the all-encompassing social study, and in some respects, the various social sciences have been spinoffs of history. History studies previous political events, former economic ups and downs, and past sociology (the relations among groups, the historic family, religious developments).

Not all historians like to consider themselves social scientists. Some universities classify history with philosophy and literature in the humanities rather than with psychology and economics in the social sciences. History, of course, shares a similar frame of reference with philosophy in tracing how people have tried to find answers to the big questions such as What is life? and What is the good society? It shares a similar frame of reference with literature in attempting narrative reconstructions of the past.

What Is History?

It is said that everyone knows what history is until he or she begins to think about it, then the surety of that knowledge waivers. In its simplest definition history is the story of the past. In several Western languages, the word for history is also the word for story: *l'histoire* (French), *historia* (Spanish), *storia* (Italian),

and *Geschichte* (German). But history in Latin is *historia* whereas story is *fabula*, and in Japanese it is *rekishi* and *hanashi*, respectively. There are other more sophisticated definitions, however.

"History is a record of things said and done."

"History is past human behavior, recorded and unrecorded, in its many varieties."[1]

"History . . . is a mountain top of human knowledge from whence the doings of our generation may be scanned and fitted into proper dimensions."[2]

"History is a continuous process of interaction between the historian and his facts, an unending dialog between the present and the past."[3]

"The study of history is the study of causes."[4]

"History is the process of selection in terms of historical significance."[5]

"History is what one age finds worthy of note in another."[6]

"History . . . brings together the results of the inquiries that the various social sciences carry on and shapes them into a comprehensive account related to the course of historic events. History, in short, by telling the much abused "story" mediates between the social sciences and the

---

[1] California Commission for Teacher Preparation and Licensing, "History Scope and Content," Sacramento: CTPL, 1974, p. 1.
[2] Carl G. Gustafson, *A Preface to History*, New York, McGraw-Hill, 1955, p. 2.
[3] E. H. Carr, *What is History?* New York, Alfred Knopf, 1965, p. 35.
[4] Ibid.
[5] Ibid.
[6] Jacob Burckhardt, *Judgments on History and Historians*, London, S. J. Reginald Saunders and Company, 1958, p. 158.

larger community of man; it is primarily through historians that the social sciences themselves may enter history."[7]

History excites many people and it bores others. The young, in particular, have difficulties seeing that the study of the past has much value for them. Of what use *is* history?

"To be ignorant of what happened before you were born is to be ever a child."[8]

"He who does not know history is fated to repeat it."[9]

"Every organized social group is guided by its recollection of the past —because knowledge of the past is the guide to acting in the present and planning for the future."[10]

The Varieties of History

In their quest for better understanding of the past, historians find it convenient to organize their discipline in a number of different ways. One of these is according to geography; thus we have American history, European history, African history, and the like. Another is according to chronology: ancient history, medieval history, modern history. More often they combine the two: seventeenth- and eighteenth-century French history, history of the Indian subcontinent before 1500, the recent history of Japan. A third variety is topical: intellectual history, the history of science, the history of education (or of America education), diplomatic history, economic history. And

some recent varieties of history include future history, oral history, psychohistory, among others.

The ancient Greeks believed that humans' fate—their history—was in the hands of the gods, and Clio was the Muse[11] of history. The ancient Greeks were also the first systemitizers of knowledge, however, and Herodotus is called the father of history for his secular narrative of the Persian Wars, the first of its kind. Until well into the nineteenth century, history served either the church or the state with biased accounts of, first, the church leaders and, later, of the national rulers. Then von Ranke and others attempted to apply the scientific method to history, insisting on massing of historical facts, the objective analysis of them, and drawing inferences accordingly.

In recent years there have been economic interpretations of history, cyclic theories of history, hypotheses about the importance of the Western frontier in the development of the United States, theories emphasizing the theme of consensus in the nation's past, and other theories stressing conflict. The constant flow of new theories of the past, many of them contradicting previously stated theories, is disturbing to the lay person who has difficulty understanding why history doesn't "show" one idea or the other to be *the* one, once and for all without some disturbing new hypothesis coming along. We must realize that each generation must write its own interpretation of the past. It reconstructs previous events in terms of its own insights and its own understandings of human behavior.

[7] Page Smith, *The Historian and History*, New York, Alfred Knopf, 1964, p. 137.
[8] Cicero, ca., 50 B.C.E.
[9] George Santayana, ca., 1920.
[10] Edgar B. Wesley, *American History in Schools and Colleges*, New York, Macmillian, 1944, p. 16.

[11] The nine Greek Muses were daughters of Zeus and Mnemosyne. These goddesses were the patrons of the arts and sciences. In addition to Clio there were Cailiped, the Muse of epic poetry and eloquence; Erato, the Muse of the poetry of life; and Terpsichore of choral song and dance. Apollo was their leader.

The Evidence-Inference Process in the Study of History: The Historical Method

History is different from the other social sciences in many respects, and its structure is of quite different order than the other social science disciplines. History is particularistic—it is concerned with particular events, particular eras, particular people. There is great reluctance among historians to make generalizations about the social scene. They would prefer, for example, to explore the causes, events, and consequences of the French Revolution than to indulge in generalizations about the causes, events, and consequences of political revolutions. Historians use social science concepts freely in their investigations of the past, but there are few uniquely historical concepts. Since we have defined structure as the imposed concepts which guide the inquiry of a discipline, the structure of history is to be found in its inquiry process, the historical method. Of course, the concept of chronology is central to the study of history (as are related concepts such as epoch and period), but just about all the other concepts used by historians are "borrowed" from other social science and humanistic disciplines, concepts such as politics, environment, monarch, economic progress, and so on.

Although history is particularistic, it is also holistic and integrative. There may seem to be a contradiction for a discipline to be both of these things because they appear to be opposites, but if we realize that most of the other social science disciplines are analytical—concerned with developing generalizations about the human condition which are neither time bound nor space bound—then we can see that history strives to integrate historical information and historical ideas so that we may understand a particular group living in a particular locale in a particular time holisticly. The analytic social sciences strive to answer the major social science questions of "What's going on?" "Why do things behave as they do?" by which they clarify concepts such as revolution or power or role behavior or scarcity regardless of whether they exist in Periclean Athens, the Paris of Louis XVI, or twentieth-century St. Petersburg. The historian, on the other hand, conducts his or her inquiries to answer the questions, "Who am I (who are we)?" "What am I (we) doing here?" in order to add to our knowledge of the political, economic, and social life of Athens, circa 450 B.C.E., of the conditions giving rise to the French Revolution of 1789, or of the life in the Imperial Russian capital during World War I.

Even if history is unlike other social science disciplines in the lack of unique concepts, it does have a mode of inquiry. Historians make hypotheses, gather and interpret evidence, and draw inferences from the evidence. The historian, like other scholars, conducts his inquiry through a series of analytic questions. Before we can pursue the nature of historical investigation, however, we need to examine the different meanings of history.

The word history carries a great burden because people use it to encompass several meanings. First, there is history-as-actuality meaning *everything* that has happened in the past. Even if we narrow history (as-actuality) down to a particular time or society, no historian can possibly have access to information about everything that happened. Much of what happens is inconsequential; future historians are unlikely to be interested in what John Jones had for breakfast on July 4, 1976 or what color pants suit Judy Smith wore to the Bicentennial picnic. (They may, however, be interested in what Americans typically ate or wore in 1776 compared with 1976.) The historian must work with the second kind of history, history-as-record: official documents, chronicles, diaries, maps, pictures, tools, eyewitness accounts, and the like. From history-as-record the historian attempts to reconstruct the past, utilizing all the pertinent evidence from which inferences can be made about the past. The reconstruction thus becomes the third kind of history, written history. It is this kind which the average person has in mind most of the time when the term history is used. History is what is in history books!

All of us live history-as-actuality every day and in a way we "make" history every day. We make it in the sense that we are part of events that may in the future prove to be of consequence. College students of the late 1960s and early 1970s were part of the college revolt of that era and their support—even passive support—of the changes advocated then are now history. Each generation and each people has to rewrite history in light of its own experiences. That's why the views of historians in the 1970s may differ from the views of historians of the 1930s, and why Americans view their own history differently than do the Soviets. It cannot be said that "only history will prove (such and such)." History is what historians say it is after they have gathered, examined, selected, verified, interpreted, and presented historical facts and information.

The average person does not think of himself or herself as poring over old documents in dusty archives in order to develop a new hypothesis about some distant epoch. Yet Mr. or Mrs. Average Citizen may find themselves in the position of going over family Bibles, old photographs, ancient letters, grandmother's recipe book, a distant cousin's diary from the Spanish-American War, or asking Aunt Mabel about the family childhood in order to find out something about their ancestry, in order to better under-

stand, "Who am I?" Although the average citizen may not write history professionally, (s)he does on occasion engage in roughly the same evidence-inference process as the academic historian in producing history-as-written-history.

What distinguishes the professional historian who writes history from the history buff who reads it is involvement in historical research? The professional historian is schooled in it, practices it, and lives it. In the process he or she produces written-history, which is an attempt to reconstruct history-as-actuality based on history-as-record. Historical research is a valuable process to know, even for ordinary people, not only for the occasions mentioned above to help us learn who we are, but because the evidence-inference process is useful outside the domain of history. What is this process in the field of history?

The first step in historical inquiry is discovering the evidence. This involves locating artifacts, public documents, receipts, chronicles, bills of lading, memoirs, diagrams, charts, and so on, on a given topic or about a given period. These are organized in a meaningful way by subtopic, chronology, or other appropriate system. The historian carries on the work through the medium of question-asking. "What is the significance of this document? With what other evidence should it be grouped? Is it valid? How can it be authenticated? What hypothesis can be developed from the evidence?" Analytical questions such as these guide the historian in the search for data and they tell historians what notes to take from their evidence. They also help provide an organizational scheme for the presentation of evidence. These questions —and an infinite number of other questions—may have their origins in the structures of anthropology, economics, geography, political science, psychology, or sociology. They may, as well, show a relationship to philosophy, literature, and the fine arts.

Let us examine a series of analytic questions about the causation of historical events:

1. What was the immediate cause for the event?
2. Had there been a background of agitation for the principles victorious during this struggle?
3. Were personalities involved on either side whose strengths or weaknesses may have helped to determine the outcome of the struggle?
4. Were any new and potent ideas simulating the loyalty of a considerable number of people?
5. How did the economic groups line up on this issue?
6. Were religious forces active?
7. Did any new technological developments influence the situation?
8. Can the events be partially explained by weakened or strengthened institutions?
9. Was the physical environment itself a factor in the situation?[12]

Now apply these to an event within your memory or knowledge and for which you can provide the evidence (e.g., detente with China, the Nixon resignation, the colonial decision to declare independence from England).

In conducting his/her historical research, the historian depends on primary sources such as first-person accounts, tax records, inventories, minutes of meetings, and the like; on authority, such as expert's interpretations of events and/or phenomena, the works of other historians, or even custom or common usage that has been supported by individuals in a position to know;[13] and logical inference. The historian prefers to use primary sources when these are available so that (s)he can authenticate them and derive and support (or reject) hypotheses from them. Primary sources — history-as-record — become scarcer the farther back

in time we go. It becomes necessary, then, to use authorities (by way of example, the Bible[14] or Gibbon[15]) when there are no primary sources available. Since primary sources may be fragmentary or non-existent, then logical inference is necessary to reconstruct the past based on limited evidence, that is, few or incomplete primary sources.[16]

Another way of describing the evidence-inference process in history is to observe that the historian constructs history out of the chaos of original historical atoms through the process of synthesis.

The Core Concepts of Social Science and History

The historian finds the integrating concepts of social science useful in studying

---

[12] From *A Preface to History* by Carl G. Gustafson. Copyright 1955 by McGraw-Hill Book Company. Used with permission of McGraw-Hill Book Company.
[13] Most of what we "know" comes from authority; we read it in a book, we saw it on television, our parents told us. We accept what we read, see, or hear in such cases because we have faith in the authoritative sources. Very few people have the opportunity, the resources, or the patience to "discover" all the great truths that we accept.
[14] The Bible has to be considered the authoritative evidence in attempting to reconstruct the life of Jesus of Nazareth although the discovery of the Dead Sea Scrolls in the 1940s and 1950s has cast new light on early Christianity. Nonetheless, the Biblical Gospels were apparently written approximately 30 to 100 years after the death of Jesus and much in the Gospels is actually secondhand accounts or hearsay.
[15] Edward Gibbon was an eighteenth century English historian who has been the acknowledged authority on the Roman Empire. Since his six-volume *Decline and Fall of the Roman Empire* was published, other evidence has become available and not all historians agree with his inferences about the Roman Empire, but he is still an authority who must be considered in any reconstruction of that epoch.
[16] A good example of the evidence-inference process based on virtually no primary sources is the statement that King Arthur and the Knights of the Round Table probably fought on foot in chain mail rather than jousting in heavy armor on chargers. There is evidence that there was an Anglo-Saxon monarch in southern England in the fifth or sixth century, but the earliest evidence of stirrups (necessary to support the heavy weight of a man in plate armor) used in continental Europe was about the seventh or eighth century.

and writing history. History also helps add to our comprehension of these core concepts (Figure 6.1).

> The Core Concepts of Social Science
>   Habitat
>   Culture
>   Institutions
>   Resources and resource allocation
>   Interaction: competition, cooperation, accommodation
>   Conflict and conflict management
>   Power
>   Technology and industrialism
>   Social change
>   Choice: values/valuing
>   Multiple causation
>
>   **Figure 6-1**

History always occurs in some *habitat* or environment, and the habitat can exert an influence on past events. The climate and terrain of East Asia (i.e., the Middle East) has a different effect on people than does the taiga[17] of Northern Russia and Siberia. Similarly, *resources* (either the presence or the lack of them) have a powerful impact on the course of history: the European Industrial Revolution began in England where coal and iron were present, and Japanese expansionism in the first half of the twentieth century was influenced by her drive to find new sources of raw materials. The level of *technology and industrialism* among the Union forces in the Civil War meant the ultimate defeat of the Confederacy.

The *interaction* of individuals, groups, tribes, or nations is the stuff of history.

---

[17] The taiga are the swampy pine and cypress forests between the treeless tundra of the Arctic and the grassy steppes to the south.

Such interaction very often results in *conflict:* conflict between political ideologies as in the French Revolution or between religious ideologies as in the Crusades; conflict between national interests as in the frequent wars between England and France and later between France and Germany; conflict between economic systems as between the Western Powers and the Iron Curtain countries after World War II. Conflict cannot long continue unabated; it must be resolved whether through peace treaty, absorption of one people or one ideology by another, the dominance of one political or economic system over another, and so on. *Power* can be a root cause of conflict; it can also be one of the means of conflict management. The interplay of power is the stuff of which the events of history is made.

The study of history is basically the study of humankind's political, economic, and social *institutions* over time. We can understand our present institutions as we see how they have developed in the past. The study of history helps us to comprehend the *culture* of diverse peoples and the knowledge of cultures helps explain the unique histories of Americans, Spaniards, East Indians, and others.

We have already indicated the possible frame of reference (in itself a cognitive structure) for the study of social science through the concept of *choice.* History can be viewed as the study of past choices that have been made by individuals, groups, tribes, or nations. If *social change* never took place there would be little interest in or need for history; we could merely study the present and be assured that it is simply an unchanging extension of the past. History is the study of the changes in societies and cultures, but it is more than the narrative description of societies, or institutions, or levels of technology. The historian tries to explain *why* events took place and *why* changes occured; (s)he is concerned with causation. Like other scholars in the social sciences, the historian is aware that events rarely if ever have a single cause, and that invariably we must seek explanations in *multiple causation*. The musket that was fired across the village green in Concord, Massachusetts, in April 1775[18] may have been "the shot heard 'round the world," but without many other causes it would not have precipitated the American Revolution.

History is a necessary addition to the other six social sciences in order to round out a comprehensive view of the social scene. Without it we are limited almost exclusively to the present in our view of social interaction and human behavior. History, more than any other field in this broad area of study, enables us to follow the development of ideas, institutions, cultures, and peoples; it enables us to grasp their interrelationships. History provides us the perspective of time, much as geography provides us the perspective of space and areal relationships.

With its ties to the humanities, history enables us to seek better answers (and better specific questions) to the broad social science questions of What's going on here? Why do things behave as they do? Who am I (we)? What am I (we) doing here? What do I (we) do next?

History and the Social Studies

History was taught in elementary and secondary schools long before there was any such thing as social studies. U.S. history is still today the most commonly offered subject in American schools, but history as history has a less prominent place in the curriculum than it had formerly. One reason for this is that the social studies draw on a variety of content, not just history, and there is more content in contemporary social studies that is drawn from social sciences such as anthropology and sociology. Another reason history is less prominent in the curriculum is that recent research indicates that children do not develop much of a historical sense, that is, a strong sense of chronology, until they are about 10 years of age. Children can and do learn about the personages and events of the past at any age from about 2 on, but they do not ordinarily develop a sense of time until they are in about the fourth or fifth grade. Consequently, in the mind of a 7-year-old, Grandma, Queen Elizabeth I, and Cleopatra could all be contemporaries because they represent the past. So, too, do the signing of the Declaration of Independence, Columbus' first voyage to the New World, and Julius Caesar crossing the Rubicon. History, then, is probably most effective integrated into general social studies until about the fifth grade or even later, after which the study of history as a separate subject might be appropriate. But certain staples of the past, such as fifth-grade U.S. history, are not as universal as they once were and some, such as ninth-grade ancient history, have almost become extinct. Some critics of the schools say that history is neither taught nor learned. Perhaps pupils of the last quarter of the twentieth century know less about some historical periods than did their counterparts of the 1920s, but a lot has happened in the past 50 years and pupils have been learning about this.

The push away from history began with the 1916 report[19] which gave the term social studies wide circulation. It was accelerated by curriculum projects in

---

[18] Even today no one knows for sure who fired the first shot nor whether it was fired by an American Minuteman or a British soldier.
[19] *The Social Studies in Secondary Education . . .,* Report of the Committee on the Social Studies . . ., Washington, U.S. Bureau of Education, 1916.

other disciplines—sociology, anthropology, economics, as well as more modern approaches to geography and political science—in the 1960s.

The major new projects for the teaching of history are most often found at the secondary level. Among these are the Amherst project in American history, the Carnegie-Mellon project for high school U.S. history, the University of Chicago project to develop instructional materials for ninth- and tenth-grade world history courses integrating history and the social sciences, and the Educational Development Center's Subject to Citizen project for eighth and ninth graders. History is incorporated in several projects of an interdisciplinary or multidisciplinary nature, such as those at the University of Minnesota and the Educational Research Council of Greater Cleveland area study projects, such as the Asian Studies Program at the University of California, also include history as well as the other social sciences. Many of these projects have been completed and are now published by various book companies.

Anyone who expects to teach history, either as a separate subject or integrated into the social studies, must give some thought to the question of how to organize it. Should it be treated chronologically, topically, a combination of the two? Should it stress biography or events? Should it be primarily political (as history has been taught in the past) or should it be economic and social? Should it emphasize specifics or should it be concerned with the broad socioeconomic-political movements? Should it emphasize the positive elements in American history or should it expose the warts on Uncle Sam (or Columbia)?

Defenders of any of the above positions can be found, but at our present state of knowledge the best procedure seems to be to stress biography for young children and events that are seasonally timely. A biographical approach has much to commend it at the junior high school level, too. Until the fifth grade, there is little point in treating history chronologically since pupils have a weak time sense. After that, a combination of the chronological and the topical works well. History is not just past politics, so economic and social history should be on an equal footing with political history. Muckraking serves little purpose with young children, but middle school youngsters should not have a distorted view of their country's past, nor of the rest of the world. History should not be learned as if it were mostly mythology and fairy tales.

The study of the past is thought to be irrelevant by some, but history is still the most commonly offered course in U.S. secondary schools.[20] Where the teaching of history stresses important ideas rather than dates and trivia it is highly relevant. History helps answer the questions, "Who am I? Who are we?" People are interested in their family heritage, and a family heritage is part of the cultural heritage. A sense of the past is important for living in the present and planning for the future. History as a subject in the schools may appear to be in retreat in the face of the advance of other social sciences, but it should always have an important and pertinent place in the curriculum.[21]

---

[20] In 1973, U.S. history courses, grades 7 to 12, had twice the enrollment (3,464,000) of the next course, world history (1,541,000).

[21] World history had increased only 5 percent from 1961 during which time total enrollment was increasing 59 percent. Even though economics, sociology, and psychology increased 102, 175, and 321 percent respectively, their aggregate enrollment totaled only 1,978,000, considerably less than the combined total of 5,005,000 for history. See Richard E. Gross, "The Status of the Social Studies in the Public Schools of the United States: Facts and Impressions of a National Survey." Unpublished document, 1976.

Geography, Social Science, and Social Studies

Ancient in its origins, geography goes back to the Greeks as an important field of study and was added to and refined by the Arabs during the Middle Ages. Advances in map making and navigation during the Age of Exploration thrust geography into prominence as a useful as well as interesting subject. The systematic observations of German geographers in the nineteenth century and the introduction of this new but old science into the German universities ushered in a new era for the discipline. In a twentieth-century world growing rapidly smaller through instantaneous communications and super-sonic speed aircraft, no one can be considered educated who is ignorant of geography.

The Nature of Geography

Geography is more than the study of the earth, despite the literal meaning of the word. It is the study of the character of place, the nature of site and situation; the study of the earth divided into its meaningful parts. "Geography is the study of space relations and is concerned with the over-all personality of place."[22] It is the study of the surface of the earth *and* humankind as they interrelate with each other.

"Geography is that field of learning in which the characteristics of particular places on the earth's surface are examined. It is concerned with the arrangement of things and with the associations of things that distinguish

one area from another. It is concerned with the connections and movements between areas. [It is also concerned with physical, chemical, and biotic processes] in complex areal relation . . . .to each other. And there are economic, social, and political processes by which mankind occupies the world's lands."[23]

Distinctions are sometimes made between physical geography and cultural (or human) geography, but they are more ways of approaching a unitary subject than they are separate fields.

Modern geography can also be understood through a series of nonexamples: it is *not* simply the names of places, the boundaries of political units, the products of countries, the lists of longest rivers (or of highest mountains or hottest places), travelogues, thumbing through the National Geographic. Places, boundaries, products, and so on, may be considered the facts and attributes that help develop understanding of geographic concepts, including the concepts of character of place and site/situation. Such facts, attributes and concepts may contribute to the development of generalizations about human beings in relation to their natural and physical environment and in their areal association.

Geography is perhaps better identified as chorography (the study of place description) and chorology (the understanding of the relationship of things and people that give character to place). Chorography is more typical of the "older" geography and chorology is more typical of the "newer" geography.

The subdivisions of geography can be grouped in a number of different

---

[22] George B. Cressey, "Geography" in *High School Social Studies Perspectives*, Boston, Houghton Mifflin, 1962, p. 83.

[23] Preston E. James, "Geography," *The Social Studies and the Social Sciences*, American Council of Learned Societies, New York, Harcourt, Brace and World, 1962, pp. 45–56.

ways. The obvious starting place is physical geography and cultural geography as the major categories. The latter (the study of man-land relationships) is now more prominent than the former (the study of the surface of the earth, its topography, climate, soils, etc.), but they are really two sides of the same coin. Geography may also be subdivided into systematic geography and regional geography. Systematic geography includes economic geography, political geography, urban geography, historical geography, and the like. Regional geography uses the major areas of the world as its organizing framework: Anglo-American geography, the geography of the Indian subcontinent, the geography of Western Europe. The dynamic character of modern geography makes it possible to divide the discipline in other ways than those listed: plant geography, the geography of population, medical geography, and the like. Cartography—map making—must be included in any scheme of geographic subdivisions.

Despite its ancient origins, geography is very much involved in modern scholarship and contemporary affairs— conservation and environmental studies, urban studies, city planning, and so on. The urbanization of populations throughout the world makes a general understanding of the principles of geography more important than ever and makes the services of geographers to planning agencies essential for rational and orderly development.

Approaches to the Study of Geography

Examining space relations and the character of place can be done through the frame of reference of physical geography or of cultural geography. There are a number of other approaches to the subject, approaches that have reflected the changing nature of geography. Among the approaches that have been used and are being used at various levels of instruction are the study of (1) countries and/or continents; (2) hemispheres: east-west, north-south, land hemisphere-water hemisphere; (3) climate zones: "torrid, frigid, temperate;" (4) climate regions: tropical rainforest, Mediterranean subtropical, etc.; (5) culture realms: Anglo-American, Islamic, among others; (6) rural and agricultural geography; (7) the urban scene.

The study of countries and/or continents has been such a standard approach for so long that it needs no discussion. It has limitations because continents are not necessarily logical cultural units and are not even logical geographic units in the case of Europe and Asia. The study of the various hemispheres has been tried in some instances, but these categories can become as rigid as continents. The division of the world into the torrid, frigid, and temperate zones was the basis for the study of geography in the early part of this century, but it had so many contradictions that the terminology became meaningless. The so-called torrid zone north and south of the equator to the two tropic lines, Cancer and Capricorn, contains more than one climate type. The temperate zone of the middle latitudes between the tropics and the Arctic or Antarctic circles contains some of the coldest and hottest parts of the world— hardly temperate. Needless to say, the frigid zone contains some areas of relatively mild climate.

A refinement of this approach has been the study of climate zones, varying in number from perhaps eight to a dozen depending upon the geographer. This approach recognizes that climatic conditions do not follow the neatly parallel lines of latitude around the world—equator and tropics of Cancer and Capricorn. A temperate marine climate such as San

Francisco, California, can exist only a few miles from the Mediterranean subtropical climate in Palo Alto, California, and both are only a few hundred miles from a dry subtropical desert climate around Las Vegas. The climate zones approach has the advantage of gaining maximum knowledge of the geography of the world through a conceptual structure that provides considerable understanding with a limited amount of factual information. Once the student understands the relationship between the climate, the typical vegetation, the range of soil types, the usual human uses of the environment, that person has understanding of, say, tropical rain forests whether found in Brazil, the Congo, Honduras, or the Malay Peninsula.

Some geographers advocate the study of culture realms. These are very large regions showing some degree of homogeneity in cultural development, most often economic and political institutions. The characteristics that distinguish one culture realm from another will be revealed most clearly in the core of the region with wide zones of transition in which there is intermingling of the characteristics of neighboring culture realms. Thus, Anglo-America—Canada, the United States, and the adjacent British Commonwealth Islands—forms a logical unit, even though of varied physical geography. So, too, does the Islamic culture realm, spreading from North Africa through West Asia[24] to the Indian subcontinent and beyond being united, in this case, by a common religion as well.

Other culture realms include the European, the Soviet, Latin America, Southeast Asia, East Asia, sub-Sahara Africa, Australian-New Zealand, and the Pacific.

The early physical geographers were interested primarily in the land, in its topography, its weather, its natural resources, and its fauna and flora. Cultural geographers are interested in these as they affect and relate to human activities. The setting or habitat of human activities has moved from a rural one to an urban setting. With this shift, urban geography has become an important approach to the discipline. The same principles and concepts are valid in urban geography as before, but there are some new ones, too. One of the concerns of the urban geographer is the journey to work. Another is the nature of urban development. Still others include the distribution of populations in the different neighborhoods of a city, different types of urban complexes, and the indices of social health and pathology found in the different sections of the city. The urban geographer must utilize knowledge from the fields of sociology, political science, economics, and others. Geography is a dynamic field and new approaches to it develop constantly. This list of approaches is not to be considered exhaustive. Some approaches may be more appropriate to certain grade levels and certain maturity levels than others, but mostly they are matters of frame of reference. For most school children, who are not going to be professional geographers, the approaches emphasizing cultural geography are more meaningful than the others.

The Structure of Geography

Understanding the structure of geography enables the social scientist to place the facts and attributes of geography into a meaningful framework. Similar to other disciplines, the structure of geogra-

[24] West Asia is popularly called the Middle East, but it is hardly that from a North American standpoint. It is about the same distance from Kansas, the geographic center of the United States, as is East Asia, hardly accurately called the Far East from our perspective. Middle East, Far East, and Near East are geographic terms all showing a geographic frame of reference of Western Europe.

phy is the body of imposed conceptions that define geography and that control its inquiries; it is the characteristic modes of inquiry of the geographer as well. Some of these concepts are shown in a framework of fundamental ideas prepared for the Social Science Education Consortium, one of the outstanding organizations in America for the development and dissemination of a knowledge in the social studies. This framework is shown in Figure 6.2.

1. Every geographic area is affected by physical, biotic, and societal forces.
2. The impact of these forces on a geographic area creates similarities among areas. These similar areas are called formal or uniform regions. They are static in character.
3. The similarities among different areas have been brought about through different combinations of physical, biotic, and societal forces.
4. An area may be kept together through a pattern of circulation binding the area to a central place. This area is called a functional or nodal region, held together by functional relationships. The functional/nodal region is dynamic in character.
5. Uniform and nodal (or formal or functional) regions are often related to each other through gravitation to the same central place. (Reprinted with permission of Social Science Education Consortium, Inc., Boulder, Colo.)

There are a vast number of geographic concepts. We can hardly expect to understand geography in any form without grasping the fundamental concepts relating to physical geography—concepts such as river valley, plateau, monsoons, fault, and the like. Man-land concepts are probably even more important to modern cultural geography, even though they may be more abstract and, thus, more difficult to comprehend. Among these are the concepts of site, situation, and the many concepts related to

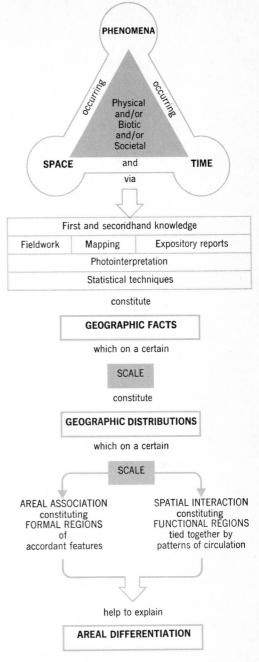

Figure 6.2 Fundamental ideas of geography.

region (areal association, areal differentiation, pattern, etc.). A region is a "natural area" with certain common characteristics or some central use. Within the region there exists a network of facilities, patterns of interaction, transportation nets, communication nets, and so on. Such interfacings may vary from very small (a neighborhood of schools and shopping areas defined by certain physical features) to huge (the Eastern Megalopolis region from Boston to Washington). A region may have subregions: the Eastern Megalopolis consists of a number of metropolitan regions, such as those of New York, New Haven, Newark, Providence, Philadelphia. Although generalizations may be made about characteristics of regions, factors leading to their development, and the like, the accordant features and the patterns of circulation in various regions help to explain areal differentiation.

Inquiry in geography bridges the social and the physical sciences. The geographer may use rigorous laboratory and quantitative techniques, much as his or her counterpart in chemistry, astronomy, and geology, but ultimately the geographer seeks answers to the human equation. More than any other research methodology survey is used to gather data on specific aspects of the physical and cultural landscape. These are plotted on maps, and analyzed for their connections among the variables. Much early evidence gathering was done by direct observation in the field. Now geographers use remote sensing. Unmanned satellites take measurements of the earth from a scanner and feed the data into a computer for use by the geographer.

The nature of inquiry in geography is related to the key questions of social science (What's going on? Why do these things behave as they do?) More than most of the social sciences it attempts to find answers to the question, Who are we? The most important geographic question is probably, Why are people where they are? Other important ques-

tions that help guide the inquiry of the geography (and help him or her select and communicate data) are, What is the character of this place (site)? How is it reflected in the culture of its occupants? How have the occupants and their culture had an impact on the site? Why did people locate these cultural objects (crops, buildings, etc.) where they did, when they did? What pattern of relationships is observable among these geographic phenomena? How have human beings changed their habitat? How has the habitat influenced human life?

Elementary children can engage in many geographical inquiry exercises. They can make "journey to school" maps for a class in which they plot the routes followed by student from home to school, noting whether on foot, in private automobiles, public transportation, or school bus. They can make land-use maps of the school environments showing residences, commercial areas, public facilities, and so on. They can plot a communications region by showing the source of newspapers subscribed to by families, the locations of radio and television broadcasting stations, and the like. Map experiences are excellent ones for children in the way they provide a bridge between concrete and abstract concepts.

Maps are, of course, important tools for the geographer. They are means by which the geographer handles his/her data and are useful in communicating his/her findings. They were first used extensively at sea, and technical developments in navigation and mapmaking coincided with the age of exploration of the fifteenth, sixteenth, and seventeenth centuries. Maps of the sea lanes were important to help sailors know where they were and figure where they were going. As land travel increased and as unknown territories in the hinterland were explored, claimed, and colonized, there came a worldwide boom in map making.

Maps are used to represent something about the physical and cultural landscape. They are *not* the terrain any more than the word or symbol is the concept. Cartography requires the understanding and use of special concepts, the most important of which are scale and projection. A map must show certain features of the landscape in a relatively small space. Different ideas about the habitat are conveyed by different scales. Consider what can be put on a piece of paper 24 inches by 36 inches, depending on whether it is of a neighborhood, a small city, a compact region such as the Puget Sound area, or larger areas such as the Far West, North America, or the world. On a small-scale map of a neigh-borhood 1 inch might represent 100 feet whereas on a large-scale map of the world 1 inch might represent 1000 miles.

A geography student must know the potential and the limitation of different kinds of map projections. Any map is an attempt to represent the curved surface and features of the earth on a flat piece of paper. Nearly all maps, therefore, distort some aspect of what is represented. (Globes don't have this problem, but there is a practical limit to how large one can make a globe and still find it useful for geography instruction.) A very small-scale map may not be noticeably off in portraying that flat surface, but the larger the scale, the more room there is for error. One kind of map, the Merca-

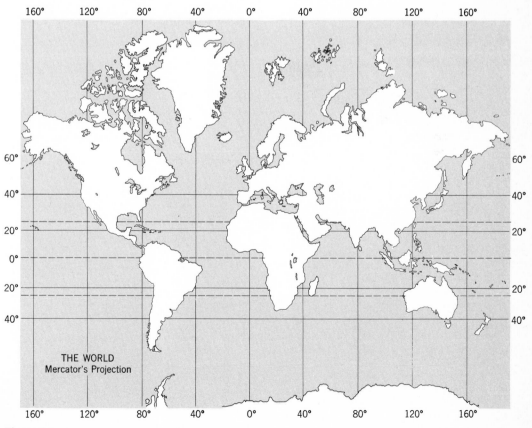

THE WORLD
Mercator's Projection

Figure 6.3

tor projection, may be useful for navigation and for showing the relationship of geographic areas according to the points of the compass. When used as a large scale map or to represent areas toward the poles, it greatly distorts area. Notice how on the accompanying map of the world (Figure 6.3) that Greenland looks slightly larger than the continent of South America. In actuality, Greenland is *one-seventh* the size of South America. Notice, too, how Greenland compares with North America in size. Then look at the second map (Figure 6.4), an equal-area map not a Mercator projection, and compare Greenland with North America. What other differences do you notice in the two maps?

Other kinds of maps may show the size of landmasses in the proper proportion but distort directions or distances.

Since it is a practical impossibility to portray everything on a map, they are used to record or indicate only certain kinds of information, or a whole series of maps may be needed to represent accurately the important information about a specific habitat. Different maps would be

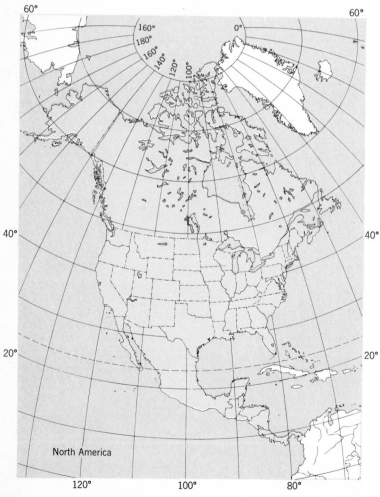

Figure 6.4

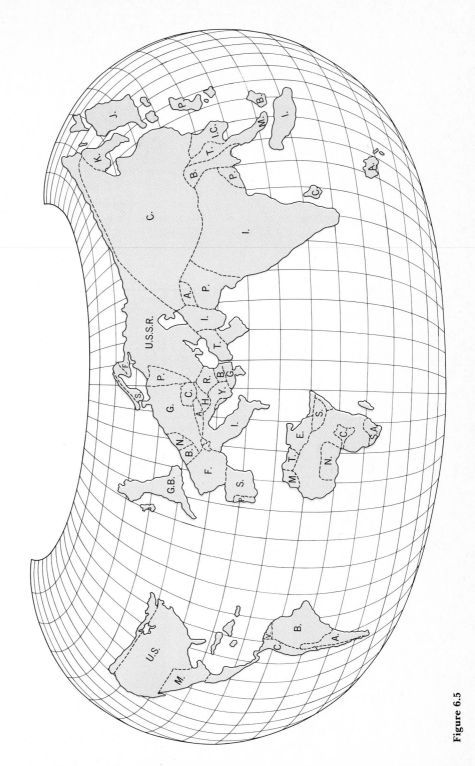

Figure 6.5

used to present certain kinds of information, be it about the physical terrain and features, the political units and divisions, the economic features, or social relationships such as the distribution of ethnic groups, income levels, or church membership.

Geographers search for improved means of recording data and communicating geographic conclusions. Some of these newer maps bear only a crude relationship to the kinds of maps we have been accustomed to seeing and using. With the increasing importance of cultural geography, maps appropriate for physical geography become unsatisfactory. The size of the world land masses bears little relationship to the population distribution, the resources, the energy

consumption, the food caloric intake, or the literacy level. A map (Figure 6.5) showing the relative size of the various nations by population has India and China much larger in area than their physical size, whereas Australia is much smaller than its physical size indicating its relatively low population density.

Carry this idea of a map a step further. Suppose that we have entirely different kinds of information than the usual geographic data that need recording in a fashion lending itself to geographic analysis. Such might be the geography of terms, or even the geography of geographic references. This principle is illustrated by the following maps (Figure 6.6) on which the size of the "place" is a function of the amount of attention de-

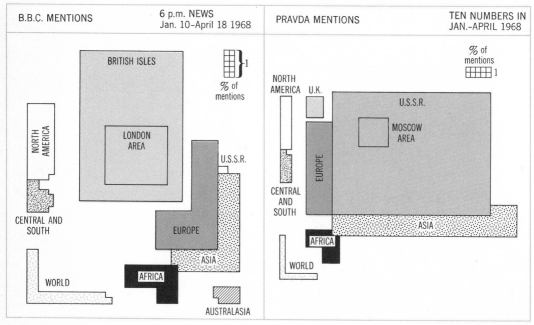

Figure 6.6 The geography of an issue of *Time* and four issues of *Rolling Stone*: copyright, 1969, *The North Dakota Quarterly*. B.B.C. and *Pravda* mentions are from "Places in the News, a Study of Geographical Information," *Bulletin of Quantitative Data for Geographers*, No. 7, July 1968. (Reprinted by permission of the author, John P. Cole, Department of Geography, University of Nottingham, Nottingham, England.)

voted to it by a different agency. On the maps show the world as seen on the British Broadcasting Company evening news, the Communist Party newspaper *(Pravda)* *Time* news magazine, and *Rolling Stone* (a journal initially devoted largely to the rock music scene and related topics).

How do we explain the difference in these maps? How do these maps help us communicate the geography of important social phenomena? What other kinds of information might be portrayed on maps of this type? What would be their general appearance?

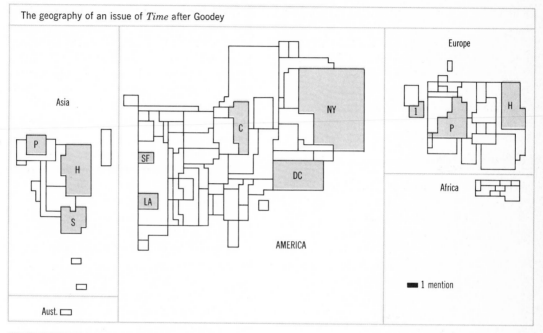

The geography of an issue of *Time* after Goodey

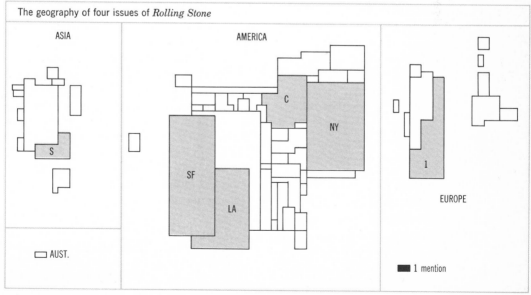

The geography of four issues of *Rolling Stone*

Geography helps illuminate the integrating social science concepts, and each of them in turn contributes to a holistic understanding of geography as a discipline. *Habitat* refers to the locale where organisms and organizations find themselves and in which they operate. It includes the physical, biotic, and social elements interacting within it. *Interaction,* both personal and social, makes up a network of contact points among human beings as they attempt to survive and prosper in their habitats. Interaction is usually of three specific types: competition (for the goods and the values which the habitat has to offer), cooperation (as a means of improving individual or group means of survival), and accommodation (making the necessary adjustments and compromises among individuals and groups where neither competition nor cooperation prevails). Human beings as social animals of necessity interact with one another, socially and individually.

Culture is the learned way of behaving (and thinking and feeling) characteristic of a group of people, a society. Culture is influenced by the character of place (e.g., Greenland has a different character than does Hawaii) and culture in turn influences the character of place (e.g., San Francisco land fill and hillside homes). *Resources*, the raw materials, actual and potential, available to humankind, may constrain a particular society in its development. They are a part of the habitat and influence and are influenced by the culture. It is no accident that the habitat of the Industrial Revolution was in those countries with resources needed for that revolution. The emergence of the United States as a world power was strongly influenced by its abundant and varied resources.

Most wars have been fought over territory (habitat) and their resources. Wars are the most terrible form of *conflict.* The industrialized North Vietnam needs the food-producing area of the south; Nazi Germany claimed that it needed living room and so took over the Saar and the Sudetenland, and when it invaded Poland for the same reason, World War II was the result. Groups within a nation may be in conflict, too, among rural, urban, and suburban habitats. But conflict can't go on forever; the nation that feels secure with the territory it has conquered (Israel and the Golan Heights, Egypt and control of the Suez Canal, Turkey and Cyprus) is then willing to negotiate. *Conflict resolution* includes the various means by which conflict is reduced or ended.

Certain natural resources contribute to the development or lack of development of nations. But it is *technology* (closely related to those human resources) that makes the real difference between development and underdevelopment. Technology leads to *industrialism;* the geographer is interested in how site and situation, areal differentiation, and spatial relations affect industrialism. Regardless of a nation's level of technology, it has *institutions* (those elements of social organization by which people carry out specialized roles and activities and which are centered around basic human needs such as governing, producing and consuming, educating, etc.). Geography influences the kinds of government—for example, the Greek city-states—throughout the world, the economic institutions such as those built on individualism and private enterprise in New England, the form of education such as casual schooling in California, and the flourishing of social institutions such as black slavery in the southern United States and Brazil.

Social change takes place as cultures become more industrialized and develop new demands on resources, as resources become exhausted, as old institutions have difficulty accommodating to increased populations, and so on. Geography, thus, may be a factor in creating conditions favorable (or unfavorable) to social change. The concept of *choice* may provide a frame of reference for the study of site and situation. People make choices regarding their occupance of a particular territory. They make choices in how they plan to modify or use their environment. Even though culture and institutions may condition people's response to their habitat, there is still an element of choice with respect to conflict, technology, interaction, etc.

Finally, the geographer, like all social scientists, attempts to investigate and understand the causative factors of why humans locate where they do and why they use their environment as they do. *Causation* is multiple rather than singular; rarely can an event or a phenomenon be traced to one cause alone. Causation in geography has moved away from the determinism of an earlier era when it was thought that a people's environment determined in an absolute fashion; thus, societies in extreme "frigid" or "torrid" climates were ordained to be "primitive" and societies in "temperate" climates were destined to be "advanced." Today, this view has been softened; the environment provides constraints and possibilities for human development, but it does not determine it.

Geography and the Social Studies

Geography has been, along with history, the staple ingredient in public school social studies, particularly at the elementary level. It remains important even though there have been significant changes in elementary social studies in the last two decades. Geography frequently remains the core of elementary social studies whether the curriculum is based on expanding horizons or on newer ideas (see next section). The content of geography is probably going to be prominent in elementary social studies whether youngsters study people of a given culture area or whether they study human activities across the world.

At the secondary level, separate geography courses have given way, in many instances, to the integration of geography with history and other social sciences in such courses as Old World backgrounds of the United States or courses in world cultures. One of the major curriculum innovations of the 1960s and 1970s was the Association of American Geographer's High School Geography Project, an attempt to restore geography to the high school. It apparently was not very successful because the teaching of courses in geography increased much less than the school population increase in the 1960s, and less than half of the public secondary schools offered geography in 1973.[25]

Although none of the major curriculum projects of the 1960s used geography as their central core, there were area studies projects in which geography was a very important element. The several multidisciplinary projects previously mentioned include geography.

Whether at elementary or secondary level, the emphasis in geography has shifted somewhat from place naming and describing to experiences that help young people think geographically and conceptually in terms of the problems of "man-land" relationships. Geography is an excellent vehicle for learning the process of social science inquiry and, in turn, for learning valuable information about the world in which we live.

---

[25] Gross, loc. cit.

Bibliography

Broek, Jan A. M. *Geography: Its Scope and Spirit.* Columbus, Ohio: Charles E. Merrill Books, 1965.

Bacon, Phillip. *Focus on Geography: Key Concepts and Teaching Strategies.* 40th Yearbook of the National Council for the Social Studies. Washington, D.C.: The Council, 1970.

Cartwright, William H. and Richard L. Watson, Jr., "Historical Study in a Changing Curriculum" in *The Re-Interpretation of American History and Culture.* 43rd Yearbook of the National Council for the Social Studies. Washington, D.C.: The Council, 1973.

Commager, Henry Steele. *The Nature and Study of History.* Columbus, Ohio: Charles E. Merrill Books, 1965.

Dye, Thomas R. "Power and History," in *Power and Society: An Introduction.* North Scituate, Mass.: Duxbury Press, 1975.

Gustafson, Carl G. *A Preface to History.* New York: McGraw-Hill, 1955.

The History Teacher. Journal of the Society for History Education, California State University, Long Beach.

Kownslar, Allan O. (ed.). *Teaching American History: The Quest for Relevance.* 44th Yearbook of the National Council for the Social Studies. Washington, D.C.: The Council, 1974.

How does economics influence our daily lives?

CHAPTER 7

The Policy Disciplines: Political Science and Economics

The social sciences attempt to find answers to some very broad and very basic questions: Why do things (people, events) behave or occur as they? Who am I (who are we, who are they)? What do I (we) do next? These question spawn an endless variety of other questions because only as we find answers to the small questions can we expect to find answers to the basic ones. Sometimes answers elude us, but in the process of looking for them we may learn how to ask better questions next time.

There can be no more important questions than What do I (we) do next? This question and the questions it generates are policy questions or questions that are designated to find answers leading to major courses of action or potential action. Policy questions are most crucial when it comes to matters of how humans govern themselves and how they produce, distribute, and consume goods and services. Political science and economics are the policy sciences. The institutions and processes involved in the distribution of power are significant determiners of

what is (and what can be) done next. So, too, are the institutions and processes involved in the allocation of available productive resources.

The value-free neutral posture of social science is important at the foundations of political science and economic knowledge. After all, one cannot know what to do next without knowing what is going on and why and the roots of one's existence. But when it comes to deciding what to do next one's values come into play. As a nation through its government and its economy decide what policies to embark on, cultural values are involved.

Policy question are not limited to the high levels of government and the corporate board room, however. The question of what to do next faces communities, neighborhoods, schools, classrooms, gangs, and cliques. In each of these the distribution of power and the allocation of resources is of concern to all members of the group and, often, to other groups and social aggregates.

Instruction in the social studies can help young people phrase questions and seek answers at their level of sophistication to these basic questions: What's going on? Why do things happen as they do? Who are we? What do we do next?

Political Science, Social Science, and the Social Studies

Every citizen is an actor in a political community. The citizen may take a leading role or only be an extra passively observing the political scene but not actively involved in it. A school, a classroom, a city, and a nation are all political communities. More and more we are recognizing that the world is a political community, too. The members of a political community share certain goals and concerns in common. They have consensus on some of the fundamental rules by which the community operates. Still there can be room in a political community for disagreement. The less autocratic a political community is, the greater the area of political disagreement.

Despite the pervasiveness of politics, particularly in a democratic society, citizen interest in politics appears to be low. Despite the fact that people must know the rules of the political communities within which they function, citizen's minimum participation in making the rules— the act of voting—involves barely half the eligible population. There is no shortage of public issues at any time; almost inevitably conflicts develop over these issues. The process of resolving conflicts over public issues is one way of describing politics.

Instruction in civics, a major part of the social studies program for several generations, has not produced a noticeable increase in citizen involvement in public affairs. Why is this? Political science is the principal ingredient in civic

education. What can we learn about it that will help us understand better the content of civic education?

The Nature of Political Science

Political science includes in its scope the formal structure of government as well as the processes and goals of politics; the informal interaction within government, and the interaction among government officials, individual citizens, and interest group representatives. There are a number of definitions of political science, three of which may be cited to illustrate the range of possible definitions.

> "Political science is the intellectual discipline that is primarily concerned with the question of how man governs himself."[1]

> "[Political science] is the systematic study of government and of the political process, from the point of view of what is, of what ought to be, and how to achieve the greatest coincidence between the two."[2]

> "Political science is the study of decisions that are made that are binding on all members of a political community."

In the minds of some people, political science is synonomous with government, but increasingly the definition of political science has been broadened to include the political process in its widest application.

---

[1] Robert E. Cleary and Donald H. Riddle, "Political Science and the Social Studies" in the *36th Yearbook* of the National Council for the Social Studies, Washington, The Council, 1966, pp. 1–2.
[2] J. Roland Pennock and David G. Smith, *Political Science: An Introduction*, New York, Macmillan Co., 1964, p. 22.

The Major Subdivisions of Political Science

An analysis of the components of political science can give us a better idea of its scope and indicate some aspects of the discipline that are not possible in a simple definition.

Governmental institutions, particularly American government and politics.

Political theory, including the history of political thought.

Constitutional law.

Politics and political parties.

Political sociology and political behavior.

International relations, that is, international politics, law, and organization.

Comparative government and politics.

Public administration.

Political scientists tend to identify with one of these areas and then to specialize in a narrow aspect of the subdivision. For example, a scholar may do most of his or her research in seventeenth-, eighteenth-, or early nineteenth-century political theory as it helped shape the American political system, including such major figures as Montesquieu, Locke, Voltaire, Jefferson, and Madison. Or the political scientist may be interested in expanding our knowledge of how children become politically socialized.

There are two broad approaches to the study and teaching of political science, which can be broken down into more specific approaches. First, there is the traditional approach to the discipline, as befits a field of study that can trace its philosophical roots back more than 2000 years to the time of Plato and Aristotle. The traditional approach to political science is actually a broad category of different approaches which have tended to close ranks with the development of the relatively new behaviorist school of political science. The four traditional ap-

proaches to the discipline are (1) the descriptive-structural, (2) the prescriptive-proscriptive, (3) the legal-institutional, and (4) the philosophical-normative.

Most people are familiar with the descriptive-structural approach since it has been so widely used in the teaching of government. The emphasis is on a description of the structure of government: local, state, and national levels; executive, legislative, and judicial branches; the number of senators and their terms of office; the steps by which a bill becomes law; and so on. The prescriptive-proscriptive approach has been a staple of public school civics instruction for decades. The desired and expected attitudes and practices of the good citizen are prescribed—the good citizen votes, the good citizen is informed on the issues, the good citizen pays taxes to support government, the good citizen always obeys the laws—and the undesirable and un-American attitudes and practices are proscribed—the good citizen eschews emotionalism in favor of rationalism in making up his/her mind on political issues, the good citizen avoids special interests and acts for the benefit of all, the good citizen downgrades the personality and concentrates on the positions of the candidate on issues.

The legal-institutional approach operates from the study of the major legal institutions of a political community; in the case of the United States this would be the presidency, the Congress, the courts, and the principal government agencies as expressed in their edicts, laws, rulings, and decisions. It had been a widely used approach for a very long time. The philosophical-institutional approach may have difficulty accepting *science* as a legitimate part of the name of the study of politics. Advocates of this approach are concerned primarily with the big questions confronting humanity, that is, the major political questions of our time and of the past. This is a speculative rather than a strictly scientific approach, probing the standards or norms by which ethical conduct in the political arena may be judged.

In recent years the behavioral approach to the study of politics has gained adherents and, in many ways, may be considered to be the dominant school of political science today. It shares much in common with the behavioral sciences to be discussed in the next chapter. It does not reject the structure of governments, political institutions, or philosophical issues in politics, but its approach to them is quite different. Its central focus is the actual political behavior of people (actors) in the political community. The behavioral approach includes studies of voting behavior of the various groups in a political community, of the interest groups (either from the perspective of pluralistic interest groups or a power elite), of propaganda and public opinion, studies of political socialization, studies of the nature of political culture, and the like. Related to the behavioral approach is the process approach. It is concerned with the political process, where the action is within the framework of a political community or of political entities. Decision making, policy making, and similar activities are political processes and are the focus of this approach.

Although one could study the structure of political science from any of a number of approaches to the discipline, our analysis is more compatible with the behavioral or process approach than with any of the traditional approaches.

The Structure of Political Science

The structure of political science has been symbolized by the use of systems analysis, largely through the work of David Easton. The systems model includes within it some of the most important concepts in political science, shown in dynamic interaction with each other typical of the operation of a system. Figure 7.1 shows the model with the necessary explanatory information.

Political Science Concepts.

Many of the concepts in a systems model are unique to a behavioral approach to political science, concepts such as gatekeepers, support, and binding decisions. Other terms in the model would be found in other approaches to political science although the actual concept might be slightly different. Among these are issues, authorities, regime, and (probably) political system.

There are, of course, many other political science concepts. Undoubtedly the central concept to the discipline is power, the authority to make binding decisions. The concept of power runs through all the many subdivisions of the discipline and an understanding of it is essential to an understanding of the structure of political science.

1. Members of society have many wants which they hope to satisfy.

2. Some of these wants will be satisfied through the economic, family, educational, and religious systems. Wants that cannot be satisfied by any of these systems are channeled to the political system.

3. As the people's wants enter the political system for satisfaction, they become demands. These demands are screened.

4. The screening process operates through formal or informal organizations. These organizations act as gatekeepers. Some of the demands vanish. Others become issues debated in the political community, a group who share a desire to work together as a unit in the political solution of problems.

5. The issues are molded by cleavages in the political community and by the authori-

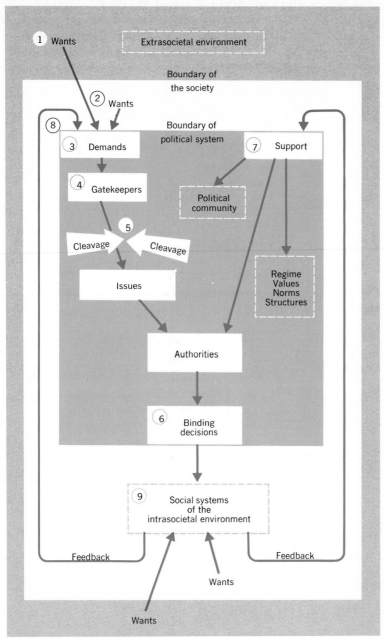

Figure. 7.1 Fundamental ideas of political science. (From *Our Working World: Cities at Work*, Resource Unit, by Lawrence Senesh. © 1966, 1967, Science Research Associates, Inc. Reprinted by permission of the publisher.)

ties who translate these demands into binding decisions.

6. The binding decisions affect the social systems and the participants in them, generating positive or negative support.

7. The support may be directed toward the political community; toward the regime, a political system that incorporates a particular set of values and norms and a particular structure of authority; and/or toward the authorities, the particular persons who occupy positions of political power within the structure of authority.

8. The binding decisions generate new wants, which appear again at the gate of the political system asking for recognition.

9. The source of the support for the political community, regime, and authorities may originate from the social systems in the forms of education, patriotism, and other mechanisms.

The concept of citizenship is fundamental for teachers of social studies in a democratic society (which is itself another fundamental concept or construct) because of the role of the public school in developing citizenship. Yet it is a concept that may take 12 or more years for students to develop, and the voting record of the public indicates that only about half of the population has internalized the concept enough to act on it at the polls. Voting is only one aspect of the responsibility that is a part of citizenship, but it is the most easily demonstrated aspect. As a construct, democracy or a democratic society is even more complex. Most upper-grade students and adults can give a simple definition, but volumes are required to go into all the nuances of concepts and generalizations which make up this construct. One rather simple description of democracy that does no injustice to its many subtleties is the statement that democracy is a system of government of shared power and shared responsibility. Freedom, which is a part of most definitions of democracy,

is not mentioned. It is not necessary to do so because freedom is implicit in the concepts of shared power and shared responsibility and it is meaningless outside of power and responsibility.

Other political concepts are easier for children to grasp at appropriate levels of maturity: monarchy—ultimate power in the hands of one person, a king or queen; law—a rule of conduct enforced by a controlling authority; or constitution—the fundamental law or principles of a nation, state, or organized body of people contained in written documents. Even these relatively simple concepts usually require a variety of experiences for children to grasp the concepts. Memorization of definitions will not guarantee that concepts are understood.

The Mode of Inquiry of Political Science

Political scientists may use any of the methods of research employed by other social scientists: field work, case studies, surveys, observation; only rarely is controlled experiment used. Philosophical speculation is a mode of inquiry, one that is used by students of politics, although it may not qualify as scientific in nature.

Regardless of the particular method used, the evidence-inference process commences with the asking of questions. Questions lead toward the kinds of data needed to provide answers and help draw inferences. Here are some questions typical of political science inquiry.

How do different groups in society—men and women, age groups, ethnic groups, religious groups, sections of the country—vote in national elections?

To what extent do voters participate in varying degrees in local as compared to state and national elections? Why?

Do children usually follow the political preferences of their parents? What accounts for possible political shifts between generations?

Do different groups in society have different perceptions of their power? What kinds of perceptions? What accounts for different feelings of political efficacy?

What is political legitimacy? Of what is it comprised? How can it be measured? What is its function in a political system?

What is the nature of a political system? What are its components? How does it *work*? What means can be used to validate it?

Each of the above is a major political question. Some can be answered rather simply by collecting appropriate data and analyzing it. Evidence may be available from census tracts or from a registrar of voters. Some of the major questions require observation of political practices followed by analysis and speculative or philosophical thinking.

Major questions come after a preliminary period of asking general questions about what's going on and why in the world of politics. They most certainly will be followed by a number of specific questions relevant to the major one: What specific evidence do I need? Where can I get it? How large a sample do I need? How will I know the evidence is reliable? From what perspective shall the data be analyzed? And on and on. These kinds of questions, leading toward answers of major questions, are used in all kinds of social science inquiry, not just in political science. Many times the inquiry process in social science leads us not to better answers than we've had before but to better questions as we continue our quest for knowledge.

The inquiry process in political science will lead the investigator more to the use of observation or survey than to other methods. The political scientist may observe political behavior in the field—in the mayor's office, on the campaign trail —or as recorded in votes or other kinds of records or by the use of public opinion surveys such as those of George Gallup or the interviews conducted by the Center for Political Studies of the University of Michigan. He or she may have to treat the data by statistical analysis or by deduction. For some purposes, the political scientist will use historical inquiry.

Elementary children can conduct inquiry activities of a political science nature. They can read newspapers for the results of elections and plot these on national, state, or community maps. They can, with their parents, visit polling places and observe behavior there. They can use their own school as a laboratory and observe the political process there in terms of student elections or by interviewing fellow students on political questions.

The Core Concepts of Social Science and Political Science

We have already identified one of the core concepts—power—as the central concept of political science (Figure 7.2). Virtually every relationship among human beings involves power, the ability (or its potential) to influence or control others.

Figure 7.2   The Core Concepts of Social Science
Habitat
Culture
Institutions—political, economic, social
Resources, resource allocation
Interaction—competition, cooperation, accommodation
Conflict and conflict management
Power
Technology
Social change
Choice
Multiple causation

People who occupy a particular *habitat* (a political community such as a city, county, state, or nation) need to develop means of social control within the habitat. The particular means of social control or government is an integral part of the *culture* and is generally harmonious with all other elements of the culture. The political culture refers to the beliefs, traditions, and practices that make up the entire process of controlling and distributing power in the habitat. The political *institution*, which includes the government and the political culture, interacts with the economic institution in terms of how productive *resources* are to be allocated and with social institutions such as education, the family, and religion. In the state and local budgets in the United States, the largest single item is education, and what is taught in schools is subject to considerable state and local government oversight through school boards and legislature. Freedom of religion and the separation of the political and religious institution are guaranteed by the U.S. Constitution, but there is government financial assistance to religious institutions in the form of the tax-exempt status of church property.

Governments act as referees to assure fair play in group *interaction*. Both competition and cooperation are encouraged under certain circumstances. Much government involvement in human affairs establishes accommodative arrangements among those involved — conciliation, compromise, adjustment. *Conflict* is apt to develop out of interaction, and, were it not for the political institution, conflict would be more widespread than it is. One way of regarding the political process is as a formalized means of *conflict management.* Many modern conflicts are the product of *technology and industrialism.* Labor, management, and agriculture compete with each other for material benefits and look to the gov-

ernment to protect their special interests. Business management may encourage technological advances as a means of maximizing profits, and labor may resist the same advances if they mean a reduction in jobs. Both may use political power to try to get their way. Advancing technology and industrialism have resulted in a considerable loss in political power in farm areas, but agribusiness is closely tied to government with respect to price supports, export licenses, and import quotas.

It has been difficult for political institutions to keep pace with rapid social change. Political and social institutions change much more slowly than the economic institution, particularly in its technological form. Yet the nature of the American government has changed drastically in the last half century. Government is involved in our daily lives in ways that few envisioned in the early years of the republic. Some argue that the involvement of government has brought with it greater opportunity, a better quality of life, and a stronger democracy giving more people a wider range of *choice.* The choices that we make are based on our values, among which our political values are very important.

The changes that have occurred in the political institution are the result of *multiple causation.* The ruling of the U.S. Supreme Court in 1954 that segregated schools are in violation of the U.S. Constitution was the product of many factors working over a number of years. A whole series of court cases on segregation in education spanning more than a decade had preceded the 1954 decision in *Brown* v. *Board of Education.* Furthermore, the arguments that convinced the Supreme Court justices in that case were many — some legal and some sociological in nature.

Political science is helpful in gaining greater understanding of the core concepts of social science. The core concepts also enrich our knowledge of political science. With them, and with the specific concepts of political science, we can generate an infinite number of generalizations, such as those above and those explaining the fundamental ideas of political science (see Figure 7-1). What other generalizations can you develop from evidence available to you and from your understanding of political science concepts?

Political Science in the Social Studies

The study of government and politics has a firm place in the public school curriculum although it has more typically gone by the name of civics. Almost every state mandates that the study of American political institutions be included in the elementary and again in the secondary grades. This is to be expected considering the prominence given to sociocivic instruction as a key function of the public schools. The famous 1916 report, *The Social Studies in Secondary Education,* recommended that civics be taught in the ninth grade and again in the twelfth grade in a new course, Problems of Democracy. These courses were widely taught until the 1960s. Civics in the elementary grades was integrated throughout the social studies, as children learned about good citizenship in the home, neighborhood, and local community, and in regions and the nation. Additional civic instruction came through units centered around important national holidays or out of current events. A major "rite of passage" for many eighth graders remained the civics test, a throwback to a time when an eighth-grade education was the maximum achievement of 90 percent of the population.

The ninth-grade civics course was in many cases a community civics course in which the community became the laboratory for the study of democracy and its political and related institutions, and it often included units on the economic system and occupations. By 1960 it was being criticized for trying to do too much and actually accomplishing too little. Consequently civics has shown the greatest decline of enrollment of any secondary school course, dropping 39 percent between 1961 and 1973 while the overall secondary enrollment was increasing almost 60 percent.[3]

The drop does not mean that the study of government and politics is disappearing from the schools. Quite the contrary. During the same interval enrollment in U.S. government increased 67 percent, an absolute growth of 580,000, second only to U.S. history. This increase reflects the added importance of the separate social science disciplines in the curriculum revolution of the 1960s. In addition to other requirements, some states mandate instruction on the United Nations and some require that at least a short period of time be spent on the study of communism. The latter is apt to be of the prescriptive-prospective type of instruction.

There have been a number of national social studies curriculum projects in the 1960s and 1970s at the Maxwell Graduate School of Citizenship and Public Affairs at Syracuse University, which has been active in exploring the major social science concepts; the Lincoln Filene Center for Citizenship and Public Affairs at Tufts University, whose studies have expanded citizenship education to include the world; and most notably at the High School Curriculum Center in Government at Indiana Universiy. The latter

---

[3] Richard E. Gross, "The Status of the Social Studies in the Public Schools of the United States: Facts and Impressions of a National Survey," unpublished document, Stanford, California, 1976.

has two major curriculum projects that have had and are having a considerable impact on high school social studies. These are the projects in American Political Behavior, which gets away from the traditional structural approach to American government by having students analyze political behavior, and Comparing Political Experiences, designed as an alternate to high school government courses and in which students learn participation skills using their schools as political communities.

In the 1970s the American Bar Association and the U.S. government's Law Enforcement Administration provided support for several law-focused education projects at both the elementary and secondary levels. Some of these projects were designed to acquaint young people with their civil rights, rights that were limited to adults until the *Tinker* v. *Des Moines* case of 1969. Others, reflecting the increased lawlessness of the turbulent 1960s, were to acquaint young people with the law and to encourage them to be more law-abiding citizens.

Fewer projects have concentrated on political science content at the elementary level, although a number of inter- or multidisciplinary projects have incorporated civics or government in their programs. Among these are the Mershon Intermediate Units, the Boston Children's museum MATCH project, the Educational Research Council's Concepts and Inquiry program, and Project Social Studies of the University of Minnesota (the eighth grade of which is devoted to "Our Political System"). The Educational Development Center's Project, From Subject to Citizen, is designed for eighth- and ninth-grade American history, but it involves a considerable amount of political science. So, too, does the Harvard University Social Studies Project on public issues for grades 7 through 12. The Committee on Civic Education at the

Universiy of California at Los Angeles has developed materials, including excellent case studies, for grades 4 through 8.

Political socialization studies of the last two decades have provided considerable insight into the process by which young people learn about political communities and how they develop various political values. These have been helpful to educators in improving the curriculum and in developing new teaching strategies to promote desirable sociocivic behaviors.

Most social studies educators agree on the importance of political science knowledge in developing competent citizens, one of the main reasons the public supports its school system. Increasing attention is given to the study of political behavior and decision making. From the contemporary view, the competent citizen is capable of making decisions, at all political levels, and is a person who has had some experience in the process, rather than being a robot who can memorize terms and passages and obey unquestioningly. A political science foundation for this kind of social studies that will develop such a decision-making citizen is vital.

Economics, Social Science, and the Social Studies

Economics, has, until the last decade or so, been only peripherally involved in public school social studies prior to the twelfth grade. True, for a long time some phase of economics has been a part of the school curriculum—bank days in elementary and junior high school, the study of community helpers (the milkman, the postman, the physician, the nurse, the librarian, the policeman or policewoman) in primary grades, and the study of the elements of production in the regions of the world as a part of sixth- or seventh-grade North American Neighbors or Old World Backgrounds. The eighth grade sometimes included major products of the various regions of the United States, and junior high school and senior high school history included the causes of the depression and something about the nature of the American economic system. Economics has also been found in courses in business economics or consumership that have been offered in secondary business departments or as part of the instruction in home economics and industrial arts. Semester and year courses in economics have been offered to seniors in many high schools since the 1920s. For obvious reasons, interest in teaching about economics picked up in the 1930s.

Why, have asked some social scientists, has such a basic human activity as earning a living and making wise choices of how we spend our money been considered as inappropriate at the elementary and most of the secondary levels? Is the content so difficult and so abstract that it takes the maturity of a 17-year-old to understand it? Is it less important knowledge than geography, history, anthropology, or sociology? The answer to all of these questions seems to be no.

For many years observers of the American political scene and practicing politicians have claimed that the economic issues are the ones that count in the voting booth. From this perspective, what influences people in choosing among candidates or in voting on referenda is how this hits them in the pocketbook—how it affects the taxes they pay, the material benefits they get from their government, measures to promote economic activity or to hold down the cost of living, the ease with which money may be borrowed, or opportunities for invest-

ment. Pocketbook issues, it is alleged, dominate in virtually all areas of life, not just the political.

Many people, not just economists, have commented on the fundamental economic illiteracy of the American people. Professional economists, working in universities, research institutes, government agencies, financial institutions, and in business—are agreed on the need to do something about this illiteracy. Many of them look to the high schools as the logical place where systematic economic instruction should take place, typically during the senior year when pupils are faced with making important decisions about their post-high school careers. Furthermore, fully 50 percent of high school graduates in the nation do not go on to college, and a large number of college students manage to avoid courses in economics. If anything is to be done about economic illiteracy, it is to be done in the public schools, particularly the last years of high school due to the abstruseness of economics requiring a certain level of maturity. Not all economists agree that economics is such an abstruse science that only mature upper high school students can profit by instruction in it. Professor Lawrence Senesh of Purdue University and later of the University of Colorado was so convinced that economic understanding is within the level of pupils of all ages that he took time out from his university teaching to instruct elementary pupils to test his ideas. As a result, he has developed an entire elementary social studies program, *Our Working World*,[4] using the structure of economics as the central threads for social studies instruction. Pupils can demonstrate their economic understanding operationally, even if they can't give neat definitions of such concepts as supply and demand curves, GNP, and opportunity cost.

---

[4] Published by Science Research Associates, Chicago.

What is economics, then, that it is so abstruse that only the most mature intellects can understand it—or—that is so fundamentally simple that a child intuitively "knows" some economics by the time he enters school and can use economics as the vehicle for extending his social science knowledge?

Ecomomics, Defined

There is probably more agreement on what economics is, at least as far as a definition goes, than on most other social sciences.

> "Economics is the study of man making choices in the allocation of resources."[5]

> "Economics is . . . the study of how society produces and distributes the goods and services it wants . . . it examines the activities that people carry on—producing, saving, spending, paying taxes, and so on—for the purpose of satisfying their basic wants for food and shelter, their added wants for modern conveniences and comforts, and their collective wants for such things as national defense and education."[6]

> "Economics is the social science that is concerned with the things that men want and how they go about acquiring them."[7]

> "The central idea of economics is the scarcity concept, namely, that every society faces a conflict between unlimited wants and limited resources."[8]

> Economics is the dismal science.[9]

The Development and Nature of Economics as a Social Science

What we now know as economics was once called political economy and was largely speculative and philosophical in nature. Present-day economics still retains its ties with political economy in that it is a policy science and it is perhaps more deductive than the other social sciences. Government leaders and lay persons alike look to economics to make analyses of economic trends to help in making policy decisions.

Economics has developed from the classic economic theories of Adam Smith, David Ricardo, and Thomas Malthus through the works of John Stuart Mill and Karl Marx to such diverse twentieth-century economic theorists as John Maynard Keynes and Milton Friedman. Over the years economics has embraced such polaristic views as classical laissez-faire economics versus Keynesian government planning economics, free trade versus national trade restrictions (tariffs), demands (private enterprise) economics versus command (government ownership and control) economics, and unrestricted economic growth versus zero population growth and environmental controls.

Among the more important branches of economics are microeconomics (factors affecting small units such as a single factory or store), macroeconomics (factors affecting an entire nation or an entire industry), labor economics, economic history, money and banking, government and economic policy (taxation, fiscal policy), foreign trade and international economics, and econometrics (mea-

[5] John R. Coleman and Kenneth O. Alexander, *Study Guide for the American Economy*, New York, McGraw-Hill, 1962, p. v.
[6] Marshall A. Robinson et al., *An Introduction to Economic Reasoning*, revised edition, Washington D.C., The Brookings Institution, 1959, p. 4.
[7] Peter R. Senn, *Social Science and Its Methods*, Boston, Holbrook Press, Inc., 1971, p. 124.
[8] Lawrence Senesh, "Organizing a Curriculum Around Social Science Concepts" in Irving Morrissett, ed., *Concepts and Structure in the New Social Science Curricula*, West Lafayette, Indiana: Social Science Education Consortium, 1966, p. 24.
[9] Attributed to Thomas Carlisle.

suring devices and techniques producing economic indicators of the health of a given economic unit).

The Structure of Economics

In addition to the imposed conceptions of economics that guide economic inquiry, certain questions give us a clue to the structure of economics. These questions, or the answers to them, help circumscribe the scope of economics. Since economics is essentially a deductive science, these questions are directed toward obtaining particular answers in specific situations, ranging from a few people to an entire nation or international bloc.

1. What will be produced?
2. How will it be produced?
3. How will things be distributed?

There is a fourth question that was asked during the expansionist period of the 1950s and 1960s: How can we provide for future growth of people's needs? This is still a pertinent question for developing nations in the 1970s and 1980s, but in the postindustrial economics the question raises additional questions about the limits of growth.

Thanks to the Social Science Education Consortium, there is a model of the economic system (Figure 7.3) which, similar to the one we have already seen on the political system, illustrates how the economic system works. In so doing, the model uses a number of important concepts, such as unlimited wants and limited resources, specialization, and market. The explanation accompanying the model puts the concepts together in a series of generalizations about economics.

Major Concepts in Economics

Lists of economic concepts may be short or long depending upon their degree of specificity. In its list of 18 major substantive concepts for social studies, the Syra-

cuse University Social Studies Curriculum Center lists six that are essentially economic in nature.[10]

1. The central idea of economics is the scarcity concept, namely, that every society faces a conflict between unlimited wants and limited resources.
2. Out of the scarcity concept a family of ideas emerge. Because of scarcity, man has tried to develop methods to produce more in less time, or more with less material and in shorter time. Various types of specialization were discovered in order to overcome the conflict between unlimited wants and limited resources. We specialize geographically, occupationally, and technologically.
3. Because of specialization, we are interdependent; interdependence necessitates a monetary system and a transportation system.
4. Men had to discover an allocating mechanism and this is the market, where through the interaction of buyers and sellers price changes occur. Prices determine the pattern of production, the method of production, income distribution, and the level of spending and saving, which, in turn, decide the level of total economic activity.
5. The market decision is modified by public policies, carried out by the government, to assure welfare objectives. These welfare objectives are determined in the United States through the political interaction of 200 million people that generates thousands of welfare objectives that can be reduced to five: attempts to accelerate growth, to promote stability, to assure economic security, to promote economic freedom, and to promote economic justice.

The industrialization-urbanization syndrome: technical advance, industrial growth, and secularization accompanied by the movement of population from the farm to the cities; with them have come the benefits of

---

[10] Roy Price, Warren Hickman, and Gerald Smith, *Major Concepts for the Social Studies*, Syracuse, New York, Social Studies Curriculum Center, 1965.

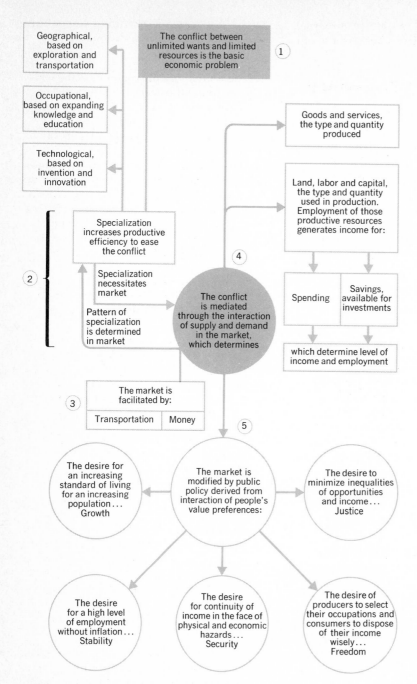

Figure 7.3 Fundamental ideas of economics.
(From *Our Working World: Cities at Work*, Resource Unit, by Lawrence Senesh. © 1966, 1967,
Science Research Associates, Inc. Reprinted by
permission of the publisher.)

higher standards of living and the detriments of crowding and alienation.

Comparative advantage (or opportunity cost): "It is impossible for any individual, political party, or nation to dictate life to such an extent as to assure total acquiescence to all outside forces. . . ." Comparative advantage extends from the child deciding whether to trade a bucket for a sand shovel while constructing a castle on the beach, to a community deciding to tax itself more (thus giving up something the money could otherwise buy) for better schools.

Opportunity cost (or alternative cost) is the idea that the same money can't be spent for two different items at the same time; spending it for one (e.g., money invested in a college education) means it can't be spent for another (a trip around the world). We have to reckon the comparative advantage of one over the other.

Input and output: Input refers to the productive resources furnished by people in producing something, and output is all the goods and services produced for sale during a period of time. The two are equal; we are rewarded for our share of input and our income should equal our output.

Saving: a financial asset or claim on some economic unit; a debt is someone else's saving. Aggregate saving, or saving for the economy as a whole, contributes to the stability or instability of the economic system.

The modified market economy: The economy of the United States is a mixed economy, being a partially private (or market) economy and partially a public (or command) economy. It includes the private functions of the enterpreneur and the public functions of the government as a market (defense and public works purchases) and as a source of capital (loans and grants-in-aid).

Almost any list of economic concepts would contain scarcity, factors of production (land, labor, capital—land refers to natural resources, labor is the effort

needed to produce something, and capital consists of manufactured things that are used to produce other things, that is, tools, machines, factories), specialization (engaging in only one part of the productive process), and market (the mythical place where supply and demand factors mediate the conflict between unlimited wants and limited resources). Even more detailed lists of economic concepts, including most of the ones above, are to be found in the 1977 report of the Joint Council on Economic Education:[11]

An extremely important but simple concept for the average citizen in a market economy is, in lay terms, the "dollar-vote" concept. It makes use of a number of the technical ideas presented in an easy-to-understand everyday context. When people spend money for any commodity or service in a private enterprise system they are registering "votes" that business people and investors "count" through the mechanism of the market to make decisions about what goods and services are to be offered to consumers and in what quantity. If people are interested in quick food service, they will spend their money for it rather than for, say, natural unprocessed foods for "scratch" cooking—or vice versa. Every dollar a person has to spend should be weighed heavily by the consumer for the consequences of his or her dollar vote. Do we want to encourage hard-core pornographic movies by our willingness to pay high prices for them or do we wish to encourage widespread participation in amateur musical productions and athletics by withholding our dollar votes from the commercial enterprises? Do we cast

---

[11] *W. Lee Hansen et al, A Framework for Teaching Economics; Basic Concepts;* Part 1 of *Master Curriculum Guide in Economics for the Nation's Schools,* New York, Joint Council on Economic Education, 1977, pp. 28–29.

our dollar votes for convenient rapid transit or do we cast them for large and luxurious automobiles that consume large quantities of gasoline? Or do we have other choices, other ways we can cast our dollar votes?

With these and other concepts, and with the proper use of the economic mode of inquiry, economists (and lay people) can develop helpful generalizations, as we shall soon see.

The Mode of Inquiry of Economics

The evidence gathered by economists is largely statistical data related to and/or elaborating on the economic concepts. It will include money costs of various items, figures on labor and employment, production statistics overall and by specific industries, productivity. It does not have to be presented in dry lists of tables, as we can see from the following charts and graphs from the Conference Board on employment and income (Figure 7.4).

There are only examples of the many kinds of data about human economic activities that are collected by economists. Of particular importance to government policy makers and the average citizen are the economic indicators that provide information about the nation's (and the world's) economic health. Much information is generated constantly and means must be employed for collecting it. Economic surveys are taken from time to time to gather data not part of regular reports from businesses and government agencies.

To assist in making inferences from the evidence, economists use models. Social scientists don't play with model airplanes or model ships, but the models they do employ use the same concept as model ships. A model is a symbolic representation, a description, or a reproduction of something on a small scale. A map, of course, is a model. Models need

not be complete, but they must contain the essential characteristics of the object represented. A model ship probably won't have an engine nor the detailed interior spaces and machinery of a full-scale ship, but it will have a hull and certain other external features. The list of concepts in Figure 7.5 is actually a model of the economic system because the schematic framework illustrates the way the economic system functions. The following model of GNP (gross national product) in the American economy is designed to help social scientists draw certain kinds of inferences about the relationship of production, spending, and taxation. (See Figure 7.6.)

Inferences from a model of GNP and from other economic models can include statements of principles regarding government expenditures and their impact on the economy, hypotheses about whether increased taxation will place a drag on the economy, and conclusions about what level of demand will attract what supplies into the market at what price, among others.

Economics and the Core Concepts of the Social Sciences

Of the 11 integrating concepts, *resources and resource allocation* are probably the ones that are most central to the discipline of economics. By now, you should be sufficiently familiar both with the core concepts and with the general nature of economics to make inferences about the relationship of these concepts to economics.

How does the economic *institution* of a country convert the resources of a given *habitat* to help satisfy human wants? What is the relationship between a culture's values and the particular system of resource allocation that is used? To what degree do the *interactive processes* of com-

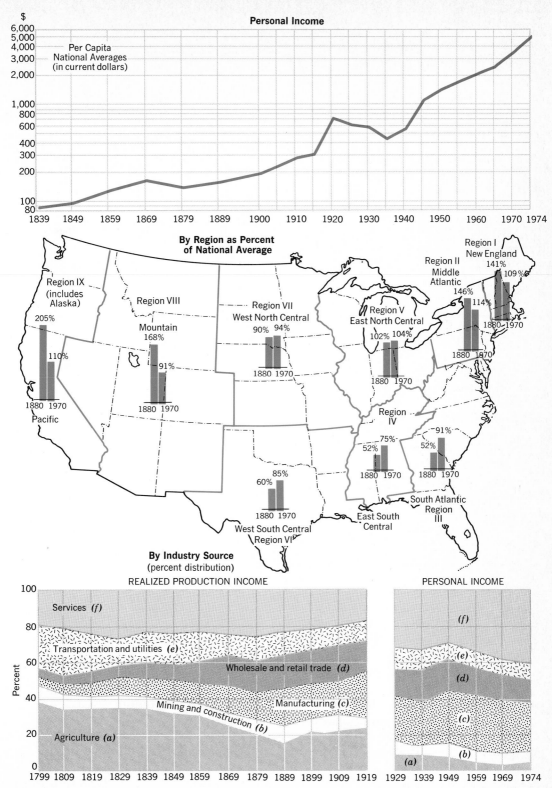

Personal Income

$
6,000
5,000
4,000
3,000

2,000

Per Capita
National Averages
(in current dollars)

1,000
800
600

400
300

200

100
80

1839 1849 1859 1869 1879 1889 1900 1910 1920 1930 1940 1950 1960 1970 1974

**By Region as Percent
of National Average**

Region I
New England
141% 109%

Region II
Middle
Atlantic
146% 114%
1880–1970

Region IX
(includes
Alaska)
205% 110%
1880 1970
Pacific

Region VIII
Mountain
168% 91%
1880 1970

Region VII
West North Central
90% 94%
1880 1970

Region V
East North Central
102% 104%
1880 1970

Region
IV
75%
52%
1880 1970
East South
Central

91%
52%
1880 1970
South Atlantic
Region
III

85%
60%
1880 1970
West South Central
Region VI

By Industry Source
(percent distribution)

REALIZED PRODUCTION INCOME

100

Services (f)

80

Transportation and utilities (e)

60

Wholesale and retail trade (d)

Percent

40

Mining and construction (b)

Manufacturing (c)

20

Agriculture (a)

0

1799 1809 1819 1829 1839 1849 1859 1869 1879 1889 1899 1909 1919

PERSONAL INCOME

(f)

(e)

(d)

(c)

(a) (b)

1929 1939 1949 1959 1969 1974

Figure 7.5 (Permission granted. The Conference
Board.)

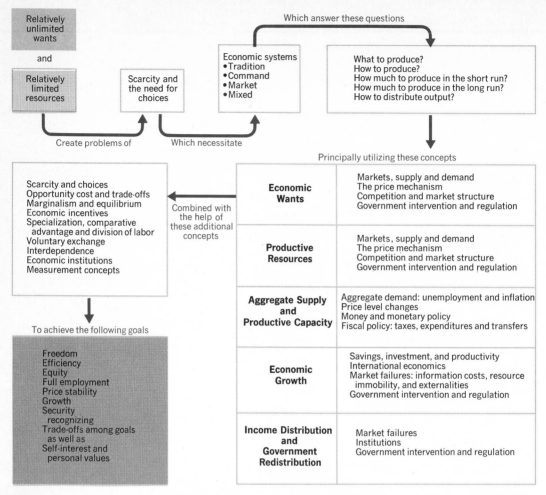

Figure 7.4   A schematic framework of economics: an approach to linking the concepts. (Reprinted with permission of the Joint Council on Economic Education, *Master Curriculum Guide in Economics* *for the Nation's Schools.* **Part 1:** *A Framework for Teaching Economics: Basic Concepts.* © JCEE 1977. **All Rights Reserved.)**

petition or cooperation help solve the scarcity problem? What is the relationship of economic *power* to political power to social or moral power? How have changes in *technology* produced social *conflict* or mediated it? To what extent has *industrialism* changed the quality of life of a *culture*? To what extent may economic *values* conflict with social values? What are some of the major *causes* of technological developments, economic conflict, and the like, and what are the major effects of these on our economic life?

Economics and the Social Studies

Social science educators have taken seriously the need for better economic understanding. In addition to the aforementioned series (p. 124) having economics as the organizing center for grades 1 through 6, *Our Working World,*

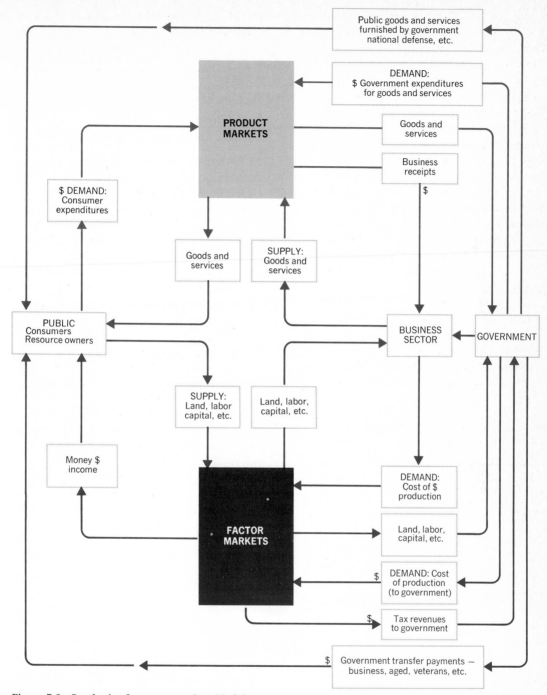

Figure 7.6   Synthesis of government into Model
II. (Permission granted. The Conference Board.)

there are several other national curriculum projects focusing on economics, most of them for the elementary grades. The University of Chicago Industrial Relations Center has had an Elementary Economics Project for Grades 4 through 8 and Ohio University has a Manpower and Economic Education project for grades 8 through 10. One project, San Jose State University's Economics in Society, is for grade 12. In addition, the several multidisciplinary projects already mentioned in relation to political science devote some attention to economics.

Economic understanding is important for social scientists and for laymen. A certain amount of it can be gained in the school of hard knocks and by everyday experience, but this must be augmented by systematic instruction in the schools, beginning as early as possible. It need not be the dismal science, either, as these selected pages from *The Adventures of Primero Dinero*,[12] published by the Office of Economic Education of the University of Hawaii, reveal.

---

[12] From *The Adventures of Primero Dinero* by Steve Jackstadt and Yukio Hamada with illustrations by John Dawson. Copyright © 1971 by Follett Publishing Company. Used by permission.

The Policy Sciences and the Social Studies

Although we call political science and economics the policy sciences largely for purposes of convenience, these disciplines are related to the other two categories of social sciences. Treatises on politics are among the oldest scholarly works in the Western World and political economy as a more-or-less systematic body of knowledge is at least 200 years old. Because of the philosophical and normative nature of these disciplines in their early manifestations they can be grouped with the classic disciplines in some ways.

On the other hand, recent and major thrusts of scholarship in both economics and political science show the influence of behaviorism. A teacher of the social studies needs to be familiar with both the traditional and the behavioral aspects of the policy sciences.

The nature and development of the behavioral sciences as foundations for the social studies is our concern in Chapter 8.

DEFINITION OF "SCARCE":

SOMETHING IS SCARCE WHEN YOU DON'T HAVE AS MUCH OF IT AS YOU WOULD LIKE.

SCARCITY WAS NOW A PROBLEM FOR PRIMO.

HE HAD MANY WANTS

... AND FEW RESOURCES.

DEFINITION OF RESOURCE:

A RESOURCE IS ANYTHING THAT CAN BE USED TO SATISFY HUMAN WANTS.

ALL HE'S GOT IS A COUPLE OF STICKS AND SHOELACES

NOW...

PRIMO IS FAMILIAR WITH THE "ECONOMIC PROBLEM"

HOW CAN I BEST ALLOCATE MY SCARCE RESOURCES TO SATISFY MY MANY WANTS?

LAND LABOR & CAPITAL

ARE GENERAL RESOURCE CATEGORIES

FROM NOW ON GANG

AS WE WATCH PRIMO IN ACTION, WE'LL BE STUDYING ECONOMICS.

DEFINITION OF ECONOMICS:

ECONOMICS IS THE STUDY OF HOW MEN CHOOSE TO ALLOCATE SCARCE RESOURCES IN ORDER TO SATISFY THEIR WANTS

NOTE ↳ IF YOU DON'T KNOW WHAT "ALLOCATE" MEANS, LOOK IN A DICTIONARY.

NOW THERE WERE REALLY BIG PROBLEMS...

.OVER WHAT TO PRODUCE.....

> MAN, THIS COULD BE A GROOVY PLACE TO GROW CHIVES 'N KUMQUATS.

> NO. IT'S AN IDEAL PLACE TO ESTABLISH A SASHIMI* INDUSTRY!

> COME ON, FELLAS, LET'S USE OUR RESOURCES TO BUILD A TRAINING-GROUND FOR GUERRILLAS.

> I LIKE ALL THIS EXCITEMENT

NOTE: SASHIMI IS RAW FISH, YUM.

HOW TO PRODUCE IT...

> HEY, MAN, WHY DON'T ONE OF YOU GUYS GET SOME COCONUTS?

> YEAH O.I., HOW 'BOUT IT?

> I GOT 'EM LAST TIME, LET ALI GET 'EM.

> ISN'T IT EXCITING?

ZZZ

AND OVER WHO WOULD GET IT.

> I SHOULD GET THE BIGGEST SHARE. I DID THE MOST WORK.

> SO WHAT! I WAS HERE FIRST!

> SOCK POW

> THIS REALLY IS EXCITING!

BEFORE THINGS GET TOO EXCITING, GO ON OVER TO THE APPLICATIONS. JUST STAY TUNED.

Bibliography

Cleary, Robert S. and Donald H. Riddle. *Political Science and the Social Studies.* 36th Yearbook of the National Council for the Social Studies. Washington, D.C.: The Council, 1966.

DEA News: For Teachers of Political Science. A Publication of the Division of Educational Affairs of the American Political Science Association, Washington.

Easton, David. *The Political System.* Publication #103 of the Social Science Education Consortium. Boulder, Col.: The Consortium, 1966.

Hansen, W. Lee et al., *A Framework for Teaching Economics: Basic Concepts;* Part I *of Master Guide for the Nation's Schools.* New York: Joint Council on Economic Education, 1977.

Kirkpatrick, Evron M. and Jeane J. Kirkpatrick, "Political Science" in *High School Social Studies Perspectives.* Boston: Houghton Mifflin, 1962.

Martin, Richard S. and Reuben G. Miller. *Economics and Its Significance.* Columbus, Ohio: Charles E. Merrill Books, 1965.

Price, Roy A. et al., *Major Concepts for Social Studies.* Syracuse, N.Y.: Social Studies Curriculum Center, Syracuse University, 1965.

Senesh, Lawrence. *Economics.* Publication #105 of the Social Science Education Consortium. Boulder, Col.: The Consortium, 1966.

Sorauf, Francis J. *Political Science: An Informal Overview.* Columbus, Ohio: Charles E. Merrill Books, 1965.

How do the behavioral sciences help us understand other people and cultures?

CHAPTER 8

The Behavioral Sciences: Psychology, Sociology, and Anthropology

The term behavioral science is of relatively recent origin although the focus of it—individuals and groups—is old. The ancient Greeks began the systematic studies that formed the basis for modern scientific psychology and anthropology, but it has only been within about the last 100 years that these fields have emerged as scientific disciplines.

Behavioral science has emerged only within the last half century to denote the central concern of one group of social scientists, the study of the nature and varieties of human behavior in a number of contexts. Earlier social scientists had engaged in descriptive studies of societies or in philosophical treatises on the human condition. Those scientists who wished to concentrate on observing, recording, measuring, analyzing, and interpreting human behavior patterns began to differentiate themselves from the social philosophers, archeologists, historians, political scientists, and others who maintained the more traditional approach to social science. Typically, the behavioral scientist quantifies his/her research, that is, makes highly sophisticated statistical measures and analyses to probe the nature of human behavior.

As we have seen, the policy disciplines of political science and economics have their behavioral aspects. The new scholarly field of psychohistory involves the use of the behavioral science, psychiatry, with a traditional discipline of history, among other examples of the behavioral influence in fields outside the normal scope of behavioral science. Behavioral science is actually broader than psychology, sociology, anthropology. It includes not only the behavioral aspects of the classic disciplines and the policy sciences, but psychiatry, physiology, and social psychology. By contrast, there are among sociologists, psychologists, and anthropologists those scholars who are more humanistically inclined and who would not consider themselves behaviorists in the strict sense of the word.

The behavioral sciences have made mixed and sometimes minor contributions to public school studies until relatively recently. As school subjects, psychology and anthropology were felt to be too advanced to study below the college level. Even sociology in the form of social problems or problems of democracy was limited to high school seniors and was not studied as a discipline. All that has changed in the past two decades.

Psychology, Social Science, and the Social Studies

Psychology has become the "in" subject of the 1970s for the "aware." It has not only take over from sociology as the most popular[1] social science among college students, but the whole field of "pop psychology" has expanded tremendously in recent years due to widespread public interest in individual behavior. There are many manifestations of this interest, not all of it scientific: transcendental meditation, transaction analysis ("I'm okay, you're okay"), the popularity of the journal *Psychology Today*, the excellent sales records of paperback books on a variety of psychological topics, and the phenomenal success of self-awareness ventures such as est, rolfing, and the Esalen Institute, among many others.

People have always been interested in themselves, but the present upsurge of interest in psychology, both systematic and pop psychology, may represent not only a turning inward, in contrast to the socially activist 1960s and early 1970s, but a concern for people as individuals as

well as for people as members of groups. During the activist 1960s and early 1970s many people were hopeful that they could reform society by overhauling — even overthrowing — its institutions. The increased interest in psychology and other related movements may not indicate an abandonment of the idea of reform so much as it does a new target for reform. Perhaps the best way to improve society is by improving people. And what discipline has greater potential for understanding their behavior — the motivations, aspirations, fears, abilities, and the like — than psychology?

Of all the social sciences, psychology is the discipline that most teachers have studied. Because of the importance of the psychological foundations of education teachers typically have two or more courses in psychology and study psychological topics throughout their preprofessional training and continue it as a part of their professional education. Thus, prospective teachers are already familiar with some of the content of psychology, at least as it applies to teaching.

Definition of Psychology; the Nature of Psychology

Whether as a scientific discipline or as a pop subject, psychology is one of the easiest of the social sciences to define. It is the systematic study of individual behavior and mental processes. The term derives from the Greek words *psyche*, meaning mind or soul, and *logos*, meaning study or disclosure. In this definition "mental" is viewed broadly, comprising emotional as well as intellectual factors. Mental health, for example, is concerned more with emotional factors of adjustment than with the purely cognitive.

Psychology is not just the study of personality, as is sometimes assumed by lay people. Nor is it the study of mental/emotional abnormalities nor of entertain-

---

[1] All the social sciences have suffered enrollment declines as the college students of the 1970s have shifted to more secure career-oriented fields such as business and engineering. Psychology has declined less than the others, partly because of the increased interest in fields such as industrial psychology, as well as interest in ourselves.

ing activities such as hypnosis. Psychology is the only one of the social sciences or even of the behavioral sciences that is concerned primarily with individual human behavior. Furthermore, it has strong ties with the natural sciences, particularly with biology, and these ties have become even stronger in recent years. An emerging field is that of psychobiology, drawing upon the work of not only ethologists (students of animal behavior), but also of human biologists and biochemists.

Psychology provides important knowledge that is valuable for everyday living. Everyone needs to have some understanding of individual human behavior — motivation, states of consciousness, emotions, personality formation, adaptive mechanisms, the growth and development of human beings. Teachers have an even greater need of psychological understanding, adding to the above such things as perception, learning, and intelligence.

Despite its value in everyday living, psychology has not been traditionally a part of the social studies to any degree, particularly at the elementary level. Perhaps the lack of psychological content in grades one through eight represents the disdain that the academic psychologist has for watered-down or pop psychology and the belief that the principles of academic psychology are too advanced for elementary and most high school students. The social studies draws from the pertinent social science disciplines. Psychology can provide a source of information for social studies programs in a variety of ways and teachers need to know something of the nature of the social studies in order to do curriculum planning intelligently.

Major Subdivisions of Psychology

Individual human behavior is complex and has many manifestations. The study of psychology, therefore, is made up of many branches or subdivisions that can provide a good indication of the scope of the discipline.

General psychology, the foundation on which the other specialities are built, includes most of the topics of a first-year college psychology course. Among these topics are such psychological concepts as learning, conditioning, motivation, perception, emotion, and personality. Learning is the process of acquiring and modifying behavior through experience and practice. A form of learning is conditioning, as exemplified by such classic conditioned reflex experiments as Pavlov's stimulus-response work on dogs. Motivation is of interest to all social scientists. It consists of the basic forces that impel people or animals to act and to do what they do in varying circumstances. Much of the earliest scientific (i.e., experimental) psychology was done on perception, the study of the complex process by which patterns of environmental energies become known as objects, events, people, and the like. Closely related to motivation is emotion, a stirred-up state of an organism, manifested in intensity of feeling, level of tension, and physiological changes in the body. Emotions are complex, ranging over anger, joy, fear, pride, grief, love, hate, misery, awe, contentment. Adolescents tend to be self-conscious about their own personalities and are interested in all aspects of personality, the characteristics of individuals and their development and measurement.

Abnormal psychology formed one of the early emphases of modern psychology, as social scientists attempted to learn more about mental and emotional disorders. It is still an important subdivision of psychology, but it has declined in importance as psychologists have directed their attention more to normal behavior. Although the dividing line between normality and abnormality in individual human behavior is often obscure, there are many more normal people than abnormal people and even people who may be defined as psychologically abnormal act "normal" most of the time.

Physiological psychology is concerned with the relationship between behavior and the function of the nervous system. Among the recent valuable investigations in the subdivision of psychology have been those on the different functions of the right hemisphere of the brain, relating to the more artistic and more free-spirited activities of individuals, and the left hemisphere, which is the center of the more logical or linear activities.

Developmental psychology has taken on new dimensions in recent years. As the study of changes in human behavior from birth to old age, its focus has been on how children develop and what their characteristics are at each stage of development. Studies have also included comparisons of siblings and twins reared together and reared apart. Generalizations that had been developed about developmental changes among the elderly have recently been called into question. As a result, developmental psychology is developing a new interest; we are learning that many of the myths of old age are exactly that. The elderly do not necessarily lose their ability to learn nor cease to be sexually active. With a population that is rapidly growing older,[2] our knowledge of psychological development in the older years needs to be expanded markedly.

Comparative psychology has been a productive source of our knowledge of many facets of individual behavior. The study of behavior and abilities of different animal species helps the social scientist to generalize about human behavior from the kinds of experiments that might not be possible with people and to develop hypotheses that can subsequently be tested with human subjects. It is also the source of interesting and valuable information about the animal world. Rats early became favorite subjects for experiments on learning, the effects of reward and punishment, the effects of crowding, and so on. Their nervous system is similar to that of humans and their small size and short gestatation period make them economical laboratory animals. Because of their overall similarity to humans, primates have been excellent subjects. Recent primatological research has included probing the language capacity and the problem-solving abilities of chimpanzees and gorillas.

Drawing on and applying the principles of comparative psychology, developmental psychology, and general psychology has been the subdivision, educational psychology. Although it is, to a large extent, an applied field, educational psychology nonetheless has a cadre of investigators who are conducting research that can help educational workers improve their effectiveness with children. Psychometry, the process of assessing and measuring mental abilities and emotional states, is another branch of psychology of great importance to teachers and counselors. Although the first systematic psychometric devices were designed to diagnose such psychological abnormalities as mental retardation, this branch of psychology is not limited to the study and measurement of intelligence. There are tests of specific mental abilities such as memory, logical reasoning, perceptual speed, and handling spatial relationships. There are also tests of aptitudes—artistic, musical, mechanical, among others—as

---

[2] The median age was 16 in 1790, 28 in 1970, almost 29 in 1975, will pass 30 in 1981, and is expected to be 35 by the year 2000.

well as of school achievement, subject by subject.

Social psychology overlaps sociology, using concepts from both psychology and sociology. The study of relationships among people in groups includes not only crowd behavior—"mob psychology"—but public opinion and propaganda. The widespread use of mass media in this century, and particularly the influence of television in the second half of the century, have been favorite subjects for the investigations of social psychologists. Another subdivision, organizational psychology, has grown in importance in recent years. Sometimes known by other more specific names such as industrial psychology or military psychology, organizational psychology applies psychological principles and techniques to the needs and problems of specific organizations. It may include the study of man-machine systems in industry or human relationships in the factory or office. In the form of motivation research it may also include probing the potential success of "hidden persuaders" in selling and advertising.

New branches of psychology are developing all the time as are new combinations of psychology and other disciplines. No list of subdivisions of psychology can be complete. To the nine already identified we conclude with clinical psychology, which provides diagnosis and treatment to help individuals adapt to their environment. Clinical psychology is closely allied to psychiatry, the psychiatrist being a medical doctor specializing in psychological disorders, the clinical psychologist being a social scientist specializing in such disorders. Both specialties are licensed by the state, but a clinical psychologist is apt to work under the supervision of a psychiatrist.

Obviously, then, there are many facets to the complex field that studies individual human behavior. As psychology has evolved as a behavioral science, it has not only developed a variety of branches, it has also developed schools of thought. Some schools may concern themselves with one or more branches of psychology to a greater degree than others, but they also represent different frames of reference as well as different emphases that have emerged in the development of psychology.

Schools of Psychology

There are perhaps four or five schools of psychology today, although a very careful analysis would reveal there are a number of schools within each of the schools! They are the structuralist-functionalist school, behaviorism, gestalt psychology or field theory, psychoanalysis, and humanistic or third-force psychology.[3] Some older schools may still have a few adherents, but the faculty psychology attributed to the Greeks and dominant until about the seventeenth century no longer has any support in the scientific community. Behavioral scientists are unwilling to accept the idea of inborn "faculties" of memory, reason, or artistry. Associationism, the school that succeeded faculty psychology, is close to mid- and late-twentieth-century principles of psychology in its attempts to explain how memory functions through the laws of similarity, contrast, and contiguity, but its recent form can be subsumed under behaviorism.

The structuralist school of psychology goes back about 100 years in attempts to probe the structure of the

---

[3] Although third force originally referred to psychology's position at the interface of natural science and the humanities, more recently it has meant the alternative psychological position between behaviorism and psychoanalysis, the leading influences on late twentieth-century psychology.

mind in terms of analyses of conscious experience such as sensations, feelings, and images. Functionalists desired to go beyond simple conscious experience and probe how the mind functions; every feeling or sensation has a function in reference to some kind of object, knowing it and choosing or rejecting it. The two most significant members of this combined school from an educator's point of view are John Dewey and Jean Piaget.

Behaviorism developed in reaction against structuralism. Behaviorists stress the study of tangible and observable behavior, not the science of conscious experience, an earlier definition of psychology. Behaviorists have stressed the stimulus-response bonds, conditioned-reflex, and theories of learning based on conditioning. Although behaviorism was probably the dominant school of psychology in the United States in the 1920s as far as education was concerned, it declined for a period only to enjoy a revival during the Sputnik Era of the 1950s and 1960s. B. F. Skinner is undoubtedly the best known of the current behaviorists, and his work on operant conditioning (the "Skinner box") and human engineering (*Walden Two*) is both influential and controversial.

The reaction against structuralism took another form in Germany and began to develop about the same time as behaviorism was developing in the United States. Gestaltists are convinced that the "mind" cannot be analyzed the way a physical scientists analyzes a chemical compound into elements or atoms. Human perceptions, responses, and learning work in organized patterns, the German word *Gestalt*. An observer not only perceives things as whole, rather than a congeries of discrete unrelated items, but tends to provide closure on partial or incomplete objects of perception. The relationship between the different parts of a stimulus, which we per-

ceive as a whole or a pattern, give us our meaning out of experience. Gestalt psychology was very influential in the new theories of education emerging in the 1930s and later. Gestalt psychology provided an appropriate foundation for the ideas of progressive education, and the "look-say" method of teaching reading was based in large part on gestalt principles.

Strictly speaking, psychoanalysis is not a school of psychology in the sense of the others. It is actually a medical method of treatment of mental/emotional disorders. As a development within the field of psychiatry it has links with academic psychology in certain assumptions about how the human organism functions intellectually and emotionally or about its dysfunctions under the impact of certain kinds of conditions. Although the teacher has little or no need for psychoanalytic knowledge in the classroom, nonetheless the impact on all of us of the work of Sigmund Freud is considerable. We have incorporated into our everyday discourse such concepts as repression, sublimation, inhibition, and subconscious, as well as other quasi-psychoanalytic terms such as introvert, extrovert, and neuroses. The work of Freud, Jung, Adler, and others has had a major impact on the discipline of psychology.

In the middle of the 1960s a new school of psychology arose both in reaction to behaviorism and to psychoanalysis. Although called by various names at various times in its development, humanistic or third-force psychology is now a widely used term, embracing a range of ideas and theories.[4] The humanistic psychologist has reacted

---

[4] Phenomenology, personalism, and existential psychology are some of the psychologies in this category. Some gestaltists share many ideas in common with humanistic psychology.

to the dehumanization that inevitably seems to take place as investigations become ever more empirical and objective and as they concentrate on minute tangible elements of behavior. Superscientific psychology has avoided, it is claimed, the very things that are most human: love, courage, happiness, faith, and all the other emotions that cannot be observed behaviorally. Research methodology, statistics, and other irrelevant treatment of human behavior does little or nothing to help the individual understand himself or herself. New or modified principles and methodologies are needed. Humanistic psychology is based on the following principles:

1. Emphasis should on the self.
2. Human beings are self-directing or self-actualizing.
3. Awareness is the most basic psychological process.
4. Psychology should direct itself to the legitimate needs of people (the problems of ego identity, self-fulfillment, prevention of violence) rather than squandering resources on problems of investigation that are most notable for their closeness to natural science methodology.
5. Psychology should be based on twentieth-century assumptions stemming from insights of physicists and philosophers rather than the nineteenth-century assumptions on which behaviorism has been based.
6. Humanistic psychology makes no pretense of being value free.
7. The ends of psychological research should be clearly thought out and should be to help enlarge individual freedom rather than help someone gain advantage and power over others.

The emergence of humanistic psychology has coincided with the upswing of interest in psychology we have already noted.

Although new schools of psychology (or economics or history) tend to emerge in reaction to existing schools and to be challenged later by another new school, supporters of a variety of schools of thought will coexist at any given time is well that they should because this competition in the marketplace of free ic is one of the best means of advancin knowledge.

The Structure of Psychol

The concepts that guide the inquir psychology have, for the most part, already been mentioned in the examination of the subdivisions and schools of psychology. Among the most important concepts and concept clusters of psychology, including those mentioned, are:

Perception, sensation, attention

Feelings and emotions

Learning, association, stimulus-response, conditioning (classical and operant)

Intelligence, cognition, psychomotor skills

Motivation, drive

Growth and development

Self, personality

Adjustment, avoidance behavior, inhibitions, defense mechanisms

Psychoses, neuroses, phobias

These and other psychological concepts are important for the teacher in the classroom, but they have not typically been a part of the formal curriculum. Recently, however, programs of study and textbooks have recognized the importance of self-understanding and included material relating to these concepts at various levels of the elementary school. Some of the concepts are being taught regardless of the name attached to them. They may be a part of the reading program, of social studies, of health, or of natural science.

As an investigator, the social scientist constantly asks questions relating to what is going on and why. The kinds of analytical questions asked by psychologists include the following:

What specific motives explain individual's behaviors? Are some motives stronger than others?

What induces fear in children? Can they be taught to overcome avoidance behavior? How?

What reactions do youngsters have to violence in films or on television? Does continual exposure make them callous to violent or potentially violent experiences in their own lives?

What physiological correlates are there of various emotions? Are emotions specific or nonspecific? Can specific emotions be induced artificially? How?

To answer these questions involves the consideration of other questions: What evidence is needed to answer the questions? How shall the evidence be treated? What conclusions shall be drawn from it?

The evidence-inference process of psychology, its distinctive mode of inquiry, relies heavily on controlled experiments, both of animals and humans. In laboratory or other controlled situations, hypotheses are tested that may involve pretests and posttests, control groups, and experimental groups. The literature of psychology is replete with monographs on experimental psychology: identification of the problem or statement of the hypothesis, the subjects used in the research (what data are needed), research design (how the data are to be treated), the results of the experiment, discussion of the research, and conclusions (what inferences are drawn from the data as treated). Psychological investigation may also conclude observations of subjects in natural habitat, but this mode of inquiry is considered less reliable by behaviorists and some gestaltists. Humanist psychologists lean more toward case histories, modes of inquiry that may be used by psychologists regardless of school. Surveys may sometimes be used by psycholo-gists to determine norms for such things as attitudes, motivations, fears, and the like, but the questionable validity of such surveys restricts their use. Social psychologists will use such research techniques, however, as a means of understanding group behavior, as well as evidence gathered from observation in the field.

Psychological inquiry may be a touchy matter when used in the classroom. Humane, simple experiments with white rats or hamsters may be conducted successfully by children on such topics as conditioning. Inquiry episodes on "safe" topics such as perception or reaction time may also be carried out on human subjects. But many school districts have policies restricting investigations into attitudes, emotions, personality, and the very concepts that are most crucial from a humanistic frame of reference. Nonetheless, even relatively small children can learn aspects of the modes of inquiry of the psychologist.

Psychology and the Core Concepts of Social Science

Because of its concern with individual behavior, psychology will undoubtedly relate to fewer of the integrating concepts of social science than do the other behavioral sciences or the policy sciences. Nevertheless, psychology does add to the comprehension of a number of these concepts and, in turn, these concepts can broaden one's understanding of psychology.

Interaction is probably the core concept most closely related to psychology and social psychology. An individual's interaction with other individuals is guided by motivations, self-concepts, abilities, and it is moderated by avoidance behavior, inhibitions, and adaptive behavior. *Conflict*, both internal and external, and its management through adjustment or psychoses or neuroses, is another important core concept related to psychology. *Habitat* influences self-concept, which in turn may shape abilities. *Technology* in its advanced form brings with it serious problems of adjustment as the individual's sense of personal accomplishment is far removed from finished technological products. Behaviorist psychologists may believe that the individual's act of *choosing* is circumscribed by years of conditioning, but humanistic psychologists disagree and elevate individual choice to an important position. Finally, *multiple causation* figures as prominently in understanding individual behavior as it does in understanding group behavior; the psychologist must look for *all* the factors that explain phenomena.

Psychology and the Elementary and Secondary Curriculum

At present the elective twelfth-grade psychology course has been expanding rapidly, more than any other single course in the social studies in high school.[5] The American Psychological Association (APA) has formed the Clearinghouse on Precollege Psychology and Behavioral Science in response to the great interest in psychology not only at the secondary level but at the elementary level as well. The increase in high school psychology courses has resulted in conferences and summer institutes on the subject throughout the nation and the formation of a number of state and regional associations. With National Science Foundation assistance the APA has sponsored the development of a number of modules for inclusion in psychology or behavioral science courses.

Two innovative projects for the elementary school make extensive use of psychological concepts and materials and maximum involvement of students. These are the Human Sciences Project of the Biological Sciences Curriculum Project and the Exploring Childhood and Exploring Human Nature units of the Educational Development Corporation. The former consists of the modules Humanself, Developing, and Learning, each of which is composed of a number of self-directing activities that can be carried out in almost any sequence. The modules are designed for sixth, seventh, and eighth graders.

Two publishers have elementary textbook series that have incorporated considerable behavioral science content, unlike those of previous years where the emphasis was on more traditional social science content. The Harcourt Brace Concepts and Values series uses psychology in a number of its text and media materials, but the psychological content is most prominent in *Sources of Identity,* for seventh or eighth graders. The Allyn and Bacon series Concepts and Values, originally developed by the Educational Research Council, is multidisciplinary, including some psychology, although not as prominently as the Concepts and Values series.

Although psychology does not enjoy as large a share of the social studies curriculum as the other social sciences, psychological content in the social studies is growing as a part of a general behavioral science movement. Even though the growth is at the expense of history and the more traditional foundations of social studies, it is easy to understand the reason for the development. What is more important than understanding the most interesting person in the world—ourselves?

---

[5] The Gross study mentioned several times previously reveals that enrollments in psychology courses have increased 321 percent between 1961 and 1973.

Sociology and the Social Studies

As important as an understanding of individual behavior is to each of us, human beings are essentially *social* creatures. True isolates, hermits in caves or religious fanatics who seek salvation through solitary meditation, are exceedingly rare. Throughout the history of humankind, people have lived in groups — families, tribes, villages, clans, nations — and many of humanity's richest experiences and most difficult problems are the result of group interaction. Both sociology and anthropology investigate the group life of human beings but in different ways.

Sociology appeared to reach the height of its popularity in the mid-1960s and early 1970s, at least on the college campus. During this period of intense demands for reform of social institutions, the study of society and its institutions seemed to be a logical means of beginning the process of overhaul. "Sunday Supplement Sociology," as found in newspapers and popular journals has, since the 1920s when it first began to appear, found a ready and large audience. Pop sociology, like pop psychology, is interesting and enlightening, although not always accurate. The number of paperback book titles dealing with popular sociology has been considerable the last several decades.

The Nature of Sociology

Sociology is the newest of the social (or behavioral) sciences, going back only a little more than 100 years by that name. Of course, scholars and lay people alike have observed group behavior, speculated about it, and written on it for hundreds of years. The nature and definition of sociology has changed over a century and a quarter, but the term has a generally agreed on definition today. There are a number of acceptable contemporary definitions, all very close to one another.

"The systematic study of the consequences of group living."

"The realm we will explore is that of men's relationships — the social structures that we build . . . the way they are formed, sustained, and change."[6]

"The study of group life and social relationships."[7]

"The scientific study of the social relations men develop in their interaction with one another."[8]

"Sociology involves the collective experiences of individuals. It attempts to describe and understand persons' social relationships with each other. Sociologists also study the social structures and social processes of groups and communities."[9]

"The empirical scientific study of the structure and process of systems of interaction among humans ('social actors,' as many sociologists tend now to call them)."[10]

Known first as social physics and then by the hybrid term sociology (from the Latin socius for companion and the Greek logos for study of), the field

---

[6] Everett K. Wilson, *Sociology: Rules, Roles, and Relationships*, Homewood, Ill., The Dorsey Press, 1971.
[7] George Simpson, *Man in Society: Preface to Sociology and the Social Sciences*, Garden City, N.Y., Doubleday and Co., 1955, p. 34.
[8] *California State Framework for the Social Studies*, Sacramento, California State Department of Education, 1962, p. 64.
[9] Robert S. Browne, et al., *The Social Scene, a Contemporary View of the Social Sciences*, Cambridge, Mass., Winthrop Publishers, Inc., 1972, p. 114.
[10] E. Merle Adams, Jr., "New Viewpoints in Sociology" in *New Viewpoints in the Social Sciences*, Roy A. Price (ed.), 28th Yearbook of the National Council for the Social Studies, 1958, p. 97.

emerged in the mid-nineteenth century through the work of the French social philospher, August Comte. He saw it as the "queen of the sciences" and the logical highest evolutionary stage in philosophy. Taken up and popularized by the Englishman, Herbert Spencer, it became almost synonymous with social Darwinism and social engineering. It took the work of the Frenchman, Emile Durkheim, to develop a scientific methodology for sociology that made it a theoretical empirical science. Polish, Italian, and German sociologists added to the principles and concepts, but so too have the many eminent American sociologists.

Contemporary sociologists are no longer concerned with identifying the building blocks of social relations, like the structuralist psychologists and the analytical chemists. They are more concerned with trying to understand the basic units of social life: groups, the family, the school, the neighborhood, the urban community. They are interested in what holds a group together and what is the source of intergroup antagonisms, that is to say, in what elements provide for social stability and which ones cause social change. Behavioral scientists observe that social behavior is patterned, not random and accidental. What explains the patterning? To attack the vast problem of understanding human behavior and the consequences of group living, sociologists develop specialties.

Subdivisions of Sociology

It is exceedingly difficult to break down sociology into its component parts in any accurate or comprehensive manner. Not only has it been a growing field of research, reflecting the great interest in the discipline, but new specialties and combinations develop constantly. The National Science Foundation recognizes the following specialties in sociology:

Sociocultural theory
Methodology
Demography and population
Rural-urban sociology
Social change and development
Social organization, structure, and institutions
   Bureaucracy
   Educational
   Familial
   Industrial
   Intergroup
   Medical
   Occupational
   Political
   Religious
   Stratification
Social problems, social disorganization
Social psychology

Notice how one of the specialties alone—social organizations and institutions—has 10 specialties within it! As comprehensive as the NSF list is it does not include all the *44* areas of specialized training in sociology offered by American and Canadian universities that are recognized by the American Sociological Association. Among these are the sociology of small groups, political sociology, the sociology of age, the sociology of knowledge, the sociology of world conflicts, and military sociology. To these might be added other subdivisions of sociology such as collective behavior, criminology, and the sociology of masculinity and femininity. One of the newest specialities is exosociology, the sociology of extraterrestrial life and of future space colonies.

A specialty does not signify a subdivision of a discipline; however, the National Science Foundation list includes two specialties that are woven throughout all the branches of sociology—sociocultural theory and methodology. Sociocultural theory as a specialty of sociology attempts to develop the theoretical bases that explain various aspects of group behavior or of social structures and/or processes. In large measure, this specialty of sociology works on the second of the broad social science questions we've identified, that is, "why do things behave as they do?" Theories are developed about population growth and distribution, about living in urban complexes, and about the changing family, among many things. The development of improved statistical methods and, particularly, computers and computer programs, has helped refine the research methodology of sociologists. With them, large amounts of data can be easily analyzed so that relationships among variables can be made more precise and can be tested for significance, a means of verifying whether the compared results are genuine or a matter of chance coming together. The nature of most of these specialties is self-evident from the categorical label or at least can be approximated from the name. A few of them would require explanations far beyond the scope of this book. Some clarification is in order, however. Demography is sometimes considered a subdivision of sociology and sometimes functions as a discipline unto itself. In either case, the demographer attempts to study such things as birth rates and death rates, the distribution of the population by age groups, fertility rates by ethnicity, social class, and other factors, and how any or all of these change over time as well as how one nation compares with another.

Rural sociology and urban sociology may actually be considered two different but related branches of the discipline, with the latter being more dominant nationwide as the nation's population has become concentrated in vast urban-suburban-intraurban complexes or megalopolises. Theories of how urban communities develop (of concern to urban geog-

raphers, as well), the impact or urban phenomena on social life, and the nature of the urban life-style are all part of this subdivision.

The study of the structure of society includes, on one hand, the study of social institutions in their many varieties—the economic, political, educational, religious, and familial institutions—all of which are part of the *overt* structure of society. On the other hand, there is a *covert* structure of society, exemplified by the relations and interaction of racial and ethnic groups and by patterns of social stratification. There are other elements in the society as well.

Modern society is filled with all kinds of organizations. No one can be free of their influence, no matter how much they would like to do so. Complex organizations such as bureaucracies and the bureaucratic red tape that go with them are not confined to governments. The complex organizations necessary to manage a growing population with expanding demands seems to increase at an even more rapid pace than the population and its demands.

There are many manifestations of the imperfect functioning of the social structure: suicide, emotional illness, poverty, crime, intergroup conflict, public corruption, environmental pollution, and war. All of these and more are studied under a variety of headings indicative of the frame of reference of the behavioral scientist: social problems, social pathology, social disorganization, deviant behavior. The results of studies of social problems are favorite sources of information for pop sociology.

The Sociological Perspective

Sociology was originally as much or more social philosophy as it was a social science, and many of its early scholars saw it as the means of providing guidelines for the improvement of human society. At the end of the nineteenth century, the Social Darwinist school of sociology was prominent in America, reflecting a society that supported the ideas of competition and the survival of the fittest. It was replaced by a school that emphasized the empirical process of identification and collection of social facts and their statistical analysis.

In the twentieth century, one approach to sociology has stressed that society exists in a state of dynamic equilibrium in which the various parts worked together and functioned to maintain the stability of the society. Humans are social actors whose conduct toward others is motivated to optimize gratification and minimize deprivations.

In the last third of the twentieth century the field of sociology is divided over the role of values in the science. On the one hand are the strict behaviorists who take the position that the task of the sociologists is to study society in the most objective fashion possible. It is the scholar's task to study society as it *is* rather than what any individual or group thinks it *ought* to be, even if this means that the investigator may get into socially controversial or unpopular topics. The sociologist must be a neutral observer and reporter; if he or she gets involved in the social unit or social aggregate being studied, objectivity is lost and the study becomes of questionable worth.

Nonsense, say an opposing group of sociologists. (Elsewhere in the behavioral sciences the counterparts of this group of activist sociologists are the third-force or humanist psychologists.) Values, norms, and beliefs guide human behavior and help shape the social structure. If sociologists act on their understandings and convictions, they are as much a part of the social evils they have investigated as those who perpetuate violence, contribute to the roots of poverty, are the causative

agents of crime, and so on. Society can never be improved if those who are most knowledgeable about social ills take a hands-off position when it comes to social amelioration.

For some, the sociological perspective is a means of maximizing knowledge about the consequences of group life through the most painstaking and most objective methods of inquiry. For others, it is using our knowledge of social structures and social processes to the end of improving the human condition.

The Structure of Sociology

The theoretical structure of sociology below (Figure 8.1) indicates a number of the important concepts of sociology with generalizations that provide us a framework for the analysis of the patterned social behavior of society. The framework lists a number of the most important concepts of sociology: organizations, groups, social system, social aggregates, social action, and role. Many sociologists believe role (and role behavior) is the central concept of sociology. To this list can be added an enormous number of concepts, only a few of which need be identified here. Some have already been noted in the subdivisions and specialties of sociology (e.g., institutions, social stratification, social change).

Groups are of two kinds, *primary groups* and *secondary groups;* the former are intimate, face to face, enduring groups such as families, old-fashioned neighborhoods, and small tribes, while the latter are voluntary associations brought together by special interests such as those found in clubs, political parties, labor unions, and the like. *Significant others* or *reference* groups are the models for our behavior particularly as we are growing up. Mothers, fathers, older siblings, and teachers are important significant others for young children, but at ad-

1. Human societies exhibit patterned social behavior that can be described and explained.
2. Much of the human behavior is guided by shared values that people voluntarily follow.
3. Also, much human behavior is guided by a set of norms and beliefs that people follow under the threat of punishment or promise of reward.
4. One important part of the social system is organizations. People work together in organizations to achieve specific goals.
5. Another important part of the social system is groups. People come together informally—some to strengthen their common values, some to strengthen their emotional identification.
6. Organizations and groups have many positions that people fill. Positions are more formal in organizations than in groups.
7. The unique way a person fills a position is his role. People play roles differently depending on other people's expectations and on their own attitudes, personalities, and life experiences.
8. Another important part of the social system is social aggregates. Social aggregates consist of people who have many socially significant characteristics in common and therefore have the possibility of developing organizations for social action.
9. Two types of forces tend to shape organizations and social aggregates. Some forces lead to stability and regularity, such as recognition of complementarity, isolation of one organization from another, compromise, and submission. Other forces lead to tension and strain, such as uneven distribution of values and power that may result in human rights revolutions.
10. Values, norms, beliefs, organizations, groups, positions, roles, and social aggregates influence human behavior and the makeup of the social system resulting in support or modification.

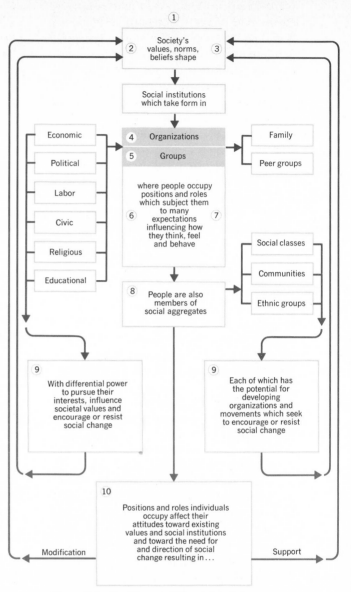

Figure 8.1   Fundamental ideas of sociology. (From *Our Working World: Cities at Work*, Resource Unit, by Lawrence Senesh. © 1966, 1967, Science Research Associates, Inc. Reprinted by permission of the publisher.)

olescence attention turns to members of the peer group and to media entertainers, or athletic heroes. Successful business people, a particular social class, scholars, writers, or other social aggregates may be reference groups for young and old alike. *Definition of the situation* refers to the social actor's conception of the social action possible in any situation. Through social conditioning people learn to define situations calling for particular patterns of behavior. Children soon learn the definition of the situation which permit some kinds of behavior and discourage others. What is rewarded in one situation is punished in another. So, too, do people learn to define the situation in church, at a ball game, at a wedding, on Halloween, on Easter or Passover, and so on. If a person is unable to define the situation, due to lack of knowledge or experience, the person is very uneasy and must either avoid it or proceed on a basis of trial and error.

Although there is a core of sociological concepts common to all sociologists, different sociologists develop or use a congeries of concepts unique to them, their specialty, their school, and their frame of reference.

The inquiry of sociologists is guided by sociological concepts framed in such questions as the following:

What kinds of groups (organizations, associations, etc.) tend to form in a society?

How is society a social and cultural system? (Or how is urban society a cultural system?)

How do the different groups in society use their leisure time? Is there more difference or more similarity when comparing sociceconomic groups, ethnic groups, and the like?

What are the features of a societal system?

What holds groups together? What pushes them apart?

How are social roles learned?

How does a society prepare or train people to become functioning members of society? What agents or agencies assist in this process?

Sociologists use many different modes of inquiry although the survey is perhaps most typical of the discipline. A survey is the orderly and comprehensive gathering of social facts about a social aggregate and some phase of its operation. Among the classic sociological surveys have been those of the American soldier, white collar crime, sexual behavior, and race relations. The sociologist also uses case studies, whether of professional thieves, gangs, a community power structure, or families. Whereas a survey is extensive and comprehensive, a case study is intensive, confining itself to a single individual, group, community, or even a segment of a community. The sociologist will use statistical means of treating the data gathered from a survey as appropriate.

Some surveys and some case studies are carried out by participant observation in which the researcher is "inside" rather than "outside" the social action. This is the anthropological mode of inquiry and will be examined in due course. The sociologist must, of course, consider the evidence needed to answer the questions, as well as how it is to be treated, and what inferences are to be drawn from it.

Some sociological topics are as controversial for the elementary teacher as are some psychological topics, if used in the classroom. Children can, of course, gather some evidence about group behavior on the schoolground, about families, or about some groups within the community. They can carry out studies by observation, interview, or questionnaire, but some kinds of interview questions may be regarded as violating the privacy of subjects and may be unwise for use for school inquiry exercises.

The fundamental ideas of sociology in Figure 8.1 utilize some of the important concepts of the discipline to analyze the structure of society and how the elements of the structure interrelate to provide support or modification for the society. So, too, can the core concepts of social science be used from a sociological frame of reference to analyze the society. Or the core concepts can be used to analyze one of the elements of the social system—a formal organization such as a labor union, a community or neighborhood, the socioeconomic system, or the family.

Families are one of the most important agents of the *culture,* providing the means by which the societies have continuity through the biological continuation of the society, and they are probably the prime unit for transmitting the culture, the learned way of behavior distinctive of the culture. The family exists in a *habitat,* partly physical in the shelter, the influencing climatic and topographic elements, partly biotic in the flora and fauna that surround the family, and largely cultural in terms of the customs, rituals, values, and so on. Human beings are constantly faced with making *choices* in all kinds of circumstances, even within the protected habitat of the family. Many of these are hardly "choices" at all because cultural behavior may be conditioned by the definition of the situation and by custom. The system of values of a culture helps shape the particular kind of family found in that society, and the pattern of choices available to individuals, operating inside and outside the family unit. One of the goals of the study of sociology can be to help individuals understand the constraints and sanctions of a culture, thus freeing the individual from artificial and unreasonable limitations on behavior and widening the range of choice open to them.

The value system manifests itself in the highly organized ways in which members of a society work toward a specific goal centered around one of the basic needs of humankind. Among these basic needs are those providing for the biological maintenance of the species—the family; transmitting the culture—education; producing, distributing, and consuming goods and services—the economy; finding meaning and motivation in the universe and expressing spiritual impulses—religion; and providing the organizational means by which binding decisions are made among the groups in society—political life. These are the *institutions* of society: the family, the institution of education, the economic institution, the institution of religion, and the political institution. Each of these institutions forms an important unit of sociological study. The organizations that develop around institutions and the groups that operate informally or covertly in society are in *interaction* with one another. Family members interact with one another, and the family (individual members and the family unit) interacts with other families and with other organizations and groups. This social process may involve cooperation, families working harmoniously toward agreed-on goals; competition, groups striving to achieve goals before others reach them; or accommodation, in which the families or other kinds of groups have worked out arrangements for separate spheres of action. Not infrequently the social pattern of interaction leads to *conflict,* in which the disagreement between families or groups over ends and means becomes personal; striving is directed not at achieving the goal but at preventing the other group from achieving it. Conflict, however, cannot go on indefinitely. Some means of managing the conflict is ultimately developed. A feud between families may end when the members agree to forget the past and to work together harmoniously or it may cease when one family eliminates or absorbs the other.

In the traditional family, the father represents *power*. His absolute authority may be resented, but it is not often questioned. In some families, however, the father is a figurehead with actual power being wielded by the mother. In modern families power is more democratically distributed among all members. At one time the family was directly involved in converting productive *resources* into goods and services and deciding how resources were to be *allocated.* Today, the family's role is that of a consumer more than anything else.

The family has been strongly affected by *social change,* particularly as manifested in *technology and industrialism.* Modern technology has reduced much of the drudgery of feeding and caring for a family and even reduced the size of the family! Some people have theorized that the traditional family is no longer a viable social group. Whether this is true or not, the family today is different in many respects than it was a half century or more ago. No single cause accounts for the differences; we must look to *multiple causation* for an explanation.

Sociology and the Elementary and Secondary Curriculum

In the social studies program that was almost universal in the United States for most of the first two-thirds of the twentieth century, sociological content was present throughout it but only to a minor extent. The study of families, neighborhoods, and communities in primary grades was interdisciplinary but certainly included sociology. Many textbooks and curriculum guides provided some social history and cultural geography in the expanding study of the North American continent in the middle and upper elementary grades and also in the Old World backgrounds of junior high school. This was true also of world geography or world history and of U.S. history in the high school years. The capstone course for seniors, Problems of Democracy, was the most conspicuous part of the curriculum drawing upon sociological knowledge.

The tremendous variety of social studies programs that exist today across the land makes it difficult to generalize about the status of sociology in the curriculum. The other behavioral sciences have increased their prominence in the social studies. The curriculum revolution of the 1960s, as manifested in the social studies, was typified by emphasis on concepts, inquiry, and the structure of the disciplines. The Problems of Democracy course for high school seniors declined greatly during this period, its place being taken by a variety of discrete courses, including sociology, as senior electives.[11] Problem solving, supposedly the heart of the P.O.D. course, had had a prominent place in the entire curriculum until the beginning of the era of the New Social Studies when the modes of inquiry of the separate disciplines came into vogue. The move toward separate disciplines that was prominent during the 1960s was most prominent at the secondary level. During this period sociology had relatively little

[11] The Problems of Democracy or Senior Problems course had the second largest percentage decline in enrollments between 1961 and 1973, 22 percent. During the same period sociology showed the second greatest increase, 175 percent! The decline is greater than it appears because the period 1961–1973 was one in which secondary enrollments increased 59 percent. Richard E. Gross, "The Status of Social Studies in the Public Schools of the United States: Facts and Impressions of a National Survey," unpublished document, 1976.

The Behavioral Sciences: Psychology, Sociology, and Anthropology   157

impact on elementary social studies as a separate subject. The federally funded Sociological Resources for Social Studies developed a number of learning episodes for inclusion either in a separate high school sociology course or individually in almost any high school social studies course. No other national social studies project is centered on sociology except for the University of Michigan Elementary School Science Education Program for the upper elementary grades, which uses social psychology as its prime subject area. Many of the others do include sociology content, even where their central focus is one of the other disciplines. Among these are *Our Working World,* for grades 4 to 6; the Boston Children's Museum MATCH project (Materials and Activities for Teachers and Children) for grades 1 to 6; the Educational Research Council of America's *Concepts and Inquiry* project for kindergarten through grade 9; the Harvard University Public Issues Social Studies Project for grades 7 to 12; the kindergarden-to-grade 12 University of Minnesota Project Social Studies; the Taba Social Studies Curriculum Project; and the Utah State University Social Studies Project on Analysis of Public Issues. Many of these projects have been taken over by publishing houses.

What the future holds for sociology in the elementary curriculum is not clear. The behavioral sciences have challenged the supremacy of the classic disciplines in the curriculum, and many people—students, teachers, and the lay public—see the value in increasing our understanding of human behavior. Thus sociological content, as a part of the behavioral sciences, is important to elementary social studies, especially in interdisciplinary or multidisciplinary programs. The emphasis on basic skills in the primary grades leaves little room for social studies, however, with or without sociol-

ogy. Furthermore, the back-to-basics movement of the mid- and late 1970s stresses history, geography, and civics, and to the extent that the movement gains momentum, sociology's contribution to the curriculum may be limited.

Anthropology, Social Science, and the Social Studies

Anthropology is a subject nearly all students have experienced in school without calling it by name. Very often American school children will study a Japanese or an African family in the second grade, American Indians in the third or fourth grade, or neighbors in Latin America in the fifth or sixth grade, prehistoric peoples in the seventh or ninth grade, and so on. Such depth studies have an anthropological base and use an anthropological approach.

Of the three behavioral sciences anthropology has probably had the greatest involvement in the social studies at all levels in recent decades. An understanding of anthropology and its contributions is essential for the teacher of social studies for our times.

Anthropology—Definitions and Nature

Even more than history, anthropology is the broadest of the social sciences because it studies humankind as a whole. Literally, the study of man, anthropology is defined most frequently as the science of man and his works. Further definitions may clarify these words.

"Anthropology is the study of our favorite subject: ourselves."[12]

---

[12] Clara K. Nicholson, *Anthropology and Education,* Columbus, Ohio, Charles E. Merrill, 1968, p. 1.

"American anthropologists consider that their subject properly encompasses the biologic, psychologic, social, and cultural aspects of man. Nothing human is foreign to them. They have embraced enthusiastically and immodestly the literal meaning of the word anthropology. . . . Not satisfied with the *science* of man, they honor many in their profession who are avowed humanists."[13]

"All social sciences are seeking the secrets of the "unconscious" structuring of human life. Some are like grammarians, some are like phonologists, some are like transformationalists (to maintain the metaphor); but the anthropologist is a linguist. He must take all these topics into consideration; he is interested in the ways that they influence one another, and in the totality of human life, society, and culture."[14]

Anthropology thus not only touches on all the other social sciences, but it merges into the natural sciences, both life science and physical science, much as does geography. According to Paul J. Bohannon, it "is less a subject than a holding company."[15] Anthropology includes the history of a historyless people, the economics of underdeveloped nations, the language structures of nonliterate peoples, the means of social control of societies without formal governments, the art and music of peoples without "higher culture."

Like most other fields of knowledge, anthropology is best understood from what the anthropologist does. He or she attempts to find answers to questions about the biocultural nature of Homo sapiens. Anthropologists conduct field studies of both preliterate and contemporary peoples, their cultures, and the components of their cultures—such as culture traits, kinship systems, and customs—that

contribute to a holistic understanding of the people.

Although we can trace the ancient beginnings of anthropology to the investigations and speculations of Aristotle in the fourth century B.C.E.[16], interest in the field was whetted first by the scholarly observations of thirteenth- and fourteenth-century travelers, and then particularly by the explorations of the fifteenth through eighteenth centuries. The discovery of exotic peoples in the New World and the Pacific Ocean Area, for example, resulted in attempts to record their customs and their social organization in a more systematic fashion than had been done previously. Modern scientific anthropology stems from the mid-nineteenth century, however, with new theories and new methodologies. Natural history studies of Darwin and others provided a basis for a whole new scholarly discipline, but they also caused a revolution in people's thinking about themselves and their place in the universe.

In the early twentieth century, anthropology shared the same impetus toward the scientific method as the other behavioral sciences, notably in the use and refinement of fieldwork among the populations studied. Before this time, anthropologists functioned mostly as outsiders visiting and observing their sub-

[13] Cora DuBois, "Anthropology: Its Present Interests" in *The Behavioral Sciences Today*, Bernard Berelson (ed.), New York, Basic Books, 1963.
[14] Paul Bohannon, *Anthropology*, Publication #106 of the Social Science Education Consortium, Boulder, Col., The Consortium, 1966, p. 1.
[15] Ibid.
[16] B.C.E. stands for Before the Common Era. There are many calendars. America's Bicentennial was in the year 7485 according to the Byzantine calendar, 5737 according to the Hebrew calendar, 4775 according to the Chinese calendar, 2729 by the Roman calendar, 2636 on the Japanese calendar, and 1354 according to the Muslin calendar. We recognize the necessity of a single system of time notation, but it should not be expressed in ethnocentric terms such as B.C., Before Christ, or A.D., anno Domini, the Year of Our Lord.

The Behavioral Sciences: Psychology, Sociology, and Anthropology   159

jects for brief periods. In fieldwork, the anthropologist attempts to study a group of people from *within*, by entering directly into all phases of their life for years on end. Fieldwork has remained the basic methological approach of anthropologists ever since.

In a sense, an anthropologist is a detective in that (s)he is trying to solve certain mysteries of biocultural man and provide explanations about human behavior. But anthropologists do a great amount of practical work as well. For example, many people have had the experience of feeling cramped and uncomfortable after sitting in old theater or auditorium seats. They can blame some anthropologists who took anthropometric measures 30 or more years ago when Americans were a little bit slimmer in the hips than they are now. (They can also blame the theater owners for not replacing the seats with ones better fitted to contemporary anatomy.) Anthropologists worked for the military services in World War II designing equipment such as military uniform sizes, aircraft seats, and the like. The armed services have had to update such items because the recruits today average a couple of inches taller and 20 to 30 pounds heavier than their counterparts 35 years ago. Anthropologists also rendered valuable service during and after World War II providing information about the different islands in the Pacific and their inhabitants and how to work with the Japanese people.

As a public investigator the anthropologist looks for clues that adds to our understanding of a tribe or a society or a nation as a *whole*. The specific cultural practices examined by the anthropologist function and are best understood as they contribute to the smooth working of the culture as a whole. The very breadth of anthropology necessitates its division into manageable subdivisons.

The Branches of Anthropology

The two main branches of this behavioral science are physical anthropology and cultural or social anthropology, and these can be broken down into further subdivisions.

Physical anthropology studies the evolutionary development of the genus Homo from its earliest origins to the present. It is related to the natural sciences because of its study of the important aspects of the biological nature of humans. Physical anthropology includes the study of contemporary "breeds" or "races" of man and of the distinguishing features of these breeds. Anthropologists have much to offer in eradicating myths about races. The more that anthropologists have tried to come up with neat classification systems of races—white, yellow, and black—the more any such classification scheme breaks down, whether of 3 races or of 12. Thus, many anthropologists today say that the distinguishing physical features of so-called races is not as important as what is inside a person's head—culture. Related to physical anthropology are such fields as ethology, the study of animal behavior, and primatology, the study of primate development and behavior. Much can be learned from Homo sapiens' closest animal relatives.

Cultural anthropology is the systematic study of the patterned behavior of human beings, particularly the culture traits (i.e., traditions and customs) and the norms of behavior. Although the conventional view of the anthropologist is of the field worker observing so-called primitive peoples in their native habitat, cultural anthropologists bring their expertise to the study of contemporary societies. Sociolinguistics has made important contributions to language in general, and language is probably the most important "invention" of man and certainly his most distinguishing characteristic. Sociolinguistics helps to decipher heretofore unknown languages for the anthropologist in the field, and it is used increasingly to understand problems of language learning of multilingual populations.

Archeology and ethnology are two fields that are of sufficient importance as to be considered by many as disciplines in themselves, despite the closeness of their relationship to anthropology. Ethnology, sometimes called ethnography, is the contemporary study of a particular group of people, a tribe, or major ethnic group. Archeology is the study of ancient and extinct peoples, the reconstruction of peoples in other settings, done largely through digging for the artifacts that survive. An archeologist must have knowledge both of anthropology and of history and contributes to both disciplines.

A pluralistic society like that of the United States provides a rich resource for ethnomusicology, the study of the distinctive music of ethnic groups, and ethnic folklore, the mythologies and other tales handed down from generation to generation of a people. As interest in folk music has increased and as Americans have taken increasing pride in their cultural heritage — Native American, African, Hispanic, Asian, or European — these two subdivisions of anthropology have become more important. Their potential contributions to the elementary social studies program is considerable, the more so as they can provide the resources for the integration of social studies, reading, music, art, literature, speech communication, and the like.

The Anthropological Perspective

One of the most important tasks of the social studies in the contemporary world is multicultural understanding. The value of anthropology in accomplishing this task is second to no other discipline. As it has developed as a discipline over the span of more than a century, anthropology has continually broadened man's view of himself.

The study of anthropology is directed toward two or three goals above all others. The primary goal is to gain an anthropological view, that is, getting inside the skull of peoples who have cultural heritages and different cultural perspectives. No self-respecting anthropologist can maintain notions of racial, ethnic, or cultural superiority or inferiority. Anthropologists themselves reject ethnocentrism[17] and expect the study of their discipline to eradicate ideas examining the world only from one's own ethnic or cultural perspective. Yet ethnocentrism had been a common feature of humans' world view for millenia. It is interesting to note the number of preliterate tribes whose name means in their language human beings, the people, or synonym — the Nez Perce or the Yahi, for example. Even though the well-trained anthropologist may eschew ethnocentrism, he or she may have preferences (for his or her own culture; the one in which he was brought up), but he or she ideally will not let this cloud the ability to view another culture objectively from the anthropological perspective and to view life from the frame of reference of that culture.

Another major goal of anthropological study is the attainment of the concept of cultural relativism. Cultural traits and institutions help survival in a specific physical and cultural environment, but what has survival value and what is right and proper varies from culture to cul-

---

[17] Ethnocentrism is one of the important concepts in anthropology. A good example of it is the use of the Christian calendar in a world that is mostly non-Christian. See page 159 for elaboration.

ture. There are few if any overall cultural practices that are universally followed among *all* peoples of the world. Although it may seem "natural" for Americans to eat certain types of foods at certain times, it is equally "natural" for Spaniards to eat different foods at different times. Such differences may be viewed as quaint by the layperson, but not by the student of anthropology. Other types of cultural practices, such as the matter of polygyny or concubines or of degrees of nudity, are taken seriously by anthropologically unsophisticated individuals in all cultures and may be matters of deep moral concern. But the student of anthropology must view them relatively. There are few absolutes of right and wrong in the world. Cultural relativism means that one suspends judgments of cultural practices in one culture based on the standards of another culture. The merits of cultural practices and cultural traits are judged within the context of the culture itself.

Studies of school textbooks used in a number of nations have found them to be heavily nationalistic, quite the opposite of cultural relativism. Once schools became state responsibilities they became instruments of developing patriotism and nationalist spirit. First history and then civics were the principal means of developing nationalism in impressionable young minds, but no subjects were free of it. Two world wars in the twentieth century stand as evidence of what extremes of nationalism can do. If schools can help develop nationalism, it is argued, they can also help develop international understanding. Progress has been made in this direction, to the delight of anthropologists and others, but there is a limit to how far state-supported schools can be expected to go in developing social studies programs and textbooks free of nationalism. A neat balance between enlightened nationalism and cultural relativism free of ethnocentrism may be desirable but difficult to obtain.

A third goal of anthropology is the attainment of a holistic view. Many cultural practices make little sense when studied as isolated phenomena. They are, along with institutions and beliefs, functionally linked to one another into a more-or-less integrated whole. Child-rearing practices or types of formal education need to be studied and understood in the context of the society as a whole. The concepts of holism and of cultural relativism reinforce each other and, in their reinforcement, add to the anthropological perspective.

The anthropological perspective of today has gone through a number of phases in trying to provide a holistic view of society and culture. At first anthropologists thought that all human cultures progressed through logical and orderly stages: hunter, nomad, farmer, artisan, manufacturer. One culture or civilization builds on another as they all evolve toward the "highest" state. An advanced technological culture is obviously "higher" in evolutionary development than a "primitive" nomadic culture.

Opposition developed to this, the cultural evolution school, however. Some American anthropologists argued that cultures do not evolve neatly, that there can be many cultures existing contemporaneously at different levels or phases manifesting different degrees of complexity. Cultures do not necessarily build on one another, nor should some be considered "higher" in their stage of development. Cultures are not like trees in a forest, it was argued, the small and immature ones at a stage of savagery or barbarism, the largest and most mature at the highest stage of civilization. Instead culture may be compared to a single tree with many branches. The lower branches on the tree are not necessarily inferior to the upper branches. Empirical studies indicate that some cultures have developed into nomadic cultures from agrarian cultures, in contrast to culture evolution theory. Furthermore, cultural development should not be equated with progress or improvement.

Modern anthropology, both American and European, has come under the influence of a different school of thought, the structural-functional. The functionalist school views cultural practices as made up of a tightly interrelated network, the whole of which can be understood in terms of the relationships of the sociopsychological needs of individuals or of the systems in society.

Recent Developments in Anthropology

Any reports of the premature demise of anthropology because the preliterate and nonliterate peoples of the world have been studied out are untrue! Anthropology is a viable field of scholarship. It is viable, of course, in helping promote intercultural understanding, which is no less important today than in the past. Heretofore unknown tribes have been "discovered" in recent decades, such as the Tasaday of the Philippines. Partly through the influence of anthropologists the rush to "civilize primitive peoples" has been reexamined and, in many cases, moderated.

The Structure of Anthropology

The fundamental ideas of anthropology of the Social Science Education Consortium can be used both as a part of anthropological perspective and as a model of the structure of anthropology (Figure 8.2). The fundamental ideas include several major concepts used in anthropology (Figure 8.3).

Anthropology uses a large number of specific concepts, some of them rather technical in nature. We have already discussed several of these briefly: evolution, innovation, ethnocentrism, and cultural relativism. A college course or two would be necessary to familiarize the reader with basic anthropological concepts. It would take many, many courses in anthropology to grasp the vast number of specific concepts in the discipline. Amazing as it may seem, however, children sometimes delight in learning long and technical terms of prehistorical creatures — human, subhuman, and reptilian — and understanding their nature.

Anthropological Inquiry

The anthropologist uses the evidence-inference process, as do other social scientists. His inquiry is also guided by questions, but of a different type. Among the kinds of questions that guide anthropological inquiry are the following:

What is culture for?

What function in a culture is served by a given culture trait? How does it help us to understand the total culture?

What kinds of kinship patterns are found in societies?

What are the values of a given culture? How do they influence the specific cultural elements (technology, institutions, etc.)?

How have particular cultural elements diffused from one place to another?

Each of these questions leads to an infinite number of other questions.

Anthropologists collect most of their evidence by means of field studies, going among the peoples to be studied as unobtrusively as possible and studying them in their natural habitat as they go about their normal activities. This may involve the anthropologist as a participant-observer, a recorder, or an interviewer, or maybe even all three. Modern tech-

1. Man may be looked upon as a mammalian, social, and cultural animal.
2. Man is a member of the human population.
3. The human population lives in an environment—a natural environment and a man-made environment.
4. The man-made environment represents a social system.
5. The purpose of a social system is to satisfy man's needs.
6. The structure and functioning of the social system are shaped by man's belief system called culture.
7. Culture affects the natural as well as the man-made environment and also affects man and his needs.
8. Culture is made up of many traditions that are the result of accumulated knowledge, artifacts, and customs.
9. To meet his culturally limited goals, man innovates (invents and borrows inventions). Innovations challenge tradition and the social system.
10. If innovation leads to complications, the social system generates further innovations.
11. Further innovations may lead to simplification.
12. The innovation may become irreversible.
13. If the simplified innovation improves man's chances of survival, then innovation becomes adaptive and evolution of culture occurs.
14. Evolution of culture may change the natural and man-made environment, and it may change man and his needs.

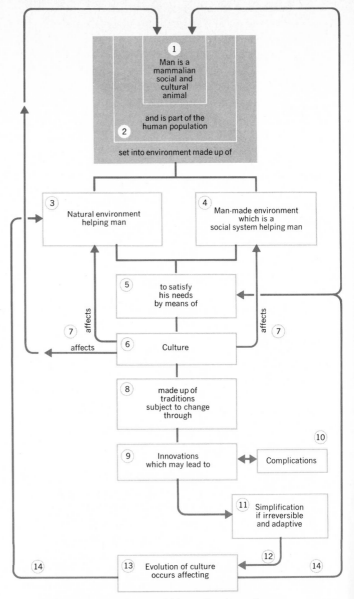

Figure 8.2 Fundamental ideas of anthropology. (From *Our Working World: Cities at Work*, Resource Unit, by Lawrence Senesh. © 1966, 1967, Science Research Associates, Inc. Reprinted by permission of the publisher.)

Figure 8.3

Some concepts of physical anthropology:

  Genotype: a group of individuals sharing
    a particular genetic makeup.
  Anthropoids: the apes most closely re-
    lated to man, for example, chimpan-
    zees, gibbons, and gorillas.
  Australo Pithecus: an extinct tool-making
    near-man of three to four million
    years ago in East Central Africa.
  Homo habilis: the first true man who
    probably coexisted with Australo Pith-
    ecus.
  Homo neanderthalensis: a contemporary
    of Homo sapiens about 35,000 to
    125,000 years ago in Europe who ei-
    ther became extinct or (according to
    more recent theories) merged into
    Homo sapiens.
  Brachycephalic: broad-headed, charac-
    teristic of certain populations in
    Northern and Central Europe in con-
    trast to long-headed (dolichocephalic)
    peoples in Africa.

Some concepts of cultural anthropology:

  Clans: one of the major subdivisions of a
    tribe, usually exogamous (requiring
    that one marry outside the clan).
  Kinship systems: arrangements by which
    descent is traced, through the father
    (patrilineal) or the mother (matrilin-
    eal).
  Polyandry: a recognized marriage prac-
    tice of one wife being united with two
    or more husbands (in contrast to the
    more common polygamous practice of
    polygyny, in which a husband may
    legally have two or more wives).

they dig for evidence of extinct cultures. Analysis of the artifacts replaces inter-viewing, but technical developments such as carbon dating, modern means of pre-serving fragile items, and the like, have been a boon to an anthropologist. Infer-ences are drawn by anthropologists by which they try to reconstruct cultures from fragmentary evidence or by which they attempt to develop generalizations about culture.

Anthropological inquiry is helpful in understanding contemporary societies. Studies have been made of the American class system, industrial plants as social systems, subcultures in technologically advanced societies, and many other simi-lar ones. Anthropologists are working as parts of social science teams in advancing our knowledge of society and culture. For example, cooperating with psychia-trists they have contributed to such topics as group motivation, the source of cul-tural drives, and the like.

The Core Concepts of Social Science

Of the core social science concepts, *culture* is central in the study of anthropol-ogy. One can, in fact, define anthropol-ogy as the holistic study of cultures or of a given culture. Anthropologists are par-ticularly interested in the norms of be-havior, the rules, which bind a culture to-gether. The *habitat* of a people has an influence on the culture, in obvious ways in contrasting Eskimo culture with Poly-nesian culture, but in more subtle ways in contrasting water rights in dry climates with wet climates.

Anthropologists are interested in studying the *interaction* process, particu-larly interaction networks. The func-tionalists among them believe that each element in a culture is best understood in terms of the whole. The parts—institu-tions, culture complexes, and customs—

nological devices have greatly aided the field of anthropology in its field studies through the use of cameras and tape re-corders. Field work is the method used by anthropologists, or archeologists, as function to maintain the life of the society even when that function is latent and unknown to the individual, such as saying "Bless you" when someone sneezes or passing out cigars or candy on the birth of a baby. The anthropologist is interested to know what governs the interaction patterns between, say, son-in-law and mother-in-law or teacher and student? Why do some societies stress competition as a mode of interaction while others stress cooperation?

The *institutions* of the family and of religion have been particular targets of anthropological study. As a result we know much more about comparative practices in these institutions among peoples around the world than we do about the other institutions. But anthropologists study economic and political institutions as well, notably among preliterate peoples, leaving modern economic and political institutions to other disciplines.

Anthropologists are interested in determining why some people value and utilize certain *resources* and others do not. This is partly a matter of the level of *technology*, but not entirely so. Water is vital to life and is a resource of great importance to all people, but oil has been used by some as an emolient, and by others as a fuel. Anthropologists are aware (but wish to learn more about the reasons) that resources such as land are held in common by a tribe in some areas, by a few nobles in others, or by private individuals in still others. The answers to the perplexities of *resource allocation* may be found in a better anthropological understanding of the concept of *power.* Formal governments are not necessary for the making of binding decisions. Custom and practices of informal social control can be as binding as statute law and pervasive police forces.

Social change, we learn from studies of culture history, takes place by innova-tion and invention, whether by developing new ways of shaping stones for arrowheads or of using integrated circuits to develop new generations of computers. Social change takes place by diffusion, as elements from cultures work their ways into other cultures. Sometimes there is conscious culture borrowing, as when a tribe replaces stone axes with imported metal ones. Sometimes it is largely unconscious, as when words from another language become part of English, French, or Japanese and the origin of the words is lost. We speak of wanting to get away from the crowded urban areas by getting off in the boondocks (from the Tagolog word "bundok"); the French patronize "le drugstore" and look forward to "le weekend"; and the Japanese enjoy "aisukurimu" (pronounced ah-ees-*kreem*) for dessert.

The *choices* made by peoples may be made by their cultures, as much as by the individuals. The understanding of values is at the center of the understanding of what makes a culture tick. Our value systems become so internalized that we can suffer considerable discomfort when coming in contact with another culture or subculture. We can suffer culture shock. A typical American may choose material benefits over the spiritual, whereas an East Indian Hindu might choose the reverse. Premarital sex among pre-nineteenth-century Micronesians provided no value conflicts, but in Puritan America this was not among the choices available without severe punishment from the society.

Anthropology and the Social Studies

Anthropological content has been a part of the social studies, both elementary and secondary, for some time, although not necessarily labeled as such, Inasmuch as cultural anthropology and cultural geography share some things in common, content from anthropology has been a part of the study of the expanding environments of children, a staple approach to social studies for many years. Recently, however, anthropology has been introduced into both the elementary and secondary curriculum in its own right as well as a part of the general behavioral science thrust of the last two decades. Several important national curriculum projects have developed excellent and extensive materials teaching important anthropological concepts and introducing pupils to the structure of anthropology. These go far beyond the examination of quaint customs or the comparative studies of families that were a part of earlier social studies programs.

Notable among these is the University of Georgia Anthropology Curriculum Project, designed for kindergarten through grade 12 but initially concentrating on grades 1 through 7 for teachers with little or no background in anthropology. Undoubtedly the most well-known, most expensive and elaborate, and most controversial is the Educational Development Center's MACOS—Man, A Course of Study. It is intended as the centerpiece of the curriculum for one year in grades 5, 6, or 7 and consists of a number of films, games, readings, and other activities that are presented with little or no commentary. Students are to make interpretations about human behavior from what they see on film and observe in readings. The controversy over MACOS comes from several quarters, but one criticism is that it presents certain human experiences graphically without moral comment. On the other hand, some social studies curriculum experts consider it to be the outstanding social studies project to come out of the curriculum revolution of the 1960s.

At the secondary level there is the University of Georgia's Anthropology Curriculum Study Project, Patterns in Human History, for grades 9 and 10. Students involved in it have the opportunity to become anthropologists through a variety of case study materials, utilizing plastic replicas of artifacts, eyewitness accounts, films, and data sheets.

Anthropological content is worked into such inter- or multidisciplinary curriculum projects as the MATCH (Materials and Activities for Teachers and Children) project of the Boston Children's Museum, the University of California World Studies Inquiry Program, the Educational Research Council's Concepts and Inquiry Program, Project Social Studies of the University of Minnesota, and the Taba Social Studies Project. Two economics projects have also made important use of anthropology in their development of curriculum.

It seems clear that an anthropological perspective is important in the modern world. The contributions that anthropology can make to the educated person are such that anthropology is assured of a place in the social studies program alongside history and geography. Only a minority of the population take a formal course in anthropology. The elementary and secondary schools have the challenge of teaching some of the important concepts of anthropology to all children and youth.

The Social Science and the Social Studies

We consider the social sciences to be the foundations of the social studies. A knowledge of each of the social science disciplines is important, most of all as we put them back together in a holistic view of the social studies.

We have limited ourselves to seven of the social sciences, but those seven are not the totality of social science. Social science is a dynamic body of knowledge, constantly growing, sometimes blending with humanities or merging with natural science. Among the fields of knowledge that we might have included had we had the space are social work, urban planning, education as a social science, environmental studies, linguistics, and cybernetics. Other fields can be expected to be added to the social sciences in the future.

We have stressed the structure of each of the social science disciplines. But we have woven them into a general social science structure. This structure consists of the eleven integrating concepts (habitat, culture, mutliple causation, etc.) and the evidence-inference process, the social science modes of inquiry. The structure is flexible enough to add other powerful concepts or concept clusters. It is also a viable framework for new social science fields.

Although we have analyzed social science as one of three broad areas of knowledge, the boundaries among these are permeable. Many social scientists are sympathetic to the focus of the humanities—the individual human being seeking the good life in the good society—by the use of the inquiry mode of the natural sciences—the scientific method.

A teacher of the social studies must have the knowledge area of the social sciences, but he/she must also develop the teaching skills to help students reach the overarching goals of the social studies. These goals are to prepare students to be well-functioning citizens in a democratic society and to make the most rational decisions possible about public as well as private issues. The development of these teaching skills is our next task in this book.

Bibliography

Anthropology and Education Quarterly. Journal of the Council on Anthropology and Education, Washington, D.C.

Berelson, Bernard. *The Behavioral Sciences Today.* New York: Basic Books, 1963.

Bohannan, Paul. *Anthropology.* Publication #106 of the Social Science Education Consortium. Boulder, Col.: The Consortium, 1966.

Oliver, Bernard. *"Cultural Anthropology"* in *The Social Studies and the Social Sciences.* New York: Harcourt, Brace and World, 1962.

Periodically. Newsletter of the American Psychological Association Clearinghouse on Precollege Psychology, Washington.

Perrucci, Robert. *Sociology.* Publication #101 of the Social Science Education Consortium. Boulder, Col.: The Consortium, 1966.

Sykes, Gresham M. "Sociology" in *The Social Studies and the Social Sciences.* New York: Harcourt, Brace, and World, 1962.

SECTION 3

Social Studies: Curriculum and Instruction

Curriculum, broadly defined as all of the learning experiences for the students that are under the control of the school, and instruction, the variety of teaching strategies or methods, are the heart of any instructional program. Presently, the social studies programs throughout the nation appear to be confused and diverse as various different states and local communities embark on different programs. In addition, the various alternative organizational patterns in the schools encourage individualization of instruction and a multiplicity of courses.

Of course, some general social studies trends run across all the grade levels and in most of the schools. For example, multicultural education and values education are getting more attention in most schools. But the movement back to the basics has hurt many elementary social studies programs as teachers spend more time on reading and mathematics and less time on other areas of the curriculum. In some cases, this has meant more concern for reading in the social studies.

Because of these diffuse trends, it is difficult to discuss the whole K-8 social studies program. For this reason, this section is divided into the following four chapters: (9) Social Studies in the Elementary School, (10) Social Studies in the Middle School/Junior High School, (11) Values Education: A New Emphasis and (12) Different Instructional Strategies or Methods.

What should be the foci of social education in
the elementary school?

CHAPTER 9

Social Studies in the Elementary School

Social Studies Trends in Elementary School

Content, what is studied in elementary school social studies, has changed in the past 10 years. Also changed are the ways used to present social studies as well as the interpretation of why elementary students should have social studies. Changes in content, instructional strategies and broad goals or learning objectives, have not occurred in all elementary schools to the same degree. Elements of change in each of these broad areas can be detected, however, in almost any elementary school social studies program. So that you are prepared to detect changes in any elementary social studies program, let us look briefly at trends in the following areas.

Trends in Content

Traditionally, elementary school students progressed through a social studies program with content arranged according to the "widening horizons" or "expanding

Environment" approach (see Figure 9.1), of their experiences and focusing on the basic human activities within each horizon or circle. As outlined by Paul Hanna and others, the social studies curriculum should start with the child's real concerns. Students should first look at their own families, their school, neighborhood, local community, state, region of the state, and then the national community. Several basic human activities such as transportation, communication, education, and so on, common to all cultures, were used to tie together the conceptional framework based on moving the child from the here and how (his/her own family and neighborhood) on to the international scene as students become older.

Thus the typical curriculum of the early 1960s for the elementary level usually centered around the topics and units in Chart 9.1.

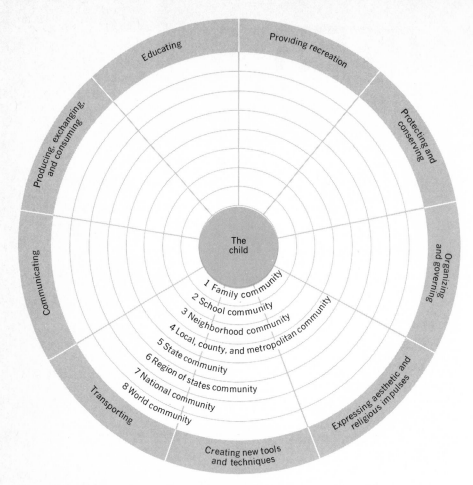

Figure 9.1   Diagram of expanding environment approach. (From Paul R. Hanna, "Revising the Social Studies: What Is Needed?," *Social Education*, 37, April 1963.)

For the most part, the content that students learned was restricted to middle-class-oriented roles and norms that organized and dictated individual interactions within these environments. Focusing in similar fashion on "basic human activities," fourth graders learned about the geography and history of their country and sixth graders broadened their scope to learning about the geography and history of the Western Hemisphere.

Organizing topics according to the ever-widening geopolitical circles of awareness made more sense before the worldwide economic, political, and social changes of the middle of this century. Before this time there were no sophisticated global communications networks, supersonic commercial travel, or acute

Chart 9.1 Typical Elementary Social Studies Curriculum, Circa 1960

Grade 1   Family, School, and Community
          Life
Grade 2   Community Studies
          How We Get Our Food, Shelter,
          and Clothing
          Transportation and Communication
Grade 3   Urban Communities, City Life
          Pioneer Communities, Indians,
          Local Communities
Grade 4   Our State, Geography of Certain
          Regions of the USA
          Geography of Other Countries,
          Great People in American History
Grade 5   Living in Early and Modern
          America
          Canada and Latin America
Grade 6   Geography, Western or Eastern
          Hemisphere
          Europe, Latin America

awareness of the limited resources and competing human needs of this planet. The horizons of children were, of necessity, confined mostly to their immediate surroundings.

Now elementary students, at least visually, are exposed to events, personalities, and environmental atmospheres from many parts of this planet. They are members of a mobile society where a typical individual may change residences an average of 15 times during a lifetime. Social studies materials reflect this new exposure and style. For example, primary students are led to compare their own family structures and norms to those of families from different cultures. Human adaption to physical environment is studied by comparing clothing and housing types in cultures from a variety of climates and degrees of industrialization. There is a notable increase in content examples from Africa, Asia, and Latin America.

Geographical and cultural comparisons in social studies content led to a greater use of all kinds of social science knowledge. Previously, content in social studies materials focused on the geography and history, especially U.S. History, of an area. Now writers, scholars and curriculum developers attempt to present topics in ways that include the perspectives of sociologists, social psychologists, anthropologists, and economists. Instead of describing production and consumption in a community, students are led to further analyze these activities in the economists' terms of the specialization, scarcity and interdependence the economic cycle represents. Broadening the knowledge base has also meant that contemporary as well as historical situations receive emphasis in newer social studies materials. Furthermore, it has meant that fewer topics are studied in greater depth than before. Chronological historical coverage has become less evident.

The multiethnic emphasis is another important change in social studies content. In the 1960s the Civil Rights Movement jolted curriculum developers and educators to a greater awareness of the school-perpetuated denial of cultural pluralism. Greater attention to the contributions and problems of America's ethnic groups is now given in school programs as a means of creating a more just society for all citizens. Newer materials attempt a wider coverage of ethnic groups in the American past and present. These materials strive to expose students to the variety and diversity of family and community life we have always had, but rarely admitted. They also explore with greater candor all types of conflicts between majority and minority groups that have punctuated every facet of our national existence. There is more stress on what really happened in our nation's history rather than simple recitations of what Americans ideals are.

Trends in Instructional Strategies

Instructional strategies in social studies have followed two extremely diverse traditions. One tradition relied on whole classes reading and reciting together from one textbook. The other tradition began with the Progressive Education movement led by John Dewey in the first half of this century. The Progressive tradition stressed learning through active involvement. In practice, this often meant that a third-grade class might actually construct a replica of a Pueblo apartment dwelling and "play house" in it as a way of exploring how this Native American group lived. Often this dramatic play promoted valuable interaction among students, but was not oriented to shed much light on the realities of Pueblo life. Newer instructional strategies rechannel both these diverse traditions toward greater emphasis on developing thinking and analytic skills.

Another pressure that prompts teachers to diversity the instructional strategies they employ is the behavioral objectives movement. Pressures for teacher accountability have affected instructional planning in social studies. Stating expected, observable student outcomes from an instructional sequence is widely practiced in most of today's elementary schools. This movement means adjustments for teachers of both the traditions described. The Progressive teacher, who promoted free-flowing creative play in an enriched environment in hopes that some of the problems of Pueblo living and patterns of that culture would rub off on the students, must now add enough structure to the study to be able to record what facts and understandings about how a group of people adapt to life in an arid climate with a scarcity of edible natural resources. The teacher who employed a read-and-recite strategy must examine whether the kinds of feedback students can demonstrate through this strategy fulfill the broad goals of using information gained through reading to confront problems and make decisions.

Continuing concern that a student's analytical thinking and problem solving skills be developed combined with the behavioral objectives movement has promoted much exploration of instructional strategies since the 1960s. Inquiry or discovery learning is the most significant strategy to result from this combination. Briefly, this strategy emphasizes active, involvement learning that is structured through students answering teacher-posed questions and being prompted to ask questions of their own about sets of data they study or collect.

Reading and reciting, as the sole instructional strategy, cannot provide for development of the various thinking processes and research skills. Therefore, instructional strategies are being modified to allow for student progress in these vital skill areas. To promote thinking skills, instructional strategies often employ an event seen from different points of view, unorganized "raw" data, incomplete sequences of events, or examples of the same concept in differing contexts. The idea behind all these devices is to structure situations that demand students to engage in thinking processes such as categorizing, defining, comparing, summarizing and generalizing. Films, picture files, audiotapes and overhead transparencies as well as books are essential pieces in the instructional arsenal that promotes thinking skills.

Special attention to valuing as a thinking process is also evident in newer instructional strategies and techniques. The analysis procedure for exploring the problems of human relationships has assumed greater prominence in classrooms. Sometimes classroom governance or individual behaviors are the focus. In other cases, commercially prepared pictures, films, and stories are used as vehicles for thinking about how others feel and what makes them feel this way. More and more, empathetic and valuative kinds of thinking are integrated into ongoing social studies content. This is particularly evident in multiethnic versions of community life and national history.

Newer instructional strategies prompt students to engage in active research techniques. Interviewing, polling, and structured observations of human interaction are some of the techniques more commonly recommended in the new social studies materials. All the skills involved in writing an individual research paper or giving an oral report are still initiated in most elementary school social studies programs.

Individualizing and personalizing instruction is another trend in recent social studies strategies. Contracts and learning centers are favorite organizational attempts used to allow for individual variety in pace and interests. Too often, unfortunately, the only real differences made in the name of personalization and individualization have been to change the group's lockstep or read-and-recite to an individual repetition of the same strategy at varying speeds. Misuses of these strategies will eventually become evident. Well-founded program will continue to employ techniques of personalization and individualization as well as direct teacher instruction of small and large groups.

Trends in Goals

The basic goal of social studies instruction remains the same as it always had been. This goal is to prepare the student for full, responsible citizenship. The wrinkle is that the definition of what is necessary for good citizenship changes with the ebb and flow of events in our country and the world. Patriotic loyalty, knowledge about national geography and history plus an ability to work well in a group effort were once considered sufficient accomplishments for instruction during elementary social studies programs. Now greater emphasis is given to developing the critical, active and empathetic components of "good citizenship" in elementary school social studies. Classroom self-governance, community work projects, and participation in setting schoolwide rules are all used as means of citizenship development.

To develop a citizenship potential, social studies instruction has always tried to focus on goals within the categories of knowledge, skills, attitudes and values. These categories are still valid. What has changed are the emphases within each category. Knowledge from all the social sciences, not just history and geography, is included. The skills area has also broadened. Thinking about data or evidence in ways similar to the ways a social scientist does is now a specific concern in addition to the older geographic locational and library research skills. Concern for individual and group responsibility continues to be given prominence. The category of valuing is perhaps the most changed. Valuing is fostered as a skill the individual needs to develop, not a set of conclusions to be adopted.

This list of trends in elementary social studies would not be complete without mention of the lamentable response given to pressures to go "back to the basics" in elementary programs. Parents and the general public alike are clamoring for more emphasis on teaching/reading skills as a basis for going beyond the "three R's". Teachers have reacted to these demands by spending more time drilling on phonic skills and reading from basal reader series. The result is a trend to diminish the amount of time alotted to social studies and science instruction. It is hard to disagree with the complaint that many students are not learning to read adequately in elementary schools. It is easy to imagine, however, that more students would develop greater interest in reading if they were allowed the chance to sample the topics social studies and science materials now offer the young mind. Certainly reading skills could be taught using reading matter and related activities from both social studies and science materials.

These brief highlights should alert you to trends to look for as you observe teaching and learning social studies. To detect evidence of change in a social studies program, find answers to these questions:

1. How much of the content is based on history and geography?
2. How much of the content is drawn from locales outside Western Europe and the United States?
3. How much comparison of family and community types throughout the world is done?
4. How much coverage is given American ethnic groups?
5. How much does the instruction rely on one basic textbook?
6. How much does the instruction promote student collection and organization of data?
7. How much does the instruction promote student choices and interests?
8. How much attention is devoted to probing human motivation and values?
9. How specific are the objectives for each grade?
10. How varied are the kinds of behaviors sought in the stated objectives?
11. How much time is spent on social studies?

We will examine each of these trend categories in greater detail in the following sections.

Curriculum Development

Curriculum development is organizing experiences and materials that will direct students toward acquiring the knowledge, skills, attitudes and values deemed essential for good citizenship. School districts usually involve teachers, subject specialists, and community representatives in elaborating a list of general instructional objectives that encompass these social studies components. This group reviews the current district program and studies presentations of other programs preparatory to an analysis of how well the program is meeting the needs of students in that district and the legal-moral requirement of the state. In their deliberations this group relies heavily on program goals suggested by State Departments of Education, the National Council of Social Studies, and statements from commercially published social studies programs, Thus, the first step in curriculum development is an assessment of what currently is happening in the program and from this assessment, this group elaborates a general statement about what they would like to see for students gains as the result of the district's program.

The second step in social studies curriculum development is to define the scope and sequence for the district's social studies program. Defining the scope means selecting topics such as the community or technology and/or social science concepts such as interdependence or adaption and deciding how much time and what detail should be devoted to each in the total kindergarten through sixth or eighth grade program. Hand in hand with defining what content shall be included goes the task of ordering or sequencing what aspects of this content students will study during each of the various years they spend in the district's schools.

The general planning process is concluded by developing unit plans for each grade or level's specified content. Units planned for teachers vary in their organization and thoroughness. At the very least, they list main points in knowledge, skills, attitudes, and values that students should learn and provide a bibliography of materials teachers may use in developing the listed learnings. Often, much more assistance is provided. Not only are student learning results and teacher resources listed, but suggestions outlining appropriate instructional strategies from a unit's beginning to its conclusion are included.

Curriculum development is an arduous, time-consuming and expensive process. As a classroom teacher, you may feel that the process of curriculum development is beyond your responsibilities. This attitude is understandable. But it is this same attitude that can lead to either mindless teaching of something you do not understand or being urged to use materials and topics that you feel are irrelevant for your students. One of the things you, as a teacher, need to know about a school district is how curricular decisions are really made in that district. It is safe to say that the more classroom teachers actively participate in curriculum development, the better the quality of that district's instructional program. The more the teacher, newcomer or experienced, knows, the better contribution he/she can make.

Patterns of Content Organization

There are several social studies scope and sequence patterns that are currently popular. They merit our closer attention since they are so widely used in the schools. You should compare these patterns by analyzing where each fits along the continuum items listed in Chart 9.2. The following pages will briefly describe four different patterns and then comment on their similarities and differences referring to the items on the comparison continuum.

Chart 9.2 Scope and Sequence Pattern Comparison Points

1. Social science disciplines

Integration _____ separation[1]

2. Concepts

Repetition _____ variety

3. Settings

Global, non-U.S.A. _____ widening horizons

1. Addison-Wesley series *The Taba Social Studies Program.*

Addison-Wesley's edition (1973) of Hilda Taba's program is for kindergarten through grades six or seven. Over 10 years were spent by the late Dr. Taba and her associates in developing and perfecting a set of materials that puts her research and ideas into a usable form for elementary teachers.

For grades one to five, there are hardbound student textbooks with the following titles: *Peoples in Families* (Grade 1), *People in Neighborhoods* (Grade 2), *Peoples in Communities* (Grade 3), *People in States* (Grade 4), and *People in America* (Grade 5). For grades six and seven, there are eight softbound booklets on such topics as **Africa, East Asia,** and **Latin America.** It is expected that the sixth-grade teacher would use four of these and the remaining four would be used by the seventh-grade teacher. In addition, there is a readiness unit of 18 study/activity posters on "Anuk's Family of Bali" that can be used in kindergarten. Furthermore, there are separate student activity books for grades three to five and test materials (duplicator masters) for grades three to five; in the sixth grade,

---

[1] An integrated approach would, for example, present a Bolivian family in terms of how the terrain affects the family's means of earning a living and social relationships. A separated approach would look at Bolivia's geography, then describe Bolivian history chronologically.

the student performance exercises and skills worksheets serve as objective tests.

These grade-level titles are deceiving. They appear to repeat the old family-to-world progression. While it is true that traditional grade-level topics remain, the focus is upon the 11 key concepts and a number of social science generalizations. Instead of chronology and mere facts, the key concepts are emphasized. In addition, contrasting examples are used. Thus, a first grader still studies the family. He/she comes to know how family members in such diverse settings as Kenya, New York City, France, and a religious commune in Canada meet their basic needs. Vivid details related by mothers, fathers, and children provide the student a realistic and personalized data base.

The heart of the program is outlined in the very extensive teacher's guides that are available for the textbooks or the separate booklets. These teacher's guides are absolutely essential if the program is to be taught according to the Taba approach.

In general, data in some form are presented to the students. Either students may read a few pages from the text or follow the audio materials which dramatize the exact words in the text. Or the teacher may read a short passage from the teacher's guide. Then using the questioning strategies outlined for the teacher, students are asked to do something with the data. This may involve answering questions, making a map, a chart, drawing pictures or taking an exploratory walk.

In particular, asking good questions is one of the primary tools that teachers are asked to use. Dr. Taba concluded that children can be aided to higher level thinking processes if teachers structure classroom discussions that move from the concrete to the abstract. Good teacher questions helped students to reexamine their own experiences and the new data that had been presented in Taba's research. In this process students could develop concepts—especially by listing, grouping and labeling—as well as learning to interpret data and moving toward generalizing and applying principles as outlined in Chart 9.3.

Taba emphasized what children learn depends depends on how they are prompted to handle the knowledge presented to them. It is not facts children need to learn, but how to organize these facts. To organize the overwhelming amount of information in the social studies curriculum, Taba used 11 key social science concepts such as conflict, cultural change, institutions, interdependence, and the like that provide the program's framework.

To be successful, the Taba program demands a teacher who does daily teacher's guide homework and who establishes observational expertise. For the program's vital core is what happens during the structured class discussions and small group activities. The teacher must become skilled at getting students to clarify their contributions and to doubt others by using logic. The teacher also must develop skills to recognize when a student has made a leap in thinking or has closed off all further data.

Some have felt that the Taba program is not doing as much as it should in terms of roles of women/girls and the contributions' of the different ethnic groups in America. For example, in the first-grade textbook on families, none of the mothers is employed outside the home. Only two-parent families are shown. Furthermore, less attention to the contributions of each minority/ethnic group results from the nonchronological approach used for U.S. history and the series coverage of cultures from Africa, Asia, Europe, Latin America, Australia, and New Zealand.

Chart 9.3 Taba's Questioning Pattern for Concept Development

TEACHER'S QUESTION	CHILD'S MENTAL OPERATION	OBSERVABLE ACTIVITY
What do you see, hear, or think?	Differentiating items	Listing
What things seem to belong together? Why do you place them together?	Identifying common properties	Grouping items
What can you call these groups?	Determining and justifying lables	Labeling

2. Harcourt Brace Jovanovich series *The Social Sciences: Concepts and Values.*

Dr. Paul Brandwein first became known as a curriculum developer in science. During the 1960s he extended his efforts to social science in the elementary school. Leading a corps of specialists and teachers from schools scattered throughout the country in seminars, materials development workshops, and classroom experimentation, the conceptual schemes model evolved.

Five general statements, or concepts, make up the bases for this curriculum model. They are broad statements accepted as being empirically true by social scientists in their accumulated findings to date. They are:

1. People are the product of heredity and environment.
2. Human behavior is shaped by the social environment.
3. Geographic features of the earth affect human behavior.
4. Economic behavior depends upon the utilization of resources.
5. Political organizations resolve conflict and make interaction among people easier.

Notice that these are statements about the way things work in human affairs, about human behavior in groups and as individuals.

The Brandwein curriculum development team used these broad statements to form the skeleton for the content of the whole series. They did this by starting with a simpler, more restricted version of each statement for the earlier levels, or grades, and adding further complexity to the statement in the higher levels. Thus, the concept statement, "People are the product of heredity and environment," gets the following progression as it is worked with from earlier to more mature levels in the series:

Level K   Children interact with the physical and social environment.

Level 1   Individuals resemble each other.

Level 2   People live in a variety of environments.

Level 3   The members of a community learn to adapt to their environment.

Level 4   People inherit and learn patterns of behavior.

Level 5   The interaction of physical and cultural inheritance results in people's adaption to their environment.

Level 6   Physical and cultural inheritance results in variation in the people of the earth.[2]

These versions of the general concept statement provided the developers with a definition of the degree of sophistication

---

[2] Paul F. Brandwein et al., teacher's manual for *The Social Sciences: Concepts and Values,* New York, Harcourt Brace Jovanovich, 1970, p. T-16.

Social Studies in the Elementary School   179

and the setting within which illustrative incidents were then developed. To give impetus to the model, the theme of responsibility was added. This theme provides a personal and group action element to the incidents described in the series' written materials and the experiences suggested in accompanying guides.

Units within each level of this scheme emphasize the ways that one or another of the Social Sciences would examine the concept-statement. In first grade or level one, students look at themselves and each other observing their body structures and physical features. By listing and comparing characteristics, they come to a first synthesis of what physical anthropologists refer to as human variability. Later, a unit in the fourth level emphasizes the psychologist's concern for the difference between learned and inherited behavior. Insight into the concept of social learning is gained by considering the uses of language and animal problem solving.

Accompanying hardbound textbooks for each grade level are filmstrips and audiocassette programs, large study prints, and detailed teacher manuals. A second edition of the series in 1975 amplified the scope of the curriculum to include books for each grade level devoted to giving students experiences in the humanities. Extension into sound, color, and action makes the series much broader. Given Brandwein's definition of curriculum as the device by which children's random encounters outside the classroom are married to nonrandom classroom encounters in the search for meaning, the inclusion of these humanities-oriented books offer a certain logic in reducing the areas in which non-Brandwein organized experiences could occur.

3. Houghton-Mifflin series *Windows on Our World.*

Windows on Our World is a kindergarten-through-sixth-grade social studies program published in 1976 by Houghton Mifflin. In addition to student hardcover texts, each grade level also has a workbook for students, packages of diagnostic evaluation and performance texts, activity cards for grades three through six, and a well-developed teacher's guide. The publisher obviously had in mind the demands on busy elementary teachers and has tried to reduce some of the tasks such as test preparation in this series.

The titles of this series do not tell the complete focus of the text. Instead, it is necessary to look carefully at the units to get some understanding of the changes in traditional curriculum patterns that have occured in this series (Chart 9.4).

As the unit titles indicate, this program has made some radical content changes as compared to the traditional elementary social studies program. This departure is more obvious on the fourth grade level with its emphasis on science and ecology, the long introduction in the fifth-grade book on American society before proceeding with the typical chronological American History approach, and the sixth-grade text with its focus on the uniqueness of human beings as compared to higher animals, acceptance of death with a touching story of Buddha helping a mourning mother, and other unique content.

Also new is the focus on global education, which is direct as one unit in the fifth grade as well as indirect in all the colorful pictures that stress the wide diversity of cultures throughout the whole planet Earth. This global emphasis puts a new look on even the primary textbooks, which, from the titles, appear to be covering the old traditional topics of the family and communities. In addition,

Chart 9.4 Scope and Sequence of Houghton-Mifflin Series

Me (kindergarten)

Unit 1 Me
Unit 2 My Family
Unit 3 My School
Unit 4 My Community
Unit 5 My Tools

Things We Do (grade 1)

Unit 1 Me and You
Unit 2 People
Unit 3 Living with Others
Unit 4 Using Space

The World around Us (grade 2)

Learning about the World
Feeling about the World
Communicating about the World
Thing about the World
Depending on the World
Acting on the World

Who Are We? (grade 3)

What Is Earth?
What Is a Human Being?
What Are Groups?
Who Am I?

Planet Earth (grade 4)

You and Your Environment
Culture and Human Needs
Living in the Air-Ocean
The Water Around You
The Land You Live On
You in the Life System
The Energy You Use
Looking Beyond Earth

The United States (grade 5)

The U.S.: People and Places
The U.S.: Our Natural Environment
Culture in the United States
The U.S. in the Global Community
The Beginnings of the U.S.
The United States Grows and Changes
The Modern United States
The United States in Today's World (Canada,
    Mexico)

The Way People Live (grade 6)

What Makes You a Human Being?
How and Why Are Human Beings Alike and
    Different?
How Does Culture Vary and Change?
Our Urbanized Earth

especially on the kindergarten through grade two levels, the open-ended questions and extensive opportunities for students to react to pictures and questions in the text makes the primary area heavily inquiry oriented.

But the program does not have a tight rationale other than its focus on the global. Content from the various social science disciplines is included, but different grade levels devote slight or great attention to the disciplines depending on the particular unit. These variations in the grade levels perhaps reflect the different sets of authors of the textbooks.

The textbooks also vary in the attention devoted to skill development. Some of the texts are quite explicit with sections in the students' textbook devoted to inferring, classification and the like. Other texts have more indirectly outlined skills such as small group discussion in the teacher's guides. The only skill consistently emphasized is map skills.

A great deal of attention went into the analysis of the reading levels for these books. Publishers report that all texts have been written on grade level. In addition, attempts have been made to avoid sexism. However, some American ethnic groups might want more attention to their specific group in the United States, even though the portrayal of the many different racial groups found throughout the world is excellent.

4. Allyn & Bacon series *Concepts and Inquiry.*

A large group of curriculum specialists and classroom teachers located in Cleveland, Ohio, schools collaborated in the development of this program. Several principles guided program development. All the social science disciplines are important, although, in fact, greater emphasis still is given to historical and geographical information. The importance of the disciplines for the learner lies in his/her working with the concepts, methods of investigation and structures rather than learning the facts produced by social sciences. Exposure to social science concepts is planned, sequential, and cumulative, as shown in Chart 9.5.

Student materials come in paperback booklets varying in number according to the titles listed in the topical content chart above. Accompanying these booklets are vocabulary and concept development ditto masters. Teachers guides are detailed and provide evaluation suggestions. The most salient feature of this series is the extensive reliance on the comparative approach. For each typical subject of the traditional self-to-world sequence this series provides examples from a variety of places and periods. Also notable are the topics chosen for kindergarten and upper grades. Famous explorers, both of the past and present, are used as case studies in kindergarten to explore man's capabilities. Fifth- and sixth-grade topics are usually found in the seventh and eighth grades.

Comparing Series

Each of the series discussed has its own particular content and organizational pat-
tern. Referring to the Addison-Wesley *Taba Social Studies Program* as 1, the Harcourt Brace Jovanovich *Concepts and Values* as 2, the Houghton-Mifflin *Windows on Our World* as 3 and the Allyn Bacon *Concepts and Inquiry* as 4, let us compare where they fall on the comparison points previously discussed (Chart 9.7). They all include more than knowledge from the disciplines of history and geography. They all attempt to repeat concepts in more sophisticated ways as the program progresses. They all include settings that are not from our own country. The Addison-Wesley and Allyn & Bacon series integrate social science concepts throughout, as does the Houghton-Mifflin series, without emphasizing to the student the name of the concept involved or the social science(s) from which the concept was derived. The Harcourt Brace Jovanovich series takes greater pains to identify the social science from which concepts are drawn and how the scientists from different disciplines use particular concepts, such as social learning, in their studies. Another difference is the definition of concept employed in the four series. Allyn & Bacon's series often specifies topics within disciplines, such as regions, urban geography, or people and their environment from geography. The Addison-Wesley series uses broad ideas or concept-statements such interdependence of peoples or how people use their environment to secure basic needs, which underlie all these topics. While the Houghton-Mifflin series shows a multidisciplinary concern, no attempt is made to explicitly develop a given set of concepts.

Repeating basic themes or concepts or ideas in even greater complexity throughout a curricular sequence has come to be known as using the spiral curriculum organization. The logical argument for this kind of curriculum structure is that through repeated exposures using a variety of situations and settings,

Chart 9.5 Selected Conceptual Content of Allyn & Bacon Series

CONCEPTUAL CONTENT
GRADE TWO THROUGH GRADE THREE

GEOGRAPHY	GRADE TWO	GRADE THREE
Globe and map skills	Continents; countries; map key; poles; equator	Map symbols; scale; aerial photos; historical maps
Earth science in relation to social science	Earth-sun relations; day and night; seasons	Earth-sun relations and climate; bar graphs
Man and his environment	Natural and cultural environment	Varied uses of natural environment in Anglo-America
Regions	Functional areas; some physical regions of the United States and Australia	Major physical regions of Anglo-America and some cultural regions
Natural resources	Some natural resources of the USA	More natural resources of Anglo-America
Circulation, or spatial interconnections	Interdependence of American communities	Exploration and expansion of Anglo-America
Political geography	Country, state, community	Historical geography of Anglo-America
Urban geography	Areas of a community; Pittsburgh, Pa.	Detailed study of metropolitan community

Permission by Allyn & Bacon, Boston, Mass.

Chart 9.6   Topical Content of Allyn & Bacon Series

Although the conceptual content of the ERCSSP is paramount, the teacher should be familiar with the topics used for case-study throughout the program.

Kindergarten: School, self, home and family, buying goods and services
                  The earth, globe, landmasses, oceans
                  Life in Japan, Mexico, Samoa, England

First Grade: Review of home and school
                  Study of transportation
                  A trip to Washington, D.C.
                  Explorers and discoverers from the Norsemen to John Glenn
                  Four great Americans: Washington, Lincoln, Clara Barton, Amos Fortune
                  Anthropological studies: Mongols, the Ganda, Tahitians, Southeast Woodland Indians
                  Geography: globe, landmasses, poles, cardinal directions, maps, aerial photos

Second Grade: Systematic study of communities: local community, Australian Aboriginies, Alaskan Eskimos
                  Study of American communities: Williamsburg (Virginia), Webster City (Iowa), Crossett (Arkansas), Yakima (Washington), Pittsburgh (Pennsylvania), Fort Bragg (North Carolina)
                  Geography: maps, continents, oceans, natural and cultural environment

Third Grade: *The Making of Our America*
                  The Metropolitan Community

Fourth Grade: *Agriculture: Man and the Land:* man as a hunter-gatherer and a primitive agriculturist; rice growing in Java and Texas; evolution of wheat growing on the Great Plains
                  Industry: Man and the Machine: growth of the canning, textile, and automobile industries; automation; problems and future of a changing world
                  Geography: scale, relief, grid, regions, climate
                  Area Study: *The Indian Subcontinent*

THE HUMAN ADVENTURE

Fifth Grade: *Ancient Civilization:* ancient Sumerians; Indus Valley civilization; ancient Egyptians; the "ebb and flow" of civilizations in the Middle East until 500 B.C.
                  Four World Views: Confucianism, Buddhism, ancient Hebrews, Greek naturalism
                  Greek and Roman Civilization: ancient Greece and Rome and their influence on Western civilization and early Christianity
                  Medieval Civilization: Islam; African kingdoms; Latin Christendom; Mongol conquests
                  Geography: latitude, longitude, historical maps, time, review of earlier studies
                  Area Study: *Lands of the Middle East*

Sixth Grade: *The Age of Western Expansion:* discoveries and technological advances; Renaissance; Reformation; rise of nationalism in Europe
                  New World and Eurasian Cultures: Maya and Aztec civilizations; European conquests and colonies in the New World; Russia under Ivan IV; Japan in later Middle Ages
                  The Challenge of Change: absolute monarchy in France under Louis XIV; growth of Parliament in England; American and French Revolutions; Industrial Revolution

The Interaction of Cultures: Western and non-Western imperialism; interaction of Western and non-Western cultures, spread of Western controlling ideas — nationalism, democracy, humanitarianism, socialism

Geography: continued use of maps and atlases; expansion of skills taught in earlier grades

Area Study: *Lands of Latin America*

Permission by Allyn & Bacon, Boston, Mass.

Chart 9.7 Scope and Sequence Pattern Comparison Points

Social Science Disciplines				
Integration ——————— 3-1 ——————— 4 ——————— 2 ——————— separation				

Concepts				
Repetition ——————— 1-2 ——————— 4 ——————— 3 ——————— variety				

Settings			
Global, non-U.S.A. ——————— 1-2-3 ——————— 4 ——————— widening horizons			

students will better internalize the basic structures of ideas that organize the different social sciences. Developers of all but the later Houghton-Mifflin series tried to put into practice Jerome Bruner's premise that Social Science ideas can be taught to students of any age if curriculum writers can summon the talent to arrange appropriate instructional devices to present them.[3]

Each of the series except Houghton-Mifflin also breaks with the traditional widening horizons of human experience sequence in the same way. The progression from self to universe is still followed. The difference is in the comparative settings presented for each step in the progression. Both the Harcourt Brace Jovanovich and the Houghton-Mifflin series develop the whole question of what it means to be human. Greater distinction between agricultural economy types and industrialized types is made in the Allyn & Bacon series. Specific attention on

world views as they are defined by major religious groups is included in this series too. In the other series, the difference this aspect of culture makes in how a society or group organizes its life and resources is present, but imbedded in exemplary settings that look more holistically on life in that particular setting. The same is true for the Allyn & Bacon series' treatment of political ideas. Nationalism, democracy, humanitarianism, and socialism are directly addressed rather than being mentioned as influences in a more chronologically oriented general description of the history of political entities.

Significance of These Series

Perhaps the most salient fact about each of these models is that each has become widely known because of the commercial preparation and marketing of student materials that put the series into consumable form for both students and teachers. Thus the steps in local curriculum development less and less often actually occur. There is a positive result from this practice. Purchase of a commercially

---

[3] Jerome Bruner, *Process of Education,* Cambridge, Mass., Howard University Press, 1960.

available program that comes with a rationale and structure already packaged saves local groups the arduous effort of "reinventing the wheel." Teachers involved in curriculum development groups have complained in the past that they were expected to perform the tasks of experts when, in fact, they were trained as generalists.

A possible negative side of local schools and districts opting to buy one or another series or select from the list of state adopted series is that the materials may be doomed to failure because no one really understands their organizational and conceptual designs. Teachers, who have not had a chance to develop with other teachers an agreed-on set of objectives for social studies, are most likely to use only what is already familiar to them from whatever materials come into their hands and fail to explore the rest. A case in point is the general dismissal of nonchronological American history found in most of these series. Thus teachers trained in more traditional structures based on the expanding horizons of human experience as seen through the grid of basic human activities will possibly ignore and reject most of the content of the newer materials.

Another factor to reflect on in analyzing these series or others not included in these pages is the validity of the curriculum structures. Three of the series reviewed here are conscious attempts to present the concepts and methods of social science in a form young students can assimilate. There is no convincing experimental evidence that supports this logical approach. There is support for the general notion that as children learn to write (express themselves) best by writing, they learn to perform intellectual tasks of listing, categorizing, and comparing best by being repeatedly asked to perform these tasks. That children learn to think by practicing thinking would be hard to re-

ject. Whether the content and methods used in the newer social studies materials is psychologically, as well as logically, learnable for students has yet to be profoundly evaluated. We really cannot say with certainty how much children respond to or apprehend of illustrative settings foreign to their experience or how much they retain of the analytic techniques these materials encourage.

Finally, in considering the significance of these series, we need to remind ourselves that no one of these series provides for all the facets of a well-rounded social studies program. It is true that each attempts to arrange for problem solving and empathy enlarging experiences within the student and teacher guide materials. To be effective, however, these kinds of skills are best developed by teachers and students using content that is provided in volume from the day-to-day living together in schools and communities. What better way to develop problem-solving skills than through group self-governance? What better way to become active in one's community than to discuss current events that seem significant on a day-to-day basis? What better way to develop understanding of one's self and one's peers than through daily sharing within an ongoing group?

The commercial series of social studies we have discussed have much to recommend them, as do other kindergarten through eighth grade series not covered in these pages. They provide young children with the substance for using and developing their abilities to think more systematically and analytically about the world around them. None of these series should, however, be used as the only ingredient of a social studies program. Any one of these series can serve as one element of the social studies program. In the next section we will examine some other sources of curriculum essential to a well-rounded program in social studies.

Although not reviewed there are other basal series for social studies that are worthy to note:

Ginn: *Ginn Social Science Series*

Noble & Noble: *Man and His World.*

Field Educational Publications: *Field's Social Studies Program*

Holt, Rinehart and Winston: *Holt Databank System*

McGraw-Hill: *McGraw-Hill Elementary Social Studies Series*

Harper & Row: *Our Family of Man*

Scott, Foresman: *Investigating Man's World*

Macmillan: *Social Studies: Focus on Active Learning*

Rand McNally: *Social Studies Through Inquiry*

Specialized Curriculum Materials

Series of basal textbooks need to be supplemented and enriched. Specialized commercial materials can round-out the social studies curriculum. Some of these materials are designed for particular grade levels. Others are meant to address only one discipline or one kind of instructional strategy or one skill area. Acquaintance with materials that allow students additional means of learning about the social world is a must for creative teaching.

1. American Science and Engineering: *Match Box Units.*

Usually, reading constitutes the most essential element in a social studies program. Reading typically is the vehicle that provides the data to the students. One of the few exceptions is the *Match Box Units* series. *Match* relies on multimedia and artifacts about such topics as the "Japanese Family," "The City," and "A House of Ancient Greece." If reading materials are included in the kit, they are materials

such as a Japanese comic book or a Japanese poetry book with translations that the teacher normally reads to the children.

An analysis of one kit, "The City," illustrates how students interact with these materials. First, the students view a film about three children in three different American cities. After this viewing, small groups of students in an unstructured situation play with the 75 wooden buildings of different functional types that they place on a board. Soon students are introduced to aerial photographs and learn how to place the wooden buildings to duplicate the aerial photograph. Students also view sets of pictures and learn to build sets of pictures upon a particular theme. In addition, students also make a walking tour of the school's neighborhood and build a model of the school as well as a map with a key for it.

Other activities include using city road maps, making a city map from photographs, identifying simple city sounds from a record and role playing an accident scene. As a final activity, students solve a problem about how to best route a new highway through their neighborhood. This unit provides 16 activities. If used in their entirety, units would take from two to three weeks to complete.

2. Science Research Associates: *Our Working World.*

The 1973 edition of these series presents a program from grades one through six with the following student text titles: grade 1—*Families*, grade 2—*Neighborhoods*, grade 3—*Cities*, grade 4—*Regions of the United States*, grade 5—*The American Way of Life*, grade 6—*Regions of the World*. In addition, each grade level has a paperback workbook, accompanying cassettes and scriptbooks, and, for upper grades, pamphlet sets. The cassettes and scriptbooks for earlier grades are deemed essential to circumvent the reading problems students of primary grades usually encounter. To use the series, then, teachers are oriented to work with a whole class since everyone listens to the same cassette together.

At first glance, the content of this series may not seem too different from the traditional social studies program. The titles are replicas of the familiar expanding-environment approach. These titles are misleading. The content of the series is drawn heavily from the discipline of economics. Lawrence Senesh, the designer of the program, is an economist. His approach calls for teaching basic social science ideas at every grade level with increasing depth and complexity each year. In the 1973 edition the first three levels of the series were revised to incorporate broader, multidisciplinary content. However, the last three levels of the series still concentrate primarily on economics.

Some communities might not adopt the series because of sexist and racist imbalances. For example in the text for first grade, *Families,* there is a section entitled "Someday." The girl daydreams about the future. What roles are shown? They are a wife, a nurse, a mother, and a grandmother. What does the boy daydream about? He sees himself as a volunteer for the community, an inventor, or having a job doing something important. Nor is there much attention given to portraying racial diversity in the series.

On the positive side, students using the program will be oriented toward the economic realities of our society and be challenged to work to improve our society. The program tries to point out that there is a gap between our ideals and our social reality. In addition, the *Teachers' Resource Guide* offers a wide variety of activities such as role-playing, committee work, and using community resources.

3. Education Development Center: *Man: A Course of Study.*

This program is designed for a one-year social studies curriculum for upper elementary or middle school students from grades five through seven. The materials include 21 student booklets, nine teacher's guide booklets, two records, five filmstrips, 23 maps, three games, 16 color films, posters, photo murals, project cards, and worksheets.

The content is drawn from current research in behavioral science and emphasizes the concepts of life cycles, adaptation, group organization, communication, and language. Various groups of subjects are used to explore these concepts. Students examine the behavior of salmon, baboons, gulls, and people. It is the stark realism of these comparisons that has upset some adult critics of the program. The sections of the program portraying the life-style of the Netsilik Eskimos has even been decried in the *Congressional Record* by a representative who objected to "teaching" children about infanticide, adultery, and genocide as reported in these materials.

In terms of following the cannons of curriculum development, this program represents a degree of sophistication and field testing rarely paralleled. Dr. Jerome Bruner, the famed psychologist at Harvard, led the development team sponsored by National Science Foundation and Ford Foundation funding. The films and other program materials are polished. The price of the program, around $1000, makes it a prohibitive option for many districts. As a well-founded experience in thinking like a behavioral scientist might, actually observing and manipulating pertinent data, this program is hard to surpass.

4. Holt, Rinehart and Winston: *People in Action.*

This is a series of four spiral-bound, black-and-white photograph collections organized by Fannie and George Shaftel. Each photograph shows some urban social situation. Often the scene captures a decision point such as a policeman apparently admonishing a boy with a ball glove who is in front of a broken window while two other boys stand by and a fourth boy runs toward an adult in the distance. Other photos present scenes for discussion that develop concepts such as why we have pet shelters. The intent of the series is to stimulate students to speculate, to explain, to verbalize feelings, to seek alternative ways to solve problems.

Role playing and the discussion that must accompany profitable role play is the methodology used in the series. The Shaftels see role playing as a invaluable vehicle for children to practice behavior under controlled conditions and to learn the value of social solutions without suffering the consequences of anti-social or dangerous actions. In effect, it gives them the "second chance" that real life rarely offers. To implement this method requires careful teacher guidance. Suggested steps and detailed questions are available for each photograph of the series in the teacher's guide. Daily use moving from one photograph to the next would be a misuse of this series. It would be most effective as the occasional prop for a sharing session. The issues this series of pictures evoke are real and appropriate for children, even though the photo settings are definitely the multicultural ambience peculiar to San Francisco.

These same authors have produced other materials designed to employ the method of role playing: *Words and Action: Role-Playing Photo-Problems for Young Children* and *Values in Action: Role-Playing Problem Situations for the Intermediate Grades* by the same publisher. All these materials are well-grounded in the role-play theory and methodology. The *People and Action* series represents the authors' best efforts at translating the theory and method into a readily consumable product for teachers to use in classrooms.

5. Rand McNally: *Going Places.*

Three sequential booklets comprise this series designed to develop map and globe skills for primary and intermediate grades. In exploring the content of space relationships the series develops these objectives:

☐ Ability to orient the map and note directions

☐ Ability to recognize the scale of a map and to compute distances

☐ Ability to locate places on maps and globes by means of grid systems

☐ Ability to express relative locations.

There is no attempt in this series to integrate geographical knowledge and skill with other areas of the curriculum.

Teacher's manuals accompany each student booklet. These are extensive and specific, carefully explaining the conceptual side of the content as well as what is known about the cognitive development of these concepts in young children. The instructional strategy employed is direct teaching of concepts followed by individual work in activity books and extended by other activities suggested in the teacher's manual. Use of this series implies that students have globes, flat maps, and atlases available in the classroom. The value of this series is its logical and thorough development of geographical knowledge. The possible drawback of this series is the effect its continued, routine and separate use might have on student motivation.

6. American Guidance Associates: *Developing Understanding of Self and Others (DUSO).*

DUSO comes in two kits, one for early childhood and one for intermediate levels. Each kit is self-contained with hand puppets, teacher's manual, cassettes, discussion pictures, story books, and role-playing cards. The kits' activities are designed to be used by regular classroom teachers in helping children better understand social-emotional behavior. Activities are structured for daily use throughout the school year. The kits are organized around these major themes:

"plementary" materials on the basis of the variety of stimuli and consequent activity encompassed. *DUSO* could be used simultaneously by various teachers. It is a well-

---

EARLY CHILDHOOD – DUSO D-1

1. Understanding and Accepting Self
2. Understanding Feelings
3. Understanding Others
4. Understanding Independence
5. Understanding Goals and Purposeful Behavior
6. Understanding Mastery, Competence, and Resourcefulness
7. Understanding Emotional Maturity
8. Understanding Choices and Consequences

INTERMEDIATE – DUSO D-12

1. Toward Self-Identity
2. Toward Friendship
3. Toward Responsible Interdependence
4. Toward Self-Reliance

5. Toward Resourcefulness and Purposefulness
6. Toward Competence
7. Toward Emotional Stability
8. Toward Responsible Choice Making.

Specific directions are given for the implementation of every session. Background theory explains and substantiates the activities. Foremost for the success of the activities is the climate established by the teacher. Guidelines presented for discussion are:

☐ Listen for feelings.

☐ Tell how you feel about things.

☐ Don't interrupt.

☐ Be with it.

☐ Talk with each other.

☐ Be positive.

The ultimate objective *DUSO* is designed to achieve is "to help the child become more aware of the relationship between himself, other people and his needs and goals. Through *DUSO* the child is helped to develop a sensitivity to the causal, purposive and consequential nature of his behavior. As the child comes to perceive the purposes and goals of his behavior, he is more likely to recognize the basis of his faulty relationships with others" (page 10, D-1 *Manual*).

Human relating is the focus as with the Shafters' materials, of these kits. *DUSO* can be contrasted with other "sup-

rounded, expensive set of ready-to-go materials.

There are many other specialized programs not reviewed here. Some worthy of note are:

Science Research Associates: *Social Science Laboratory Units*

Random House: *Peoples/Choices/Decisions*

Ginn: *Your Rights and Responsibilities as an American Citizen*

Asian American Studies Central: *Ethnic Understanding Series*

Media Sources and Social Studies

Textbooks designed as basal series and other specialized materials concentrating on social studies are essential materials for basic, sequential student learning in this curricular area. These specialized materials are often considered the building blocks for constructing the edifice of social knowledge. However, other materials are as important. To fit our metaphor, perhaps these other materials can be likened to the mortar that sustains the larger chunks of knowledge and makes them fit together in a more satisfying fashion. The materials we have in mind are the media. What a student reads about in "trade books" (children's literature broadly defined) and sees on film or television can help him/her piece together the topics and concepts studied in social studies. It is the teacher's art that employs media sources as an unsurpassed aid for making the social studies real on the one hand, and for applying social studies knowledge, on the other hand, to better understand the media and real life.

Children's Trade Books

Community and school libraries house an almost limitless resource for social studies teaching. This resource is growing explosively. In 1975 alone, nearly 2500 new juvenile titles of all categories were published in the United States! Categories most useful as social studies resources can be classified in the following way:

1. Nonfiction	2. Fiction
Biography	Historical
Travel	Adventure
Geography	Human relations
History	Folk tales

Children's trade books can be used as supplemental individual reading or shared orally with the whole class. They can be used to introduce, enrich, or even convey the main content load of a topic or problem that the teacher and/or the class wish to focus on in social studies. Literature can bring past events and the present to the lives of students. Literature is usually more people centered than much of text material. It can give fresh insight or empathy for the ways of life of our culture—past and present—as well as cultures of other places and times. In addition, such reading enables students to gain and improve their reading skills.

The primary advantage of orally "sharing" trade books is that the problem of diverse reading abilities is greatly alleviated. Still, care must be taken to select the right book for the occasion, and furthermore, to abandon a book when it does not catch the students' imagination. If books are assigned as part of social studies reading, care should be taken that student enthusiasm for reading is not killed by the burden of reporting on what was read. Book reporting can be done orally and pictorially as well as in written form.

Books for Different Purposes

To sample the possibilities trade books offer social studies teaching read the following minireviews. Note the range—from fiction to nonfiction, from description to analysis, from personal to public—of issues and genres these reviews represent.

An all-time favorite often used to enrich the study of geography in middle grades is Holling C. Holling's *Paddle-to-the-Sea* (Boston: Houghton Mifflin, 1941). Through the progress of a hand-carved Indian in a canoe toward the Atlantic Ocean from Lake Nipigon above Lake Superior, readers learn about all aspects of the Great Lakes' geography: currents, seasonal changes, locks, saw mills, water transportation systems, narrows, and falls. The book is illustrated realistically. Detailed drawings assist the readers' understanding of such concepts as the Great Lakes' drainage system, what is inside a big tanker ship, and how natural resources are related to industry along the Great Lakes' water system. Students respond to Holling's device of the adventures of an inanimate object, the Indian carved in a canoe, encounters as it gets tossed about by currents and winds and picked up by curious humans along the way. They are helped to conceptualize by such visual analogies as showing the drainage system of the lakes as a series of connected bathtubs along a hillside.

Books of historical fiction are excellent means to bring alive another period of time for students. Esther Forbes' *Johnny Tremain* (Boston: Houghton Mifflin, 1943) stands for many students as their most vivid memory of what life was like in our revolutionary era. Daily routines of 11- to-14-year-old boys apprenticed to a silversmith in Boston provide the setting. Through the eyes of another young person students become involved with the important events of the time. The Committee of Public Safety and such personages as John Hancock and the Adams brothers come to life for readers because of Johnny's fateful accident that keeps him from performing his apprentice duties and leads him through a series of mishaps, even jail, as he looks for work and eventually finds it as a messenger for the rebellious colonists.

Books of historical fiction tend to concentrate on the positive heroics and heroes of the eastern seaboard during the colonial period and the frontier men of the Anglo-American westward expansion. There are exceptions, and a growing number of them, to this focus. One is *The Bloody Country* by James and Christopher Collier (New York: Four Winds Press, 1976). Set on the banks of the Susquehanna River in Pennsylvania after 1750, the book is a fictionalized account of the actual conflicts between settlers competing for occupancy of the fertile land. The events unfold through the perceptions of young Ben Buck. This is not a one-sided portrayal of the good whites against the bad Indians, but a realistic portrayal of the violence that was part of the westward movement of Europeans on this continent.

Revisionist history and more comprehensive coverage of our multicultural society are becoming available in picture and easy-to-read books. An example is Johanna Johnson's *Who Found America* (Chicago: Children's Press, 1973). This book is an exemplary antidote to the customary excesses practiced on October 12. It could be done in a one-session "read" that would put Columbus into a larger perspective. The text starts with the hypothesized movement from Asia of the first humans to populate this hemisphere. Then it encapsulates, with text and illustration on each double page, each of the successive "discoveries" of this hemisphere halting at the War with England and concluding,

> "Who had found America? All of them.
> All kinds of people have kept on finding
> American ever since. YOU find America
> one way or another every day."

All Us Come Cross the Water by Lucille Clifton (New York: Holt, Rinehart and Winston, 1973) exemplifies one approach to multiculturalism. The reader follows Ujamaa, an urban black boy, through an experience in self-identity. The message to be explored through this book is imbedded in the following conversation between Ujamaa and an old black street man called Tweezer:

> "I ask him, 'Tweezer, we from all different parts of Africa, how we gonna say what country we from?'"

> "Tweezer say, 'We from all them countries, Ujamaa. All off the same boat.'"

> "I say, 'Some people tell me we wasn't all slaves.'"

> "He say, 'Wasn't none of us free though. All us crossed the water. We one people, Ujamaa . . . All us crossed the water.'"

For black students coping with the cross pressures of identification with both America and Africa, this book provides a low-key *entré* to discussion of the confused feelings of being *from* a place and not *of* it. Nonblack students can, through sensitive exploration of the theme by the teacher, become more aware of the identification dilemmas people from different places and cultures must resolve in this country.

A different way of providing students a view of our multicultural society is illustrated by such books as *A Week in Henry's World: El Barrio* (New York: Crowell Collier Press, 1971). Henry and his family live in a small Harlem apartment. Their lives are defined in part by their environment and personal finances. Little children do not play outside alone, toys are scarce, apartments are crowded. But, contrary to what an outsider may believe, a family like Henry's has some control over its life-style. This photographic essay illustrates that there is joy in growing up in Harlem and there are family rituals that can prevail.

This kind of black-and-white photobook serves different purposes for different kinds of student groups. For Puerto Ricans *El Barrio* is a chance to see themselves realistically portrayed without prejudicial stereotyping in picture and print. For non-Puerto Ricans, *El Barrio* allows a view of a culture that might otherwise remain unknown or be misunderstood by primary to intermediate students.

Document collections compiled in books provide teacher quick access to primary sources. Many of these are devoted to multicultural concerns. *Let Me Be a Free Man: A Documentary History of Indian Resistance* edited by Jane B. Katz (Minneapolis: Lerner Publications, 1975) covers voices of the Native Americans from the beginning of their conquest by the Europeans in 1607 to the present.

The Native American point of view from any phase of our history can be readily gotten at through collections such as this. Most of the statements make no pretense at objectivity. Rather, the statements represent the Native American side of their story. Teachers using this and other documentary sources would get more mileage from this kind of material by following these steps:

1. Preview the significance of the selection with students.
2. Read selection orally to class, pausing to clarify words and comprehension frequently.
3. Discuss why person making statement felt as he/she did.
4. Discuss how people from other groups would have reacted to the statement.

In general such collections of documents should not be assigned as individual reading and never as a whole book to be read. Specific, edited selections can be successfully used by individual students when they are read onto audiotape and accompanied by written questions that guide the listener's attention.

Trade books on historical topics can be found in fiction and nonfictional forms. Ann McGovern's *If You Sailed on the Mayflower* (New York: Four Winds Press, 1969) answers all, or certainly most, of the questions a young student might have about the Pilgrim's venture. For example, in answer to, did the Pilgrims have any medicine, the text replies with specifics:

> ". . . Suppose you cut yourself. Your mother would make a medicine from the wild daisy. She would mix it with animal fat and smear it on your cut . . ."

Such an approach is sure to delight and intrigue students as is the fictional mode used by Jean Fritz in *George Washington's Breakfast* (New York: Coward-McCann, 1969). In this tale the reader follows George Washington's modern-day namesake, approximately 11-year-old George W. Allen, in his search to discover just what Washington usually ate for breakfast. Readers also learn a lot about all aspects of Washington's life and how to conduct historical research as well.

Children's trade books are one of the best means for providing the emotional distance necessary to examine the whole range of interpersonal relations and personal problems relevant to growing young people. For the group of children having trouble keeping friendships, there are books like Charlotte Zolotow's *The Unfriendly Book* (New York: Harper and Row, 1975) in which one girl systematically cuts down any positive quality her friend mentions in another person. Very quickly the point, that liking others is a two-way street, is made. The best reference source for selecting the right book for the particular human-relations problem a teacher wishes to try bibliotherapy on is *Reading Ladders to Human Relations* edited by Virginia M. Reid (Washington, D.C.: American Council on Education, 1972). Books are briefly reviewed under appropriate problem categories such as creating a positive self-image, appreciating different cultures, coping with change. The only drawback to this valuable guide is that the last edition came out in 1972 and therefore, the wealth of titles published about human relations since then are not included.

It is true, that within the past few years more and more books are being published that attempt to deal realistically with such heretofore unmentionable topics as death, divorce, handicaps, and interracial marriage. Rose Blue's *A Month of Sundays* (New York: Franklin Watt, 1972) describes preadolescent Jeffery's reactions to his parents' divorce. Everything changes for Jeffery. In a few short days he moves from an affluent suburban life with Mother as a housewife to an apartment in New York with a working mother and a Sunday father. Jeffery suffers and learns to adjust and appreciate new outlets.

Part of the new realism in children's books is directed to redefining traditional roles. For example, no longer are authors automatically portraying all boys as the characters in the story that are aggressive problem solvers. In her picture book, *William's Doll,* Charlotte Zolotow (New York: Harper and Row, 1972) presents a typical boy who desires to own and caress a doll. No matter how much William is belittled and sidetracked into "boyish" activities, he still wants a doll. Finally, Grandmother comes on the scene. She responds to William's plight and gets him a doll. She explains to William's bewildered father that William needs a doll so that he can practice being a father!

The other side of the coin is humorously presented by Miriam Schlein in *The Girl Who Would Rather Climb Trees* (New York: Harcourt Brace Jovanovich, 1975). Melissa is William's opposite. Being 10 or so, she solves the problem of her elders foisting a role on her in a more sophisticated way. She informs grandma and mother that her unwanted doll is asleep, and goes out to climb some more trees while dolly naps.

The "humanistic" new books have not met with universal critical acclaim. Some charge that the new "stories for free children" err on the side of preachiness for whatever the author's particular social soapbox is.[4] One thing is certain. Sexual, racial, and status stereotyping will continue to concern trade book writers, textbook and media publishers, and con-

---

[4] For an excellent discussion of this issue amply illustrated see Margaret B. McDowell. "New Didacticism: Stories for Free Children," *Language Arts,* 1(54), 41-47.

sumers for some time to come. It is a reflection of the societal ferment on these issues. Life-styles are changing. People are questioning their traditional assumptions and premises.

The most extreme and organized illustration of this concern is the evaluation begun by the Council on Interracial Books for Children on children's books in terms of how the books portray "human and antihuman values."[5] Although teachers probably will not agree with subjecting every book to an evaluation of how it represents these values—racism, sexism, elitism, materialism, individualism, ageism, conformism, and escapism, for example—teachers should be aware of this kind of movement.

The few samples of children's trade books reviewed here, in reality, do not adequately picture even the tip of the iceberg of resources these books represent for social studies teaching. Librarians, curriculum guides, and book review digests can help extend and maintain the teacher's awareness of newer titles. Whatever the teacher's source of updating, the value of children's trade books to any problem or topic being discussed under the guise of social studies cannot be overemphasized. Trade books prompt the student to employ his/her imagination. They are cheaper and more easily scheduled than any other media. They should be a basic component of social studies teaching and learning.

Classroom Celluloid

Motion pictures and filmstrips and recordings are favorite means of adding variety to social studies. Indeed, the poten-

tial authentic sound and action have for bridging the gaps between where the students are and other people, places, times, and circumstances is beyond comparison! Often, however, the potential celluloid and magnetic tape have for extending student consciousness is not realized. There are several related reasons for this. One is that films are shown with little regard for matching the level of sophistication of the media and the students. Another reason is that scheduling and media budgets do not permit a smooth-flowing, sequential development of themes or topics. In this case, films frequently serve as entertainment only vaguely related to study.

Even when better conditions for selection and scheduling prevail, we often fail to get the most mileage possible from a film. There are some time-proven guidelines to correct this situation. First, teachers need to prepare students for viewing or listening by outlining what they are expected to learn from the session. This may be done by:

☐ Discussing what is already known about the subject and lead into what might be expected from the viewing or listening.

☐ Introducing key words in orally and visually and explaining their meanings in the context of the film or record.

☐ Developing a list of questions to be at least partially answered by film or record.

Usually films are shown in their entirety before discussion begins. A second showing may be recommended to clear up questions or doubts students have. To fully develop the potential films and records have for imparting information, follow up activities such as these should be employed:

☐ Dividing into small groups to answer questions posed before film and comparing group results with whole class.

☐ Taking a field trip for which the film or record served as an introduction.

[5] Council on Interracial Books for Children, *Human and Anti-Human Values in Children's Books*, New York, Council on Interracial Books for Children, 1976.

☐ Giving a written or oral check test covering the major points.

☐ Asking students to obtain more detailed information about ideas in film or record.

All these steps apply to using media sources in independent study situations. Even if the student views or listens alone, it is important for him/her to discuss what was seen and/or heard with someone who had the same experience. It is in the sharing of insights that students become aware of what they know and what they still need to find out more about.

Television

In its convention during February 1977, the American Medical Association declared that "television violence is both a mental-health problem and an environmental issue." We are all familiar with the calculations that tell us how much television American children watch. Children under five average 23.5 hours a week, which, by the time they are ready to graduate from high school, they have spent 15,000 hours in front of the television set. Only sleeping occupies more of their time! What effects does such immersion have on the intellectual and emotional growth of young people?

Social studies teachers must take cognizance of the positive and negative effects the tube has on their students. On the positive side, television allows children to become acquainted with a span of personalities, cultures, and events that contribute to making a village of our planet. On the negative side, the manners and morals pervading so much of television programming can promote less than healthy learning expectations and social attitudes. Children who watch television learn in a passive manner. Even educational programming promotes this learning mode. Sesame Street entertains

in order to instruct. Its flashy, quick changes are designed for short attention spans. Commercial television exposes children to a degree of violence and commercialism that denies most of the virtues — honesty, loyalty, and conserving — that we publicly espouse.

What Can Teachers Do?

Short of cutting the plugs off the sets in student homes, what steps can teachers take to make our blue-hazed tranquilizer into a more positive intellectual and emotional force for students?

1. Plan viewing with students. Use your Sunday newspaper television supplement or *T.V. Guide.* Bring it to class and study it with students to alert them to what is good.

2. Discuss viewing with students. Use sharing time to discuss the special viewed the previous evening. Be sure to bring up questions about different viewpoints. Have your wall map and globe ready to pinpoint where the program took place. Use student researchers to report from encyclopedias and other sources what further they found out about topics presented on the assigned program.

3. Analyze social issues by capturing how they are portrayed on situation comedies or police shows. Here is an observation guide developed for schools in Chicago by Prime Time School TV, a nonprofit television reform ogranization (Chart 9.8). Other issues such as male-female roles, consumer intelligence, parent-child relations, treatment of older people, and so on, can be analyzed with equal success. Data from student observations can be used to question the reality, legality, and morality of what is portrayed on television.

4. Communicate with parents about television viewing program. Just as parents have been appreciative of teacher hints on homework help and reading assistance, they will welcome knowledge of what school is doing related to television viewing and even questions about programs

they might discuss at home. The national Parent Teachers Association is running a television reform campaign. The issue might be one your local parent-school group would like to study.

5. Seek programming outlines from commercial and public stations. Excellent teacher guides are available for many of the public educational series such as "Inside-Out." Commercial networks have even printed scripts of dramatized documentaries for school use.

Following one or several of these suggestions may mean the rescheduling in an already crammed school day of blocks of time. It may mean breaking into your orderly unit plans with topics that do not fit. The argument in favor of trying some of these suggestions is that by discussing what students see on television, you are building a bridge between home and school, between two often segregated realities. Bringing television into the classroom can be used for social studies and general learning enhancement.

To our minds, however, orienting students to engage in more active and diverse activities in their nonschool time

is a better goal than teaching better television viewing. But, half-a-loaf is better than none at all. Television is here to stay. It is a window on the world. Teachers should take advantage of it and use it to help achieve their students' social studies learning goals.

Newspapers

Classroom sets of biweekly or weekly newspapers are often used as part of the social studies program. Subscriptions are relatively inexpensive and promoters guarantee controlled reading levels and coverage of age-related interests. Students usually like the comics and cross-word puzzles that are added attractions to the news and feature stories.

Frequently, these newspapers serve as "filler" for that ten minutes before recess when students have finished their "work." This practice diminishes the effectiveness of junior newspapers in two ways. First, since they are saved to be used as "fillers," they tend to lose whatever newsworthiness they might once have had by the time they reach the students. And second, students tend to be

Chart 9.8 Student Data Recording Chart

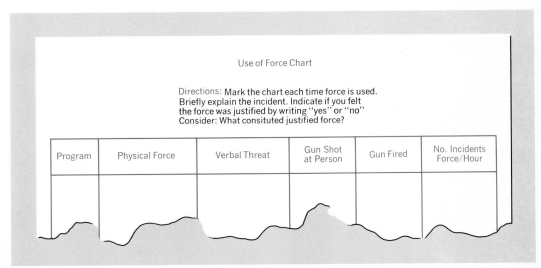

Use of Force Chart

Directions: Mark the chart each time force is used. Briefly explain the incident. Indicate if you felt the force was justified by writing "yes" or "no" Consider: What consituted justified force?

Program	Physical Force	Verbal Threat	Gun Shot at Person	Gun Fired	No. Incidents Force/Hour

less than enthusiastic about anything passed out to them for the purpose of "keeping them occupied" until the bell!

Junior newspapers can be used profitably when they are given status by the teacher. Feature articles should be treated as reading lessons. News articles should be related to other sources of information students have or can develop about the topics covered.

Hopefully, schools can become involved with the local or regional daily or weekly newspapers. The public relations departments of newspapers usually sponsor a newspaper education program which assists schools in teaching students how to "use" the newspaper. Programs that show students how to solve problems and encounter amusement and information in a real, adult newspaper are available to students from the time when they begin reading independently. Reading the adult version of the news is in itself a motivation to most students. Certainly, junior newspapers have their place in a classroom or school program. Ideally, they should be used to promote news gathering from the regular newspaper, periodical, television and radio sources.

A favorite activity for middle grades is comparison of newspapers.[6] Newspapers can be compared from cities within the United States, cities from around the world, county seats within your own state and present and past issues from the local newspaper. One way of initiating this comparison is to write letters. Students should write friends or relatives who live in other cities asking that they send a copy of their hometown newspaper. If students have parents or relatives who travel, they should ask them to pick up a newspaper for the class from the cities they visit. For those students to whom neither choice is available, newspapers can be requested directly from publishers listed in *Editor & Publisher International Year Book,* which gives newspaper names and addresses.

Following are sample points of comparison students can make on the newspapers they collect.

1. What types of headlines do you find? Are they sensational as to size of type and content? Are they conservative as to size of type and content?
2. Does there seem to be a system of story continuation from page to page? Do you find any newspapers using the layout similar to the local paper?
3. How effective is the use of pictures on the front page?
4. From a quick look at the front page, what can you surmise about the town/city politically, economically, and/or culturally?
5. How many international stories, national stories, local, and/or state stories do you find on the front page?
6. Is the layout of news stories and pictures on the front page different from your home town newspaper? How?
7. What wire services are listed as being used on the front page stories . . . AP, UPI, N.Y. Times Service, and so on?
8. Does the newspaper have a women's/family section? Is it called Women's or Society Section or does it carry a more family-oriented name for this section?
9. Are weddings features or minimized as to number and length of stories and accompanying pictures?
10. Make a list of the syndicated columnists and local columnists used, as well as syndicated cartoons, reviews, and so on, in the family/women section.
11. Evaluate the editorial and op-ed pages (opposite editorial). Does the newspaper have an op-ed page? Which items are informational? Satirical? Humorous?
12. Classify the editorial(s) as to local, national, and international in content.
13. Compare two newspapers of the same data as to editorial subject and viewpoint.

---

[6] Vicky Deggs of *San Jose Mercury-News,* San Jose, California, developed these ideas as part of the Newspaper in the Classroom program sponsored by that paper.

14. Looking at both editorial and op-ed pages, does there seem to be a reasonable balance of opposing viewpoints?
15. Look at the advertising in the pages of your newspaper? If you were given only the ads from this paper, what could you tell about the town/city?
16. List "national" ads (placed by the manufacturer or distributor of a product). Compare amount of space to advertising by local businesses.
17. What types of sports are covered in the sports section of your newspaper? Do they use major sports columnists that are syndicated? How do they handle the coverage of sports in their own areas?
18. Is there a front-page index adequate to guide you through the newspaper with minimum time and effort?

Other newspapers that are fascinating to compare are the large city papers directed to specific ethnic and/or language groups. For example in the Los Angeles-Long Beach area the following language groups are served:

Arabic—*News Circle,* 626 N. Beachwood Drive, Los Angeles 90004

Armenian—*Asbarez,* 1501 Venice Blvd., Los Angeles 90006

Chinese—*American Chinese News,* 763 North Hill Street, Los Angeles 90012

Danish—*Bien (The Bee),* 4540 Hollywood Blvd., Los Angeles 90027

German—*California Staats-Zeitung,* 221 E. Pico Street, Los Angeles 90015

Neue Zeitung, 9571 Hidden Valley Place, Beverly Hills 90210

Hungarian—*Californiai Magyarsag,* 105 South Western Ave., Los Angeles 90004

Italian—*L'Italo-Americano,* 810 N. Broadway, Los Angeles 90012

Japanese—*Kashu Mainicni,* 346 E. First St., Los Angeles 90012

Korean—*New Korea,* 1368 W. Jefferson Blvd., Los Angeles 90007

Spanish—*La Opinion,* 1436 S. Main Street, Los Angeles 90015

Swedish—*Veckoblad,* 4967 Melrose, Los Angeles 90029

Yugoslavian—*Yugoslavenski Americki Glasnick* (Serbian and Croatian) 1632 Brooklyn Avenue, Los Angeles 90033

Special reprints of historical newspapers were published by a number of newspapers as part of the Bicentennial celebration. Products of this effort are still available and well worth the nominal fees charged for them. Some are:

Newspapers and American Independence @$3
Minneapolis Star-Tribune
425 Portland Avenue
Minneapolis, Minn. 55415

1776 July 26 Reproduction
Virginia Gazette
Williamsburg, Va.

Founding Fathers @$1
Christian Science Monitor
One Norway Street
Boston, Mass. 02115

Historic Impressions, Authentic Reproductions of Rare Antique Newspapers @$5
Robert Sharp Design Associates
Youngstown, Ohio 44512

Leaders in Crisis
Independent, Press-Telegram
Sixth and Pine
Long Beach, Ca. 90844

Bibliography

Banks, James A. *Teaching Strategies for the Social Studies.* Reading, Mass.: Addison-Wesley, 1977.

Ellis, Arthur. *Teaching and Learning Elementary Social Studies.* Boston, Mass.: Allyn & Bacon, 1977.

Jarolimek, John. *Social Studies in Elementary Education.* New York: Macmillan, 1977.

Gillion, M. E. et al. *Practical Methods for Social Studies.* Belmont, Cal.: Wadsworth, 1977.

Martorella, Peter. *Elementary Social Studies as a Learning System.* New York: Harper & Row, 1976.

Maxim, George W. *Methods of Teaching Social Studies to Elementary School Children.* Columbus, Ohio: Charles E. Merrill Publishing Co., 1977.

Oliner, Pearl M. *Teaching Elementary Social Studies.* New York, New York: Harcourt Brace Jovanovich, Inc., 1976.

Seif, Elliott. *Teaching Significant Social Studies in the Elementary School.* Chicago, Ill.: Rand McNally, 1977.

Welston, David A. and John T. Mallan. *Teaching Elementary Social Studies.* Chicago, Ill.: Rand McNally, 1976.

How can the social studies program best help
middle/junior high school students?

CHAPTER 10

Social Studies in the Middle School/Junior High School

The Middle School and Junior High

Before discussing the social studies curriculum, let us define what is meant by the middle school and the junior high school. What images pop into your mind when you hear these words? Many perceive that the middle school is more child-centered and innovative while the junior high school is more subject centered like the high school. Both the middle school and the junior high school are the institutional structures between the elementary school and the senior high school.

One of the first problems is to define what grades are included in the middle school or junior high school. The middle school, like the junior high school, is a different structure in different communities and school districts. In some school systems, the middle school consists of grades 6-7-8, the most common pattern. In other cases, the middle school includes grades 5-6-7-8. Instances exist of middle schools following the pattern of grades 6-7-8-9, 5-6-7-8-9, 5-6-7, and 6-7. Junior

high schools typically have had three grades (7-8-9) as well as two years of junior high school (7-8). Other variations include having the junior high school start with sixth grade (6-7-8) or having two years beginning with the sixth (6-7).

Thus, you cannot define the middle school or the junior high on just the grade levels it contains. However, supporters of the middle school believe that it, in contrast with the more subject-oriented junior high school, is characterized by being more child centered, open to innovation, and more concerned with self-actualization. These advocates believe that the middle school is identified by the following: ungraded classes, core classes or unified curriculum, team teaching, more efforts made to individualize the curriculum for various types of students, increased use of electives, independent or semiindependent study plans, module scheduling, small group-large group organizational patterns, smoother articulation with the elementary and senior high school, improved guidance programs, and a more dedicated staff that understands young people.

Nevertheless, the educational innovations of the 1960s and the 1970s have not just been confined to one administrative level—the middle schools. It is not fair to impute to the middle school all the innovations. However, when the middle school is established by choice with a principal able to choose a staff that is supportive of the middle school, it is more likely to be innovative than a middle school started by administrative fiat and without much planning by teachers and the community.

In addition, when a middle school is established with a new physical structure, it is far more likely that it has more technology, movable walls, and other features that can lead to a better learning situation than compared to an older physical plant. However, the advantages of a new physical plant accrue to any level of administration: junior high, elementary, senior high as well as a middle school. Initially, both teachers and students may be more willing to try something new in a brand new school.

In trying to characterize the middle school, it should be realized that within the middle school (as well as the junior high), a wide variety of administrative organizations may exist. Thus, in many school districts, the younger children in the middle·school (fifth and/or sixth graders) may spend more time in a self-contained classroom while the older seventh, eighth graders, and in a few cases, ninth graders, move more in a departmentalized pattern of seeing different teachers each period. However, some middle schools, even for older students, still have a block of two or three periods, called the core or various other names in which one teacher is expected to correlate several subject areas and is supposed "to know" the students. Usually, this core teacher is given the responsibility for the day-to-day guidance function of the students.

The late 1960s and 1970s witnessed a rapid increase in the number of middle schools throughout the United States. However, many middle schools were established more for a consideration of financial expediency, building needs, and efforts to end desegregation rather than to follow the general philosophy behind the middle schools. Some school districts, especially ones with declining enrollments in the junior high schools, simply added one or two earlier grades to the existing structure of the junior high school so that there would be better use of the physical plant that had been designed for specialized areas such as art, music, science, and physical education.

Many school districts are considering what are the advantages (if any) of a middle school, as compared to a junior high school. Again, because of the wide variety in the schools themselves as well as the wide range of students they serve, it is obvious that some students, being more mature, are probably better suited to a junior high school or a middle school where more independence is stressed than the traditional self-contained elementary classroom. In a similar manner, many less mature students (often males) are probably better off in a self-contained classroom.

Ideally, students should be allowed to enter a higher administrative level of schooling when it is appropriate for their needs. This might mean in practice that girls would be allowed to move faster on the educational ladder than boys. However, presently we do not have reliable tests to measure if an individual is "mature" enough for the next educational level. Because of the administrative headaches plus possible stormy parental reception, little has been done to break the normal lockstep automatic promotion of students from one grade level to the next. The only important exception is, of course, the growth of nongraded classrooms, many which are concentrated at the primary level. In effect, neither the middle school nor the junior high school have solved the problem of the wide range of differences in the maturation levels of girls and boys to an institutional setting. But a good middle school, in general, probably has more electives and minicourses. These middle schools try to allow students to explore different options.

But does the philosophy of the middle school make a difference? The various claims that the middle school or the junior high school is "better" have not been supported by the limited amount of research that has so far been completed.[1] In comparisons between the middle school and the junior high school, the research has not shown significant differences in student achievement in the various subjects or in the attitudes of the students. Of course, it is possible that our present evaluation instruments are not sophisticated to show the real differences that do actually exist between the middle school and the junior high school. In addition, the immense differences among both middle schools and junior high schools make comparisons difficult.

The basic issue then is not whether to have a junior high or a middle school, but how can the school be set up to best serve the needs of this age group. Orga-

nization as such, of course, is never as important as what actually happens in the classroom. Ideally, the organization of the school should help teachers and students work together to achieve the purposes of the school. Just name changing or adding a year or two probably do not change the typical class situation too much.

In effect, this means that a typical social studies program in the middle school might not vary too much from that found in the upper elementary school or junior high school. The major academic subjects — English or language arts, social studies, mathematics, and science — are required to some degree in almost all middle schools as well as junior highs. Again, the extent of departmentalization might vary in school schools, especially at the fifth- and sixth-grade levels, as well as the number of electives available. Of course, the student body and its characteristics would have an important effect on the social studies program.

Organizational Patterns

We have mentioned the wide variety of organizational patterns that exist in middle school/junior high schools. Common for many middle schools and some junior high schools are core or block time programs in which an integration of social studies and language arts is to take place. Only rarely do some schools attempt to integrate language arts and the social studies with science, mathematics or other subjects.

However, although classes may be called "core" there is often a wide variation on how much integration of social studies and the language arts actually does occur. Since most teachers have not

[1] Carl H. Glissmeyer, "Which School for the Sixth Grader, the Elementary or the Middle School?" *California Journal of Educational Research 20*, September 1969, pp. 176-185; Thomas E. Gatewood, "What Research Says About the Middle School," *Educational Leadership*, **31,** December 1973, pp. 221-224; J. W. Wiles and J. Thomason, "Middle School Research 1968-1974: A Review of Substantial Studies," *Educational Leadership*, **32** March 1975, pp. 421-423.

been trained to integrate social studies with other subject areas or vice versa, there is always a tendency for teachers to stress their own academic major or their own interests. In addition, many junior high school teachers really wanted to teach in the high school and, in effect, model the high school in their teaching style. Thus, rarely are the core/block periods innovative.

Therefore, it is not surprising that often many core classes have a period of language arts and then a period of social studies with very little relationship between the two content areas although the teacher and the class remain physically together. In other classes, however, teachers try to integrate. Students may be encouraged to read books, magazines, and other materials related to their social studies' unit. Oral reports, small discussions, research papers, written homework, current affairs, essays, and the like may all focus on a social studies unit such as Kenya or American local government. Sometimes there is an integration of the two subject areas during a given unit but not during the next unit where the teacher may wish to devote time to grammar without using sentences from social studies content.

In most junior high schools, social studies is taught as a separate subject with only accidental correlation with other subjects. Often the social studies class meets once a day for one period. However, more schools at the junior high level are using a double period every other day or some other variation to increase the time block at a single meeting. In some cases, the large block of time is not interrupted but sometimes a recess, a break of a few minutes is used.

The most innovative organizational format, open classrooms with learning centers and individualized instruction, has tended to emphasize separate subject areas. Typically, the learning centers or

the projects have concentrated on one subject area such as science or the social studies. Apparently, it has been difficult for teachers to set up centers or contracts which correlate or integrate different subject areas.

In the coming years, all types of programs will be operating throughout the nation. However, in the long run, instead of focusing on the polemics of what organization is best, it might be more worthwhile to examine the actual curriculum and instruction of the social studies programs for young people of this age group.

Trends in the Middle School/Junior High School

As previously mentioned, in the early 1960s the expanding-environment approach became firmly rooted in many elementary schools as many national textbooks adopted this conceptual approach. In this framework, the social science disciplines were usually not taught as separate subjects but an attempt was made to integrate the findings of the social sciences into the conceptual scheme. Thus, such topics as families and schools were not taught with a separate discipline approach in the primary grades. However, as students moved more into the fourth, fifth, and sixth grades, a heavy dose of history and geography usually dominated the social studies curriculum, often to the exclusion of other social sciences such as sociology, anthropology, and economics.

In the junior high school, most courses, with the exception of a few core classes, were taught as separate subjects. At the typical classroom level, up to the 1960s, the separate subject approach emphasized a heavy dependence on one textbook, rote learning of facts, and little development of social studies skills.

As for content, Moreland reported in 1962 that in his sample of 179 school systems throughout the United States, the most frequently required social studies courses were as follows (Chart 10.1):

Chart 10.1 Sample of Required Social Studies Courses[a]

GRADE LEVEL	SUBJECT	NUMBER OF DISTRICTS
Grade 7	World geography	28
	American history— geography	28
	American history	27
	Geography	21
	State history— geography	21
	Social studies	14
	State history	13
Grade 8	American history	105
	American history— state history	19
	American history— civics	17
	American history— geography	16
	World geography	10

[a] Willis D. Moreland, "Curriculum Trends in the Social Studies," *Social Education*, **26** February 1962, pp. 74-75. Courses in which less than seven districts reported for a given grade have not been included in this table.

Thus, in the 1960s, at least in terms of required courses, seventh graders were most likely to be exposed to a geography or a history course. Eighth graders were almost universally taking an American history course or a variation of it.

What trends are observable today? Dr. Richard Gross made a national survey about the status of the social studies. He found that state requirements in 1970 and 1975 revealed that only 1 state increased requirements for social studies during this period, 4 reduced requirements, and 30 reported no changes. But requirements at the local level seem to show a very changed pattern. Approximately one-fourth of the districts reported a decrease in social studies requirements. In some instance, state and local history requirements as well as mandates for U.S. government and economics have cut into history courses.

The Gross Survey reported that many elementary teachers were spending little time on social studies. Indeed, it appears that administrators give more support to secondary social studies programs while the elementary school has only average to little encouragement for social studies. The position of social studies at the middle school/junior high school level remains unclear. United States History remains a dominant course at the seventh- and eighth-grade level. But this course may also include content on law, citizenship, state and local history, as well as consumer and career education.

Thus, as compared to earlier periods, the social studies curriculum at all levels, including the middle/junior high, appears to be in a flux. In some cases, there are drops in required social studies courses or more options within the social studies requirements.[2]

Textbook Trends

In addition, a careful examination of a few representative textbook series may also point out the current trends in middle school/junior high school social studies. As previously mentioned in the elementary section, there is now a much broader spread of the social sciences than was typically found in the 1960s elemen-

[2] Richard E. Gross. "The Status of the Social Studies in the Public Schools of the United States: Facts and Impressions of a National Survey," *Social Education*, **41**, March 1977, pp. 194-200, 205.

tary and junior high school social studies textbooks. Anthropology, economics, sociology, and political science are now given much more attention. While the expanding-environment approach is still used in some elementary-junior high school textbook series, there is now a much broader range of non U.S. cultures.

As in the elementary level, some middle school/junior high school textbooks use a multidisciplinary approach. In other words, the social sciences are treated consecutively in separate units and are not integrated. For example, in 1972, *The Social Sciences: Concepts and Values* series under the leadership of Paul F. Brandwein released two textbooks that could be used in the junior high school. The titles and chapters are as follows (Chart 10.2):

Chart 10.2   Example of Multidisciplinary Approach

Level Seven: Sources of Identity[a]

Chapter 1. Man as Individual (psychology)
Chapter 2. Man as Group Member (sociology)
Chapter 3. Man in Culture (anthropology)
Chapter 4. Man as Policy Maker (political science)
Chapter 5. Man in His Environment (geography)
Chapter 6. Man as Producer (economics)

[a] Harcourt Brace Jovanovich, Inc., *The Social Sciences: Concepts and Values* Series, 1972. New edition expected in 1977; can be purchased as a whole volume or a separate units with each chapter a complete unit.

Level Eight: Settings for Change

Chapter 1. Man in Groups (sociology)
Chapter 2. Man's Attitudes (psychology)
Chapter 3. Man's Governments (political science)
Chapter 4. Man's Settlements (geography)
Chapter 5. Man's Economic World (economics)
Chapter 6. Man's Changing Cultures (anthropology)

What is your reaction to these chapter headings? Perhaps the first thing you noticed was that this textbook series did not have a specific text devoted to the study of U.S. history. Yet, as you are well aware, traditionally on the eighth-grade level, U.S. history has been the traditional content area. In other words, this series has not emphasized U.S. history for either the fifth or the eighth grade.

However, this does not mean that the *Concepts and Values* series neglects U.S. history. Starting with Level 3 (third grade if the class has excellent/very good readers), content is taken from U.S. history. For example, on Level 4, the concept "Social Control" is illustrated by content about the California miners and vigilantes. On Level 8, "Crisis and Response" has material on the Great Depression and the New Deal. But the text also includes how the Great Depression influenced the course of history in Germany. In other words, content from U.S. history is not organized in the traditional chronological approach but serves mainly to illustrate concepts from the various social sciences.

In contrast to the multidisciplinary approach of the *Concepts and Values* series, the *Concepts and Inquiry: The Educational Research Council Social Science* program published by Allyn & Bacon uses an interdisciplinary approach. The interdisciplinary approach, in effect, refutes the usefulness of the unique, separate social science structure of the various social science disciplines. It is, in fact, a more integrative curriculum approach. The interdisciplinary approach can focus on such topics as prejudice or technology and examine the particular topic by including content from any social science discipline that appears to be fruitful in explaining the topic.

Here is the topical content for the *Concepts and Inquiry* program for the junior high level (Chart 10.3).

Chart 10.3   **Example of Interdisciplinary Approach**

Seventh Grade
Technology: Promises and Problems
Nations in Action
Choices and Decisions: Economics and Society
Lands of Africa (area study)
Eighth Grade
Either the hardbacked text, *The American Adventure*, Volume 1 or the three separate booklets from the text
The Early Years (20,000 B.C.-A.D. 1763)
The Forming of the Republic (1763-1825)
Expansion, Conflict and Reconstruction (1825-1880)
(In press, Volume 2) 1977
Into the Twentieth Century
Making of Tomorrow

What are the striking features of the *Concepts and Inquiry* program? First, you notice that content formerly found in higher grade levels in the traditional 1960 curriculum has moved downward into the lower grades. For example, the founding of the United States, usually in the fifth grade, is officially placed in the third grade. Topics such as Ancient Civilization, Greek and Roman Civilization, formerly located around the seventh grade, have moved down to grade five. This movement of content is especially noticeable at the seventh-grade level. The former emphases of the seventh grade upon geography/history of the United States/world have greatly diminished.

But, in many cases, teachers have kept the traditional content despite the series' recommendations. Many teachers have made this choice because of the reading level of the social studies textbooks. In the past, studies have indicated that even average students have had difficulty reading the typical social studies textbook. In fact, the new social studies textbook series, with their greater emphases on different social sciences, concepts, and inquiry, are placing even more demands on reading skills that demand

not only comprehension but analysis as well.

Two major studies by Roger Johnson in 1970 and 1973 indicated that the average reading level of a social studies textbook on the elementary level was increasing. In addition, Johnson found that the range of reading levels, often several grade levels within a textbook, was also increasing.[3] Thus, although the new textbook series are intellectually far superior to the rote-learning procedures of earlier decades, many teachers have found the new materials difficult to work with. Lemlech found in a survey of 200 elementary Los Angeles area teachers that teachers believed that the reading of social studies materials was the students' greatest learning problem.[4]

However, it appears that the publishers responded to the complaints that the reading level of social studies textbook was too difficult for the average students. In many cases, they encouraged teachers to use materials that had nominally recommended for lower grade levels. Since almost all textbooks are not labeled with grade level designations, this posed no difficulty. It also meant that a teacher on the seventh-grade level might be very pleased with using Concepts and Inquiry material such as the fifth-grade booklets on *Medieval Civilization* or *Four World Views* (major religious beliefs). In effect, this meant that content had not really moved downward. The traditional content was being taught although it was in a new format.

In addition, most of the major publishers revised their series and gave care-

---

[3] Roger E. Johnson. "Teachers Beware: Elementary Social Studies Textbooks Are Getting Harder to Read." Paper read at the National Council for the Social Studies–CUFA Conference, Atlanta, Ga., 1975, p. 1.
[4] Johanna K. Lemlech, "Elementary Social Studies: An Evaluation," *California Social Studies Review,* **12,** Winter Issue 1974, pp. 39-44.

ful attention to the reading problem. In fact, Roger Johnson reported in 1975 that in his evaluation of five major elementary social studies series that the average reading level had been simplified. Furthermore, the range of reading levels within a given text was also less than in 1970.[5]

The partial solving of the reading problem has meant that the *Concepts and Inquiry* program, like many other textbook series, is now probably more helpful to students. The availability of separate booklets instead of one large textbook probably encouraged many middle school/junior high school teachers to choose several different topics, often unrelated in terms of a rationale, instead of sticking to a geography orientation or using a chronological approach. The more widespread use of many discrete topics in the junior high school is, of course, related to the mushrooming of minicourses in senior high school social studies classes.

In addition, the *Concepts and Inquiry* program, because it was still producing material up to 1977, has been able to adopt to new trends such as more inclusion of minority groups and more consideration to problems facing American society. For example, pollution can be studied in *Technology: Promises and Problems* and problems of some minority groups in *Prejudice and Discrimination.* This emphasis has probably helped this project to gain national acceptance at the middle school/junior high level as well as at the elementary level. Furthermore, the booklets appear especially attractive and motivating for students.

An example of a possible topic that middle school/junior high school teachers now might choose is law-related educa-

tion. This field was practically unheard of 10 years ago, especially at the elementary and junior high school level. However, both private and federal sources have funded many law-related projects for use at all grade levels. Houghton-Mifflin's *Justice in Urban America* series is one of many projects that is available for the middle school/junior high school level. There are six separate booklets on poverty, consumerism, housing, crime, youth, and the law.

In summary, what trends seem to be evident from textbooks at the middle school/junior high school level? Most of the publishers' textbooks now reflect more of the new social studies with more emphasis on inquiry, concepts, and the methods of investigation by the social sciences. However, little exist in terms of sequence and continuity from one grade level to another. In addition, the traditional grade level allocation is seriously being challenged. Presently, at the sixth- and seventh-grade levels there appears to be no consensus on content allocation. The wider availability of different materials on different topics as well as the popularity of every teacher doing his or her "own thing" has probably encouraged this trend.

Thus, almost anything can go on in the middle school/junior high school level although the eighth grade, often because of state requirements, still is more likely to focus on U.S. history. On the other grade levels, it is possible to find units on Africa, technology, economics, law education as well as traditional topics such as Latin America or backgrounds for Western Civilization.

Thus, the middle school/junior high school social studies curriculum appears to be in a flux and no clear-cut patterns exist. The lack of continuity and sequence is a problem since effective learning requires building on previous experi-

---

[5] Roger E. Johnson, ibid., p. 5.

ences. This is especially true of skill development such as reading and small group discussion. On the other hand, the availability of more options available to teachers and curriculum planners can ideally better meet the needs of different students. The emphasis upon multicultural education also is very promising. However, all these developments in social studies textbooks and media do pose a challenge to middle school/junior high school teachers.

Bibliography

Books

Bossing, Nelson L. and Roscoe V. Cramer. *The Junior High School.* Boston: Houghton Mifflin Company, 1965.

DeVita, Joseph et al., *The Effective Middle School.* Englewood Cliffs, N.J.: Parker Publishing Co., 1970.

Eichhorn, Donald H. *The Middle School.* New York: The Center for Applied Research in Education, 1966.

Grooms, M. Ann. *Perspective of the Middle School.* Columbus, Ohio: Charles E. Merrill Books, 1967.

Hansen, John H. and Arthur C. Hearn. *The Middle School Program.* Chicago: Rand McNally and Co., 1971.

Hertling, James E. and Howard G. Getz. *Education for the Middle School Years: Readings.* Glenview, Ill.: Scott, Foresman and Co., 1971.

Kindred, Leslie W. et al. *The Middle School Curriculum.* Boston, Mass.: Allyn & Bacon, Inc., 1976.

Moss, Theodore. *Middle School.* Boston: Houghton-Mifflin, 1969.

Pumerantz, Philip and Ralph W. Galano. *Establishing Interdisciplinary Programs in the Middle School.* Englewood Cliffs, N.J.: Parker Publishing Co., 1972.

Ramano, Louis G. et al., *The Middle School.* Chicago, Ill.: Nelson-Hall, Co., 1973.

Stradley, William. *Practical Guide to the Middle School.* Englewood Cliffs, N.J.: Prentice-Hall, 1971.

Articles

See 14 articles in special issue "Middle School in the Making" in *Educational Leadership,* **31,** December 1973, pp. 195-244.

Why is values education important?

CHAPTER 11

Values Education: A New Emphasis

One of the most important trends in the social studies at all grade levels is values education or moral education. A vast majority of parents approve of this emphasis. However, different people mean different things by values or moral education. For some, it means the ability of students to develop their own standards. For others, it may mean conformity to the laws of our society.

Values have always been part of any school curriculum. However, in recent years there has been a renewed interest in "values" and "valuing." While definitional problems exist on the meaning of values, most teachers define values as the criteria for determing levels of goodness, worth, or beauty. Examples of values are honesty, freedom, trust, and rationality.

The most publicized approach is the value clarification approach of Sidney Simon and his colleagues. The purpose of this approach is to help students become aware of and to identify their own values and those of others. The value clarification approach allows students to use both rational thinking and emotional awareness in examining their personal

behavior patterns. In addition, students are encouraged to identify and to become aware of their own values and the interrelationship among values, to uncover and to resolve personal value conflicts, to share values with others, and to act according to their own values choices.[1]

The value clarification approach, in effect, relies on the wisdom of the human being to decide which values are positive and which are negative. The individual becomes the initiator of action within the society and the individual can change his/her environment. In other words, internal rather than external factors are seen as the prime determinants of human behavior.

To achieve the goals of the value clarification approach, teachers use a wide variety of methods. These methods include the following: large and small group discussion, rank orders and forced choices, listening techniques, songs, artwork, games and simulations, and jour-

---

[1] Sidney Simon, et al., *Values Clarification: A Handbook of Practical Strategies for Teachers and Students,* New York, Hart, 1972.

nals. However, the technique that best models the value clarification approach is the self-analysis reaction worksheet.[2] Here, the student is asked, for example, to list 20 things that he/she loves to do. The student then codes his/her answers according to cost, whether his/her parents like the activity, and other categories.

Because of the probing of the students' personal values, Simon's value clarification approach has been controversial. Fears are expressed about invasion of students' privacy. However, other values education approaches do exist. One is action learning.[3] As outlined by Jones, Newmann, Ochoa and Johnson, action learning extends the value clarification approach by putting more emphasis on action taking both inside and outside the classroom. In addition, action learning views values as formed from the interactive process that goes on between the person and society. In effect, values are influenced by society although the individual is encouraged to become an effective doer in society.

Thus, proponents of action learning do not just emphasize personal values. Instead, in the action approach, students are taught skills to become active participants in society. Their schooling is not seen as preparation for some more distant adulthood, but students are encouraged to act upon their values now.

Ochoa and Johnson regard action learning as a circular model in which individuals may enter at any stage (Figure 11.1).[3]

Kohlberg's moral development scheme is another well-known value approach. Kohlberg believes that there are three levels, six stages in the development of moral reasoning. These stages are listed in Chart 11.1:

According to Kohlberg's theory, an individual's growth through the sequence

Chart 11.1   Kohlberg's Levels of Moral Development

Level 1 Preconventional
  Stage 1 — orientation toward punishment; obedience to rules to avoid punishment
  Stage 2 — orientation toward satisfying needs of self primarily; obedience to rules in order to obtain rewards, get favors
(dominant in middle class children between the ages of 4 to 10)

Level 2 Conventional
  Stage 3 — conformity to stereotypical images of good behavior; conform to avoid disapproval of others
  Stage 4 — "law and order" orientation, orientation toward fixed rules, authority; conformity to avoid censure by authorities and resultant guilt
(dominant in preadolescence)

Level 3 Postconventional
  Stage 5 — social contract, awareness of relativism of values; conformity to standards agreed upon by whole society
  Stage 6 — orientation toward ethical principles which are universal and consistent such as justice, equality of human rights, respect for dignity of and value of the individual

(appears first in early adolescence)[a]

[a] Lawrence Kohlberg, "Moral Education in the Schools: A Developmental View," *School Review*, **74**, 1966, pp. 1-30; Lawrence Kohlberg, "Moral Development and the New Social Studies," *Social Education*, **37**, May 1973, pp. 369-375.

[2] This analysis of the various values education approach is heavily depended on Douglas P. Superka and Patricia L. Johnson, *Values Education: Approaches and Materials*, Boulder, Colo., ERIC Clearinghouse for Social Studies/Social Science Education, 1975.
[3] W. Ron Jones. *Finding Community: A Guide to Community Research and Action.* Palo Alto, California: James E. Freel, 1971. Fred M. Newmann. *Social Action: Dilemmas and Strategies.* The Public Issues Series. Columbus, Ohio: Xerox Education Publications, 1972. Anna S. Ochoa, Patricia Johnson. Paper given at the National Council for Social Studies Annual Convention, Atlanta, November, 1975.

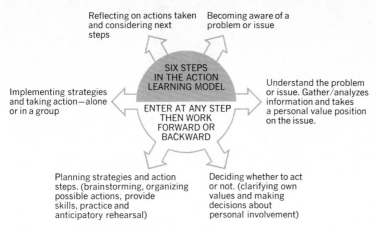

Reflecting on actions taken and considering next steps

Becoming aware of a problem or issue

SIX STEPS IN THE ACTION LEARNING MODEL

ENTER AT ANY STEP THEN WORK FORWARD OR BACKWARD

Implementing strategies and taking action—alone or in a group

Understand the problem or issue. Gather/analyzes information and takes a personal value position on the issue.

Planning strategies and action steps. (brainstorming, organizing possible actions, provide skills, practice and anticipatory rehearsal)

Deciding whether to act or not. (clarifying own values and making decisions about personal involvement)

Figure 11.1 Action learning model.

of the six stages appears to be always in the same order and to be present in all types of cultures. However, the individual's rate of movement through the stages varies. Individuals can understand all stages up to their own, but seldom more than one stage beyond their own. Individuals progress through these stages in the same order although any individual may stop at a particular stage.

In other words, Kohlberg and his associates want to help students to move to a higher moral reasoning stage. If a junior high school student, Manuel, is operating at stage 2, it is desirable to help the student to move to stage 3. This requires that the student, Manuel, hear some of the arguments at the higher stage of moral reasoning. If Manuel's own family and peer group operate primarily at the stage 2 point of development, it is unlikely that Manuel can move to a higher stage of moral reasoning. Therefore, according to Kohlberg, the school should make a deliberate attempt to facilitate moral stage changes. Kohlberg's theory assumes that the higher moral stages are better than lower ones.

Teachers set the stage by the presentation of moral dilemma episodes. These episodes usually involve one central character in a difficult, open-ended situation. They may be drawn from history, such as should Tom help a runaway slave or should Elaine warn the Indians of an attack by white people. Or, they can be drawn from problems of students such as cheating, drugs, and unfair school rules or social problems such as the role of the police, pollution problems, and the honesty of government officials.

The episode is usually read or dramatized to the whole class. Usually the episode has several available choices. Then, students are asked what *should* the central character in the story do?

Students make their tentative choice of action, usually by raising their hands. The teacher, on the basis of the students' choices, then divides the class into small discussion groups in which all members share the same value position. In the small group discussion, the group may list all the reasons they have for their position. Often they rank these reasons and eventually select the best reason for their value choice.

Variations exist but often the teacher brings the small groups together and asks probe questions that raise specific issues and examines other positions and their universal consequences. In this process, it is very likely that a given student will hear arguments that are on both a higher and lower level than he/she presently operates. In effect, individuals may become more conscious of the inadequacies of their present stage of moral reasoning and move toward a higher stage. As is obvious, this values approach is structured by the teacher and relies primarily on the moral dilemma episodes discussed in small groups.[4]

In addition to the values clarification approach (Simon), the action approach, and the moral development (Kohlberg), many social studies experts have recommended the analysis approach.[5] The purpose of this approach is to help students use logical thinking and scientific investigation to decide value issues and questions. The value analysis approach focuses on social issues rather than individual or personal issues. Topics likely to be used might include the roles of women, pollution, racial problems, and having a responsible government.

This approach is probably the most commonly accepted among social studies teachers. It uses a wide variety of techniques such as case studies, debate, research, and small discussions. Regardless

of the vehicle used to stimulate students, the purpose is always to demand that students give reasons and evidence for their position(s). In other words, a rational-analytical approach is used to value issues.

There is also a fifth values education approach. Parents are often concerned about drugs and other pressures on their children. As indicated before, most parents now want the schools to teach values. However, many parents advocate the inculcation approach that tries to instill or internalize certain values in students. The inculcation approach may use modeling, positive and negative reinforcement, scolding, providing incomplete or biased data as well as such teaching techniques as role playing or simulations.

Therefore, many communities and states have mandated that a certain amount of time be allocated to values education. Often content on drugs, alcohol, tobacco, and family life are included in the values education teaching. Often the values elements are incorporated into the social studies class.

However, different things are being done under the heading of values in the elementary school. Read the descriptions below. Which of the five major values approaches (values clarification, action learning, Kohlberg's moral development theory, values analysis, and inculcation) appear to be reflected in the following examples.

Activity 1. A school was having problems with firecrackers set off in the halls. The students formed a security council that patrolled the halls.

Activity 2. Each class member sits in a circle and is given an orange. The students are given a few minutes to carefully observe their oranges and later asked to identify them, eyes closed, from among a batch. The purpose is to teach observation skills

---

[4] Barry K. Beyer, "Conducting Moral Discussions in the Classroom" *Social Education*, **40,** April 1976, pp. 194-202. See also other articles in this issue devoted to Kohlberg's approach to moral education and especially the critique of the Kohlberg approach by Jack R. Fraenkel "The Kohlberg Bandwagon: Some Reservations," pp. 216-222.

[5] See the following as examples of the values analysis approach: Jack Fraenkel, *Teaching Students to Think and Value*, Englewood Cliffs, N.J., Prentice-Hall, 1973; Maurice P. Hunt and Lawrence E. Metcalf, *Teaching High School Social Studies*, New York, Harper, 1968; Donald Oliver and James Shaver, *Teaching Public Issues in the High School*, Houghton-Mifflin, 1966; and Hilda Taba et al., *A Teacher's Handbook to Elementary Social Studies: An Inductive Approach,* Menlo Park, Calif., Addison-Wesley, 1971.

to note details and to show how oranges, like people, are not all alike.

Activity 3. Students are asked to name 13 appliances (a baker's dozen) that use electricity. After jotting down the names of the appliances, the student is told due to the energy crisis, it is necessary to eliminate all but the three appliances that are most important. Students then share their reasons for their three choices with other members of the class or a small group.

Activity 4. The teacher reads the following story. Steven sees his best friend Tom using "crib sheets" during a test. After marking the tests, the teacher tells the class that she thinks that some of the students cheated. The teacher asks all students who know anything about the cheating to speak to her privately. What should Steven do?

Activity 5. Mr. Morrison, the social studies teacher, uses a booklet on women. The booklet focuses on the societal value conflicts between equality and traditional sex roles and continually asks students what they believe public policy should be in regard to associated issues such as child-care programs, laws related to marriage and divorce, the Equal Rights Amendment, women as officeholders, and the treatment of young women in the courts. The students engage in a variety of activities: reading, small group discussions, surveying the child-care facilities in their community, and examining how the media portrays women.

Activity 6. Ms. Balzano gives her students a lecture on the dangers of smoking. In her lecture, she tells her students that she does not smoke and that students should model their behavior after her and the other non-smokers on the faculty. Ms. Balzano does not allow any discussion on this topic.

Activity 7. Students play the game "Empire" in which in the course of trading, many students "deal" in slavery and smuggling. During debriefing, Ms. Hernandez asks students why they traded in slavery and smuggled.

Of course, often it is difficult to say that one activity exemplifies one particular value approach. But the interest in values education as part of the school's responsibility appears to be an important trend although there is not enough data to support the superiority of any one approach. However, there are also some strong criticisms of trying to teach values or morals in the school.

Some believe that the values clarification approach of Sidney Simon is immoral since it allows students, often very young and immature students, the right to choose their own values. Other critics believe that it is almost impossible for teachers to hide their own feelings and own value system. In effect, teachers may give more attention to students who have the "right" answers according to the teacher's philosophy. Their voice or body language may also convey to students that the teacher believes that some responses are "better" than others.

Perhaps the most serious impediment in the way of values education is the climate of opinion or the hidden curriculum that exist in any school. If grades are considered important, students may cheat without any qualms. Or if the message is given that in sports one should win at any price, rules will be broken. In such situations, it is not likely that values education will make much progress. In many cases, it would be worth the time for schools to focus on some of the situations which appear to be in the way of students' ethical development.

However, despite its difficulties, values will probably continue to be an important part of the curriculum. More textbooks and media will probably focus on open-ended and more value-related questions. Values education also probably promotes more discussion on such sensitive issues as discrimination, women's rights, and the like.

Bibliography

Castell, J. Doyle and Robert J. Stahl. *Value Clarification in the Classroom: A Primer*. Pacific Palisades, Calif.: Goodyear Publishing Co., Inc. 1975.

Hall, Brian P. *Value Clarification as Learning Process. A Guidebook of Learning Strategies.* New York: Paulist Press, 1973.

Kohlberg, Lawrence. *Collected Papers on Moral Development and Moral Education.* Cambridge, Mass.: Harvard University Laboratory for Human Development, 1973.

Hawley, Robert C. and Isabel L. Hawley. *Human Values in the Classroom.* New York, New York: Hart, Inc., 1975.

Kirschenbaum, Howard and Sidney B. Simon. *Readings in Values Clarification.* Minneapolis, Winston Press, 1973.

Meyer, John et al., eds. *Values Education: Theory/Practice/Problems/Prospects.* Waterloo, Ontario, Canada: Wilfred Laurier University Press, 1975.

Shaftel, Fannie and George Shaftel. *Role Playing for Social Values.* Englewood Cliffs, N.J.: Prentice-Hall, 1967.

Shaver, James P. and William Strong. *Facing Value Decisions: Rationale-building for Teachers.* Belmont, Calif.: Wadsworth Publishing Co., 1976.

Superka, Douglas P. and Patricia L. Johnson. *Values Education: Approaches and Materials.* Boulder, Colo.: ERIC Clearinghouse for Social Studies/Social Science Education, 1975.

Which instructional strategies are facilitated
by a field trip?

CHAPTER 12

Different Instructional Strategies or Methods

General Considerations

The time schedule does put restraints on what teachers can do. Larger blocks of time are often better for large group presentations, simulation games, projects, and individualized instruction. Teachers on a fixed time schedule always have to keep in the back of their mind when the bell will ring so that they can give closure to their instruction.

This is particularly true of the middle school and the junior high school. Probably the most common organization is the fixed time period of a class that meets every day, at the same time, Monday through Friday. In these schools, the first period may start around eight-thirty and last for about 50 minutes. A five-minute break usually exists between periods.

To break the traditional everyday class periods, some middle schools/junior high schools have moved to a different schedule on A and B days. Students and teachers have different classes on each A or B day. Monday may be an A day and Tuesday a B day. In some schools, the social studies class will meet for two periods on an A day but not meet at all on a B day. In other schools, the social studies class will meet every day although the time it meets may change. A or B days may start (or end) at different times.

More flexible teachers, regardless of grade level, do work around rigid schedules to make the best learning situations. They may run a simulation game for several days with each day having a trading/gaming session. Or they may group their class so that they can work with a given group of students while other students are doing something else.

But even in the same organizational time pattern within a given school, enormous variations exist of instructional strategies or methods used by teachers. Some of these differences are partly explained by the materials the teacher has available. Typically, the middle school/junior high school teacher has more choice and more supplementary materials.

Thus, in the elementary grades, it is common that each student has a hardcover social studies textbook. Often all third graders in the school have the same textbook. In addition, a given series may be used for several grade levels with some attempt to have sequence and continuity in the program. But the elementary level also has been influenced by the philosophy that "every teacher should do his/her own thing." Many elementary teachers are not following the prescribed program of the district.

A wider choice exists on what materials are used at the middle school/junior high school level. In the same school, different instructors of United States History may use different textbooks or materials. In some classes there may not even be hard cover textbooks in the classroom. Instead, there may be more extensive use of paperback and teacher-produced materials.

But teacher orientations, more than materials, are fundamental to explain the wide variations in what different teachers consider to be a "good social studies program." Some teachers have students read the textbook orally for their main activity in the social studies program. Others may develop a contract system with students on what they will accomplish during their social studies class.

What ideas about a good social studies program are illustrated in the following examples.

Activity 1. In a unit on India, after a speaker who is a yogi expert, the class, lead by the teacher, try out various yogi exercises.

Activity 2. In a unit on developing nations, students are asked to volunteer to fast for a certain number of hours. The volunteers are to keep a record about how they felt.

Activity 3. The students construct boats that will be used in their unit on "The Harbor." They will use the boats in dramatic play to see some of the problems in controlling traffic in a large harbor.

Activity 4. Each student on a committee researches a topic on colonial life—the postal service, medical services, etc. and the group then presents their report to the class.

Activity 5. Students, in a unit on human development, visit day care centers in the community. Following a guide, they observe the behavior of young children.

Activity 6. The teacher sets up an experiment to see if a given student will submit to group pressure.

Activity 7. Students in a junior high school outline their chapter of a social studies textbook.

Activity 8. Students read children's literature related to the unit they are studying.

Activity 9. Students read conflicting accounts of a given event or read about different points of view of various people on a given issue.

Activity 10. The teacher and students take a field trip to the local bakery.

Activity 11. Students play a simulation game in which they are put in the shoes of a minority group.

Activity 12. The teacher invites a police officer to the class to speak on bike safety.

As you can see, a wide variety of different instructional methods of strategies exist for teachers. What determines which method a teacher should use? The following considerations are important in setting up learning experiences.

1. An analysis of the teacher's own strengths, background, experiences, and interests. Usually, it is helpful for a teacher to use methods in which he/she feels comfortable and secure. However, teachers should try out different strategies or methods to see if they might be better and more effective for certain students. Indeed, usually a variety of methods is best for helping students to learn social studies.

2. An analysis of the students' wide diversity in background, experiences, and interests. Primary grade teachers may orally ask about interests of students. In the middle grades or junior high, brief surveys, often illustrating the methodology of social scientists, can be effective in finding out where students are at the present time.

3. A consideration of time and place. Some rooms are not designed for simulations. The last hour of the day on Friday may not be conducive to having students listen attentively to a record or a tape. The first week of school has a different climate in the classroom than the middle of the semester or the end of the year.

Chart 12.1 might be helpful for this purpose of finding out about students' interests.

Chart 12.1   What Is Worth Knowing?

Directions: Read each item. If you believe an item is important to know or learn, place a check in the space before it. If you think knowing or learning an item is of little or no importance, mark it with a -. When you have marked each item, look at the checked items only. Then rank the first three items (or as many as your teacher tells you) from the most important to the least important with number 1 being most important.

_____ 1. Who the first president of the United States was.
_____ 2. How to work effectively on a committee.
_____ 3. How to think.
_____ 4. To respect the worth and dignity of all people.
_____ 5. What causes pollution of the environment.
_____ 6. How to do research.
_____ 7. How to resolve a conflict between two people.
_____ 8. What the causes of the Civil War were.
_____ 9. How to curb pollution of the environment.
_____ 10. Understanding of other peoples and other nations.

You, of course, could add any other statements that you may think are of interest to your students.

Working with students in analyzing their own data may be very helpful. If students believe that it is important to know facts such as when Columbus "discovered" America, it probably will be difficult, at least initially, for a teacher to focus on inquiry and its related skills. Unless students can realize why a topic, skill, or value is important or relevant to them, most generally do not make much of a commitment to learning.

Are there any other considerations that might influence what methods a teacher would use? Of course, textbooks and related materials and media might make a difference. It is difficult to set up a unit on Bali if you do not have materials on Bali. It is probably important if students are studying about Africa, that a map (either in a textbook, a paperback, or on the wall) be available to the students. Some basic materials and media are helpful if students are to achieve a certain degree of competency in skills and understanding.

But does the nature of the subject matter make a difference? Perhaps 15 years ago, more people would have said that if you taught history or geography certain methods would be more appropriate for different subjects. While it is true that each of the social sciences and history do have central concepts and methodologies, probably there are no methods that are just reserved for a given subject. Thus, the case study of an individual in a dilemma is not reserved just to law-related education.

Methods and techniques such as questioning, role-playing activities, small-group work, and questioning are appropriate and useful in all social studies classes. For the same content, one teacher may rely heavily on one textbook while another, using a more inductive approach, might involve students in setting up questionnaires to gather and to analyze their own data about a particular hypothesis on how students spend their own money.

Teachers almost must at least think about how much attention should be given to the role of minority/ethnic groups, including women. Even if both the teacher and the students have little interest in this area, the *Curriculum Guidelines for Multiethnic Education*[1] of the National Council for the Social Studies strongly recommend that it is a responsibility of all teachers at all grade levels to spend more time on ethnic studies. All students, regardless of their backgrounds, should have some learning experiences on the various American ethnic groups. Students should be aware of the diversity within a given group, the historical and cultural background of the group as well as its present status in society today. They should become aware that different ethnic groups see issues from different points of view. Students should understand the whole ethnic experience and not just be exposed to an historical or heroes approach.

In many communities, multicultural education is a sensitive issue. Some communities have set up parent/community advisory boards that now are dictating exactly what topics at what time of the academic school year should be emphasized in social studies classrooms. In many cases, parent groups have moved into this area because they have felt that the schools were doing very little. On the opposite extreme, communities exist that encourage the schools to do nothing to recognize the fact that we are a multicultural society.

In addition to multicultural education, teachers at all grade levels must consider what content is mandated by the state or local community. In recent years some states have mandated certain courses or emphases such as career education or drug education. While state and local mandates have been part of the

American educational scene for sometime, in some communities there is also a movement toward accountability. In other words, can the teachers show that students really did increase their career awareness or knowledge of consumer education? It is most likely that the required or mandated courses or topics are most likely to be the ones in which some degree of accountability is stressed. This is especially true if the school district is receiving state funds for specific purposes. When teachers know that they are held responsible for teaching students certain knowledge, skills, and values, their methods usually focus on making sure that students will perform satisfactorily on any tests or other forms of assessment.

All of these considerations influence what kind of method of strategy a given teacher will use in setting up learning experiences. The teacher, the students, the climate in the classroom, and even the number of students within the class make a difference as well as the time and setting. And most certainly required or mandated topics may influence how a teacher teaches.

A further point also should be noted. No teacher can be an expert in every social science discipline nor in interdisciplinary topics such as ecology. Awareness of this fact should lead to the development of more team teaching or closer working relations with fellow teachers. In the past, not much "sharing" has gone on among elementary and middle/junior high school teachers. Thus, although several teachers may teach the same content such as U.S. history, frequently teachers guard their "successful" ideas so that no other teachers can "borrow" them.

Unfortunately, team teaching, in some cases, has in practice involved a minimum amount of real planning and cooperation among teachers. Teachers, in

---

[1] National Council for the Social Studies, *Curriculum Guidelines for Multiethnic Education,* Washington, D.C., NCSS, 1976.

this situation, merely take turns teaching larger groups. In addition, personality factors are most important in the success of team teaching or any of its variations. Too frequently, administrative fiats for team teaching have established teams with little regard to how teachers get along with each other.

Teachers, in looking over their goals and their content, should consider if other members of the staff could do a better job in certain areas while they could do a better job if they concentrated on other topics. They must consider if they can use paraprofessionals or volunteers from the community in their program. However, planning is essential for successful team efforts.

If teachers work together, often it influences their own teaching methods as well as teaching style. What you do with 60 in the class is not the same as if you have 25 students. Teachers working as a team do not usually have as much freedom in their teaching strategies as compared to traditional teachers in self-contained classrooms. Some teachers find this loss of "independence" not worth the gains of specialization and interaction with other staff members.

Thus, we have examined the many influences on what methods a teacher may use. Different instructional strategies are used by different teachers. Let us look more carefully at some of these methods or strategies that are perhaps more particular to social studies. Each method represents one route to more successful learning results for your students. Each involves teacher direction of student thinking processes. Yet all teaching methods do have some common elements. They involve preparation on the part of the teacher, concern with motivation, setting up the learning experience, and some assessment to see if the students have gained in understanding, skills, or changed values.

Questioning

How are we sure that students understand what they read or view or hear? We usually check by asking them questions. Research tells us that the form and sequence these questions take and the atmosphere in which they are posed are crucial to verifying where students are and helping them get beyond that point.

There are four effective kinds of teacher behaviors that encourage positive student participation in discussions. One is nonjudgmental teacher acceptance of student responses to a question. The more you say, "No," "Someone else?" or "That's wrong," the less likely students will be to venture responding to your questions. An incorrect response can be met several ways: you state the question another way, you restate the answer offered to see if you understand, you suggest a connection between the answer and the question, you call for further ideas on the question. A second technique for loosening students up in discussion is to probe the student's response by inviting the respondent or someone else to give an example of what is meant. A third technique is the sacred art of listening to students. Let them finish. Show you are listening by eye contact or head nodding. Insist that others listen too. A fourth technique is to accept silence after you have asked a question. Thought requires time; allow for it to happen.

On the cognitive side, these pointers should guide your planning for a discussion. First, you have your objectives well in mind. This is what separated a bull session from a discussion. A bull-session wanders from topic to topic according to whatever the participants' interests lead. A structured discussion usually has the objective of formulating a concept or a generalization. There are patterns of questioning for a concept or a generalization for guiding a group toward these higher levels of thinking.

Imagine that your objective was to expand the definition of family held by your second graders, a concept development thinking task. Previously they have shown that they have internalized the mother, father, children — nuclear definition of family. This is curious as several students come from single parent homes. You arrange four large, colorful pictures for the discussion. One is of an older woman and a young child fishing, one is of an adult male serving two children at the kitchen table, one is of an extended Mexican American family picnicking in the park, one is of an elderly woman walking her dog. Your questioning sequence is as follows:

1. "What do you see?" Present and discuss each picture in turn.
2. "How are these pictures alike?" "Different?"
3. "Are these all pictures of family groups?" "Why?"
4. "How do we know when we are seeing a family?" "What kinds of things do members of a family do for each other?"

Through this sequence of questions your students have differentiated picture details, identified common properties and formed new criteria for grouping together common properties.[2] Your objective led you to formulate a very specific sequence of questions that focused the group's attention. A prepared sequence of focusing questions is the second pointer for leading profitable discussions. Think through how you will develop your objective by asking questions rather than telling. Write down your sequence on a small note and use it as a reminder as you move the group's thought processes toward your objective.

A third pointer for conducting profitable discussions is to set the ground rules and expectations before you begin. Will the students have to write a definition or summary based on the discussion? Can they participate spontaneously or should they wait to be called on? Groups experienced in discussion will not need to be reminded of these basics each time, but until habits are formed the teacher needs to review his or her expectations. Teachers often give up on groups that are inexperienced with the discussion format. The problem usually is that teachers themselves are not careful about specifying behavior standards they expect students to follow.

Sometimes questioning, especially of low-level questions, is called recitation. Recitation is a question and answer interaction between the students and teacher. Usually, the teacher is the only one who asks the questions and students typically have responded with answers from the textbook.

You know that questioning can lead to higher levels of thinking. The type of questions asked by the teacher limits the possible responses of the student. Low-level memory questions on the products of Brazil call for little thinking on the part of students. On the other, a sequence of questions starting from a low level of fact level can cause students to think about generalizations on the problems of developing nations or the relationship of natural resources to a nation's standard of living.

Questioning is a part of effective teaching. However, it is also essential to get students to ask some questions. In actual practice, the number of questions asked by students is small compared to the questions initiated by the teacher. Yet often effective student learning comes from asking good questions.

---

[2] Hilda Taba et al., *Teachers' Handbook for Elementary Social Studies*, Menlo Park, Calif. Addison-Wesley, 1967, 92.

Initially, student questions are often on trivial or irrelevant points. But teachers can use student questions as lead-ins to have other students respond. Breaking the pattern of teacher speaks, student Sam answers, teacher speaks, student Ramona answers is very helpful. Instead, try to encourage the pattern with the teaching asking "What do you think?" followed by comments of students Jose, Rae, and Lorraine. Usually good student questions increase total student responses.

Lecturing

One of the oldest methods of teaching at all grade levels is lecturing. Even primary teachers, well aware of the attention span of their children, do some lecturing or talking to their students. Typically, in lecturing the teacher has some knowledge — a concept, information not available to students in their textbooks, an orientation to the unit, and the like — that he/she wishes to get across to the students. Lecturing assumes that the students are motivated and willing to receive the message. Unfortunately, in actual practice, often students are not motivated and as a result, retain little of the information given in the lecture since they were not actively listening.

Yet while the lecture technique has several disadvantages, especially overused, it can be very effective in some situations. Teachers should remember the following:

1. There should be a focus or organization to the lecture. In general, students have to be told what they are going to hear, get the message, and then receive a final summary of the message. The main concept may be that urban areas have a wider variety of occupations than rural

areas. Too frequently, students do not understand the purpose or rationale of the lecture and have difficulty in putting the pieces of information — jobs like air control officer, foreman, or computer operator — together.
2. Arouse and maintain interest by the use of effective questions, use of audiovisual materials, humor, showing the relationship of the content to their own lives, and effective pacing. Be especially careful not to lecture too long and at too slow of a pace. Too frequently, long lectures turn students away from careful listening.
3. Be alert to the interest of your audience. Avoid looking up to the ceiling but use good eye contact with students to see if they appear to be listening and understanding what is being said.

Inquiry

Inquiry, is essentially an umbrella term covering inductive learning, discovery learning, and problem solving. Inquiry assumes that real learning starts when an individual perceives a blocked goal or becomes aware of a new situation that does not fit his/her previous experience. The person then engages in "inquiry" to solve the problem.

This teaching method encourages students to think as contrasted with the traditional method of telling students what they are suppose to know. Inquiry, of course, replicates to some degree the procedures of scientific method. Usually there is an identification of the problem, development of hypotheses, data collection and data analysis, and some tentative conclusions. Most commonly we require students to collect, organize, and interpret data to answer questions.

For example, what does the data in Chart 12.2 suggest to you about the social climate in California between 1845 and 1860?

Chart 12.2 Inquiry Data Sample

NEW TOWNS IN CALIFORNIA		POPULATION IN CALIFORNIA	
		Year	Non-Indians
Whiskeytown	Rough and Ready	1847	15,000
Hangtown	Digtown	1850	92,598 (60,000 miners)
Fiddletown	French Gulch	1852	223,856 (25,000 Chinese)
Dutch Flat	Chinese Camp		
Mormon Bar	Placerville		SAN FRANCISCO
		1848	1,000
		1860	56,000

To answer this general question you would probably make a series of statements, or hypotheses, such as:

"California was a violent place during this period."

"There was segregation during this period."

"Miners settled with others of their ethnic or religious group."

Proving any one of these statements would require that you go beyond this initial evidence. This process would lead you to collect more information and weigh it against your initial statements. What you have done in verifying or changing your initial conclusion is called doing inquiry. Its steps replicate to one degree or another the classic procedures of scientific method.

Whenever we arrange problem situations that require students to collect, organize and interpret data, we are teaching through the inquiry process. Several conditions must be present for students to conduct meaningful inquiry. First, the students must be intrigued by the problem. Historical problems, such as the illustration above are most difficult for students to respond to. Second, students must feel they are in a climate where they can disagree with each other and the teacher. Third, inquiry techniques are not appropriate when the question has a right or wrong answer or when the teacher feels there is one right answer to

the problem or question. Situations prompting students to conduct inquiry should be open ended. They should promote the exploration of alternative conclusions.

Conducting polls, interviewing, observing behavior, measuring are all useful methods of data gathering that elementary and middle school/junior high school students can conduct. Methods of organizing data usually require charting or graphing or pictorial grouping and verbal interpreting. Structured discussions using focusing questions that ask students to make summary statements about the data they have collected or studied and compare these statements to their original statements about the problem or topic are appropriate for bringing inquiry to a summation.

Setting up fruitful inquiry is a difficult task for most teachers since the students must be intrigued by the problem. Therefore, many teachers have turned to published material. Let us look at an example of commercially prepared inquiry material, designed especially for students in the third through sixth grades.

In a minisociety program, the teacher sets up a scarcity situation in which the students' wants are greater than the resources available in the room to satisfy these wants. The teacher encourages dissatisfaction about not having enough of a particular item or activity. After enough students complain, the students and teacher get together to identify the problem. Often students discuss the advantages and disadvantages of different allocative strategies such as a lottery method, need, "first come, first served," and prices. Generally a price system is started and students work out a formula to receive an income based on certain classroom behaviors such as coming to class on time, productive work, and not being disruptive to others. As students receive income, they then can buy and sell goods and services that are desired in the classroom.

In their participation in their own minisociety, students must constantly assess their values and their financial position. Will they have enough money to bid at an auction or to buy certain goods or services? Or will there be enough demand in the class for an individual or group to start a newspaper or a business that will be profitable? Typically, individuals and partners in the class set up different financial institutions such as banks, loan companies, as well as government agencies to regulate the working of their miniature society. In addition, many go into business by making arts and crafts, selling services such as dancing lessons, or providing entertainment with board games.

In a minisociety, students are constantly required to think about what decisions they should make. Yet the particular format that each class' minisociety evolves depends on the interests and skills of the students and indirectly upon the teacher. The process is open ended in that typically different classes do different things to solve their problems in a minisociety.[3]

The minisociety inquiry experience could last for weeks or even a whole year. However, most inquiry exercises that are set up by teachers can be completed in a shorter period of time. However, in general, inquiry exercises, by the very nature of data collection and analysis, often take much longer than traditional methods such as viewing films or questioning. For example, inquiry could start out by a chart showing from 1776 to the present the life expectancy at birth of American men and women, or the percentage of women in the labor force. From these data, students might consider the roles of women and men in our society. Or a table on black and white incomes, or male and female incomes could be used as a springboard to inquiry. Students would be asked to give possible interpretations, explanations, or hypotheses to explain the data. In many cases, students during inquiry become more aware of possible value conflicts in our society.

While stressing the many possible advantages of the inquiry method, especially its motivating power to help students to think, the demands upon the teacher should not be ignored. Many social studies teachers as well as students have had little experience in using such skills as making a hypothesis, collecting data and analyzing their data. As a result, many teachers have felt unsure of themselves and have been reluctant to try material which demands that teachers have skills in inquiry teaching. Unless they are given help with in-service training, workshops, attendance at conferences, it is not realistic to expect teachers to change radically their behavior in the classroom.

Dramatic Techniques

Experiences in active exploration of how others feel about a situation is imperative if students are to develop skills of empathy and problem solving. Dramatic

---

[3] Marilyn Kourilsky, *Beyond Simulation, the Mini-Society Approach to Instruction in Economics and Other Social Sciences,* Los Angeles, Educational Resource Associates, Inc., 1974.

play, role play, and simulation gaming are techniques that structure the exploration. Each involves student discussion led by the teacher. Yet each goes beyond discussion and involves students in assuming parts of the situation. Student attempts to act out a solution demand creativity. Play calls upon students to respond to their inner voices and the reactions of others' interpretations. Pure discussion rarely accomplishes the creative response. Let us look at each technique briefly.

Dramatic play poses no initial problems to students. It is a technique that allows students to explore a setting they are studying in terms of what actual people in that setting do and how they might conduct themselves. As stimuli students need appropriate music, realia, and pictures. Thus, students would play in open-ended fashion at organizing a Plains Indian buffalo hunt, running a dairy farm, or managing an airport. The bicentennial year did see many social studies classes across the nation involved in recreating, often with attempts at accurate costuming, historical events, or time periods that had occured in their community.

Debriefing should always follow such sessions to find out, "What did we learn through our play today?" "Would things actually happen as we portrayed them?" "What do we need to find out to make our play more realistic?" "How might we do this?"

Role playing, by contrast, aims to explore alternative solutions to problem situations. Role playing aims to gain deeper understanding of social relationships of one's self and others. It has been effectively used to show conflicting values on given issues. Favorite stimuli for role plays are unfinished stories and films or pictures that portray dilemmas.

Teacher structuring is vital for guaranteeing student involvement, direction and analysis. Basic structuring steps are these:

1. Teacher sets stage with "Have you ever . . . ," question about dilemma area to be presented.
2. T: "How did you feel in this situation?" "Today, we're going to hear a story about _____ who got into a similar jam. Think about how you feel as I read."
3. Stop story at conflict point, "What is the problem here?"
4. Ask how each person in the story feels and why.
5. Call on volunteers to assume roles and play out a solution.
6. Discuss solution in terms of its realism. Ask for other interpretations until alternatives are exhausted.
7. Summarize by asking, "What would you conclude about the problem we have been exploring?"

However, some teachers have noted that certain students are reluctant to volunteer to role play. In some cases students feel uneasy about their performance before the class. In most cases, it is easier to get students to role play in historical situations such as the Constitutional Convention rather than a personal dilemma.

However, historical situations involving famous figures are less productive for role play than contemporary problems. Often students cannot free themselves of knowledge of what happened. Their role playing becomes an attempt to duplicate all facts accepted as "the way it was." Better success can be obtained by using "John Doe" characters caught up in a historically significant moment, such as brothers from Kentucky with opposing views about staying in the Union at the onset of the Civil War.

Simulation gaming allows for students dramatic creativity within prescribed limits. As the term suggests, a similation game presents a group of students with descriptions of a situation, roles they must assume as players, rules to follow and steps they must take that involve problem-solving allowing someone to "win" the games. Rules, roles, and situations are designed to imitate real-life problems.

Games and simulations have achieved a great deal of acceptance in some social studies classes, especially for older elementary school children and those in junior high school. Within the last 10 years, there has been an enormous increase in the number of commercial games including some relatively inexpensive ones. Many teachers have modified ideas from commercial games into their own simulations. Students have been involved in games about pioneers to those simulating international problems.

A simulation game sets out the rules for winning, role descriptions and positions, and steps for playing the game. A simple game example is the Purples and Pinks. This game designates a few students as privileged and the rest as deprived. It is usually played during an entire school day. The privileged have special treatment. They have more recess, better food, better work conditions, and so on, than the deprived students. Debriefing demands that a connection between how this experience made students feel and how similar circumstances might have an effect in the real world be made. The objective of this technique is to allow students a simulated experience with a set of variables they are studying about through secondhand sources.

In using a game or simulation, the teacher has a different role. The teacher often plays the role of a mediator, umpire, or an observer. The teacher keeps an eye on the whole scene to see how the various participants are behaving. Most important, from these observations, the teacher sets up a debriefing experience at the end of the game to see what the students have learned.

While games often have a fun element, it is essential to evaluate if most students seem to be gaining some insight from playing the simulated game. Usually the game has some major concepts as well as skills that the students are expected to achieve. Unless students are achieving these goals, games are a waste of both the teacher and students' time.

Games also present certain difficulties to teachers. Sometimes a student(s) may become too emotionally involved and even engage in aggressive behavior. In other cases, some students may feel that they do not have important roles and do not participate actively. Normally games greatly increase the noise level of the class that may disturb other teachers. Furthermore, certain games require more space than the conventional classroom has.

To have a successful learning experience, the teacher must understand the purpose and the rules of the game. If it is a commercial game, it is absolutely essential to read the teacher's manual or know the game. For this reason, many teachers prefer to attend a conference or to see the game played before trying it out by themselves.

Games, like role playing or any other teaching method, are not guaranteed to be successful. Teachers should consider if they have the skills as well as the physical resources and time to have a successful game. More important, they must evaluate to see that the game is really contributing to student learning.

However, dramatic techniques—dramatic play, role playing, and simulated games—allow students to learn about social situations by "living" or "doing" them. They promote active learning in social studies as manipulative materials do in mathematics. These techniques should be employed as an integral part of the unit being studied. Loosening students up for participation demands a gradual program that moves from exercises in responding to rhythm to pantomiming actions to interpreting emotions. The care taken in preparing students for dramatic techniques as well as discussions and debriefings can be a richly rewarding experience.

Small-Group Techniques

If a student is a member of a class with 25 or more members, he/she has only a small chance of participating at a given moment. However, if the teacher divides the whole class into small groups of five or so, each student has increased significantly his or her possibility of active listening and speaking. Small-group discussions therefore are one of the most important techniques that social studies teachers at all grade levels can use.

Many students, who are always the listeners when discussion is conducted with the whole class, bloom in small-group work. Small-group brainstorming is an effective way to gather input and increase interest in a new question or topic put before the class. For example, divide the class into groups of four or five or groups of two or three in the primary grades. Then give the groups 10 minutes to explore questions such as, ways to cut energy costs or ways to make people new to the group feel at ease or listing objects and supplies necessary for heading West by wagontrain. Compare the variety and quantity of results obtained in this fashion to those, concerning a similar question, obtained from the whole class. Brainstorming in small groups is useful for initial open-ended exploration of a question or topic. It is not normally an adequate way to guide students to concept formulation or generalization.

Mrs. Garvey felt her fifth-grade class needed to become more aware of the ne-cessity for group cooperation. She used small groups to get at this problem. Pieces of a cut-up tangram were given to each member of each group. Instructions prohibited any verbal or written communication between members of the small groups. The task was for the groups to assemble the pieces of the tangram. Mrs. Garvey observed acts of cooperation and noted them on paper as the groups worked. Finally, every group completed its task. Students then discussed what helped and hindered their group's progress. They discovered that groups did better when there was turn-taking and facial communication between all group members. The lesson took about 35 minutes. The awareness that working in small groups gave the students lingered for days.

One of the errors that teachers make with using small groups is not giving students enough background to have a small group discussion. Too often teachers just place students into small groups and say "Discuss problems in the Middle East" (or some other nation, the local community, etc.). This is much too vague and often students do not have enough background to have a fruitful discussion on the Middle East.

More effective is to write out a paragraph or two giving some data for each small group. For example, the teacher could summarize data on the number of people with malnutrition in the world and the amount of food that American dogs consume. Students then could focus on questions such as should Americans be allowed to have one or more dogs, especially larger dogs. Since many students have dogs as pets, this question is likely to involve the students.

It is also essential to choose exercises in which students are likely to disagree or have different points of view. No real discussion can take place if all in the group agree on what should be done. Examples of people caught in dilemmas are often most effective since it is unlikely that all students will agree on what should be done to an individual caught shoplifting or, in an earlier time period, helping runaway slaves.

All individuals have to interact in small groups—in their families, with friends, at work, and at clubs and organizations. In small-group discussion, students can gain skills in listening to others, seeing weaknesses in others and their own arguments, and coming to decisions. However, small-group discussion skills do not develop overnight and teachers must provide many opportunities for their students to practice small-discussion group skills.

Other Methods

Other methods and strategies also exist for social studies teachers, especially those that try to individualize instruction. Learning centers can be used for social studies teaching. Loosely defined, a learning center is an area in a classroom or some part of the school where there are a wide variety of different materials and resources. Students are to take more responsibility for their own learning.

Among the advantages of a learning center is that students can work at their own pace and often with some options on what they are to do. Among the disadvantages of this method are the enorous amount of time required for teachers to set up learning centers. In

addition, many teachers have found that they must spend a great deal of their time in record keeping to monitor the progress of each student. Often, unless aides, student teachers, or volunteers are enlisted, the clerical work may become al-

most unmanageable. A further point is that some students do not appear to be responsible and independent so that they can work on their own.

Group investigation or student committees are another strategy used by some social studies teachers. This is an extension of a small discussion group but there is a commitment to working for a longer period of time on a given project. Successful committee work requires a high level of skills on the part of the students to work together and to develop their own leadership. In practice, not all small committees are able to "put themselves together." Too frequently, a few more able and better motivated students do all the work for the committee since the whole committee often receives the same grade.

Other methods include supervised study, review or drill sessions, and evaluation techniques. Some people also include using outside speakers and media as specific methods. Regardless of what is defined as methods or strategies, it is usually best if the teacher has a wide repertoire of methods and strategies than to rely or overuse one or two methods.

These brief descriptions of each technique should be thought of as the yeast for raising your creativity in classroom planning. The surest way to guarantee failure is to employ one of these techniques to the exclusion of the others. Be brave! Experiment with all of them. Invent your own variations. By experimenting with these teaching techniques you will develop that sixth sense possessed by the master teacher who continually provides appropriate challenges for his or her students.

In summary, changes of both title and substance have taken place in social studies programs from kindergarten to eighth-grade level. There is more experimentation with organization structure, materials, and teaching methods than before. Still, it is rare to encounter a school where the students, parents, and teachers are satisfied with the current social studies program. The search for better ways of educating our society's young people to enter successfully the realm of citizenship will continue for the foreseeable future.

Bibliography

General Methods

Cooper, James M. et al., *Classroom Teaching Skills: A Handbook* and also by the same authors *Classroom Teaching Skills: A Workbook.* Lexington, Mass.: D. C. Heath and Co., 1977.

Gilstrap, Robert L., and William R. Martin. *Current Strategies for Teachers.* Pacific Palisades, Calif.; Goodyear Publishing Co., Inc., 1975.

Hyman, Ronald T. *Ways of Teaching.* Philadelphia, Pa.: J. B. Lippincott Co., 1970.

Social Studies Methods

Banks, James A. with Ambrose A. Clegg, Jr. *Teaching Strategies for the Social Studies.* Reading, Mass.: Addison-Wesley, Co., 1973.

Zodikoff, David. *Alternative Teaching Models in Social Studies Education.* Dubuque, Iowa: Kendall/Hunt, 1976.

SECTION 4

Inquiry Learning in Social Studies

Inquiry is one of the most potent concepts that can be used to guide the organization of social studies programs. Inquiry is about process or strategy. As a strategy for organizing learning experiences, the structure inquiry provides can ensure greater learner involvment with nearly any topic. It can be used as an overarching structure for curriculum development or in bits and pieces as the time and materials and content warrant.

This section has two purposes. It details the steps of the inquiry process and it illustrates these steps with examples from various grade levels and social studies topics. Chapter 13 relates everyday decision making to the inquiry process. Chapter 14 carries the steps of the process into action by providing reader-involving examples. Chapter 15 continues the process into the analytic steps exposing techniques for interpreting the data produced by the investigative process.

What analysis can students make of television
programs?

CHAPTER 13

What Is Inquiry?

Dimensions of Choice

"The only sure things in life are death and taxes." "Life is just one *9#?% thing after another!" These are popular expressions of the fact that uncertainty is a constant part of everyone's daily lives. Throughout the uncertainty that surrounds us, everyone's life is also filled with moments that require choices to be made. Some of these choices require more thought than others. Some choices have great consequences. Some choices affect certain people more than others. And some choices are in the form of attitudes and opinions rather than direct actions. Read the following instances. They help to exemplify the dimensions of decision making.

The Mobile Society

Hank is about to graduate from Midwestern University with a degree in electrical engineering. His girlfriend is a sophomore majoring in music. M.U.'s School of Music is one of the best and Mary is anxious to complete her course. In interviews on campus Hank has received three job offers: as a project assistant in research with a small firm in Huntsville, Alabama; one as an assistant to the plant operations engineer in an industry located 60 miles from Midwestern University; and one with a 80-member engineering section of Algomated Electric Products in San Jose, California.

Hank knows he is lucky to have several opportunities from which to choose. Even so, he is having trouble reaching a decision. Here are some of the elements Hank is weighing. He has visited the West coast. On one hand, he thinks he wants to live there, and on the other hand, he feels the job would not offer much challenge. He wants to be near Mary, but the job near M.U. is a dead-end position. The job in Huntsville would be exciting, but insecure. All his family lives near the city where M.U. is located. What choice should Hank make?

Causes and Prevention

Dr. Nichols is one of a team of public health doctors trying to discover what cause the death of so many who attended the American Legion convention in Philadelphia during the summer of 1976. Once the connection between multiple deaths from similar symptoms (high temperatures, headaches, the fluid invasion of the lungs) and attendance at the convention had been established, the task became one of examining all possible commonalities between the victims. Dr. Nichols is part of the team assigned to run all known tests on tissue samples taken from the victims. Other team members are interviewing still-living conventionaires, checking what they had eaten and how they are feeling. Still others examined victims' food scrapings and blood samples. What is the cause? A virus? A poison? Is the sickness contagious? Is this the beginning of the dreaded Swine Flu epidemic that has been predicted?

Dr. Nichols acts as a team member. He passes along the results of his cell counts to the rest of the team. There are meetings in which data from all facets of the investigation is shared in an attempt to put together a diagnosis of the sickness that is causing too many deaths. After a week, there is still no definite answer. But the team has arrived at two tentative conclusions:

☐ The sickness is not contagious because, as yet, no one outside those attending the convention has died from the same symptoms.

☐ The sickness is not the dread swine flu since no virus identifiable with this flu has been found.

The detective work continues. Dr. Nichols has to decide whether to run all his tests again to see if he missed identifying some element of significance the first time around. Examination of several hundred slides is painstaking. Dr. Nichols wonders what link his lab work can provide the team in diagnosing this killer sickness and suggesting steps that will prevent further outbreaks of it.

Gratifying Tastes

Rosario is single and has always wanted a sports car. At 25 she is already a training supervisor with the telephone company and has good prospects for further promotions. Her salary easily allows her to support her basic needs of food, clothes, and an apartment. She is in the process of deciding between an Alpha Romeo Alpheta and a Porche 924. Her parents feel she should use her extra money to buy a home or travel or make investments. They would prefer almost anything that was not a sports car! But they have accepted the fact that Rosario must lead her own life and that she can afford to realize her dream of owning a sports car. She has narrowed her choices. Here are some of the comparative data she is considering:

Brand	Basic Price	MPG
A-R Alpheta	$9,000	23
Porche 924	$10,500	23

HP	"Breeding"
110	A-R sports tradition
95	Audi engine, VW suspension

Rosario has driven both cars. The Alpheta handled like a dream. Her friend Lucas tells her, however, that A-Rs are very delicate to maintain in top running condition. Driving the Porsche was a smooth experience too. Two of her friends have more expensive model Porche's and swear that they can't be beat. Meanwhile, Rosario is gathering more information about each from the car magazines. What should be the principal basis for her decision?

How Does a Good Program Look?

Doris Pavlovich is currently vice-president of the PTA at her son's middle school. As such her neighborhood friends are urging her to take a stand on the school's new social studies program. Her closest friend, Joan, daily questions her own daughter on what topics are discussed in class and what assignments are given in the social studies. She tells Doris that the teacher shows films about life in urban ghettoes and Indian reservations and leads the class to compare the content of these films with the guarantee of the Bill of Rights. Other neighborhood women corroborate this story with further examples that illustrate the negative opinion of our country the new social studies program is developing among students. Doris has not realized that there was anything amiss in the new program. Just last spring the PTA committee had sat with the teachers and helped plan a multicultural component that would be added to the social studies program the following fall. She promises to look more closely into the matter.

That evening Doris asked her son, John, how the social studies class was going. John said, "There's a lot to read. But I like the class discussions. They really make you think."

"What do you read for this class?"

"Oh, mostly paperbacks. Like *I Know Why the Caged Bird Sings* and stuff."

"What's that about?"

"It's about how tough it is to grow up as a Black woman in this country. And, how Blacks have some of the same problems we do, only worse. You know,

there's a lot about this country that needs to be changed!"

Her son's last statement alarmed Doris. Was school making her son into a malcontent right under her nose? Maybe the neighborhood women were right. Now she was sure she should investigate more closely what was going on in this new school program.

Reflecting on the Cases

Let us look at the dimensions of choice relevant to each of these cases as they relate to Chart 13.1. Hank was consciously turning over in his mind the factors important to him in his choice of where to accept a first job. Most of the data he used was private—his family's location, his girlfriend's plans, his geographical preference, his professional possibilities. However, the consequences of his decision will affect not only him, but all those people closest to him. Even more personal is Rosario's decision. She is self-supporting and fairly affluent. Her decision may use certain public claims about auto performance or she may negate her previous examination by "falling in love with" the feel of the Alpheta on her next test drive. The consequences of her decision will affect primarily the way she budgets her own income for several years to come and the sales performance of some automobile dealer in any given month.

Dr. Nichols and Doris Pavlovich are engaged in decisions that have greater consequences for others. Both their data sources are public. Although the extent to which Doris will use sources beyond her own reactions and take time to examine the issue is not clear. Certainly, Dr. Nichols is proceeding with utmost care using all the techniques at his command

Chart 13.1 Dimensions of Choice

Decision period:	automatic ←——to——→ examined	
Data:	private ←——to——→ public	
Consequences:	self ←——to——→ others	

to make sense of his tissue slides. He will not keep his findings private. He will also describe the procedures he uses to his team members as a double-check on the validity of his findings.

Each one of these cases is relevant to some degree to events in our own lives. Everyday we are faced with making decisions and choices. Everyday, we are affected by the decisions and choices made by others. In our complex, urbanized society we are inundated with decisions of all kinds. Some complain that our kind of market system overburdens us with having to spend time on choices that ought to be automatic. Every choice, they say, is like choosing among the 31 flavors of ice cream at Baskin–Robbins. Many people sharing the belief that life is too complex act by joining rural communes or in some way dropping out of the technological marketplace our fast-changing, complex, mobile society has spawned.

Whether you agree with those who define our economic system as wasteful is for you to decide. The data you use to formulate your attitude may be composed entirely of how you personally react to certain situations. Our point is that, to the degree that you employ public information to consciously examine an issue as it relates to you and others with whom you are involved you are doing inquiry learning.

What Is Inquiry Learning?

The processes we go through to reach a decision or formulate an opinion are the quintessence of inquiry learning. In a common sense way, inquiry learning has been practiced as long as people have been engaged in human activity. Through trial and error the ancient Egyptian artisans learned that glass amulets could be made by applying the right amount of heat to a mixture of lead, certain kinds of sand and then pouring the resulting molten substance into clay molds. By sustained observation of chimpanzees in their own environment, Jand Goodall was able to make meaning of the communication patterns and social hierarchies among these animals as well as prove that they were tool users. Whenever a person uses evidence to reach conclusions he or she is *probably* engaged in inquiry learning because the *ways* evidence is gathered and the kinds of evidence used determine whether the inquiry meets the requirements of being scientific.

Check the items below that exemplify scientific inquiry.

_____**1.** A physician tells a mother who has called that her infant has a cold upon hearing that the infant has a runny nose and a fever.

_____**2.** Upon walking through a high school campus and seeing most of the long-haired students in blue jeans, tennis shoes, tee shirts a foreign visitor comments that American youth are promiscuous.

_____**3.** A police chief places a dog in every patrol car after noting that crimes of assault and burglary have decreased on beats where dogs have been used for the last two months.

_____**4.** A concerned mother limits her daughter's television viewing upon reading in the newspaper that Ann Landers feels television strains children's eyes.

_____ **5.** A politician spends most of his campaign funds on spot television ads after reading a sample survey that shows voters remember candidates names from television more than from other sources.

_____ **6.** A 12-year-old boy, anxious to build his body, buys Toast-Toasties cereal because all his friends eat it.

You should question whether the physician was being scientific. He or she may have reached a conclusion before knowing enough about the child's symptoms. The foreign visitor committed a similar error by attaching a concept or label he or she already had of what promiscuity looks like to a group of students whose behavior the visitor had no chance to observe. The police chief is in danger of making a similar mistake. Crime rates may have decreased due to factors other than the addition of dogs to patrol cars. The chief should check to see if all other factors—such as frequency of patrols, previous arrests in the district, number of citizen complaints—were the same in the district.

Basing decisions on valued others' opinions, be they members of your clique or revered personalities or sacred writings, is not scientific inquiry. Following an astrologist's or some authority's word of advice may or may not be a useful solution. A scientific inquirer would ask Ann Landers on what kinds of tests or experiments she bases her helpful hints. In our list, the politician comes closest to basing his decision on evidence arrived at by more scientific inquiry.

Thus we can begin to list some characteristics that define what scientific inquiry is not.

1. It is not basing a conclusion on any one source.

2. It is not basing a conclusion on any one sample of evidence.

3. It is not basing a conclusion on preconceived definitions.

4. It is not basing a conclusion on uncontrolled experiments.

5. It is not basing a conclusion on traditional means of solutions because they usually work.

As these examples suggest, there are several ever-present roadblocks to the practice of inquiry learning. These roadblocks, or impediments, to arriving at knowledge through the process of inquiry are as old as human history. Consider how vital a part of our own sensory perceptions play by remembering that for untold centuries people believed that the sun revolved around the earth. All they had to do was observe day dawning and night falling to see the truth of this description. Or consider how our values and experiences color what we see that is different and cause us to stereotype. We conclude that, for example, tropical peoples must be lazy since they habitually sleep during the heat of the day. We are using values esteemed by our culture—eight hours of continuous work—to judge another cultural habit when the climate, diet, need for work, daily routines, and valued activities prevalent and sensible to the practice of the *siesta* are unknown or disregarded by us.

The edicts of religious and revered authorities represent another source that defied learning by inquiry. Those who accept the Biblical version of human creation on this earth as literal, holy truth are usually not anxious to examine, with an open mind, Darwin's and other natural scientists' ideas about how species evolved on our planet. Closing off certain topics or issues as not open to question or interpretation denies the process of inquiry.

Although these roadblocks to inquiry-derived knowledge—not being able to examine from varius perspectives, using preconceived labels to explain new situations, and refusing to question an interpretation or law—are older than the process of inquiry, they are still very much with us today. We should identify these roadblocks with red flags when examining how we know about the real world.

Now we are ready to look at what scientific inquiry is. Scientific inquiry is the process of testing hypotheses about what is true in the real world. In other words, scientific inquiry is an inductive process that confirms or denies the truth of statements about things as they are in reality. Knowledge produced by the scientific process of inquiry is held to be true until evidence to the contrary is gathered. Thus the kind of inquiry one does in geometry or calculus or logic is not appropriate for scientific inquiry. These systems demand deductive reasoning to prove the truth or falsity of a statement. In *closed,* deductive systems, as the syllogism demonstrates, conclusions must follow if the first two premise statements are accepted. Scientific inquiry allows you to guess that if inductive statements 1 and 2 are true, then possible statement 3 could also be true. You can never know whether all teachers are authoritarian unless you go out into the world and test enough teachers' behavior to substantiate your guess or hypothesis.

Arguments

DEDUCTIVE	INDUCTIVE
1. All teachers are authoritarian.	1. Bill is a teacher.
2. Bill is a teacher.	2. Bill is authoritarian.
3. Bill is authoritarian.	3. Therefore, all teachers are authoritarian.

Social science inquiry attempts to describe and explain the social world. Both the natural and physical scientists and social scientists test their hypotheses by gathering empirical data, that is, evidence that can be counted from real items or

acts. In contrast to natural or physical scientists, social scientists have constraints on how they are able to proceed since their subjects cannot be controlled under rigid laboratory conditions. Therefore, the social scientist resorts to testing hypotheses about the social world by collecting evidence from large, representative numbers of people and trying to find patterns among the many factors present in the data.

The phases of inquiry have been described in a variety of similar models, with from 4 to 12 steps composing the entire process, even since John Dewey popularized his five-step model in the 1930's:

Steps in Scientific Problem Solving
1. Define the problem.
2. Suggest alternative solutions to problem.
3. Formulate hypotheses for testing.
4. Gather data to support or negate hypotheses.
5. Select tentative, supported hypothesis or reject unsupported ones.

In the 1920s, R.W. Hatch[2] suggested that elementary school children could be helped to conduct inquiry learning by following these four simple steps:

Hatch's Steps for Problem Solving
1. Find the facts.
2. Filter the facts.
3. Follow the facts.
4. Face the facts.

More recently the steps taken in the Social Science Inquiry process have been conceptualized as components of a cycle. Notice how the deductive style is integrated into the general inductive model in Figure 13.1. We may observe that our co-workers become edgy and argumentative during the long, hot, dry season.

---

[1] John Dewey, *How We Think,* Boston, Heath and Co., 1933.
[2] R.W. Hatch, "The Project-Problem as a Method for Teaching History," *Historical Outlook* (now *The Social Studies*), June 1920, pp. 237-240.

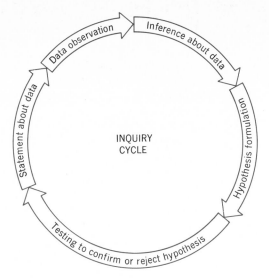

Figure 13.1 Inquiry cycle.

The labels on the inquiry cycle diagram, clockwise: Data observation, Inference about data, Hypothesis formulation, Testing to confirm or reject hypothesis, Statement about data. The center reads INQUIRY CYCLE.

From this observation we may guess that weather types affect employee behavior. In order to test this assertion, we will have to deduct definitions of what weather periods and types are related to what kinds of employee behavior. By collecting evidence of employee behavior during the weather types we have defined we can confirm or deny our original inference about the relationship weather has to employee behavior. The cyclical model of the process we use to formulate an understanding about our problem is more complete and sophisticated than the other two. However, the other two models are adequate as outlines to the process.

None of these outlines is sufficient to help guide students. Each step of the process of making better sense of the changing world about us, another definition of inquiry learning, demands a number of important considerations from teachers. The rest of this section examines in detail how to promote this way of knowing. But perhaps a parenthesis to consider the school's role in inquiry learning is in order.

Inquiry Learning in School

The decision examples used to introduce this topic were purposely taken from everyday occurrences familiar to most of us. All of us are confronted daily with conflicting advice and values, more data than we can assimilate and demands to make hundreds of decisions. Some of the decisions we make are private. They are questions of taste or preference. Some are public. They affect others. The Western world's Judeo-Christian ethic affirms that the more potential our decisions have for defining how another human lives, the more care we ought to take with our choice making. It is this concern for the consequences of our acts and opinions that many be called the roots of good citizenship in our society.

If our society were composed of people who shared uniform notions of what was best and how to live, we would perhaps have an easier time nurturing the qualities of good citizenship in schools. However, cultural diversity is a fact of our national existence. Furthermore, the idea that diversity is a strength is espoused in our best moments as we warmly reflect on our favorite Chinese restaurant or Jacuzzi session after swimming. Yet, the nature of our society is competitive. Diverse cultural or interest groups and subgroups are in continual conflict over the share of power their interests will have in decision making. Citizens are bombarded with opposing arguments and discrepant data on how to provide better schooling for all the nation's youth or how to structure an economy that benefits all the people, for example. Obviously, schools cannot resolve society's problems. But we contend that schools exist to transmit cultural heritages and to promote the skills and attitudes of reflective citizenship essential for the continuance and improvement of our society.

We feel that inquiry learning is essential to each of these broad goals in our society. For too long the social knowledge our schools taught consisted of basic "facts" about the world, particularly our country. These facts were mostly of a bland, descriptive nature. Consciously or not, this historical-social content usually excluded mention of non-white Anglo-Saxon perceptions of our national experience.

Recently, schools have begun to select content that shows greater awareness of the various ethnic/cultural perceptions and experiences. Of course, the impact of this broadening of content is felt most directly in the social sciences and social studies programs. Yet we have not known quite what to do with this "new" content except to relate it to students in a way that arouses as little hostility as possible. Thus students are often allowed, indeed required, to privately make up their own minds when presented with conflicting views on the right of migrant workers to organize unions or the pricing policy followed for energy sources.

Our position is that schools should foster both a knowledge of the pluralistic-conflictual nature of our society and the skills that will better enable the student to assume the role of humane, reflective member of that society. We feel that training in the techniques of Social Science inquiry best equips students to deal more adequately with the uncertainties and dilemmas that are part of all our lives. To accomplish this training demands that students be allowed or, better yet, provoked to question, to direct their own investigation, to experience conflict, to make errors of judgment, to become accountable for these errors. In other words, learn by inquiring. For school people and parents to develop the tolerance and skills necessary for guiding young people through episodes of inquiry learning is a big order. We hope the following sections provide some insightful guidelines and detailed examples of how this might be done.

Bibliography

Banks, James A. *Teaching Strategies for the Social Studies: Inquiry, Valuing, Decision Making.* Reading, Mass.: Addison-Wesley, 1973.

Beyer, Barry K. *Inquiry in the Social Studies Classroom: A Strategy for Teaching.* Columbus, Ohio: Charles E. Merrill, 1971.

Ehman, Lee, Howard Mehlinger, and John Patrick. *Toward Effective Instruction in Secondary Social Studies.* Boston: Houghton Mifflin, 1974.

Ryan, Frank and Arthur Ellis. *Instructional Implications of Inquiry.* Englewood Cliffs, N.J.: Prentice-Hall 1974.

Why is it necessary to organize data?

CHAPTER 14

What are the steps in Inquiry Teaching?

Starting the Inquiry Cycle ⟶ Asking the Question

Starting the inquiry process is undoubtedly the most precarious step. You must think through two problems before you are ready to attempt to engage students in the process. One problem is how to structure a question and generate a hypothesis or hypotheses from it. The other problem is how to select inquiry episodes that will interest your students. Let us think more carefully about each of these problems.

Formulating the Question

There are two elements of the inquiry cycle involved in asking the question. One is the defining of the problem or purpose for the inquiry. The other is formulating the tentative answer, the hypothesis, to the question or problem. As teachers, we need to learn how to identify and formulate questions that can lead to inquiry.

Compare question 1 to question 2.

1. How many people live in New York City?
2. Why are Northeastern cities like New York growing more slowly?

Question 1 can be answered quickly by turning to the appropriate page in the *World Almanac*. The answer is a matter of little dispute, except perhaps, to question the reliability of the U.S. Census procedures for counting people. Question 2, by contrast, invites a variety of responses that help to explain the steady to declining population counts of Northeastern cities.

Now compare these two questions.

2. Why are Northeastern cities like New York growing more slowly?
3. What is the future of cities?

We could collect empirical data from recent suburban and city censuses, corporate tax rates, union wage agreements and days of work lost due to strikes, city crime rates and welfare burdens, and the like, to substantiate our guesses as to why the population of these cities is not increasing at its former accustomed rate. To get at this problem would demand a lot of searching. Even so, question 2 is more manageable than question 3. As it stands, question 3 is too general for students to seek specific data to answer. Suppose we decided what types of cities we wanted to examine to get at question 3. We would still have difficulty as the question asks us to project the trends we can identify about cities into the future. City planners and futurists engage in this as a professional activity. But questions of this broad, general nature are at best difficult to handle as a classroom inquiry project.

Which of the following questions would promote hypothesis testing, or inquiry?

_____ A. How did Gerald Ford become President of the U.S.?
_____ B. How do people feel about Star Trek?
_____ B_1. Why do people like Star Trek?
_____ C. What were the changes in shipping patterns between Europe and the New World from 1750 to 1850?
_____ D. How many times has Elizabeth Taylor been married?
_____ E. What are the effects of eating foods with red dye on children's behavior?
_____ F. Which is better: strawberries or peaches?
_____ G. For high school students, what is the relationship between driving a car and academic achievement?

If you checked A, you should redefine your idea of what constitutes an inquiry question to questions that cannot be answered by using already available, accepted facts. Finding out how people feel about Star Trek allows several guesses to be made and checked against the data. Finding out why people like Star Trek will confront us with two problems. First, we will need to see whether people like Star Trek, or which people do, then, once Star Trek fans have been uncovered, we can address the question. B is a question that could inspire inquiry as it is. B_1 needs to be restated to something like: What kinds of people like Star Trek?

Question C could engage a specialized historian for years. It probably demands too much detail to be useful in a classroom. Surely, question D may arouse curiosity and even dispute about whether to count marriages by different husbands or by different moments, but it is not a question broad enough for social science inquiry. Again, question E is probably too specialized a question to consider in a classroom if students are to collect their own data. F is a question of personal taste and not one of discovering relationships as most fruitful inquiry questions do. Guessing, or hypothesizing as in G, about possible relationships between driving a car and school grades is a question on which inquiry could be used.

In summary, questions technically amenable to inquiry have two qualities. They should ask for more than an already available fact. They should, for our purposes, be general enough to allow nonspecialists to pursue them.

Moving from the Question to Stating Hypotheses

The process of knowing by inquiry departs furthest from answering questions in a common sense way in this step of the process. To formally pursue knowledge in the mode of inquiry requires that the investigator state his or her guess, or hypothesis, about the outcome of the question before gathering data that will help to address the question. Actually, setting out these expected answers gives greater direction and purpose to the ensuing investigation. Let us examine what this would mean for the questions we just evaluated as being amenable to inquiry.

Question B. How do people feel about Star Trek?

Hypothesis 1. Escapists like Star Trek.

Hypothesis 2.   Star Trek does not appeal to people over 40.

Hypothesis 3.   People like Star Trek.

Hypothesis 4.   Star Trek deals with the unknown.

Hypothesis 5.   People favor space exploration.

Question G. For high school students, what is the relationship between driving a car and academic achievement?

Hypothesis 1.   High school students should not drive cars.

Hypothesis 2.   Driving does not make any difference in the grades a student gets.

Hypothesis 3.   Driving teaches more responsibility, which also makes for higher student achievement.

Hypothesis 4.   Driving affects grades.

We can see that all hypotheses about question B pertain to Star Trek except 4 and 5. The fifth hypothesis would necessitate a separate inquiry as to which people favored the space exploration program. The fourth would require a judgment in the familiarity of Star Trek's apparatus and plots. The first three hypotheses, however, are more directly related to the original question. Three is most obvious. Two would require that we identify the ages of our respondents. And one would require us to ask respondents questions that allowed us to classify them as escapist or nonescapist. Thus, we would need to spend some time on defining what an escapist is for the purposes of our inquiry. The act of defining of terms is a very necessary part of hypothesis elaboration. If we have not come to an agreement on the preferences and activities that identify escapists, we cannot proceed to separate escapists from the rest of the population except by asking the respondents to identify themselves as escapists or not escapists.

Question G is more typical of a social science inquiry since it asks about what kind of relationship exists between two variables. Hypothesis 1 can be thrown out immediately because it goes beyond the question to assert an opinion about the variables. Nor is Hypothesis 5 useful since it gives no definition of what relationship exists between the variables of driving and student achievement. The third hypothesis confuses the purpose of inquiry. Should we seek to substantiate the first part or the second part of the statement? Or both? We would have more direct answers to the question by pursuing Hypotheses 2 and 4 as they state relationships between driving and achievement.

These rather technical aspects of initiating the process of inquiry are nicely summarized by Ryan and Ellis.[1] They suggest the following guidelines for stating problems and hypotheses:

1. The problem must be one that can be answered by gathering data.
2. The problem should be stated clearly, with terms defined if necessary.
3. The problem should be further refined by the statement of hypothesis or hypotheses.
4. The question or hypotheses should be based on a rationale.
5. The problem should not be beyond the scope of the investigator's resources.

Planning for Inquiry Incidents

A basic skill in how to state questions that generate researchable hypotheses is a necessary ingredient for your success in planning inquiry episodes for students. But this technical skill alone will not guarantee your success with the inquiry process in the classroom. To have success with this step of the cycle in the class-

---

[1] Frank Ryan and Arthur Ellis, *Instructional Implications of Inquiry*, Englewood Cliffs, N.J., Prentice-Hall, 1974, p. 18.

room you will need to be clear about how to interest your students and what your learning objectives for the students are. Addressing this learning problem, common to planning for any mode of instruction, is crucial to your success with inquiry.

"Turning Them On"

We just learned that not all topics can fulfill the technicalities the process of inquiry requires. It is also true that students will not necessarily be interested in pursuing questions that *do* have inquiry potential. How do we build a bridge between these two, often opposing, needs?

One possibility is to use student concerns as topics for inquiry. Knowing that your students are great television followers or that they are avid Little League fans or that they are "down" on cops and "the Government" can help you spark them to inquiry. In general, you should look for aspects of your students' concerns that can be used to make students react with these kinds of feelings:

☐ Perplexity concerning conflicting and inconsistent data.

☐ Emotional concern relating to a lack of solutions for societal or individual problems.

☐ Perplexity relating to the holding of incompatible beliefs (intrapersonal or interpersonal).

☐ Difficulties in establishing the consequences of a belief or action.[2]

For example, relating recent data on the amount of time children spend watching television and the aggressive behavior evidenced by avid viewers might be a useful springboard to inquiry on the problem of how television affects us. Or, in the second instance, inviting an opponent of Little League competition to

speak to the group could lead to an examination of competition in our society. Responding individually to the following questionnaire and then discussing it is a means of building on the negative feeling about government to examine how we feel about government.

What Is the Government Doing?
Check items you think the government is now active.

_____ Supports school lunch programs.

_____ Pays pensions to disabled veterans.

_____ Collects income taxes.

_____ Guarantees farmers certain prices for milk, grain and beef.

_____ Provides reservations for Native Americans.

_____ Prosecutes terrorists, income tax evaders and bootleggers.

_____ Guarantees everyone a minimum wage.

_____ Pays more employees than any other employer.

_____ Provides health care for everyone.

Class responses will permit you to get into the issues of why we have the attitudes we do about the government. Another possibility is to employ the episodes available in commercial materials. These episodes are meant to be used as openers to unit sequences of study for that set of materials. Various devices evoke cognitive dissonance of some sort in the student. The following episodes illustrate just two of the many inquiry openers you can find in these materials.

Here is an example from the *Holt Databank System*[3] recording that relates an actual description of an American picnic by people of a village in West Africa.

---

[2] H. Jerald Shive, *Social Studies as Controversy*, Pacific Palisades, Cal.: Goodyear, 1973.
[3] William R. Fielder, Editor, *Holt Databank System. Inquiry About Cultures: Teacher's Guide*, by Roger C. Owen, New York, Holt, Rinehart and Winston, 1972, pp. 12-13.

"For a year or so my wife and I, and several other Americans lived in a mining camp near a very small village in the rain forests of West Africa. We were quite cut off from the things we were used to. Even a day's journey would not have brought us to a shop, restaurant, or movie theater because the roads were poor. And we had no television—only a transistor radio. So we had to make our own good times, with small parties and picnics, and on Saturdays, if the weather was good, we always went there. The spot was a large table rock that jutted out over a bend in the river. The view from the big, flat rock was magnificent, especially at sunset. We would cook our supper over a campfire and have a wonderful time, American style. Imagine our surprise when we heard the way the people of the village described our picnics:

"These foreigners have a strange ritual that they must follow on a special day of the week. They always go to the big rock over the river, so obviously it is sacred to them in their religion. They all watch the sun go down, and as it sets, they sing a very strange way. We think the singing is meant to cast a magic spell. Then they light a fire. When it is burning brightly, they open a bundle and take out a lot of long, brown, human fingers. Each person puts a finger on a spear and cooks it in the fire and then eats it. Some eat two or three fingers. We do not know where they get them. But we must watch out and protect ourselves against such people."

After discussing the recording the teacher asks students to speculate why what other people do often seems strange to us. The answers or suggestions or guesses, if you will, are a form of hypothesis stating what can be used to guide further study of customs and cultures.

In *Comparing Political Experiences*,[4] a secondary text, the following exercise is used with students for hypothesis formation.

Dave and Mary drove down a country road late one night. On their way to a friend's house in Bromley, they became lost. They left home two hours earlier for what should have been only an hour's drive. Now realizing they were lost, Dave and Mary wondered what to do. They wanted to go to Bromley as quickly as they could. Except for the map in the glove compartment, there was nothing else to help them. They could drive for another thirty minutes before they would run out of gas.

"How can we get to Bromley?" Dave asked.

"We should make the best guess we can about how to get there," Mary responded. "We don't have enough gas to go on for long, I checked the map about fifteen minutes ago. From the looks of it, we should head north the first chance we get. If we want to get to Bromley, then this map will be useful."

"No, Mary. Let's just keep driving east. I have a feeling that if we want to get to Bromley, then we should keep going straight."

"Dave, we can do more than just wander around. If we use this map, we'll at least know where we're headed."

---

[4] Judith Gillespie, Stuart Lazarus, and John Patrick, *Comparing Political Experinces*, Bloomington, Ind. Center for High School Government Curriculum Development, 1979.

The teacher then asks whose advice they would take, Dave or Mary and why. In the discussion about Dave and Mary's problem of how to get to Bromley, the teacher points out that the two suggestions represent hypotheses about how to get to Bromley. Again, it is pointed out that a hypothesis is a tentative answer to a problem. Additional evidence about the hypothesis can confirm or reject it. According to *Comparing Political Experiences,* a useful hypothesis is *precisely stated, makes direct reference to a problem,* and *offers a new idea about the problem.*

The teacher would, then, proceed to ask if Dave's hypothesis was precisely stated. Was Mary's hypothesis precisely stated? Was Dave's hypothesis related to a problem? Was Mary's hypothesis related to a problem? Did Dave's hypothesis offer a new idea about the problem? Did Mary's hypothesis offer a new idea about the problem? Who stated the most useful hypothesis?

A class discussion, accepting student responses, usually shows that most students believe that Mary's advice should be taken. While both Dave and Mary state a hypothesis, only Mary introduces a new idea, the map. By heading north, they can find out whether or not the map is a help to them. In other words, both Dave's and Mary's hypothesis was precisely stated. Dave's hypothesis was, "If we want to get to Bromley, then we should keeping going straight." Mary's hypothesis is, "If we want to get to Bromley, then this map will be useful." Both Dave's and Mary's hypothesis are also related to the problem of how to get to Bromley. But only Mary's hypothesis offers a new idea about the problem. She states the problem, but she also brings in a new idea, the map. Solving the problem depends on whether or not the map helps. If they don't get to Bromley, then they can conclude the map was of little help.

The following are particularly recommended for examples of beginning an instructional sequence with problem definition and hypothesis elaboration.

Elementary

1. Addison-Wesley: *Taba Program in Social Science*
2. Educational Development Corp.: *Man: A Course of Study*
3. S.R.A. *Social Science Labratory Units*

Secondary

1. Macmillian: *High School Geography Project*
2. Ginn: *American Political Behavior*
3. Macmillian. *Anthropology Curriculum Study Project*
4. Denoyer-Geppert. *From Subject to Citizen.*

However, your school may not have these materials as they may not "fit" your course of study or they are too expensive. Even if you cannot use them in your classroom, you would expand your own powers of planning by studying how inquiry episodes are structured in some of these materials.

Where Are You Going?

In our discussion to this point, we have left untouched the most basic question about instruction. Before you worry about turning on your students or begin to analyze the technical side of the inquiry process, you should ask yourself just what your students should be learning from the use of the inquiry mode. What are your objectives?

Social studies teachers have a particularly hard time with this question as it related to inquiry. For, strictly speakly, inquiry relates to processing data, and our traditional orientation in social studies has been to instruct so that students will amass what we consider to be significant information. We believe both ways of knowing about the social world are important and that they can be combined. Look at the following objectives. Check the ones that call for using the question-asking, hypothesis-formulating step of the inquiry process.

_____**1.** Students can list factors influencing inflation.
_____**2.** Students can state problems about environment after viewing filmstrip, "The Earthknowers."
_____**3.** Students can locate principal routes of westward movement.
_____**4.** Given several artifacts, students can state hypotheses about life in ancient Athens.
_____**5.** Students can relate several things they learned from each of the following sources: parents, school, television.
_____**6.** Students can identify a researchable hypothesis.

You should have checked 2, 4, and 6. In our view, objective 2 is valid as it is. However, it does not necessarily lead into a hypothesis-formulating step. Objective 4 appears to be an appropriate first step into the Match kit[5] materials sequence on inquiry into the conditions of ancient Greece.

We would question 6 as a short-range objective on pedagogical grounds. Teacher enthusiasm for the rigor involved in formal social science inquiry is not likely to be contagious to students if the process is presented divorced from concerns of students or as integrated steps concerning the topics students are studying. Reserve exercises that teach and reinforce this kind of skill for college classes in research methods or as follow-up application-type exercises a student needs to pursue a problem in which he or she has already developed an interest.

---

[5] Children's Museum of Boston, *Match*, Unit "A House in Ancient Greece," Boston, American Science and Engineering, Inc., 1969.

As a long-range objective, number 6 is clearly a skill, for our values, that students should acquire during the course of their schooling.

The key to good instruction is to blend problem definition and hypothesis-formulation, or any part of the inquiry cycle, into the topics and content to which we feel students need exposure whenever the use of these processes seems logical and efficient. Logically, these steps should initiate a new topic or unit or the exploration of a problem relevant to your students. To be efficient, these steps should be used when data sources to examine are readily available and when we feel the topic to be investigated merits the time this step of the cycle requires.

What Does It Look Like?

Now it's time for you to be the judge. Read this edited classroom transcript. What comments do you have about the adequacy of the session?

Native Americans—Fourth Grade

Objectives: 1. Students can compare pictures.
2. Students can hypothesize about pictures.

Mr. Hill: Writes word "Indian" on the chalk board. "I am interested in sharing what image the word brings to your mind. I'll accept one or two work descriptions. O.K., Joe?"

Joe: "Wild, long hair."

The teacher nods his head or points to various students and records the contributions which include:

teepees	tomahawks	long hair
wild	moccasins	horses
jewelry	reservations	buffalo hunts
dancing around a fire		papoose

Finally, he stops and asks, "How do you suppose we were able to make up this list?"

Myrna: "Simple, everyone knows about Indians."

Mr. Hill: "How does everyone know?"

Kelley: "I see 'em all the time on television." A chorus agrees and various individuals mention specific movies and Indian characters they've seen.

Teacher places large picture of Plains Indian scene on the chalkboard railing. "Is this the way Indians look?"

Most students agree.

Mr. Hill places a second picture, a Pueblo scene, in view. "How about this? Is this the way Indians look?"

Many students agree. Marilyn raises her hand, "Well, some lived in bark houses too. And some didn't wear any clothes!" The chorus giggles.

Mr. Hill: "Marilyn, you seem to know a lot. Let's see if some of these pictures I'm placing on the board are the ones you have in mind.

"Now take a careful look at these five pictures. I'd like first to have you tell me how the list you made compares to the pictures."

Carey: "Not all of them have long hair, and only the one has any turquoise jewelry."

Luke: "I don't see any buffalo hunts or dancing around the fire."

Mr. Hill: "Why do you suppose that's true?"

June: "Maybe there are more of those kinds of Indians."

Mr. Hill: "Who else has some ideas about this?"

Kelley: "Like she said, That's the kind we see in all the movies."

Marth: "Oh, we don't either. We see Apaches. They ride horses, but they don't have teepees and stuff."

Mr. Hill : "But, would you all agree that these pictures are all of Indians?"
Class responds affirmatively.

Mr. Hill: "Well, if they are all Indians, I

wonder if we could make some guesses about why they look so different."

Molly: "Maybe they come from different places."

Mr. Hill: "Could I say, 'Indians from different places look different? O.K., what else might explain why these Indians appear different?"

Carey: "Indians dress different because they have different animals and plants around them."

Terry: "I bet that Indians from cold places wear more clothes than Indians from hot places."

Mr. Hill: "What else do you notice besides clothes?"

Joe: "Some Indians build more permanent houses. Some live in things they could build easy or carry with them."

Mr. Hill: "Would you care to guess why?"

Joe: "Maybe some liked to move a lot."

Molly: "Or, maybe they just knew how to build one kind."

Mr. Hill: "What shall I put down as a guess, or hypothesis about why Indians had different kinds of houses?"

Mr. Hill: "O,K., now we're getting into some good thinking. Now I'd like you to work for a few minutes in groups of two or three. Each group is to write down as many guesses about what made these Indians different. We will keep these guesses and use them as we watch a film about Native Americans in the past tomorrow morning."

Reflecting on the Episode

Mr. Hill evidently knew his students would respond to free association. And he must have felt that they held fairly stereotypic images of native Americans or he would not have begun the lesson as he

Chart 14.1   Data for Inquiry

Selected Income and Employment Characteristics of Asian-Americans over 16:		
	JAPANESE- AMERICANS	CHINESE- AMERICANS	FILIPINO- AMERICANS
Total Employed	263,972	113,562	131,555
Professional, technical	19%	25%	24%
Service, not household	11%	20%	19%
Farm labor	2%	0.3%	7%
Mean annual income	$6,001	$5,195	$4.862

Source: Washington, D.C.: U.S. Government Printing Office, 1973.

did. In fact, he might well have begun with the picture exploration anyway. Starting here would have prevented him from going off on the tangent of why we have the images we do of Indians.

But, did he accomplish his objectives? As much as we know from this excerpt, it looks as though he did. Questioning allowed him to guide their observations or differences. He might have spent more time on this, before going into the formulation of statements about what these pictures mean. On the positive side, he did explore some statements with the whole group before setting smaller groups to the task.

The real test of meeting his second objective will come in the next class session when the small groups share the statements they have produced.

We would be remiss if we concluded this section without noting that not all springboards, episodes aimed toward involving students with a problem, need to lead to formal hypothesis formulation. For inquiry to proceed, it may be quite adequate for the students to sense conflict or to express a question. Therefore, we have seen that inquiry learning cannot proceed without the skillful teacher guidance and preparation of relevant, motivational materials.

Getting the Evidence

Gathering evidence to use in solving a problem or substantiating a hypothesis prompts us to address two questions: What kind of data are we getting? How do we go about getting data? These sections will help answer these questions.

What Have We Got?

What do the following items mean to you?

Item 2. *Indianapolis Telephone Directory,* January 1950.

Marion County-Indianapolis Telephone Directory, January, 1975.

Item 3. Electrical sources used by Mary Souza during one day: lights in house, coffee maker, mixer, can opener, refrigerator, stove, dishwasher, garbage disposal, garage door opener, telephone, pencil sharpener, Xerox machine, typewriter, hairdryer, record player, television, radio, exhaust fan.

Item 4. Set of Salinas High School annuals from 1940 to 1970.

Unless you are easily led to fantasy, these items in and of themselves probably meant little to you. The reason is quite simple. You have not formed a question in your mind that these items—data and data sources—can help you to resolve. And this is the first point we need to make about the "getting evidence" step in the inquiry cycle.

Evidence of all kinds about every subject surrounds us. Most of this evidence or data has no meaning to us until we have a problem or concern. It is our focus or question that gives significance to these data. For example, until we decide to move from a rented apartment to our own home, we probably do not use the kinds of data found in Chart 14.2. Yet data pertaining to home ownership is continually present.

Once we begin gathering evidence to aid our problem solving, we need to be aware of two distinctions about the evidence we gather. Let us examine some typical home advertisements to alert us to the different kinds of evidence that are mixed into something as ordinary as a real estate announcement. For each ad, list the data that are factual in the blanks below.

A
DECOR & CLASS
Beautiful 3 bd., showplace located on foothill setting, custom drapes, lovely shag carpet gives you real pride in this home. Only $35,000. Sunset Properties.

C
VETS NO DOWN
4 bdrm, 3 ba., new prof. paint $37,950 is below market. Loan can be assumed. Hurry! Ram Realtors.

A_____
_____
_____
C_____
_____
_____
_____

B
SUPERB VIEWS
3 bd, 2 1/2 ba, 2 balconies, full AEK, elec. garage opener, secure prkg. for trailer/boat/RV. Finest TH in development. Owner had 1st choice. $46,250. Tom Jordan Properties.

D
SHARPEST Willow Glen Charmer 2 br, 1 ba., huge din & liv rm. Upgraded cpts, drps, paneling new driveway, roof. Quiet st. $57,750. Lincoln Realty.

B_____
_____
_____
D_____
_____
_____

How do you know when data are factual? Usually, factual data is considered to be whatever can be seen by anyone, or counted or weighed or verified from a publicly accepted source. Our anwers to which data were factual in these ads looks like this:

A
3 bd, foothill setting, custom drapes, shag carpet, $35,000.

C
Vets no down, 4 bdrm, 2 ba, new prof. paint, $37,950, loan can be assumed.

B
3 br., 2 1/2 ba, 2 balconies, AEK, garage opener, $46,250.

D
2 br, 1 ba, new driveway, roof, $57,750.

We included such items as custom drapes, new professional paint, new driveway, and roof because we can use our practiced eye to check them or we

Chart 14.2   Sources and Kinds of Data

DATA SOURCES	KINDS OF DATA
Real estate want ads	House descriptions
Real estate agency	Lot size
Banks	Tax evaluation rate
Savings and loans	Neighborhood character
Building Inspectors	Prices of houses
County assessor	Interest rates on loans
Title company	Cost of title transfers
Termite inspector	Moving company rates
Maps	Utility and maintenance costs
House-owning friends	Local bargaining procedures
Building codes	Items to inspect in house
Local planning board	Nearness of shopping center

can bluntly ask the seller to show us the bills proving the paint and driveway jobs are new. We included the prices as they are public asking prices; we are aware these prices do not necessarily represent true, verifiable values.

The items we did not see as factual are still data. These are bits of information—showplace, real pride, secure parking, below market, upgraded, quiet—about the image the realtor wants to project. These are called inferential data. These are not based on facts, but instead on feelings about facts. They are still useful to our inquiry into which house to buy. However, we would do better not to rely heavily on this kind of data to guide our choice about which houses to actually go out and see.

This distinction is a very important one in inquiry learning. To reinforce it, check which of the paired statements below is inferential.

_____ President Ford arrived at the Republican Convention in Kansas City on Sunday.

_____ The ambitious President arrived early at the National Convention.

_____ Russians' showing at the Olympics demonstrates how competitive they are.

_____ Members of the U.S.S.R. Olympic team won more medals than any other country.

_____ Bygone School District's bond elections have been defeated three years in succession.

_____ Citizens of Bygone School District are not interested in education.

Did the words "ambitious," "competitive," "not interested" bother you? If they did you are developing the skill of distinguishing between fact and inference. From now on you should be putting your own red flags on statements that interpret or go beyond evidence that can be empirically validated.

Knowing whether the data we gather as evidence to answering a question is firsthand data or interpreted data can be useful. Firsthand data are called primary sources. Interpreted data come from secondary sources.

To distinguish between primary and secondary data sources, let us examine the following situations. Mark the items in each that you consider to be primary sources.

Situation A. Several students are investigating land use in their community. They have assembled these sources of evidence:

_____ 1. Series of aerial photos of community

_____ 2. Film *Suburban Sprawl* based on local community growth

_____3. U.S. Census figures for county for twentieth century

_____4. Packet of editorials on land use from local newspaper files

_____5. Packet of land sale bills copied from County Museum display

Situation B. Class is examining India's population explosion from these sources:

_____1. Visiting Indian student

_____2. Copy of Indira Ghandi's speech to United Nations' Conference on the Human Environment at Stockholm, 1972

_____3. United Nations statistics on birth rates, mortality rates, average daily protein consumption, and so on

_____4. Film on India's family planning program

_____5. Textbooks on India

Situation C. Class is studying the labor movement in the United States. They have:

_____1. Simulation game on Haymarket Riots

_____2. Film *Sacco and Vanzetti*

_____3. Textbooks on U.S. history

_____4. Biography of the Reuther brothers

_____5. Statistics on union membership since 1930

_____6. Teamster circular on "Why Organize?"

Primary sources in Situation A are 1, 3, and 5. Sources 2 and 4 give the students valuable, but interpreted data about how land is used in their community. Even though the film, *Suburban Sprawl*, purports to be a documentary, the filmmaker selected the footage to present this community as an example of poor planning by city fathers and voraciousness on the part of land developers. Situation B allows students three contradictory primary sources—1, 2, and 3. And so does Situation C with sources 1, 5, and 6.

Both kinds of sources provide valuable evidence for inquiry learning. However, in recognizing when we are dealing with secondary data we alert ourselves to

the fact that someone else has organized the data and is telling us what he or she thinks about them.

In summary, to improve our chances of collecting fruitful information, we will need to gather data from a variety of sources. Distinguishing between factual and inferential and furthermore, between primary and secondary sources, is useful when we evaluate data.

How Can We Get It?

Cliches on travel posters often attempt to lure us into taking a trip by promising that "getting there is half the fun." So it is with the data gathering segment of the inquiry cycle. Learning how to use the techniques for gathering data may be the most memorable experience of the inquiry cycle for students. There are a variety of data gathering techniques that should be considered as possibilities before the data gatherers take off on their search. Students should consider the appropriateness of these techniques to the problem being explored. First, to provide you with an array of techniques, let us list and briefly define several techniques. Then, we will consider which techniques might be more appropriate for several different problems. Furthermore, we will suggest some guidelines for launching students in various techniques. And, finally, we need to discuss the issue of teacher versus student gathering of data.

Some Data-Gathering Techniques

1. Observation. This way of getting evidence requires that the inquirer look at an event or circumstance such as a meeting, a junior league ball game, a parade, or a bar scene to note the elements significant to his or her inquiry. For example, to look at how we learn to compete, an investigator could note verbal and body comments by players, coaches, students in the stands, and adults in the stands. If we have participated in team sports, we could provide our own views about learning to compete as evidence. Or we could read accounts by athletes and coaches on competition such as the Jerry Kramer biography on famous coach Vince Lombardi, *Lombardi: Winning Is the Only Thing*. Whether the investigator directly observes or uses the observations of others, useful evidence can be gathered through this technique.

2. Interview. Some of our best insights to public personalities come from the technique of the interview. Think of the format of the television shows "Today" or "Issues and Answers?" or "Meet the Press." The interview allows the investigator to interact with the subject, to ask for clarification, to request a reaction to a related subject. Interviews are excellent devices for allowing others to sense how it felt to witness an airport terrorist attack or an earthquake, the National Open Golf Tournament or the arrival of Air Force One.

3. Questionnaire. Structure and number of respondents distinguish the questionnaire from the interview. The questionnaire structures items and responses that aim at exploring how respondents feel about issues. Often, they are not open ended. This limits the investigator's ability to probe for the reasons certain responses were given. But it makes it easier for the investigator to count or tabulate the data if there are only a limited number of choices. To make up for this possible limitation, questionnaires usually request respondents' personal data on age, income, sex, race, religion, and so on. Comparisons of male and female, Protestant and Catholic questionnaire responses are then possi-

ble. Questionnaires take less time to administer and analyze than interviews. Also, questionnaire data becomes more reliable the more representative the respondents to it are of the population being studied.

4. Role Playing. Understanding, in the sense of the affective, how people act in dilemmas can often grow through the projective device of the role play. All versions of this device—from the openended incident to the more structured roles of simulation games—can produce data regarding personal motivations and how compromises or power is used in decision making. Unless the participants and observers discuss and debrief the events of the role play, indeed, they should be replayed for different possibilities of action to emerge, the student tends to forget the data detail or remain ignorant of how the data is connected to the problem focus.

5. Case Studies. The idea for this technique evolved from the tradition in legal training of requiring law students to look up and analyze decisions leading up to a particular case. The same notion of comparison of separate individuals as they relate to a selected issue is what guides the case study way of gathering data. This technique is particularly appropriate for allowing students an indepth view of the variability of human behavior since case studies usually show an individual caught in a dilemma. The fact that a case study personalizes a problem facilitates crossing the barriers of time, geography, and culture for students.

6. Original Documents. Copies of anything written by or for people in a period we are studying constitute original documents. Examples known to us all are diaries, constitutions, and all manner of official treaties or decrees or papers and personal letters. Gathering data from original documents is the customary realm of the historian. Reading such sources for substantive data is difficult going for most of us nonhistorians. However, we do better when we read to get a feeling for the period the document represents.

7. Artifacts. An artifact can be any object used by people. Usually we classify things from the past as artifacts, but objects collected from the presentation can be artifacts as well. Your family photo albums, items in Goodwill stores, bumper sticker collections and old phonograph records are artifacts that could allow us ample data to use in speculating about our recent past.

8. Secondary Sources. We repeat this category here just to remind you that study of textbooks, films, tapes, and so on, is a perfectly legitimate technique for evidence gathering. Certainly, these sources are the most obvious and plentiful ones available to students in schools. What distinguishes using these sources in inquiry learning is the spirit in which they are used. That critical attitude of questioning—how the author(s) or director got his or her or their information, what was his or her background, why did he or she want to write or film this particular subject—should guide data gathering from secondary sources.

Problems ⟷ Techniques

Fitting appropriate data gathering techniques to questions or problems tests two things. First, your knowledge of possible sources relevant to your problem is tested. The second element tested is your ability to organize and guide students in various techniques appropriate to the defined problem. Planning for and implementing data gathering are what is involved. Even the most dramatic collection of data sources about a topic will not, in and of itself, spark profitable student inquiry. Inquiry learning cannot be teacher proofed. Successful inquiry depends on the teacher's skill in launching and organizing student evidence collection.

Planning for Data Gathering

Look back over the eight techniques briefly described. Which one(s) would best fit the following questions?

Your Ideas

1. How did people feel about their government and themselves during the period of the Depression?

_____

_____

2. What was our community like a generation ago?

_____

_____

3. How do students feel about permitting boys and girls to try out for all school sports teams?

_____

_____

4. What will the proposed airport expansion mean for our city and county?

_____

_____

5. How does colonialism affect peoples of developing countries?

_____

_____

Our Ideas: Fitting the Technique to the Problem

1. The film, *Grapes of Wrath,* distributed by Films Incorporated, 1144 Wilmette Avenue, Wilmette, Illinois 60091, is an excellent opener to this problem. All American history textbooks have general descriptions of the events during the Depression and most give interpretations of why it happened. Jackdaw Kit(All), *The Great Depression,* (New York, Grossman, 1972), provides copies of such period pieces as food ads, a *Daily Worker* issue, political cartoons, family portraits, and so on. Studs Terkel's *Hard Times,* New York, Pantheon Books, 1970, gives oral histories of people who lived during the Depression.

2. Aerial photos, newspaper articles, interviews with community oldtimers, old city maps.

3. Interviews with both sexes of athletes and nonathletes, questionnaires, observations of players in mixed team sports.

4. Interviews with people for and against expansion, clippings from local paper, statistics on airport volume, noise and pollution reports, role play various citizens who will be affected.

5. Textbooks on several developing countries such as *Inquiry into World Cultures* series with volumes on Brazil, Kenya, China, and India (various authors, Englewood Cliffs, N.J., Prentice-Hall, 1975), interviews with foreign students or political scientist specializing in topic, simulation game such as "Empire."

6. Listening to the songs and music of the 1930s to discover relationships to conditions of the Era. Use, for example, *Songs from the Depression,* Pete Seeger, et al., Folkways Records, FH5264.

Naturally, you could not be as specific about sources that would allow students to use one or another technique to gather data. What we hoped you would feel, however, through this exercise is that the technique of evidence gathering depends largely on the kind of problem being pursued. For example, historical topics and topics concerning other cultures demand greater search, on the teacher's part, for sources that are comprehensible and can be made available

for more than one day or one period so that students have a chance to become acquainted with the film or pictures or slides. Whereas, topics suggesting interviews and questionnaires demand that students have the ability and permission to go where necessary to practice these techniques.

Implementing Data Gathering

Let us imagine that we have some of the data sources we need to begin data collection, or in other cases, that we have decided which techniques best fit addressing the problem at hand. How do we go about getting students profitably engaged in this step of the inquiry process?

1. Depression—High School

Assigning any of these sources without guidance in the form of study or discussion questions would almost ensure that many students will have no examined recollection of what they viewed or read. *The Grapes of Wrath* is a powerful, emotional experience. However, you are viewing it for the purpose of bringing the Depression closer to the students. Ask that students take mental or written notes while viewing the film to answer questions as:

☐ Who did these people blame for their situation?

☐ How much did they know about national events?

☐ What did the Depression do to interpersonal relationships?

☐ What ideas helped the various characters in times of stress?

To get a bird's-eye view of how the world continued to go on in spite of the economic woes of most people, students

Great Dust Storm Subsides In West

But Falling Winds Still Leave the Farm Belt in Grip of Drouth—Crop Conditions Acute.

MORE AID FOR FARMERS

Time for Signing of Wheat Production Control Contracts Is Extended Until May 16 — Dust Reaches Washington.

Chicago, May 11 (AP)—With falling winds, the greatest dust storm in 20 years subsided today, leaving good Minnesota and Dakota top soil on office desks and parlor rugs in several states as far east as Pennsylvania. The extensive drouth, which pulverized the soil for the winds, had not abated, and the condition of crops in rainless states became more acute. Experts estimated that wheat, oats and hay must have rain within a week.

Some traces of the dust storm were reported in western Pennsylvania and other places, but at St. Paul, where yesterday 10,000 tons of soil floating over the city reported clean air today.

It was estimated that the winds had brought into Chicago 12,000,000 pounds of soil, more than 3 pounds each for every man, woman and child. Temperatures over the middle west were down, some as low as freezing, but no forecast gave hope for rain within the next two days.

Short Wheat Crop Looms for Kansas

This Year's Yield Now Estimated At 99,362,000 Bushels, Bigger Than in 1933 but Far Below Normal.

CROP CONDITIONS POOR

Is 60 Per Cent of Normal As Result of Ravages of Drouth, And Pests — Other Crops Also Suffer.

Topeka, May 11 (AP) — Kansas' winter wheat crop this year, based on a condition 60 per cent of normal as of May 1, was estimated today by the state board and federal department of agriculture at 99,362,000 bushels, compared with 57,462,000 bushels last year and 175,876,000 bushels, the 1927-1931 give-year average.

Chart 14.3 Excerpt from Old Newspaper

could do a topical analysis of news from newspapers of the period such as this copy of the Emporia Kansas *Gazette* of 1934, seen in Chart 14.3.[6] How much of the news is about the economy? What kinds of economic news are included?

Hard Times is full of data about all manner of topics. Students will need orientation to gather appropriate evidence. Students can choose several interviews and collect data on the same questions from each interview read. Questions similar to those used to guide viewing *The Grapes of Wrath* would be in order.

2. Community Change — Middle Grades

Chronological aerial photos or maps are excellent data sources for this topic. Often Chambers of Commerce, the U.S. Geological Survey, or local land title offices have photos and maps that can be used. These sources should be displayed over a period of time so that students can go back and back again to them for evidence. As in reading for comprehension, guiding questions that move from identification to comparison are useful. For example: What places or objects can you name? (See Figure 14.1.)

For a topic like this students can identify people who have lived a long period in the community to interview. Students need some help in interview technique. Whether you decide to have the "old timer" to class for a mass interview or to promote student interviews outside school with various contributors will depend on the availability of local "old timers" and the time you can devote to arranging for students to conduct their own interviews. The happiest procedure is to establish with students answers

to these questions in planning the interview:

☐ What do we want to know?
☐ Who should we interview to find out?
☐ How do we conduct the interview?

Have student teams practice with other students before actually going to interview. Each team should take a list of the agreed-on questions to use as cue cards during the interview he or she conducts. The invitation to be interviewed should be made a day or so in advance of the actual interview. Most adults prefer to know the questions they will be asked before the interview. Tape recording interviews is an excellent idea as the data remain available beyond the moment of the interview. Be sure interview teams thank the people they interview.

3. Mixed Team Sports — Junior High

As with the previous item, student participation is essential in developing and applying a questionnaire. Small-group work can be used to brainstorm a limited number of items for consideration. Ask for statements, not questions from these groups. From this collection, you can lead a discussion about the implications for data these items can generate. There are matters of complexity and length to debate. Students can help restate items making them simpler to respond to and interpret. Try your own hand at restating the following items.

1. Only girls who are jocks want to play tough, competitive sports with boys.

   _____

2. All students should be treated equal.

   _____

3. Boys and girls are made different and they should not have close, physical contact in team sports.

   _____

---

[6] Historic newspaper reproductions such as this excerpt are available from many newspaper publishers. This paper, *The Emporia Gazette*, appears in its entirety in *Jackdaw Kit(All) The Great Depression*, New York, Grossman, 1972.

Figure 14.1 Photo of Santa Clara Valley. This aerial photo from 60,000 feet was taken in 1972. (Eros Data Center of U.S. Department of the Interior, Geological Survey, Sioux Falls, S.D. This photo provides a variety of projections of nearly any quadrant requested.)

Restating to get at one main idea is not always easy. The loaded language—girl jock, tough—in item one may confuse the issue of ascertaining whether only very athletic girls would be anxious to partici-pate in mixed sports such as football. Something like, "Athletic girls want to play all mixed team sports," might neu-tralize the response. Or, "Most girls prefer to play on girls' sports teams," may state the issue your students wanted to address.

Item 2 is not necessarily related to the problem. Students may want to use the item as a respondent consistency check against an item specific to the issue of whether separate is equal treatment in sports participation. In the event of such a sophisticated rationale, leave the item in except to change "all students should be treated equal," on the final questionnaire version. Item 3 can be clarified by eliminating the detracting *vive la diferánce* section so that only one idea is stated in the item, "Boys and girls should not have close physical contact that team sports demand."

There are two more tasks that the class should have a part in before the students are allowed to get questionnaire responses. One involves eliminating the redundant and unnecessary items. Another is the task of setting up a manageable answer format. For easier analysis, three choices—agree, cannot decide, disagree—are adequate, although some secondary students are able to handle the more sophisticated, five-choice Likert scales. This task is best done by a small group rather than the whole class.

The other task is to decide on a sampling technique. Bring up the question of sample bias by imagining with the students what the results would look like if only members of the all-male school football squad, or spectators at a football game or only freshmen, and so on, were to respond to various questionnaire items. Would it be important to know whether questionnaire respondents are male or female, freshmen or seniors, sports minded or not? Should this information be coded on the questionnaire? Deciding how to get a representative sample without asking every student to respond is a vital exposure for young social scientists.

4. Airport Expansion (or any controversial, current issue)—Middle Grades to High School

After initial gathering of information through news clippings, interviews, reports, and so on, students often get a better sense of the controversialness of the issue if they are put in roles. Through role playing, students learn about the various factors, often having little to do with the controversy in focus, that affect decision-making. To prepare for this kind of data-gathering demands that the teacher construct a conflict situation. Such stituations can involve more than one person and have an action sequence suggested. Following are materials developed around an actual situation. Names have been fictionalized. Read the role descriptions noting how internal conflict and interpersonal conflict has been built into them.

5. Colonialism—High School

Reading from secondary (data already interpreted) sources is one of the most widely used activities for data input concerning topics of other times, cultures. We use the word input intentionally here. For, if we do not give some reasons for reading to students, we cannot be sure that data alone are meaningful. For useful output to occur, we need to provide, forgive the mechanistic metaphor, a program.

Following is one of the many short interpretative data sources of the kind students could read to help them get a better hold on an issue of this kind. See Figure 14.2 and accompanying article. This article deals with the continuing relationship of former African colonies with their colonizers.[7] Factual recall

---

[7] John Grimond, "Europe's African Legacy: Mostly Bad, Some Good," *The New York Times*, May 2, 1976. © 1976 by the New York Times Company. Reprinted by permission.

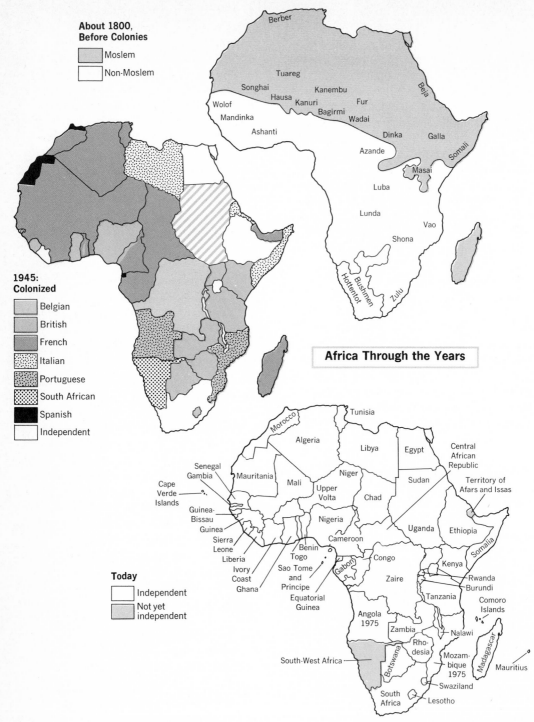

About 1800, Before Colonies

- Moslem
- Non-Moslem

Berber

Tuareg

Songhai
Hausa   Kanembu
Wolof   Kanuri
Mandinka   Bagirmi   Fur
Ashanti   Wadai
Dinka   Galla
Azande   Somali
Masai
Luba
Lunda   Vao
Shona
Bushmen
Hottentot   Zulu

Beja

1945: Colonized

- Belgian
- British
- French
- Italian
- Portuguese
- South African
- Spanish
- Independent

Africa Through the Years

Today

- Independent
- Not yet independent

Morocco   Tunisia
Algeria   Libya   Egypt   Central African Republic
Senegal   Mauritania   Niger   Sudan   Territory of Afars and Issas
Gambia   Mali   Upper Volta   Chad
Cape Verde Islands   Guinea-Bissau   Nigeria   Uganda   Ethiopia
Guinea   Cameroon   Somalia
Sierra Leone   Benin   Congo   Kenya
Liberia   Togo   Gabon   Rwanda
Ivory Coast   Sao Tome and Principe   Zaire   Burundi
Ghana   Equatorial Guinea   Tanzania   Comoro Islands
Angola 1975   Zambia   Malawi   Madagascar
South-West Africa   Rho-desia   Mozam-bique 1975   Mauritius
Botswana   Swaziland
South Africa   Lesotho

Figure 14.2   African political boundaries.

helps, such as listing European countries and their former African colonies and listing good and bad things European countries did in these colonies, should be elaborated.

In addition to factual reading guides, students should specifically be led to speculate on such questions as: What prompted the author to write on this topic? What points of this article would upset a person from Zaire or Kenya or South Africa? What evidence of a European background do you detect in the article? List any inferential statements the author makes.

Space does not permit more examples to make our point perhaps more clearly. In summary then, let us be more straightforward. We feel data gathering skills must be taught. Furthermore, to gain the most benefit from this phase of the cycle, students need specific help in how to approach data sources. All this structure may go against your persuasions about inquiry learning. You may feel that for inquiry learning to be the real thing, students should formulate their own problems and find their own data sources. Let us deliberate further about the place of teacher direction in inquiry.

Shoreline Role Play

1. Read the editorial and think about: What is the issue? What are the alternative solutions? What would possible community reactions be?
2. Join with others to form a city council of five. Pick a role description and study it. You are a city councilperson. Your task is to discuss with your city council colleagues whether to hold public hearings on airport expansion. After discussion, your council should vote. Each member's vote for or against hearings should be recorded.

Does Shoreline Need New Airport Facilities?
by Herb Culp

For nearly one year, the City Council has been discussing whether or not to build new city airport facilities. Conflicting opinions about this issue have been presented to the City Council.

The Council meets tomorrow to discuss the airport issue. Responsible citizens of Shoreline must contact their councilmen and urge them to support airport expansion.

Our present airport is large enough to serve a city like Shoreline. Money for airport expansion can be put to better use building new schools and parks. While only a few higher-income people would benefit from enlarging the city airport, all of Shoreline citizens would benefit from new educational and recreational facilities. The people of this city need money to rebuild an earthquake-proof system of elementary schools. Our city needs a larger library and more adequate bus transportation.

In addition, expanding the city airport would greatly increase air traffic in our city. This would cause discomfort to the people of Shoreline, since more and bigger jets landing here mean more noise and air pollution. Therefore, we must urge the City Council to reject the proposals to build new airport facilities here.

—excerpted from *Shoreline Mercury News*

Role Descriptions
Max Douglas

Mr. Max Douglas is an aeronatutical engineer with the engineering-consultant firm, Branis Corporation located in Shoreline. His corporation has done a study on the issue and does not propose an entirely new air terminal at this time. He feels, however, that by 1990 with

Shoreline's continued growth rate an entirely new facility capable of handling international carriers will be needed.

He cites the figures that in 1952 only 9 percent of air passengers for the whole Bay Area came from Shoreline. Last year over 40 percent did. In round numbers, this meant that 750,000 Shoreliners flew somewhere last year. Many had to drive 45 miles to San Fancisco to get a flight because they could not get reservations at Shoreline's Municipal Airport.

Branis found that jet noise in the airport neighborhood, one mile from the runways showed that the noise never exceeded 50 decibels, which is not harmful.

Carlos Mesa

Mr. Carlos Mesa is the newly elected chairperson of Shoreline's City Council. He represents the east side of the city which is predominantly Mexican-American. Mr. Mesa is a successful small businessman. He grew up in the city and attended Shoreline High School. His small restaurant features Mexican food. He is thinking of opening a branch on the west side of town near the airport.

Marshal Levy

Mr. Marshal Levy is director of the Safe and Sane Airport Committee. He lives in a residential area not affected by proposed expansion plans. He is a former pilot and moved to Shoreline upon his retirement from commercial flying. Here are his reasons for opposing increased air traffic in Shoreline:

—Jet planes pollute the air with carbon monoxide and nitrogen oxides which produce smog, lung disease, and hurt our local truck-garden industry.

—Jet landings and takeoffs produce noise levels of up to 110 decibels. Medical experts have told us that an 85 decibel level, if continuous, is enough to create serious emotional disturbances in people.

Walter Simke

Mr. Walter Simke is President of the Shoreline Chamber of Commerce. He has presided over the city's ten-year growth in industry and commerce. Mr. Simke takes full credit for turning Shoreline from a sleepy agricultural neighbor of San Francisco and Oakland into a center for light steel industries and other electronic-based industries such as IBM.

Mr. Simke feels that for Shoreline to continue attracting commerce the airport facilities must be expanded. He also knows that an expanded airport facility creates jobs.

Ann Clark

Ms. Ann Clark is chairperson of the Airport Committee of Shoreline's Sierra Club. She feels that airport expansion will ruin two invaluable public facilities—the Sands Wildlife Refuge and Placer State Hospital for the mentally ill—and much of the truck-farming done near the airport. She is currently organizing houseowners living near the airport to oppose further airport expansion. She has a petition to this effect signed by 829 residents of the affected area.

What Is To Be Gathered by Whom?

Without elaborating the complete argument favoring the inquiry approach or distinguishing between types of inquiry approaches, let us take a few lines here to discuss the role of the teacher in the data gathering phase of the process. As rules of thumb we argue two points.

1. Teachers are responsible for assembling data sources and planning study questions that will aid student use of them.

This rule of thumb does not dismiss the importance of library research skills. But, we ask you to consider whether this kind of activity is necessary or appropriate for every topic. Many an opportunity to discuss our individual reactions to a provocative or controversial film or set of data everyone has been exposed to will be lost if all the students are off on their separate research trails in the library.

2. Teachers are responsible for training students in how to acquire information or data.

By the same token, we have seen much good community will unnecessarily lost through excessive and unplanned use of data gathering modes such as interviewing and sample surveys. We have also seen good students floundering with good materials because they had inadequate guidance about how to use them. Teacher source gathering needs to be followed by planning for how students can be enabled to gain the most from the gathered sources.

Proverbs and old sayings sometimes help us remember a point. To summarize, we will try three. We agree that techniques of data gathering are like life where variety keeps things interesting. But we also know that "The proof of the pudding is in the eating," which translated to our age read "garbage in—garbage out," or as some crusty pedagogue would say, "Planning is everything my dear!"

Summarizing the Evidence

In *Cannery Row* John Steinbeck compared the clutter of data in Hazel's mind to the snarled fishing tackle on the bottom of his rowboat. Sinkers, line, hooks, old bait containers, floats, and gaffs were so tangled no one was sure about the content. Unless we do some ordering of the data we gather, our mental images about them will tend to become like the confused mind of Hazel, all snarled and tangled. In the last section we discussed several data gathering techniques. This section looks at how data gathered from these various techniques might be processed or organized.

1. Observations. Here are some observation results and possibilities for organizing them.

A. First graders have been studying families in various cultures. They have lists of who lives with each family studied. To allow easier use of data on these lists the teacher shows them how to do family tree diagrams of the households they studied (Figure 14.3). The students

India	Mexico	A.	B.	C.
			U.S.A	
Nine children	Seven children	Two children	One child	Three children
Mother	Mother	Mother	Mother	Father
Father	Father	Father	Grandmother	
Father's mother	Grandmother			
Father's father	Two aunts			
Father's uncle	Servant			
Uncle's wife				
Servant couple				

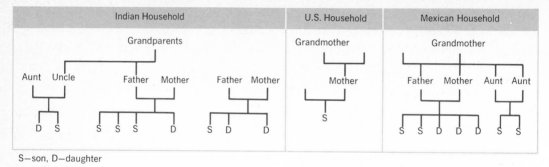

S—son, D—daughter

Figure 14.3   Family structure comparisons.

diagrammed their own household members as well as those they had studied. Once they understood the significance of the tree branches, they were careful to attach grandparents and children to the proper sides of the diagram.

B. Students observing behavior of several types at a football game have lists of tallies. For example, one student's tallies:

This kind of data need to be combined and averaged so that it can be illustrated as Figure 14.4 shows.

2. Interviews. Interview data are not easily made visual. The chart is the most amenable form for making interview data succinct.

A. Students have read various interviews about the Depression from *Hard*

Action	Adult Fan	Female Student
A. Yelled instructions	/////////	//
B. Cheered	/////////////////	/////////////////
C. Clapped hands	////////	/////////////////////
D. Talked to neighbors	/////	//////////////

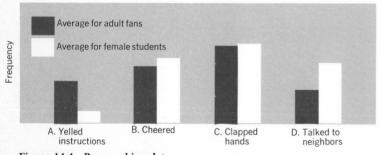

Figure 14.4   Bar graphing data.

270 Inquiry Learning in Social Studies

Chart 14.4 Sample Retrieval Chart: Reactions to the Depression

SUBJECT	WHO BLAMED?	AWARENESS OF NAT'L. EVENTS	PERSONAL RELATIONSHIPS	IMPORTANT BELIEFS
Blacky Gold (car dealer)	No one mentioned	None mentioned CCC jobs	Orphaned	Hard work, obedience, conformity
Caesar Chavez (pres., United Farm Workers)	Banker, labor contractors	Not mentioned	Close family	Family unity
Jim Sheridan (old, nervous illness)	Government	Yes	Alone	Save yourself
Edward Santander (teacher)	Not mentioned	Yes	With family, grandparents	Unionization, restore country's wealth, share

Times. Chart 14.4 shows how they compiled their data.

Retrieval charts such as the one above are good devices for visualizing interviews. The matrices of the chart should cross the persons interviewed with the categories of opinion considered important to examining the hypothesis. For example, if we had hypothesized that people undergoing the hard times of an economic depression would want to revolt against the government, we would find, in the "Who blamed" column of these data, little support for our revolutionary hypothesis. Only Jim Sheridan participated in the Bonus March on Washington and made direct comments about blaming the government for the people's woes.

3. Questionnaires. Survey and questionnaire results can be portrayed in a variety of ways. Let us imagine the following results to these items on the mixed team sports issue.

Item A. Men and women should be allowed to try out for all team sports.
       Yes   No opinion   No

Item B. Men and women should be allowed to try out for the football squad.
       Yes   No opinion   No

Item C. Man and women should be allowed to try out for the swimming team.
       Yes   No opinion   No

For Item A the total results were: Yes, 40; No opinion, 5; No, 72; totaling 117. For Item B the total results were: Yes, 12; No opinion, 3; No, 102; totaling 117. For Item C the total results were: Yes, 90; No opinion, 1; No, 26; totaling 117. Numerical data such as these are more meaningful when presented in tables with percentages as well as the "raw" numerical totals. The manipulation of data to arrive at this kind of table (Table 14.1) consists of tallying responses by category and figuring the percentages each respond category represents of the total number of respondents in that category. Care should be taken to represent both the actual and percentage counts on the tables. Unwarranted interpretations are often made when only percentages appear on tables.

The breakdown into respondent categories is a cumbersome task without the aid of data processing equipment. When schools are equipped to process these kinds of data, students should have the chance to integrate their card punching-data processing skills with this class project. In schools not equipped to involve students in the mechanized processing of data, questionnaires are best kept short, item responses narrow and respondent comparisons limited. A small group should be given the task of hand tallying the results in the latter case.

What Are the Steps in Inquiry Teaching? 271

Table 14.1 Data from Questionnaire Item

Item A. Men and women should be allowed to try out for all team sports.

	YES	NO OPINION	NO
Total 117	34%	4%	62%
	(40)	(5)	(72)
Men 57	29%		71%
	(17)	(0)	(40)
Women 60	38%	8%	54%
	(23)	(5)	(32)
Sports oriented 50	42%		58%
	(21)	(0)	(29)
Nonsports 67	28%	7%	65%
	(19)	(5)	(43)

If one of the learning objectives requires that students learn to put together a table, then the raw number results can be distributed in class. The teaching role becomes, then, to do an illustrative table for the whole group using their data and to assign the rest of the tables as student work. Can you make a table from these data (Table 14.2)?

Table 14.2 Data Conversion Exercise

Item B. Men and women should be allowed to try out for the football squad.

	YES	NO OPINION	NO
Total 117	(25)	(17)	(75)
	—%	—%	—%
Men 57	(12)	(2)	(43)
	—%	—%	—%
Women 60	(13)	(15)	(32)
	—%	—%	—%
Sports oriented 50	(21)	(1·2)	(17)
	—%	—%	—%
Nonsports 67	(4)	(5)	(58)
	—%	—%	—%

Your percentages for each line should total 100.

Data gained initially from such group choice-making techniques as presented in the role play on airport expansion can also be organized in table form. Recording of group votes on such a chart allows each member of the larger group to see how others voted. Carlos Mesa role players A, B, and C will immediately want to know why Carlos Mesa D voted "yes".

Chart 14.5 Airport Role-Play: Council Votes on Public Hearings

COUNCIL ROLE	COUNCIL GROUPS			
	A	B	C	D
Carlos Mesa	No	No	No	Yes
Max Douglas	No	Yes	No	No
Ann Clark	Yes	Yes	Yes	Yes
Walter Simko	No	No	Yes	No
Marshall Levy	Yes	No	Yes	Yes

Not all surveys will produce data as complex as the mixed sports questionnaire. Surveys of favorite sports teams, television shows, or subjects in school are often used to collect data. Results of these surveys are excellent materials for graphing. Let's assume the following data on favorite school subjects.

BOYS (21)		GIRLS (17)	
Math	16	Math	8
Language	1	Language	4
Science	4	Science	3
		Social Studies	2

Bar graphs are easy to construct and technically appropriate for this kind of data (Figure 14.5).

When individuals are keeping counts that go over a period of time such as daily calorie intake, number of electric appliances used daily, annual rainfall or Gross National Product the histogram or line graph is an appropriate way to convey their findings.

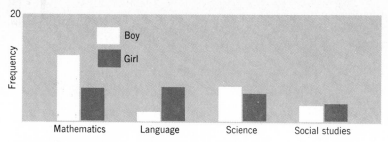

Figure 14.5   Bar graph of favorite subjects in
Mrs. Tennyson's room.

Day	1	25
	2	17
	3	33
	4	42
	5	35
	6	15
	7	19
	8	25
	9	21
	10	18

These data are a personal tally of times electricity was used in a day that can be translated into a graph like the one in Figure 14.6.

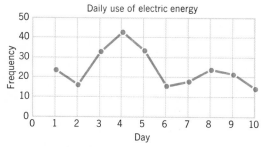

Figure 14.6   Histographing data.

Data confined to portions of a whole—a 24-hour-day, portions of a budget, a 365-day-year—can be organized into area or circle graphs (Figure 14.7).

Data that break into some very small percentages, or that have more than six or seven categories are difficult to portray through these graphs (see Chart 14.6). For example, these data are perhaps best presented as a list perhaps accompanied by a graph that shows the class division of Brazilian society without trying to break these into proportionate visual chunks (Figure 14.8).

If we had tried to show 2 percent or 1 percent on this graph, it would have been impossible to read. Had we presented only the graph, much meaningful data would have been obscured. In this case, a combination of listing and graphing serves both clarity and precision.

4. Case Studies. As with the interview, portraying data gathered from studying cases is probably best done on a chart like Chart 14.7. The purposes of the inquiry should orient the content of

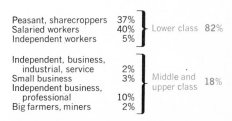

Chart 14.6   Class and Occupation in Brazil

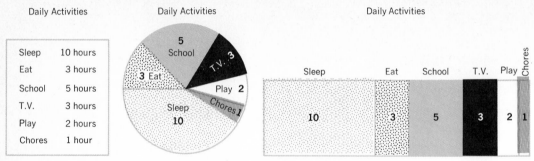

Daily Activities	
Sleep	10 hours
Eat	3 hours
School	5 hours
T.V.	3 hours
Play	2 hours
Chores	1 hour

Figure 14.7 Comparison of proportional graph.

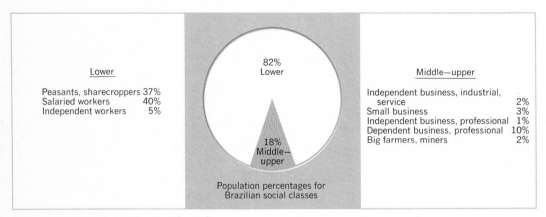

Figure 14.8 Combining charts and graphs.

Lower

Peasants, sharecroppers 37%
Salaried workers   40%
Independent workers   5%

82%
Lower

18%
Middle—
upper

Population percentages for
Brazilian social classes

Middle—upper

Independent business, industrial,
  service   2%
Small business   3%
Independent business, professional 1%
Dependent business, professional 10%
Big farmers, miners   2%

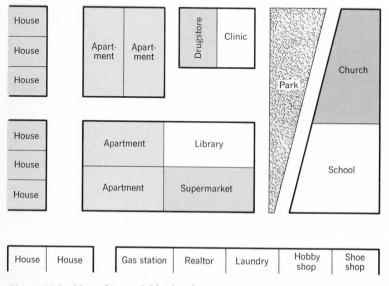

Figure 14.9 Map of our neighborhood.

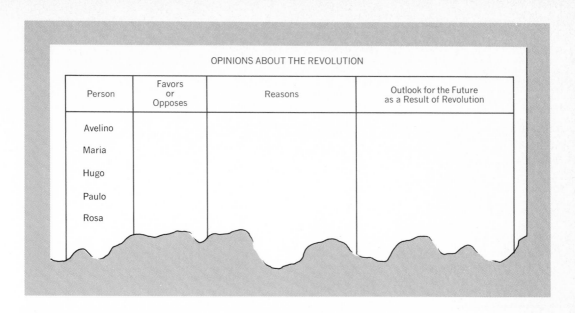

OPINIONS ABOUT THE REVOLUTION

Person	Favors or Opposes	Reasons	Outlook for the Future as a Result of Revolution
Avelino			
Maria			
Hugo			
Paulo			
Rosa			

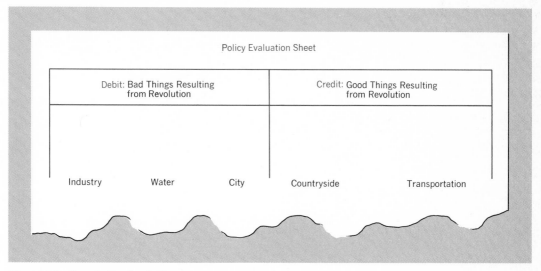

Policy Evaluation Sheet

Debit: Bad Things Resulting from Revolution			Credit: Good Things Resulting from Revolution	
Industry	Water	City	Countryside	Transportation

Chart 14.7   Sample Retrieval Charts

the chart. These examples are from a case study approach to the Brazilian revolution.

By listing their observations in categories and developing color codes or symbols for these categories, the observational data can then be plotted for these categories, the observational data can then be plotted on the outline map.

Mapping is also a useful way to convey data gathered about local communities by students (Figure 14.9).

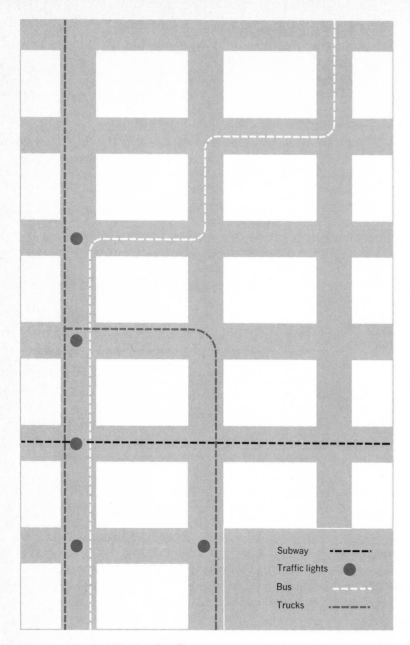

Subway	– – – –
Traffic lights	●
Bus	– – – –
Trucks	– – – –

Figure 14.10 Neighborhood traffic patterns.

Outline maps of the community being studied can be used to mark something as simple as where various students live or as complex as what traffic patterns are throught the local streets (Figure 14.10).

Using blank outline maps to organize data such as in the study of colonialism can display collected data very effectively. Mapping of this sort promotes more than listing. Global conceptualization and pattern inferences are possible when data are organized in comparative geographical contexts.

Our objective in the past few pages was to display a range of data organizing ideas and apply these ideas to various kinds of data. We looked at the following data-organizing schemes:

Charts	Graphs
Family tree	Bar graph
Retrieval	Histograph
chart	Circle graph
	Bar graph

Tables	Maps
2 × 3 and mul-	Local outline
tiple cell stables	World outline
	Route marking

This is only a sampling of the means we can use to organize the data we gather into comprehensive forms.

Check your ability at selecting appropriate forms for presenting data by suggesting which form would fit the following sets of data.

Situation A:

Problem: How was the neighborhood changed in the past 20 years?

Hypothesis: The neighborhood has become more mobile.

Hypothesis: The neighborhood has a greater variety of people.

Data Gathered:

Businesses Closed	Businesses opened
One dry cleaning store	One motorcycle shop
Five mom-and-pop markets	Four real estate offices
Two 5 and 10¢ stores	One large supermarket
One ladies dress shop	One carry-out pizza parlor
Four neighborhood bars	Two drive-through, fast-food restaurants
One gas station	One hi-fi store

Census Statistics for Neighborhood

	1950	1970
	3750	3221
Nonwhite	35	195
Spanish name		573
Under 18	1870	1002
People per household	5.5	4.0

Data Organization Suggestions: _____

_____

_____

Situation B:

Problem: How do people feel about the E.R.A.?

Hypothesis: Most high school students do not know what E.R.A. means.

Hypothesis: Woman will be in favor of the Equal Rights Amendment.

Data Gathered:

Results of states ratifying procedures to date:

☐ List of steps to get an amendment to the U.S. Constitution.

☐ Interviews with students' mothers on feelings about the E.R.A.

☐ Survey results from several homerooms selected at random on four-item questionnaire about E.R.A.

Data Organizing Suggestions: _____

_____

_____

Our Ideas

Situation A data on change in neighborhood businesses could be plotted on a neighborhood outline map. The Census figures could be presented as a simple table or they could be represented with area or circle graphs in percentages.

Situation B data suggest several forms of organization to us. The steps that must be followed to amend the U.S. Constitution could best be visualized by a numbered flowchart that labeled each point to be passed. A table listing the states with categories for checking off which had ratified or failed to ratify could visualize the legal status of the E.R.A. Hopefully, students asked their mothers several key questions. Responses to these questions could than be tallied. If the responses were of the "yes" or "no" quality, then a table would portray the results. On the other hand, if responses were more varied, the more open retrieval-chart format would better fit the data. Questionnaire results are natural materials for table construction.

To this point we have made no distinctions concerning the capabilities learners have for dealing with these forms of organizing data. We have given some attention to elementary students in the examples used to illustrate one or another means of organizing data. We need, however, to give further consideration to just which of these skills an elementary student can be expected to develop and how can these skills be initiated.

Beginning Data Organization

Organizing and summarizing data is a skill. Like phonic or grammar rules,

teaching these skills in isolation from real concerns of students guarantees that student interest will be low to apathetic. However, you may recall that earlier we have said teaching skills for acquiring and handling data is a teacher responsibility. Are these two statements contradictory? We think not. Within the dynamic of inquiry learning there are moments for direct skills teaching to occur. If we could abstractly sequence one of these moments, it would go like this:

Skills Teaching Sequence

1. Experience that creates problem.
2. Sample from which rules are derived.
3. New samples.
4. Correct new samples.
5. Reinforce by repetition on another sample.

Let us see how this abstract sequence might look in a real lesson.

Pictographs in First Grade

Background: The class is studying family roles. They have collected data about their families that they want to compile in various ways. For this purpose, Mrs. Flannigan feels they need a direct lesson on making pictographs.

Objective: Students can arrange data in pictograph form and can relate information from a pictograph.

Materials: Flannel board, felt-backed animal cutouts, plastic bags with collections of paper clips, buttons, paper stars for each child, paper for each child.

Procedure:

1. Ask about pets. "Remember the information we collected in our interviews with our families? Today we are going to see how we can share some of the information in a way we can all see and read."
2. "How could we make a picture that would tell others how many of each kind of pet we have?"

3. Collect ideas—accept all. Stimulate further to consider sharing this information quickly to people who cannot read.
4. "Let's see if you can help me organize this information about our pets."
5. Hold up dog. "How many have this kind of pet?"
6. Place cat on board. Going through same procedure, allowing student to place appropriate number on flannelboard of each kind of pet families have.
7. "Who can read this picture we made?"
8. Change quantities and have other students read graph.
9. Pass out plastic bags and papers and have students arrange these and make own graphs of plastic bags contents.
10. Evaluation: Check individually for layout and reading of content.
11. Closure: "We have some more data about our families we need to add to our booklets. Could we make pictures like this that would tell others about our families?"

Each step in the skills teaching sequence is followed in this lesson (Chart 14.8). Note the chance for individuals to repeat the skill using their own data that is easily checked by the teacher. Then the skill is reinforced by further chances to use it in the closure step of the lesson when the students are asked to select more data from their own collection to portray in a pictograph.

The essential element for successful skills teaching is that of relevance of the data to the learner. Charting or graphing becomes a fascinating activity for elementary students when dealing with data pertinent to the students. Some good possibilities of data sources interesting to nearly all elementary school students are shown in Chart 14.9

Chart 14.9 Data Possibilities for Elementary Students

Health records: height, weight
Class birthdays: frequency and distribution
Planets and their moons
Animals and their characteristics
Individual time budgets
Team statistics
Kinds of food and amounts eaten
Ways allowance is spent
Seed growth records
Pet growth and eating records
Individual reading, T.V. viewing records
Weather records: temperature at different times daily
Individual progress records in spelling, physical skills

Some of these data are cumulative, everyday occurrences have nothing to do with

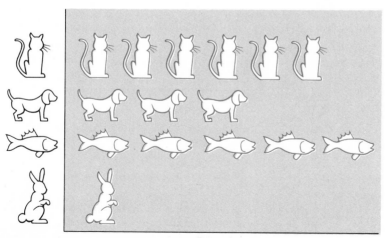

Pets we have

Chart 14.8 First-Grade Pictograph

social studies. All of these data can stimulate student interest, however, in observation, measurement and pattern seeking. Certainly, these activities are the essence of inquiry learning.

Numerous references and curriculum guides chart the desired sequences which students will learn the data organizing skills. As a general guide primary students can be expected to manipulate such formats as pictographs, simple bar, area and circle graphs, rhebus-illustrated retrieval charts, simple diagrams, time lines, school and neighborhood maps, and world maps detailing continents, oceans, altitude. Most elementary students continue to operate at Piaget's concrete level. They need symbols that have direct resemblances to their real referents. They need to manipulate quantities that are easily countable. For most primary students, perceiving that one person can be both a father and an uncle or that a person lives in a city, a county, a state, and a country all at the same time needs graphic and repeated demonstration.

Elementary students can work with organization of maps and simpler tables, charts, and graphs. They will need the direct assistance of a teacher in data organization skills. This assistance does not need to squelch a student's sense of discovery any more than teaching him or her skills in writing mechanics need wilt a budding author's creativity. Familiarity and comfort with various schemes for organizing data are essential to the more important step in the inquiry process, which must follow the organizing step. That step is deciding what the collected and organized data mean.

Making Inferences

"All Indians walk in single file; at least the one I saw did." Of course you have heard this old "chestnut" and others like it. Have you ever stopped to analyze this statement in terms of the inquiry process? It is the kind of inference making this statement represents that the inquiry process is designed to inhibit. What this statement does is generalize about a whole group of people on the basis of inadequate data.

Another example of the central role inference making plays in our lives is the television series, "All in the Family." We all laugh with Archie Bunker's social analyses. They are made to seem outrageous in the context of a television series. When he tells Edith that "Pollocks are dumb," or, "Hippies are radicals," we laugh because we identify with Archie. He is Everyman trying to maintain his self-respect under circumstances that seem difficult, even alien to him. He has never been exposed to more objective ways of making inferences and generalizations. Yet, being human, he insists on making inferences despite Meathead's continued appeals to "reason." The crux of this series is the friction and frustration that occurs between the fast-changing social world and our attempts to make sense of it.

"All in the Family" allows us to see how the common sense practice of inadequate and inappropriately informed inference making has produced many of the social and cultural stereotypes that plague human relationships the world over. Practice in the process of inquiry will not solve all these age-old human difficulties. But practice in inquiry, especially in the part of the process that concerns inference making, can offer students a better chance to question the world around them and put it into a more objective framework.

There are two skills in inference making that we need to stress with students. One is the skill of translating the data into adequate verbal descriptions.

The second is the skill of questioning the adequacy of the data for the statements made about them. In reality, these skills are highly interrelated; however, we will separate them here for purposes of emphasis.

What Do the Data Say?

Let us return to the first-grade lesson on developing graphing skills with family pet data. Following are some statements the students made in discussing what they had found out about their pets. Check the ones you feel can be supported by the pictograph data (Chart 14.10).

_____ **1.** We have 15 pets.
_____ **2.** Fifteen people have pets.
_____ **3.** Our class has a lot of pets.
_____ **4.** Nobody has a hamster.
_____ **5.** There are more cats.
_____ **6.** We like cats the best.
_____ **7.** Cats are easier to have than dogs.
_____ **8.** Most of us live in apartments.

Strictly speaking, you can verify items 1, 4, and 5 using data from the pictograph.

Items 2, 3, 6, and 8 require more data than is presented in the pictograph. We would have to check whether some students had more than one pet to be able to support item 2. Item 3 requires us to sample other groups of first graders to compare their numbers of pets to ours to define whether our class has "lots." Item 6 asks for a poll of which kind of pet each student likes best. Item 8 would need the same kind of process to see in what kinds of dwellings students reside. If item 7 means, "We think cats are easier to care for than dogs; therefore, we tend to have more of them as pets," a simple show of hands could be used to verify the statement. However, if it means what it says, to substantiate it would require a whole new inquiry. We would have to look into dog care and cat care. It is another hypothesis, another question.

Are you confused? Don't despair! All this and the next exercise are meant to do is distinguish between statements that

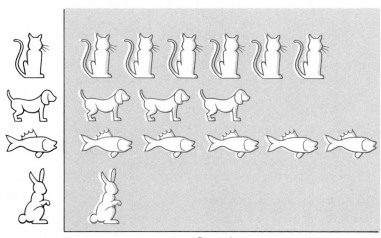

Pets we have

Chart 14.10   Pets We Have

read data and statements that *interpret* data. Statements that read data are really verbalizations about charts or tables or other organized graphic information. Stating and writing out what the numbers and pictures say is a translation skill. It should precede the more sophisticated activity of deciding what the data mean. To separate the two, perhaps this snatch of "Midnight Cowboy Theme" lyrics can help:

> "Everybody's always talkin' at me,
> I don't hear a word they're sayin',
> It's only the echoes of my mind."

Substitute the word "data" for "everybody's" and you have what we are trying to overcome. Before listening to the echoes of our minds, we need to hear what the data says. Now, check the statements below according to whether they (R) read the data or (I) interpret it.

_____ **1.** Three-fourths of Brazil's population is lower class.
_____ **2.** Brazil's society is run by a few very wealthy people.
_____ **3.** Salaried workers do not earn enough to be part of the middle class in Brazil.
_____ **4.** Big farmers are important people in Brazil.
_____ **5.** Brazil's service industry is small.
_____ **6.** Brazil's service industry is not well developed.
_____ **7.** The largest groups of people in Brazil are peasants and salaried workers.
_____ **8.** Brazil's salaried workers are not unionized.

Did you mark R's on items 1, 3, 4, 5, and 7? Each one of these can readily be supported from the percentages categorized under lower class and upper-middle class. Why are items 2, 6, and 8 interpretations? To assert that Brazil has a few wealthy people is a translation, or reading of the data. To further declare that they run the country is an inference. These data do not negate this declaration, but neither do they tell us about the

way power is distributed in Brazil. Item 6 is based on a comparison of Brazil's social structure to that of other countries. It relates to data beyond this chart. So does item 8. This item is based on the model of some industrialized countries where unionization has allowed workers enough power to force themselves into better socioeconomic status. These data do not tell us about the organizational status of Brazil's workers, only their social and economic status.

The skills of making statements about the data, or as we have termed it, reading the data are seen as hairsplitting and nitpicking by many people. Indeed it is! And our argument is summarized in the following generalization. The more care we have when reading data, the greater are our chances of not drawing unwarranted conclusions.

What Do the Data Mean?

Making meaning of anything entails relating the evidence to what we know and what others have found out about the issue in question. In one sense, making inferences from data is a recapituation of the total inquiry process (Figure 14.11). It is the step of the process during which whole new avenues of inquiry are perhaps begun. In another sense, this step is very similar to the hypothesis generation stage when students are led to guess about why a problem or situation exists. The diagram of the inquiry cycle merits repeated study for it conceptualizes this point. In using data we can collect to draw inferences, we make statements about reality that are actually further hypotheses. The hallmark of knowledge that the inquiry process generates is its transient or tentative nature. Scientific in-

Figure 14.11 Inquiry cycle.

quiry produces knowledge that is "true until proven to the contrary."

Let us look again at some of the statements we labeled as inferential in the previous two exercises.

☐ Our class has a lot of pets.

☐ We like cats best.

☐ Most of us live in apartments.

☐ Brazil's society is run by a few wealthy people.

None of these statements can be called wrong. They can be substantiated or negated by data beyond those presented in the two graphs. A full-blown inquiry process, then, would ensure that students gather data from various sources in order to make better inferences, or statements about the problems they are pursuing.

For example, to substantiate the inference that a few wealthy people run Brazil the students could qualify this inference by further ones based on reading excerpts such as the following:

A. "The sixties were simply terrible. It's hard to really understand how we managed to survive these ten years of affliction, anxieties, crises and upheavals during which we had seven Presidents of the Republic not to mention a triumvirate that lasted two months.

"One of the Presidents resigned, another was deposed and two died. Of the five left alive three have had their political rights taken away . . .[8]

B. "This is the deeper tragedy of Brazil. While the military government solidified its position, the masses continue to endure indescribable poverty. Thousands have starved during a year-long drought in the northeastern part of the country. Intestinal parasites, tuberculosis and malnutrition are destroying the health of millions . . .

"The percapita income hovers around $350 a year, but 80 percent of the people receive far less than that and many millions live outside the economy altogether."[9]

These sources are both secondary, or inferential, accounts of the way things are in Brazil. They lend support to the assertion that only a few people have power in Brazil. But still we would want clearer data before we could infer that these few people who appear to control the country are the wealthy and not the military. What are some other sources we might examine to formulate a more valid inference? The list should include offical Brazilian government policy statements and political scientists' analyses of who has power in Brazil. To guarantee that our inferences are well founded, we need to be alert to a variety of data sources while

[8] Marilo Mello Filho, *O Desafio Brasileiro,* Rio de Janeiro, Bloch, 1971, Introduction.
[9] James Armstrong, "The People Are Doing . . . Badly in Brazil," *The Christian Century,* January 6, 1971, p. 14.

realizing we will never be able to gather all possible data.

Even recognizing that all the data about a particular issue is impossible to gather, we must take care that the data we do gather is representative. Deciding how representative data are is a skill essential to better inference making. The *Chicago Tribune* headline, "Dewey Defeats Truman" is one of the classic examples of improper inference due to lack of attention to how representative the data were. Harry Truman was the underdog in the 1948 Presidential election. Newspaper owners and publishers, who were largely for the Republican candidate, Thomas Dewey, used data from a telephone poll conducted shortly before election eve. The majority of the people telephoned responded that they planned to vote for Dewey. They probably did. But Truman won handily. So the data themselves were not false. They just were not representative of the electorate, since, in 1948, a telephone was more of a luxury in that only the more prosperous people had them in their homes.

Getting representative data is a whole science in itself. There are graduate level courses in universities on techniques of social research and business firms whose special expertise is conducting scientific opinion polls. Basically, this science involves selection of small groups of individuals who represent the larger group. The science is called sampling. Through sampling representative groups a picture of what the larger group feels or prefers can be inferred. This technique allows researchers to collect data more quickly and cheaply than if they were to go to every individual in the population being studied.

The composition of the sample from which the data is drawn is crucial. The more the sample resembles the larger group it represents, the greater confidence we can have in the validity of the sample data. Here are some examples of statements made from data. For each statement write what you think you should know about the sample before accepting the validity of these data-based statements.

1. Americans prefer small cars.

2. Americans reject busing school children as a means of integration.

3. Welfare recipients do not want work.

4. Women taking birth control pills have higher incidence of cancer.

5. High school seniors now have lower SAT scores and poorer English composition skills than 10 years ago.

Our Reservations

1. To have greater confidence about this statement, we would like to know how representative of the American car driving public the sample was in terms of urban, suburban, rural and age groupings of young singles, family rearers, and older drivers.

2. Who was interviewed? Was it rural parents who expect their children to be bused to school, urban minority parents, suburban white parents, nonparents? Were respondents from areas mandated to bus by the courts?

3. How many welfare recipients are ablebodied and possess salable skills? How many attempts on the average does the ablebodied welfare person make to seek employment?

4. How long have records been kept? How representative is the sample of women according to different ages, economic statuses, childbearing, pilltaking, and non-pilltaking?

5. Did as many high school students used to take the SAT as now take it? Are more students completing high school than before? Is as much English composition taught in high schools now as before?

When making inferences about data referring to larger groups of people such as the population of the United States or the college students or high school teachers or the rich, the following characteristics have been found to be significant indicators of differences within these larger groups.

Typical Indicators Used in Social Research

Income	Sex	Religion
Age	Geographical	Marital status
Profession	Region	Educational level
Political affiliation	Racial or ethnic identification	

Naturally, these characteristics are related. They often come in clusters that have come to be almost traditional pointers to certain attitudes and behaviors. These clusters account for our expectations that, for example, white, college-educated women are more likely to identify with the Women's Liberation Movement or that high-income, college-educated men vote Republican. But times and issues change, and with them change the traditional expectations we have of social variables such as race or religion. Thus, knowing about who provided the data becomes very important when we try to understand what the data mean. A striking case in point is the voting behavior of unionized laborers in recent Presidential elections. Traditionally, this group has given solid support to whomever the Democratic Party runs for office. This bloc vote has crumbled since the 1968 national elections. The inference some analysts make to explain this shift is that many workers, such as plumbers, have moved from the "have nots" into the ranks of those citizens who want to protect what they have in our society. Therefore, the Republican Party becomes more appealing.

Perhaps this inference does not adequately explain the fact that many unionized workers are no longer voting according to our traditional expectations. Perhaps there is a more insightful inference yet to be made that will account for new facts. It is this continual reassessment of the facts to arrive at a better understanding that best represents inference making. We should always visualize inference making as similar to crossing a frozen river when the thaw is beginning. One must move from place to place, choosing only those spots that will support weight instead of spots that look solid but would break when stepped on. Sometimes it is better to stay on the slushy parts. At other times the solid chunks are safer. The careful river crosser will survey several routes before embarking and then test each footing with a pole or branch before stepping. And furthermore, if the river must be recrossed, to avoid an icy dunking, the same procedure, not the same route, should be followed.

Bibliography

Banks, James A. *Teaching Strategies for the Social Studies: Inquiry, Valuing, Decision Making.* Reading, Mass.: Addison-Wesley, 1973.

Beyer, Barry K. *Inquiry in the Social Studies Classroom: A Strategy for Teaching.* Columbus, Ohio: Charles E. Merrill, 1971.

Chapin, June R. and Richard E. Gross. *Teaching Social Studies Skills.* Boston: Little, Brown and Company, 1973.

Educational Systems Research, *Data Bank Kits: Materials for Social Science Inquiry.* Shrewsbury, Mass.: ESR, 1974.

Ehman, Lee, Howard Mehlinger, and John Patrick. *Toward Effective Instruction in Secondary Social Studies.* Boston: Houghton Mifflin, 1974.

Fraenkel, Jack R. *Helping Students Think and Value: Strategies for Teaching the Social Studies.* Englewood Cliffs, N.J.: Prentice-Hall, 1973.

Gross, Richard E. and Ray Muessig, editors. Curriculum Bulletin #14, *Problem Centered Social Studies Instruction.* Washington, D.C.: National Council for the Social Studies, 1971.

Massialas, Byron G., Nancy F. Sprague, and Joseph B. Hurst. *Social Issues Through Inquiry: Coping in an Age of Crises.* Englewood Cliffs: New Jersey: Prentice-Hall, 1975.

Muessig, Raymond H., editor. *Controversial Issues in the Social Studies: A Contemporary Perspective. 45th Yearbook.* Washington, D.C.: National Council for the Social Studies, 1975.

Ryan, Frank and Arthur Ellis. *Instructional Implications of Inquiry.* Englewood Cliffs, N.J.: Prentice-Hall, 1974.

Shive, H. Jerrald. *Social Studies as Controversy.* Pacific Palisades, Cal.: Goodyear, 1973.

Is inquiry always motivating?

CHAPTER 15

Constraints of Inquiry

Semantics and Data-Based Statements

No one would deny that, in general, the way in which a thing is said is secondary to what is said. How many times have we been frustrated by a speaker who we felt was "all heat and no light." That is, one who spoke at length, and perhaps elegantly or appealingly, but who left us with a sense that issues had been evaded, or not resolved. We want to know where a speaker stands. We are interested in the substance, not only the form of his or her ideas.

This same atittude also turns off many people to the results of social science research. Research findings are often dismissed with remarks such as "I already knew that! All they did was quantify common sense," or, "Why don't these guys take a stand; say 'yes' or 'no'. All social scientists do is equivocate."

There is a generality, a less than certain nature in social science statements. Read the following social science data-based statements, or generalizations.

Social Science Generalizations

1. People living in groups *tend to* cooperate.
2. Republicans *are more often* white, middle to upper class, and business people.
3. Prices *usually decline* when demand is satisfied.
4. Members of minority subcultural groups *more generally have* strong cultural ties.
5. Children *vote more frequently* according to their parents' political identification.

Notice that none of these statements has a simple, active verb unfettered by a qualifying adverb. There are patterns in human behavior. For example, if a person is hungry, he or she will seek food. However, in what way the food will be sought or how much food will be sought, or how the personality will be affected by hunger, and so on, are not totally predictable. Thus, the necessity for the less than certain nature of social science statements.

Perhaps a day will come when knowledge about how people act becomes so predictable that simple, affirmative statements, such as, "Water boils at 100°C," can be made about human acts. Aldous Huxley foresaw what kind of society this kind of social science knowledge might produce in *1984*. Huxley predicted that by 1984 so much would be known about human behavior that this knowledge could be used to control the thoughts and acts of all humankind. We would be willing to wager, however, that 1984 will come and go and the social science knowledge will not have reached the awesome proportions Huxley predicted.

Humans will continue to behave in much less than totally predictable ways. There always seems to be an exception to any rule of behavior among our species. We celebrate this fact of human existence. And we hope students will gain an appreciation of the limitations this humanness places on the generalizability of data-based statements in social science inquiry. We must develop a tolerance for ambiguity while continuing to seek relationships among human phenomena. In sum, results of social science inquiry can offer us the power to move beyond an incident-by-incident means of making sense of the world. However, social science inquiry results do not, and will not, permit an orderly foreknowledge of human interactions.

What Does This Mean for Teachers?

In the developmental process of learning to read, the student connects symbols to sounds for which he or she already has meaning. In learning to make inferences, the student connects meanings to symbols in a developmental process. It is only by degrees that students can deal with the subleties of the meanings they give to these symbols.

During elementary grades, it is essential to learn to "read" the data, in the sense we used when we discussed "reading" in the section on organizing data. Once the students begin to handle abstractions, in the Piagetian sense, the teacher's role in guiding inference-making changes. Students should be exposed to the case that conflicts with their conclusions. Often the teacher acts as a devil's advocate to cast doubt on the finality

or the validity of student inference statements.

Factors of the times, cultural orientations and group identification are constantly in play when we try to make meanings from data.

Questions that Test Inference Statements: Probing Validity

1. Would these same conclusions be true of other groups like the group we studied?
2. Would this statement have been true in your grandfather's or grandmother's time, or long ago, or 50 years from today?
3. Would students from another culture say what we have said about these data?
4. Would these same conclusions be reached if we had studied other kinds of groups or instances?

By responding to these kinds of queries, students doing inquiry learning will be exposed to the restraints on the inferences they make from data. Learning to see the necessity for tentative and partial conclusions when making generalizations about human interactions is the capstone of the scientific attitude. The following dialogue exemplified the teacher's role in promoting multifactor, less than absolute inference making.

A Classroom Example

Ms. Gonzales' seventh graders are studying the Presidential campaign. They have learned about the Electoral College. They know that:

☐ State electoral college totals represent a combination of that state's congressmen plus its two senators.

☐ States receive their number of congressional seats according to U.S. Census results.

☐ States may not split their electoral votes. They must cast all their votes for the presidential candidate receiving the most votes cast in that state, even if the total is only one vote more than another candidate's total.

☐ It is possible for a candidate to win the election with fewer popular votes than another candidate. This has happened twice in our history (Hayes-1876, Harrison-1888).

They have hypothesized that Presidential candidates will visit states with greater electoral strength more frequently. Furthermore, they hypothesized that candidates will carry the states they visited more frequently as well as the states near where the candidate is from. As of October, 1976 they kept running accounts of Gerald Ford and Jimmy Carter's visits to powerful electoral states, as shown in Figure 15.1.

On the basis of these data and the importance of the regional identification, students predicted that Ford would carry Michigan and Ohio (Figure 15.2).

The class has charted the election returns and this is the dialogue that went on the day after the final results were in.

Ms. Gonzales: "Did you all finish your electoral maps? Let's see how our second hypothesis, that a candidate would carry the states he visits more frequently, came out."
Dan: "Carter won Texas and he went there more times than Ford. Ford won California and he went there as many times as Carter."

Alabama 9	Idaho 4
Alaska 3	Illinois 26
Arizona 6	Indiana 13
Arkansas 6	Iowa 8
California 45	Kansas 7
Colorado 7	Kentucky 9
Connecticut 8	Louisiana 10
Delaware 3	Maine 4
Florida 15	Maryland 10
Georgia 10	Massachusetts 14
Hawaii 4	Michigan 19
	Minnesota 10
	Mississippi 7
	Missouri 12
Montana 4	
Nebraska 3	Tennessee 10
Nevada 3	Texas 26
New Hampshire 4	Utah 4
New Jersey 17	Vermont 3
New Mexico 4	Virginia 10
New York 41	Washington 7
North Carolina 11	West Virginia 6
North Dakota 3	Wisconsin 11
Ohio 25	Wyoming 3
Oklahoma 8	District of Columbia 3
Oregon 6	
Pennsylvania 27	435 Representatives
Rhode Island 4	100 Senators
South Carolina 8	3 District of Columbia
South Dakota 4	538 Total electoral votes

Becky: "And Carter won New York, Pennsylvania, and Illinois where he made more visits than Ford."

Ms. Gonzales: "What about the other states we charted?"

Skip: "Carter lost Michigan and took Ohio where Ford visited more."

Ms. G.: "Right. Who can summarize this for us?"

Figure 15.1 Graphic a campaign.

Visits in state:

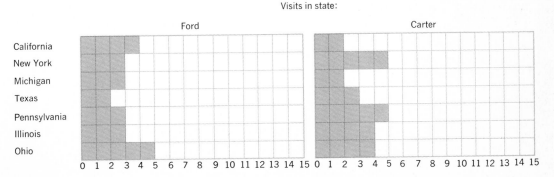

Ford   Carter

California
New York
Michigan
Texas
Pennsylvania
Illinois
Ohio

0 1 2 3 4 5 6 7 8 9 10 11 12 13 14 15   0 1 2 3 4 5 6 7 8 9 10 11 12 13 14 15

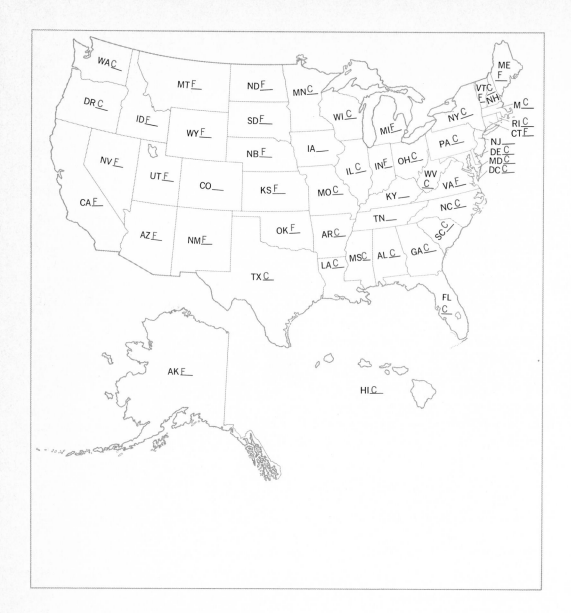

Figure 15.2 Recording electoral votes. Electoral College data map.

Ruthy: "Well, that's six states where the candidate who visited most won and one state where the candidate who visited more lost."

Ms. G.: "What do these data tell us about our hypothesis then?"

Becky: "It was right more often than it was wrong."

Chorus: "Yeah."

Ms. G.: "So you all agree that our hypothesis is supported?"

Chorus: "Sure."

Becky: "Over half, like I said."

*Ms. G.: "Who can tell me what percent five is of seven?"

Juan: "Seventy percent, if you want to know."

*Ms. G.: "Good! Is that enough to allow us to say that for every campaign that when a candidate visits a state more than another he will carry that state's electoral votes?"

Becky: "Well, over half is enough to win in a democracy isn't it?"

*Ms. G.: "Yes, in many cases. But my question is about our hypothesis, not a democracy nor an electoral college."

Earl: "I don't think so. How about the other states. It's not enough just to talk about the seven big ones."

Ms. G.: "What do you think about Earl's comment?"

Juan: "But I kept a record of the visits in other states for myself. Look, most were visited only once or twice or not at all by both candidates. I don't think there's enough difference to tell in the rest."

Ms. G.: "Hey, you're really into this! How many others did what Juan did?"

"You're the only one. Well, then, let's see if I can repeat what you're suggesting as a way to share your work with the rest of the class. Your research shows that most other states received nearly equal visits by the candidates, so they don't help us to support our hypothesis?"

Juan: "That's what I think."

Ms. G.: "Class?"

Sylvia: "Well, I think we can still say more visits means more votes."

*Ms. G.: "O.K., let's put ourselves into the position of campaign managers to someone running for President. Would you be willing to advise your candidate that he could win the election by spending a lot of time in the powerful states?"

Don: "Not me! There's more to it. I'd have my candidate spend his money on television ads. They can get to more people."

Skip: "Television isn't enough. He's got to meet people in person. My Dad met President Ford once and that impressed him more than any T.V. thing."

Sylvia: "You bet! That's why I think our hypothesis is right."

Ms. G. "Would you want to state it just as it is?"

Sylvia: "Yes."

Earl: "I wouldn't. I think we should say something like 'Personal visits to states is one of the things important in winning the electoral votes of a state.' "

Ms. G.: "Let's write that down and see what we think."

Notice the points at which asterisks were placed in the dialogue. Ms. Gonzales was introducing doubt in each instance. If she had not prompted the group to look at their data from another angle, the group would have accepted an easy, obvious, and perhaps erroneous inference. Perhaps acceptance of the obvious inference would have been more satisfying to the students. However, we feel that Ms. Gonzales was right on target. Her questioning encouraged some students to engage in critical thinking. If she continues to use this approach, more of her studetns are going to question the inferences they make and, hopefully, the inferences they see others making. They will be learning the "semantics" of social science inquiry.

Implications of Inquiry Learning

The process of guiding students to conduct social science inquiry has been examined step by step. Now, we need to take a giant step away from the techniques and examine the broader picture this approach to learning presents. Elements in this broader picture—classroom dynamics, curriculum planning and the relationship of values to inquiry—will be discussed in this section as a means of assessing the impact of inquiry learning.

Classroom Dynamics

The inquiry learning mode demands a teaching role that differs from the "knowledge dispenser" definition we have come to accept as traditional. This is not to say that under the inquiry mode of learning techers are relieved of responsibility for student learning because students should be freed to discover what they can. One version of inquiry best known as the "discovery" method does allow more ambiguity about the content objectives of learning (Chart 15.1). The objectives of the discovery method is to allow the student to "mess about" with materials and come up with whatever

conclusions he or she can fron the experience. The emphasis in discovery learning is on the manipulation of materials, or on process in the broader sense.

The continuum lines above express the difference between discovery learning and our version of inquiry learning. On the first continuum the difference between discovery and traditional concern with defining content objectives is extreme. Our version of inquiry would have content objectives almost as tightly defined as in what is usually understood as the traditional read-recite mode. Looking at the second continuum we see the emphasis on process objectives to be minimal in the traditional mode and most carefully structured under our version of inquiry. As it is defined in this book, inquiry learning does have definite content and process objectives. Promoting both kinds of objectives perhaps puts the teacher under more pressure than he or she would have under the traditional or discovery modes of instruction. To promote this kind of inquiry learning, teachers must become experts in asking questions that guide students to become better consumers of knowledge produced by others and to become better producers of their own knowledge. (*Note:* For further detail and logical conclusions on this topic please see sections on questioning Social Studies in the Curriculum and Instruction, Section 3.)

For the inquiry mode to proceed in a classroom, teachers must formulate their

Chart 15.1   Comparing Modes of Instruction

CONTENT OBJECTIVES

Undefined	x DISCOVERY	x INQUIRY	x TRADITIONAL	Defined

PROCESS OBJECTIVES

Unstructured	x TRADITIONAL	x DISCOVERY	x INQUIRY	Structured

questions in sequences that start with factual recall and eventually lead to comparisons, summations and making inferences or generalizations. Objectives of questioning vary as illustrated in Chart 15.2.[1] Students cannot conduct inquiry until teachers learn how to develop their content objectives by asking questions sometimes instead of always telling answers. These questioning techniques are the cognitive skills a teacher needs for inquiry to proceed.

These are affective skills and sensibilities teachers also need for inquiry learning to flourish in a classroom. Sensitivity to students' personal dignity and worth as thinkers is a prerequisite feeling teachers have to promote in classrooms if any real inquiry can take place there. Every teacher is entitled to his or her personal style and means of establishing rapport with students. We agree heartily with the old N.E.A. bumper sticker that said, "Teachers Are People Too!" Since we are

Chart 15.2 Levels of Questioning

PURPOSE	TYPE OF QUESTION	STUDENT ACTION DESIRED
VI. Divergent thinking	Open-ended	Gives many possible predictions
V. Evaluation as to the quality of a relationship or conclusion	Judgmental	Tells which of two or more alternatives is best according to clearly specified criteria
IV. Formation and/or identification of relationships and conclusions	Synthesizing or summarizing	States a relationship or connection among previously unrelated data
III. Analysis of the reasons behind an action	Explanatory	Gives reasons why a given individual or individuals acted in a certain way, a given event or events occurred as it (they) did, or a certain effect or effects resulted.
II. Organization of data	Descriptive or comparative	Describes, compares, contrasts, or compares and contrasts data
I. Acquisition of information	Recall or recognition	Gives correct answer

Permission by Addison-Wesley Publishing Co., Inc. Menlo Park, Cal. Tab A Teacher's Manual Program

[1] Jack R. Fraenkel, *Helping Students Think and Value:* Englewood Cliffs, N. J., Prentice-Hall, 1973, p. 178.

people, all the more reason we should do some introspection on a regular basis about our effect on the people in our classes. Ask yourself how much the items on this list are a part of your interactions with students.

Positive Teacher-Student Interaction Techniques

1. Allows students to finish answers.
2. Addresses questions to class, not individuals unless for purposes of calling back a wanderer's attention.
3. Accepts no answers and wrong answers without ridiculing students.
4. Listens to all student answers.
5. Incorporates student names and contributions in continuing dialogue.
6. Allows occasions for "speaking out" directed by students.
7. Responds to incorrect responses by further probing, restating own question, or relating answer to another question.
8. Admits uncertainty or errors and compliments students who help in clearing them up.
9. Gives students time to think before demanding responses.
10. Encourages students to ask questions.

Another feeling that must infect classes where inquiry learning flourishes is the feeling that conflict is normal. Where differences are not aired or expressed, inquiry learning seldom prospers. The whole ethic of scientific inquiry hinges on becoming ever more aware through promoting versions, often conflicting, of what data mean. Promoting this ethic with students may be the most trying task a teacher has.

A Case in Point—What Would You Do?

High school freshmen, mixed racial group in school recently integrated, are studying the U.S. judicial system. One of the Tuesday class events is a report on Monday's Supreme Court decisions. The

decision of upholding white workers' accusation of reverse discrimination for not being allowed to return to work with black workers who were laid off at the same time has just been reported.

James: "Good news! It's about time the whites got back some of their rights."

Steve: "Watch it, whitey! You're askin' for trouble . . ."

What should the teacher do? Which of these four options would you choose?

Option A. "O.k. That's enough! Both of you cool it. Now, let's move on to that filmstrip we have scheduled. Get ready to take notes."

Option B. "You seem to feel differently about this decision. Let's take a vote and find out how the rest of the class reacts."

Option C. "Do you think the reactions James and Steve have expressed will be expressed by others when they hear about this decision? Why?"

Option D. "You two were quick to express strong reactions to this decision. I would like us to examine what's behind your reactions. Could we hear why you have the feelings you do from each of you or people that agree with you?"

Which did you choose? Choosing the avoidance route may be the first impulse, the most comfortable reaction. Unless there is no discipline established at all with the group, this is the wrong response. Reponse B may be even worse! Teachers often feel that a substantive issue is resolved by a show of hands. This is a wrong-headed choice for two reasons. First, these students cannot resolve or change a Supreme Court decision. Second, even if they could, not all are informed well enough to vote. A classroom vote on such occasions only elevates the conflict and cements the ignorance present in the group on this issue.

Adequate choices are C or D. Choosing C or D would depend on your relationship with the class. Is it a group with which you have a feeling of trust? Choice D may be a good response. Choose C if it is a group that needs to remove the issues from two people in the class to a more distant perspective in order to have a calmer discussion. Neither of these choices will resolve the "rightness" or "wrongness" of the Court's decision. Both these choices, however, will promote an exploration of why we perceive events differently and why we have social conflicts.

We have not made a separate point of "setting the rules for discussion." There is a certain ambivalence on our part about those classroom decorations entitled, "Rules for Discussion," or even worse, "Rules for Good Listeners." It is the spirit, not the decorative classroom poster that matters. Rules set down on posterboard tend to get used year after year. Since incoming students do not help make the "rules," they tend to ignore them. To be sure, some basic canons of courtesy and fair play need to be discussed and probably rediscussed with each group of students we have. But classrooms are not parliaments where laws are made for generations that follow. And rules of order should not be used or allowed to stifle verbal conflict about significant issues.

It is impossible to overemphasize the impact that teacher skills in questioning have on classroom climates and dynamics between teachers and students. By examining the ways in which we structure questions for different purposes, the responses we make to student contributions and the general trust we build between ourselves and our students, we can ensure a better classroom climate for inquiry learning.

Curriculum Planning

The best argument against organizing instruction that permits inquiry learning is that this mode of learning is time consuming. Compare the topics covered in a more traditionally oriented read-and-recite course outline to the topics it is possible to deal with through the inquiry mode. Inquiry means emphasizing fewer topics in greater depth. To decide how far you plan to employ the inquiry mode, you should consider the following issues.

1. What are district expectations about process and content objectives for my level or area?
2. How difficult will arranging for out-of-class or "different" inquiry activities be?
3. What kinds of curriculum materials are available?
4. What experience have these students had with inquiry-like learning?
5. What beliefs about how learning occurs do you have?

Briefly, let us examine each of these questions in turn.

1. Many school districts have complete outlines for the knowledge and skill components learners are to master for each level within that district. If this outline is based on concepts, such as justice, supply, and demand, and the like, inquiry learning is more easily planned. If, on the other hand, the district outline is a chronological approach based primarily on historical knowledge, using inquiry learning to "cover" the sequence may take more time than is available during the school year.

2. A second, realistic question to check into before launching into inquiry activities that require students to conduct polls or surveys outside their immediate classroom group and class times, is the question of administrative and parental openness to this mode of instruction and learning. You should discuss your ideas with your principal or department head. Find out how much red tape is involved. How much red tape can be cut or routinized to make planning these activities less burdensome for you? As surely your

principal will remind you, informing and gaining cooperation from parents will be a key to your successful implementation of inquiry learning. Ask yourself if you are willing to assume this responsibility in curriculum planning.

3. Look into the sorts of curriculum materials you have for your students before you jump very deeply into inquiry. Several newer text series available at all levels (see Chapters 9 and 10) are meant to be used as components of inquiry learning. If you are not sure about those at your disposal evaluate them in terms of these points:

☐ Presents varied points of view.

☐ Identified sources for further information that students can pursue.

☐ Incorporates primary and secondary sources.

☐ Asks students to separate fact from opinion.

☐ Asks questions that stimulate more than recall thinking.

☐ Asks students to organize and make meaning from data.

Of course, you should expect to enrich your instruction with such elements as film, guest speakers, hands-on student activities, and resource books. Do not imagine, however, that you alone will have the time to create all your own materials appropriate to inquiry.

4. Knowing what experiences the students have when they come to you is one of the commandments of teaching. It is particularly important to know when deciding how much inquiry learning you can plan. As we said earlier, skills in inquiry need to be taught. Do not expect to accomplish all the hypothesis stating, data gathering, data organizing, and inference-making skills in one day. This is too much to hope for even in one unit or one year!

We believe that, although we have discussed inquiry learning as a cyclical

process, steps within the process can be worked on within the context of more traditionally oriented units. Hypothesis stating and testing, for example, could be a fine way to introduce and conclude a traditional unit on the Civil War. Data gathering on occupations could add an element of inquiry to a typical community study unit. The list could go on and on. Inquiry, for purposes of skill extension and good instruction, can be used in many contexts and according to the processes of the method relevant to those contexts.

5. Think of a time in your life when you knew you were learning. What made you learn? What kinds of things do you learn? Do you remember details or do you remember how to look up the details again if you need them? You must, by this advanced stage of your own learning career, have some feelings about what situations inspire learning and what is important to be learned. We think that the process of inquiry learning satisfied most of our biases about how best to stimulate learning. We would like to cite research to prove our contention, but feel that most research is inadequate to this large question. Before you do adopt the practice of inquiry learning, you owe it to yourself to examine your thoughts on these basic questions we have asked about learning.

Course planning is a complex, individualistic activity at best. Hopefully, focusing on these five questions will help you examine your own view of the impact inquiry learning can have on curriculum planning.

Values and Inquiry

Inquiry learning is always presented as an objective means of seeking knowledge. Some proponents of it have argued that inquiry learning denies vested interests and parochial values. Some even say that.

the method is value free. This argument is incorrect at least so far as the first charge is concerned. Inquiry learning represents the vested interests of scientific values. Under these values all topics are open to investigation.

Scientific-Scholarly Values

Skepticism	Open-mindedness
Tolerance for ambiguity	Tentativeness of of inferences
Objectivity	Free and open inquiry
Respect for evidence	All truth and beliefs are open to question

Representing the values they do, it should not be surprising to discover that inquiry materials, techniques and attitudes are not welcome everywhere by all people. A classic case of the impact inquiry can cause in a community was the furor in Tennessee over a high school teacher introducing Darwin's inferences about evolution of the species to his classes. The controversy culminated in the Scopes trial that pitted the two great lawyers of the day, William Jennings Bryan and Clarence Darrow, against each other.

We see the film, *Inherit the Wind*, based on this trial and probably wonder at how the issue got so out of proportion. We tend to look on the conflict between value systems this case epitomized as ancient history. We should not be deceived. The Scopes trial was in 1925, but the conflict between the value systems it symbolized remains alive today.

A recent example of the continued existence of this conflict between value systems over the use of inquiry is the controversy surrounding the curriculum materials developed by Harvard Psychologist, Jerome Bruner and his associates called MACOS, for *Man: A Course of Study*. The principal objective of the course designed for middle-grade students is to promote student inquiry into what is "human" about the ways in which members of our species behave. To this end developmental patterns of various species such as salmon, gulls, apes, and Netsilik Eskimos are compared. The Netsilik culture represents the contrary case to most of our value definitions about marriage, aging, and group customs.

Proponents of inquiry learning have seen MACOS as one of the most probing, sophisticated sets of curriculum materials et developed and marketed. Not everyone agrees. Here are some remarks Representative Conlan (R–Arizona) put into the *Congressional Record* about MACOS.

"Mr. Chairman, MACOS materials are full of references to adultery, cannibalism, killing female babies and old people, trial marriage and wife-swapping, violent murder and other abhorrent behavior of the virtually extinct Netsilik Eskimo subculture the children study.

"Communal living, elimination of the weak and elderly in society, sexual permissiveness and promiscuity, violence, and other revolting behavior are recurring MACOS themes.

"This is simply not the kind of material Congress or any other Federal Agency should be promoting and marketing with taxpayers money.[2]

And in another article Representative Conlan further states,

"By examining the values and behavior of the alien culture of the Netsilik Eskimos in a favorable light, MACOS teaches children cultural and moral relativism and leads to

---

[2] *U.S. Congressional Record*, April 9, 1975, p. H2585.

moral confusion among today's young people.[3]

Representative Conlan is not alone in opposing MACOS and other inquiry materials and techniques. This congressman and many others sincerely feel that the school's mission is to impart knowledge and to instill respect for basic American values. These values usually are articulated as loyalty to country, pride in the free enterprise system, and obedience to laws and authority. Any procedure within the school that has the impact of opening these values to question is often seen as subversive to the school's mission, and perhaps to the preservation of our society.

Whatever you may think about the values Representative Conlan urges school to define, there are other values that need to be defended as well. The rights of freedom of speech, equal protection under the law, and freedom of religion are even more basic to the preservation of our society. All these rights are compatible with the values of scientific inquiry.

We feel that these legitimate rights offer strong support for the practices described in this book as inquiry learning to take place in our schools. Having made this assertion, we hasten to add a limitation. The concept of democratic pluralism is also a value crucial to the well-being of our society. If we accept pluralism, we accept every person's right to believe what he or she wishes so long as his or her beliefs do not endanger or interfere with the safety or liberty of others. Under the concept of pluralism, scientific values, which the inquiry learning process represents, are as worthy as other value orientations.

There are different ways of knowing. Arriving at knowledge through the inquiry process is one way. We feel that the techniques of inquiry offer students a very powerful set of analytic tools for making sense of the world about them. Practicing inquiry will not bring peace of spirit or righteousness of mind to students. Instead, the impact inquiry learning can have on students is in the form of a greater skepticism, a more critical attitude. We feel there are qualities that will serve future citizens as well, if not better than many other value orientations schools might foster.

---

[3] John B. Conlan, "MACOS: The Push for a Uniform National Curriculum," *Social Education*, **39,** 6 October 1975, pp. 390-391.

Bibliography

Beyer, Barry K. *Inquiry in the Social Studies Classroom: A Strategy for Teaching.* Columbus, Ohio: Charles E Merrill, 1971.

Ehman, Lee, Howard Mehlinger, and John Patrick. *Toward Effective Instruction in Secondary Social Studies.* Boston: Houghton Mifflin, 1974.

Fraenkel, Jack R. *Helping Students Think and Value: Strategies for Teaching the Social Studies.* Englewood Cliffs, N.J.: Prentice-Hall, 1973.

Gross, Richard E. and Ray Muessig, editors. Curriculum Bulletin #14, *Problem Centered Social Studies Instruction.* Wasington, D.C.: National Council for the Social Studies, 1971.

Ryan, Frank and Arthur Ellis. *Instructional Implications of Inquiry.* Englewood Cliffs, N.J: Prentice-Hall, 1974.

Shaver, James P. and William Strong. *Facing Value Decisions: Rationale Building for Teachers.* Belmont, Cal.: Wadsworth, 1976.

Ubberlohde, Carl and Jack R. Fraenkel, editors. *Values and the American Heritage: Challenges. Case Studies and Teaching Strategies, 46th Yearbook.* Washington, D.C.: National Council for the Social Studies, 1976.

SECTION 5

The New Focus in the Social Studies

Despite the diversity in social studies programs throughout the United States, certain new trends in the social studies have emerged in recent years. In some cases, however, these topics are not really "new" but have always been on the periphery of social studies education. This section focuses on the present status of such topics as environmental education, multicultural education, career education, consumer education, law education, and the like that have received increasing attention but have left many teachers confused on how they could implement some of these new topics into their own social studies program.

ENVIRONMENTAL EDUCATION

ECOLOGY
and God's World

What are the goals of environmental education?

CHAPTER 16

Environmental Education

Rationale

What is environmental education? Before directly answering this question, let us first examine the three predecessors of environmental education: nature study, conservation education, and outdoor education.[1] In schools, nature study generally was limited to the identification of birds, trees, and flowers. But conservation education was broader in scope, focusing on the wise use of resources or trying to "save" natural resources. However, conservation education usually highlighted science and ignored the political aspects of environmental problems. Human conservation tended to be overlooked.

The increasing popular outdoor education movement stressed giving students firsthand experience beyond the confines of the classroom. In some primary class-rooms, outdoor education meant growing gardens/plants either outside or inside the classroom. In other cases, especially for the middle grades, outdoor education involved camping or staying overnight(s) in a more primitive setting than most students' homes. In such programs, typical activities were identification of wildlife and plants during guided hikes, visits to interesting natural sites, studying the stars at night, or learning how to use a compass. The site of outdoor education was usually limited to a recreational/ wildlife area with a low density of human beings. These outdoor education programs also often had other goals such as improving student-teacher relationships and introducing students from an urban environment into a more rural setting. However, these outdoor education programs usually did not touch on urban environmental or political problems.

In contrast, environmental education is much broader than its three predeces-

---

[1] Virginia Stehney, "Environmental Education: What It Is and What Schools Can Do About It," *Social Studies Review,* **13** No. 3, 1974, p. 3.

sors. The federal government has defined environmental education as the education process dealing with people's relationships with their natural and man-made surroundings, and including the relation of population, conservation, transportation, technology, and urban and rural planning to the total environment. In a more social action statement, Dr. William B. Stapp defined environmental education as "aimed at producing a citizenry that is *knowledgeable* concerning the biophysical environment and its associated problems, *aware* of how to help solve these problems, and *motivated* to work toward their solution.[2]

Using the above definitions, environmental education includes the social sciences as well as the other sciences. In addition, environmental education is envisioned as problem-solving, issue-centered learning. Environmental education is also seen as too important to be confined to a single grade level, age group, or to a single discipline. One-time crash programs will not do the job.

Therefore, consensus now seems to be developing that the following are the basic characteristics of a good environmental education program:

1. A *multidisciplinary* approach, with an emphasis on the interrelationships of human and nature.
2. A focus on *contemporary problems* (both people-made and natural) relating to the urban and rural environment.
3. An incorporation of the *nonformal* as well as formal education processes and utilization of resources outside the classroom, often featuring cooperation between the school and community.
4. Development of understanding and *attitudes* as well as information.
5. Involvement of all age groups.
6. A participant-process curriculum that allows the students to learn "how to

learn" about new situations, to weigh alternatives, and how to test solutions.

What about the the other hazy terms that are frequently used in environmental education? Ecology is the multidisciplinary science that studies organisms at home, especially the interrelationship between organisms and their environment. Most ecologists are concerned about ecosytems, the relationship of living organisms and their nonliving environment. In particular, ecologists are concerned with the destruction or the upsetting of ecosystems that are interrelated for the most part. Pollution to an ecosystem occurs when there is an addition in bulk to the system of nutrients already present or the addition of undesirable toxic substances. Informally, pollution refers to the poisoning of the air, water, landscape, or society.

Of course, it has been the depletion of our natural resources and the contamination of our air and water that have motivated much of the concern for environmental education. Many people now realize that the Earth's resources are limited. The exploration of space probably quickened this understanding. Photographs of the Earth revealed a finite and beautiful planet, a spaceship that depended on its human inhabitants for its safety and protection.

The concern for our precious planet implies a broad view of environmental education from population problems to the impact of industrial wastes upon the oceans. Many school systems and teachers believe that they have a good environmental education program. Actually, a close examination may show that it is really a hangover from the days of nature study, conservation education, and outdoor education. Specifically, these programs are likely to be weak in including the political aspects and the skills needed to solve environmental problems and some key issues may be neglected.

[2] Ibid., p. 3.

The Problems of Awareness and Controversial Issues

Since the mid-1960s, the public has been bombarded in the media about the harmful effects of various forms of pollution and other environmental problems. Many citizens have suffered directly from the harm and the inconvenience caused from the pollution of air, water, or noise as well as the price increases resulting from the energy crisis. Yet, are most Americans, including your students, acutely concerned about the dangers to our atmosphere, biosphere, and hydrosphere? How do they view environmental problems?

One's general background, including age, plays an important role in one's willingness to accept the fact that a serious problem exists. It is often convenient for both adults and young people to ignore certain problems and to hope that they will quietly go away. While many young people, especially white, middle-class students, are very concerned about environmental problems, teachers cannot assume that all pupils are equally motivated about environmental problems.

For example, some black leaders see the ecology movement as "ludicrous from the black perspective." To these blacks, the ecology movement appears to emphasize physical amenities such as middle-class standards of cleanliness, health, and beauty. Minority groups also fear that ecology policies could cut back on economic growth. Furthermore, some young people may not want to study population problems because of the possible implications for their own future.

From these examples, it is clear that often it is necessary to work with students to create an awareness of environmental problems. Sometimes it is effective to col-lect data from the local community on the volume of noise in the neighborhood or the amount of energy resources that the families of students use in a given time period. Or students can take pictures or films of litter and rubbish on local beaches, lakes, parks, streets or the lack of trees/plants in certain urban areas.

Of course, the question of criteria or values cannot be ignored in environmental education. A littered beach or alley may look "normal" to students or adults who have grown accustomed to seeing it that way. A further problem about awareness in environmental education is that some environmental problems are not obvious—water or soil may not look contaminated.

Even after some of these exercises, some students (and adults) still may not think that environmental problems should have a high priority compared to other issues such as providing jobs or curbing inflation. If this is true, teachers may have to respect the students' point of view even if they do not agree with it. Attempts to frighten students about our poisonous environment or gloom/doom statements may backfire—students may just become passive and believe that the road down to extinction is inevitable. Furthermore, trying to impose one's own values upon students usually is not very effective.

Environmental education frequently leads to controversy and as with other controversial issues, it is necessary that students understand the differences underlying the value conflicts. Thus, the question of who will "gain" and who will "lose" must be considered as when the values of economic well-being or improvement in the quality of life conflict. For example, an old factory may give out dust, smells, noise, and other forms of pollution on the community. If it is too expensive for an older plant to meet new antipollution standards, the workers who may lose their jobs, in effect, pay a heavy price in the war against pollution. Yet too many classes ignore this issue and only consider big industry as the "bad guy." This view, of course, ignores the fact that all of us, to a greater or lesser degree, are also polluters. How many of us are willing to abandon our cars or stop having barbeques, which also contribute to air pollution?

Students need also to become sensitive to the fact that conflicting interests also play a role on the international scene as well as in local and national environmental issues. Developing nations usually view pollution problems differently than industrialized nations. Poverty is often a main problem in developing nations. For example, India's Indira Gandhi believes that developing nations must first raise the standard of living before they can seriously worry about pollution. A so-called "dirty" plant may be better than no plant at all. In a similar manner, many of the developing nations feel differently about what some call the most serious ecological problem of the world, the population explosion. Furthermore, the worldwide competition for the limited amount of energy raises questions on how these resources should be allocated. How would your students feel if Americans were limited to energy resources on the basis of our population (about 6 percent) instead of consuming about one-third of the world's resources?

Who will pay the cost in both preventing and cleaning up the environment is also important for students to think about. Almost all experts agree that curbing pollution will be expensive. What will individuals and nations have to sacrifice to have a cleaner and safer environment? Will we be forced to change our life styles? In all cases—local, national, and international—people must find fair and equitable ways to solve environmental

problems without causing too much economic and social dislocation. This may be the price we have to pay if our precious planet is to survive. Ultimately the young will make decisions about environmental problems. To do a good job, youth will at a minimum have to understand the issues and the value conflicts behind environmental problems. In addition, they have to have skills to function in our society so that their decisions can have an impact.

Environmental Education: The Primary Grades

Children first view the world from their own egocentric perception of personal experiences. It appears that the earth is flat and most presume that their homes will continue to be adequately heated in the winter. As they mature, young people can add other viewpoints to their own and become increasingly aware of the variety and complexity of the world around them and especially cognizant that humans and the natural environment interact with each other.

Therefore, one of the priorities of environmental education on the primary level is to make students sensitive to their environment. Often this takes the form of collecting data about the weather: Why does it seem hazy? What is smog? Using field trips and walks as well as media, students can understand what is meant by such concepts as a river, a lake, a hill, or an island. On their short walks and excursions, students should be helped to realize that their local area is only a tiny part of the whole world. Of course, much of this awareness of the environment fits in with the more traditional recommendations (but not always implemented) for the development of geographical and science understandings.

In addition, acquaintance with the local neighborhood often can show the changes that are occurring in the use of land. Are new homes being put up? Are certain structures changing their use by being reconverted into a new business? What happens when there is a fire? In these cases, students should be encouraged to think about the consequences of the new land usage. If housing is put up, it may mean less open space in the neighborhood. The new factory may cause additional traffic as workers get to their jobs. A simple analysis of costs as well as benefits about land usage is often helpful in making students aware that humans can change the natural environment with different consequences to individuals, the community, and the natural environment.

But awareness of the world is not only gained through rational analysis. A poem may describe a snowflake. Music and songs can try to simulate the falling rain. Stories and can tell about accidents and weather—hurricanes, floods, earthquakes—and their effects about humans. Pictures, photographs, and literature can often contribute to an appreciation of the uniqueness and beauty of our precious planet. Pictures on a storybook about life in the Netherlands, for example, can help young children grasp the delicate balance between people and nature. Attractive children's books on environment such as Gail Haley's *Noah's Ark* are also useful.

To make students become more aware of environmental problems, many teachers (and this is not only limited to the primary level) have emphasized that the school grounds are also part of the environment. After viewing their own litter, many classes have initiated litterbug campaigns. To sharpen interest, students have made posters or slogans, presented skits for other classrooms, and have started contests for the classroom that collects the most litter and has the cleanest area. Sometimes the litterbug campaign actually extends beyond the school as students clean up and feel responsible for another environment.

Many teachers also emaphsize that many classroom resources can be wasted: paper is recycled, lights turned off when not being used, and the like. Also showing young children where many products come from such as bread or the parts of an automobile can promote an understanding of the enormous amount of resources that most Americans consume. Students have also examined the school's as well as their own family garbage cans to check on the amount of waste—unfinished lunches—as well as seeing the amount of packaging—cans, bottles, containers—that results in a disposal problem.

Thus, young children can become more aware of their environment and begin to recognize environmental problems. They also can become motivated to try to solve such environmental problems that are within their reach—the prime goals of environmental education.

The Intermediate Grades

Awareness of environment at the intermediate grades often focuses on air, water, and land. Here students may study how these resources affect them, the misuses of these resources, and how decisions must be made about using these resources. In addition, the natural environment is tied together with living things with an introduction to the concept of ecological chains or system. Energy and the solar system also are frequently included as content at these grade levels. The availability of attractive interdisciplinary social studies-science textbooks such as *Planet Earth* (Houghton Mifflin, 1976) have encouraged more teachers to try to combine social studies and science at these grade levels.

In addition, intermediate grade students also frequently study about people in different cultures, both historical and contemporary.[3] Thus, students may have a unit on the local Native American Indians who lived in their area, the American pioneers, or living in modern-day Kenya or Japan. Although the emphasis is primarily descriptive, teachers can ask probing questions on what do people do to provide goods and services to each other, what tools or technology are or were used, and what are the peoples' beliefs about natural resources. From these questions, students can become more aware that different cultures have different values and different technologies and that this plays an important role in how different cultures use their natural resources. Comparisons and contrasts with various cultures, including their own, can help students to see that human beings have had a wide range of alternative life-styles that have had different effects on the environment.

Although students at the intermediate grades usually become more knowledgeable about recognizing environment problems throughout the world, a focus upon the local community can improve awareness as well as allowing students to increase their skills in collecting and analyzing data. Students can design and use questionnaires asking their fellow students in other classrooms to check what they think about the condition of the community's air or water. Adults in the local community can also be sampled. Or students can ask adults in the neighborhood what are the three biggest advantages as well as the three greatest disadvantages in living in their community. Often the responses reveal concerns about environmental problems.

From the local data on environmental problems, the class (either as individuals or as small groups) can probe on the causes of the problem(s). Use of local resource people and local newspapers may be helpful since, for example, it is possible that the causes of pollution are not obvious or are not of local origin. After reviewing their data, students should be encouraged to take some small step that might contribute to the solution of the problem. This might be to place more garbage cans in the school area or to write to the city council asking that some change be made. Regardless of what is done, it is important to make students feel that their efforts can count.

Junior/Senior High School

At the junior/senior high school level, more of the science courses now emphasize environmental education, ecology, conservation, environmental science, and environmental health. Unfortunately, especially at the senior high level, there may be drops in enrollment of science courses and not all students are exposed to as much science as needed.

In some schools, a science and social studies teacher have team taught an ecology course. Some teachers have reported that this elective course has attracted a wide range of students—science interested students with good backgrounds as well as the more typical students with more limited science backgrounds. The wide spread in abilities within the class has caused some difficulties as some students want more technical data about the chemical composition of polluted water

---

[3] Morris R. Lewenstein, "Teaching Strategies," *Social Education 37*, November 1973, pp. 609–611.

while others are not at all interested in this particular aspect. Popular topics for these courses have been "How Can We Solve the Energy Crises" and local pollution problems. A few classes have also started organic gardens and have included an ourdoor education component into the course.

If environmental education is part of the curriculum, it is most often incorporated into existing social studies and science classes. In particular, urbanization, population, and the "food crisis" have been popular springboards for environmental education in social studies classrooms. In addition, U.S. history classes at both the junior and senior high school have many possible topics such as the conservation movement, which can be exploited by some teachers. Geography classes are also a natural avenue for teaching land usage, and major ways to utilize natural resources.

When the social studies department itself has initiated an elective course on environmental education, it often has some emphasis on law education. Frequently, case studies have provided a vehicle for analysis of environmental issues for students. In addition, simulations on environmental problems such as New Highway, Land Use, Planning the City of Greenville, Political Pollution, Smog, Atlantis II, Balance, and the Garbage Can have been popular. Furthermore, a few social studies classes have used science fiction and futuristics. Students are encouraged to speculate on what our society will be like in the year 2000 and whether or not they would like to live in such a society. Some courses with units in urbanism also have stressed whether or not planning is necessary in terms of the future.

Increasingly, publishers have produced many relatively inexpensive paperbacks on such topics as urbanism, population, and the energy crisis. Most of the materials have stressed understanding and awareness of value conflicts in environmental education. Only a few have really moved into the area of teaching students on how to participate as citizens in society.

However, *The Comparative Political Experiences*[4] (the federally funded project of the American Political Science Association) has produced a general skills kit for a one-semester course. Here students are not only exposed to environmental content, but are guided in participant roles with application activities in both the school and community settings. The five roles that are specifically taught are the following: observer, supporter, advocate, facilitator, and organizer. These roles, of course, move from minimal involvement to direct action. After students learn criteria for evaluating role performance, they act out the roles in class during the simulated activities. Students are also taught such particupation skills as to bargain, convince, trade, or confront and the probable consequences of each of these methods.

Environmental education does require that students know how to function politically in our society. How far the schools can move in a climate where alienation from political institutions has increased is debatable. But environmental education in its commitment to develop the means to solve local problems places both the teacher and students in a more activist position than most social studies teachers traditionally have played. To do this job, teachers need the support of their districts with statements of academic freedom clearly outlined.

To be effective, environmental education must take advantage of all the op-

[4] Judith Gillespie and Stuart Lazarus, *Comparing Political Experiences Political Issues Skills Kit Experimental Edition*, Bloomington, Ind., 1975.

portunities to relate learning experiences to actual local environmental problem solving and improvement. It places a premium on flexible and hard-working teachers. Environmental education also must expand beyond the classroom to make full use of all community resources – museums, libraries, local business and industry, parks, organizations devoted to outdoor education, and conservation and ecology groups. Thus, indeed, environmental education poses a great challenge to the social studies teacher as well as other teachers from grades K to 12.

Resources

Sources of National Information

American Camping Association, Martinsville, Ind. 46151

American Forestry Association, 919 17 St., N.W. Washington, D.C. 20036

American Nature Association, 1214 16th Street N.W., Washington, D.C. 20036

American Petroleum Institute, 1271 Avenue of the Americas, New York, N.Y. 10020

Atomic Energy Commission, Education Services, Oak Ridge, Tenn. 37830

Conservation Foundation, 1250 Connecticut Avenue, Washington, D.C. 20036

Environmental Science Center, 5400 Glenwood Ave., Minneapolis, Minn. 55422

Garden Club of America, 15 East 58th St., New York, N.Y. 10022

Izaak Walton League of America, 31 North State St., Chicago, Ill. 60610

Keep American Beautiful, 99 Park Avenue, New York, N.Y. 10016

League of Women Voters, 1200 17th St., Washington, D.C. 20036

National Audubon Society, 1130 Fifth Ave., New York, N.Y. 10016

National Education Association, 1201 16th St., N.W., Washington, D.C.. 20036

National Wildlife Federation, 232 Carol Street, N.W., Washington, D.C. 20036

Public Affairs Committee, 381 Park Avenue South, New York, N.Y. 10016

Scientists' Institute for Public Information, 30 East 68th Street, New York, N.Y. 10021

Sierra Club, 1050 Mills Tower, San Francisco, Cal. 94104

Superintendent of Documents, Government Printing Office, Washington, D.C. 20402

U.S. Department of Agriculture, Conservation Service and Forest Service, Washington, D.C. 20025

U.S. Department of the Interior, Bureau of Reclamation, Fish and Wildlife Service, National Park Service, Water Pollution Control Administration, Washington, D.C. 20025

Wild Flower Preservation Society, 3740 Oliver Street, N.W., Washington, D.C. 20015

Regional Offices of Federal Agencies

Several of the federal agencies dealing with environmental problems have regional offices. In addition, the Department of Agriculture has at least one agent in every county of the nation. Look in your phone directory under U.S. Government–Agriculture, or County Extension Agent.

State Agencies

All states have now set up agencies dealing with air pollution, water control, parks, and recreation as well as other environmental areas. Write to your state capital for further information. In addition, state universities are increasingly doing more work on environmental problems.

Local

Check the phone directory for possibilities of local groups (Environmental, Conservation, Ecological Organizations) as well as local government agencies (see City, County)

Bibliography

Dade County Public Schools, Miami, Fla. *Social Studies: Eco-Politics 1971.* For grades 10-12.

Diablo Valley Education Project, Orinda, Cal. *Environmental Issues Conflict Unit.* For secondary school with four major units.

Green Bay, Wis. *Project 1-C-E: A Supplementary Program in EE-Social Studies, K-12.* Topics that can be applied to courses in civics and local government, world history, U.S. history, plus energy use, interdependence, natural resources, and air and water pollution.

Minnesota State Department of Education, St. Paul, Minn. Environmental Education Curriculum Materials, 1972. Selected Resources for Environmental Education, 1972.

National Association for Environmental Education, P.O. Box 1295, Miami, Fla. 33143. Units for the intermediate grades.

National Education Association, 1201 16th St., N.W., Washington, D.C. 20036. *Environment and Population.* (No. 381-12016 $3.75 paper). A sourcebook for teachers.

New York State Department of Education, Albany, N.Y. 12200. *Handbook of Environmental Education Strategies.* Strategies for the middle school, junior and senior high school.

U.S. Department of Health, Education and Welfare. U.S. Office of Education. *AIDS to Environmental Education.* Grades 7-9 and 10-14.

U.S. Department of the Interior. Bureau of Land Management. *All Around You.* An Environmental Study Guide. Stock No. 2411-0035. Superintendent of Documents, U.S. Government Printing Office, Washington, D.C. 20402

Which is the best buy?

CHAPTER 17

Consumer Education

Rationale for Consumer Education*

Everyone is a consumer. Even the kindergarten child consumes goods and services and usually has some influence upon what clothes, toys, cereals and foods are purchased in his/her family. Yet all of us are aware that we have not always made wise choices in how we spend our money. Sometimes our car—either a new or old one—does not give good performance. Clothing may fall apart after a few normal washings. Often we may not be buying the best food for ourselves or our families in terms of either nutrition or price.

In addition, inflation in recent years has put more pressure on consumers throughout the nation, and especially the poor and those on fixed incomes. Furthermore, the concern about both the energy crises as well as environmental issues has made some people and organizations more worried about what values are reflected in our economic choices for goods and services. Fiscal problems, especially of cities but also at other levels of the government, have also made more citizens concerned about what services and what priorities should be made in spending their tax dollars.

Consumers both on a personal level and in their role as citizens now live in a more complex society and in their lifetime have to make many choices about new products and issues that their grandparents never dreamed about. In addition, people now enter into more legal contracts as in the widespread use of credit cards. Yet probably a vast majority of high school graduates have not been taught how to read contracts, do comparison shopping, and to know the legal remedies for fraud.

Haphazard, informal education learned from the hard knocks school of experience has been costly for many youths as well as adults. In response to the ignorance of so many consumers, a few states have mandated that all students must have some instruction in consumer education before they graduate from high school. Consumer protection groups on both the national, state, and local level have pushed for more inclu-

---

* The federal government uses the term, consumers education. It is too early to see what term will become accepted, consumer education or consumers education.

sion of consumer education topics at all levels of the curriculum. Business groups have also been "concerned" that students understand the basic concepts of our economic system. In addition, federal money from vocational education has served as a stimulus to consumer education.

Yet consumer education has several different meanings. Some years ago a consumer advisory council to the President outlined the following goals for consumer education:

1. "A rudimentary understanding of the market economy and the consumer's position in it, particularly the responsibility to make intelligent choices;
2. "Knowledge of standards of quality and an ability to translate the technical jargon often used by manufacturers and advertisers into everyday language;
3. "Knowledge of sources of information about products;
4. "Knowledge of existing legislation and regulatory agencies that serve consumers;
5. "An alertness toward fraudulent and misleading advertising and all other fraudulent schemes;
6. "General understanding of the legal rights and recourse of consumers;
7. "Knowledge of certain goods and services, and what features to look for when making buyer decisions."[1]

What do you think of this list? Some social studies experts think the above list stresses a passive role of "let the buyer beware." Instead, they feel more attuned to the objectives outlined by an earlier National Council for the Social Studies (NCSS) statement.

Consumer education should:

1. "enable the individual student continuingly to develop values and standards of choice-making which will help him to understand and live the democratic way of life;
2. assure the acquisition by students of information, skills, and practical competencies, particularly in connection with buymanship, utilization, and budgeting;

3. equip students to study, plan, and act to improve the social and economic mechanisms upon which we depend."[2]

In other words, the NCSS statement of 1945 stresses a more positive role of consumer education in that citizens should be more concerned with public policy and what the government as well as local groups can do to protect the consumer. The NCSS statement on consumer education is in tune with Ralph Nader's and other groups attempts to report data on the local level on such consumer topics as fraudulent repair practices, retail price comparisons, a bank interest survey, the elimination of "bait and switch" advertising and the like.[3] The NCSS definition also stresses more the need for the individual to act on his/her commitments and values rather than just be a shrewd buyer of goods and services. Consumer education as defined here requires a high degree of knowledge and skills as well as an understanding of one's values in making decisions.

But regardless of what definition is used for consumer education, almost all agree that the subject area is of prime importance to all students as well as adults in the community. It can include a great variety of active learnings from applying old-fashioned propaganda analysis techniques (bandwagon, plain folks, name calling, and the like) in assessing TV advertisements to checking comparative packaging with the new metric content and traditional measures. Given the significance of consumer education, why have not all students from grades K to 12

---

[1] John T. Kehoe, "Consumer Education: A Necessary Remedy, "*Social Studies Review,* **12** Winter Issue 1974, p. 5.
[2] Editorial "The Consumer: Another Forgotten American?" *Social Education,* **38,** October 1974, p. 498. NCSS has not updated its rationale for consumer education.
[3] Donald K. Ross, *A Public Citizen's Action Manual,* New York, Grossman, 1973.

learned some of the basic principles of consumer education? One reason is that most teachers have not taken a consumer education course themselves and are not always aware of how they could incorporate consumer education into some of their existing units. Second, consumer education has been on the sidelines of the curriculum and has not been a basic subject in most schools.

Where Does Consumer Education Belong?

The three basic ways of implementing consumer education are the following: (1) an interdisciplinary effort, (2) an integrated component or unit in the regular course material, and (3) a separate consumer education course, usually only possible at the secondary level.[4] Let us discuss some of the advantages as well as disadvantages of these various ways of implementing consumer education.

First, consumer education, by its very nature, is not just limited to social studies classes. It is also an important element in homemaking classes, business, and math classes. The interdisciplinary nature of consumer education does not pose a problem for the elementary teacher in a self-contained classroom. On the elementary level, it is usually essential for a school to check where (if anyplace) teachers are presently stressing any part of consumer education. A K to 6 or K to 8 program of consumer education should be implemented since consumer education is too important just to leave for one grade level. One or even several units in

the elementary school probably are not sufficient for a skill that will have to be used throughout a person's lifespan.

Usually it is helpful for the district or school to have a consumer education workshop where teachers can present interesting ideas on what worked in their classroom. From these discussions, teachers can see areas where they can extend consumer education into units they already have developed. Units on safety education might be extended to a discussion on how to shop for toys. Or students can listen to all the "words from the sponsor" that they encounter in a given week as they study about media in language arts. Units on the family might discuss how different families have different values and how this influences their economic choices. In addition, if some grade level allocations of consumer education topics can be agreed on within a given school, it avoids duplication and extends the learning experiences of the students.

On the junior and senior high school level with its departmentalization, the question of who is responsible for consumer education is a more serious organizational problem. Often a good first step on the secondary level is to form an all-campus team or committee with a member from the three or four subject areas most directly concerned with consumer education. This team then can investigate what emphases (if any) consumer education is presently receiving in the curriculum and how many students are presently taking these courses. Consideration often must be given to dropouts, and in many schools, the need is for the course(s) to be concentrated at the ninth- or tenth-grade level.

In some cases, an interdisciplinary course is most effective. For example, a business teacher and a social studies teacher may team up for a consumer education course. Typically, in this case, the

---

[4] David Schoenfeld and Anita Kanis Schwartz, "Integrating Consumerism" into the Social Studies Program," *Social Studies Review*, **12** Winter Issue, p. 11.

business teacher emphasizes contracts, cost of credit, insurance plans, and money management. In contrast, the social studies teacher may focus upon consumer protection agencies and legislation, value clarification exercises, and community action research. Or a homemaking teacher may team with a social studies teacher. When there is team teaching across subject area lines, it often results in a richer and more informative course than if just one teacher taught the course. The U.S. Office of Education reports that enrollment in consumer education, regardless of who was teaching the course, rose from 77,000 students in 1960 to 1961 to 413,000 in 1972 to 1973, a substantial increase beyond the population increase of the high schools.

If an interdisciplinary course is not possible, a consensus needs to be formed among secondary teachers on what responsibilities each subject area has to consumer education. Thus, the math department may concentrate on budgeting while the homemaking courses may focus on the packaging and labeling of foods and other products. The important thing, if there is not a separate course, is to make sure that the minimal topics of consumer education are included someplace so that most, if not all, students in the secondary school will encounter consumer education.

A further problem faces the secondary level social studies department in regard to consumer education. Consumer education clearly has some elements in American history, government courses as well as sociology and psychology. But more than the other social sciences, economics has important relationships with consumer education. Should consumer education be an essential part of the economics course? Typically, many teachers of economics have emphasized the economic understanding of the discipline of economics apart from the use or applica-

tion of knowledge from the discipline. Thus, the linkage of economic understanding and the application of consumer education has, in many cases, been very weak.

Abstract or dull economics courses would be improved if more emphasis were given to the individual consumer and the problems that a typical consumer encounters. Many economics courses would be of greater interest to students if portions of the course were on the individual householder, investor, saver, borrower, and other roles that the students are now playing and are likely to play. Combining economics and consumer education makes good sense, especially if the teacher preparation is strong for this combination.

Regardless of what format is used for consumer education—whether units in regular courses or a separate course(s) are used with or without interdisciplinary emphasis—the important thing is for the whole school to do some thinking about the implementation of consumer education into the curriculum. Typically, much needs to be done. Teachers and other staff members should make lists of their available resources and allocate some of their budget to the gaps in consumer education. In many cases, the new consumer educational materials and media would be very effective in some classrooms. Some of the law and the consumer education materials have high interest value and are very informative. In addition, some of the elementary filmstrips on consumer education are outstanding in their motivational as well as use of economic concepts.

Teachers also may need additional in-service training or course work in consumer education. Continual assessment of the effectiveness of consumer education is necessary to insure that it is meeting the needs of the students. Again, all of these activities assume that consumer education is integrated into the K to 12 curriculum.

The "How" of Teaching Consumer Education

Preaching to students about consumer education (or any other topic) is not usually too effective, especially if the teacher and students have different values. More promising is moving the students out of the classroom. Often, however, students do not have to go too far—the school itself can be used as a laboratory for investigation. Many students and their teachers have found it profitable to turn a "consumer education" eye on what is sold on campus. What is available to students and teachers for a snack or at lunchtime? Is it junk food and empty sugar calories? If so, should any changes be made? It may be profitable to investigate who benefits economically from the sale of food on campus.

Along with heavy use of speakers from the community, students in consumer education have also worked in the local community. Students may do comparison shopping at the local stores. They may investigate what health services are available to the community. Or students may watch what happens in Small Claims Court.

If students do investigations of the community, it is essential that they do not use sloppy procedures in data collection, especially if they expect the community to receive their reports with some degree of credibility. Careful checklists such as a food market survey or the cost of credit survey should be made carefully by the students and the teacher. All students should use the same form and all should be given careful instructions on how to

obtain the data. Usually, it is advisable for students to work together in teams of two so bias can be controlled. With good clear forms, even primary students can participate in consumer education surveys. This is especially true of the "yes or no" type questions such as the does the store provide free delivery or does the store offer a check-cashing service.

Most teachers have reported a great deal of success when students have collected data from the community. Students often learn more from these activities than if the teacher gives moralistic sermons on what a careful shopper should do. Traditional methods as well as some creative ones can also be effective. Students can be asked to furnish a hypothetical house or decide on what bike or automobile to purchase. They can become familiar with various consumer valuational publications and reinforce key skills in obtaining and evaluating information. In addition, specialized text materials like how to balance bank statements or fill out income tax forms are useful to all students.

Most Americans believe that consumer education is a practical area that must be stressed more in the schools. A wide spectrum of community groups support consumer education. Consumer education enrollment at the secondary level has increased within the last 10 years or so. However, consumer education is not yet part of the curriculum for every student. A great deal more still remains to be done.

Resources

School and Community

1. School staff members such as the nurse to talk on health or driver ed staff to discuss the purchase and maintenance of a car.

2. Health service personnel (health officials, pharmacists, nurses, etc.) on health care services and labeling and advertising of drugs.
3. Insurance agents on all types of insurance.
4. Merchants on credit charges, refunds, guarantees, and other issues.
5. Better Business Bureau on consumer fraud.
6. Real estate agents on buying and leasing property.
7. Consumer protection agencies.
8. Federal agencies with local field offices in your area: Environmental Protection Agency, Food and Drug Administration, Office of Consumer Affairs, Department of Agriculture, and so on.
9. State/local level on consumer affairs, attorney general, Bureau of Standard Weights and Measures, Health Department, Public Utilities Commission, as well as local political representatives.[5]

---

[5] This list is heavily modified from Stewart Lee's "Sources and Resources in Consumer Education," *Social Education,* **38,** October 1974, pp. 519-523.

Bibliography

Consumer Periodicals and Newsletters

Some of these would be very desirable for the library.

Changing Times, The Kiplinger Magazine, Editors Park, Md. 20782.

Consumer Reports, Consumers Union, Orangeburg, N.Y. 10962

Consumers' Research Magazine, Consumers Research, Bowerstown Road, Washington, N.J. 07882

FDA Consumer, Superintendent of Documents, U.S. Government Printing Office, Washington, D.C. 20402.

Everybody's Money, Credit Union National Association, Inc. P. O. Box 431, Madison, Wisc. 53701

Consumer News, Superintendent of Documents, U. S. Government Printing Office, Washington, D.C. 20402

ACCI Newsletter (American Council on Consumer Interests), ACCI, 238 Stanley Hall, University of Missouri, Columbia, Mo. 20005.

Media & Consumer, P. O. Box 1225, Radio City Station, New York, N.Y. 10019

Materials for Teachers

Available from Consumers Union, Orangeburg, N.Y.

Consumer Education Materials Project
Early Childhood Consumer Education
Elementary Level Consumer Education
Secondary Level Consumer Education
Consumer Education in Junior and Community Colleges
Vocational and Technical Institutes
Adult Consumer Education in the Community
Preparing the Consumer Educator
Approximately 80 pp. each. Cost: $3 each.

Enriching the Curriculum Through Consumer Education. For the elementary school. Lincoln Elementary School Teachers. Euclid Board of Education. 651 E. 222 St., Euclid, Ohio 44123. $5

Suggested Guidelines for Consumer Education: Kindergarten through Twelfth Grade. President's Committee on Consumer Interests. Superintendent of Documents. U.S. Government Printing Office, Washington, D.C. 20402, 1970. 58 pp., $.65.

Consumer Education: Its New Look. "The Bulletin of the *National Association of Secondary School Principals.* October 1967. Available from Consumers Union, Orangeburg, N.Y. 10962. 116 pp., $2.00.

Why are speakers often effective in explaining
about their jobs?

CHAPTER 18

Career Education

Rationale

Career education came into prominence on the educational scene in the early 1970s as the U. S. Office of Education focused more attention and funds into this area. What were the reasons for this new emphasis? One was the growing feeling that a wide gap existed between the "irrelevant" schools and the world of work. This gap, it was felt, limited many students in obtaining employment. In other cases even when students obtained jobs, they were disappointed or made poor career decisions.

Particular concerns were expressed about the high unemployment rate of minority students and the dropouts from high school who were mostly without salable skills or training. It was hoped that career education in the schools could make all students, and especially women and minority groups who have been traditionally outside the opportunity structure in terms of high income and responsible jobs, more aware of the opportunities for career development. In particular, it was felt that these disadvantaged or handicapped students as well as many others, needed a more positive self-concept of themselves so that they could achieve more control of their life-style, including employment.

In addition, parents and the community were generally favorable to the concept of career education. Countless surveys have found that most adults believe that the most important function of the secondary school and the college is to prepare individuals to get better jobs. Yet about 80 percent of high school students take academic or general courses that do not directly equip them for any specific employment. Thus, although most educators typically believe in the goals of general education, students and their parents often want the schools to have a greater vocational emphasis so that young people can obtain employment.

Furthermore, the changing and rapid pace of economic development of our society indicates that most people will have more than one career. To be accurate, career education should be called careers education since it is a lifelong process. Many more adults now change their jobs at midcareer. Many women and a few men who are homemakers face reentry problems as they return to paid employment. Therefore, a flexible attitude toward career development is essential since gaining full-time employment at the age of 18 or 22 is not usually the end of one's career preparation. Fewer people now stay at the same job all their life or remain employed at the same business or institution.

Thus, career education in the schools was seen as the answer to many problems: that of eliminating poverty and reducing the number of individuals/families on welfare, reducing the number of students who drop out of high school, obtaining full employment and higher status jobs for women and minorities, satisfying employers who complained about ill prepared job applicants, and making better use of people power so that the United States could complete in world trade.

But not all educators were enthusiastic about career education and having a closer link between school and work. Some teachers feared that career education was an attack on the intellectual or academic subjects. Others worried about the wisdom of exposing students to career development when both the job market as well as values may change radically by the twenty-first century. Will the Protestant work ethnic be as strong in the future? Do we really know what type of skills and attitudes an individual will need for employment in the future? Still others were concerned that career education programs would fit students into "pigeonholed" jobs rather than promoting individual development. In other words, career education, it is still feared, would subordinate the real interests of children to the needs of business and industry.

Others feared that career education might force students too early to make decisions that might lock kids into dead-end jobs. Still others thought that career education would take time away from the basic subjects. Furthermore, some critics believe that a broad liberal education allows students to adapt to the market better than specific vocational skills.

These concerns bothered many educators. While some believed in career education, they were not certain if the schools were the best place for doing this important job. Might not the basic skills of reading, writing, and arithmetic be the main function of the school that would promote entry into the job market? In addition, many educators were worried that the curriculum was increasingly becoming overcrowded and wondered what should be eliminated if another new subject area was put into the curriculum.[1]

These various issues about career education, of course, have not been resolved and are not likely to be so in the near future. However, it is important for you, an educator, to think about the place of career education in the schools. Your decision probably partly depends on what is meant by career education.

Definitions of Career Education

In the early 1970s, career education was deliberately left vague by the U. S. Office of Education so that it would not stifle the creativity of schools throughout the nation. All that was originally suggested in 1971 by Dr. Sidney P. Marland, Jr., the Commissioner of Education at that time, was the following:

> "What the term 'career education" means to me is basically a point of view, a concept — a concept that says three things: First, that career education will be part of the curriculum for all students, not just some. Second, that it will continue throughout a youngster's stay in school, from the

[1] Frank L. Ryan, "Introduction," (to the section on "Career Education — Viable or Vulnerable?"), *Social Education,* **39,** May 1975, p. 305.

first grade through senior high and beyond, if he so elects. And third, that every student leaving school will possess the skills necessary to give him a start to making a livelihood for himself and his family, even if he leaves before completing high school."[2]

This hardly clarifies the meaning of career education. Career education, whatever it may be, is according to Marland, necessary for all students from kindergarten through however long they stay in school, and that all students, even high school dropouts, should receive sufficient skills to make them employable.

Of course, some educators were troubled that career education promised too much that could not be realized, given the present organization and financial support of the schools. These educators stressed that the schools cannot fit students into the job market if jobs do not exist. Furthermore, some asserted that the schools just cannot provide sufficient skills or change basic attitudes to make high school students employable if they drop out before completing high school. Often employers will not hire dropouts who they perceive to be undependable, and to be poor workers even if they have marketable skills.

What does career education then mean? The American Association of Colleges for Teacher Education has used the following three criteria for career education programs: (1) inclusion and integration of academic and vocational education, (2) fusion of guidance and instruction, and (3) systematic use of the community and its personnel resources in the instruction and guidance processes. This definition implies that career educa-

tion permeate all the grade levels including academic subjects.

Another definition is that career education is a process to orient all students to the world of work and to help them prepare for their chosen vocations. Career education is also to be a coordinated and articulated program, with a strong guidance component, that will provide students with information about the 15 general vocational job clusters—transportation, communication, business and offices, agribusiness and natural resources, marketing and distribution, environmental control, marine science, consumer and homemaking, construction, health, public service, hospitality and recreation, manufacturing, personal services, fine arts and humanities—and specific jobs within these job clusters.

Thus, career education would make students aware of the job market as well as the necessary training and skills needed to obtain employment. How much actual occupational preparation at the high school level that the schools were to provide varied with the needs of individual students as well as the commitment of the local schools and state to vocational education. A few school systems set up expensive centers—a computer center, an aircraft hangar with a plane, greenhouses, TV studio, and the like—for use of high school students during the day and adults during the evening.

Others defined career education as basically everything—a process of decision making that involved work, leisure, family, and the community. In effect, here career education became life career development with a heavy stress on self-development.[3] According to this defini-

[2] "Marland on Career Education: Questions and Answers," *American Education,* **7,** November 1971, p. 25.

[3] Lorraine Sundal Hansen and W. Wesley Tennyson, "Career Development as Self Development: Humanizing the Focus for Career Education," *Social Education,* **39,** May 1975, pp. 304-307.

tion, students are expected to become career managers of their whole life. One problem with this definition is that the term is so general that schools could say that they have career education and really change nothing. Still another definition is that career education comprises coping or survival skills that would lead students to a satisfying, self-confident life. Presumably, this might include anything from learning how to balance a checking account or reading the classified ads to find an apartment. This definition might also include effective use of one's leisure and using political power as a citizen.

From these various definitions, most states formed their own definition of career education since federal funds—over 80 million between 1969 to 1976—for career education were distributed through the states. The states' responsibilities were generally to gather, catalogue, and disseminate information on career education as well as to design training programs and prepare assessment designs. Four states—Michigan, Iowa, Louisiana, and Kentucky—now require their public school systems to have career education programs. Eight states also contribute their own monies for career education. About 9000 of the nation's 17,000 school districts have moved into some type of career education program—an astounding increase within a short period of time. However, a wide diversity presently exists among schools on what is being done in career education.

Despite the differences in career education definitions, most educators believe that the elementary grades should concentrate upon a broad awareness of occupations with more in-depth exploration at the middle school/junior high school level. Then, actual career preparation would take place at the high school as well as the college level. Using this developmental model, elements of career education could be provided for every student at all grade levels.[4]

The Social Studies and Career Education

Again, as in consumer education, multicultural education, and other new popular areas, the field of social studies was seen as a promising area in which career education could be incorporated into the existing curriculum. True, career education was a natural for vocational/industrial arts teachers in the high school. But vocational/industrial arts teachers typically consisted of about 30 percent of the high school staff at most while about 70 percent of the staff were academic or general education teachers. Furthermore, many students in high school took no vocational/industrial arts courses during their entire four years of high school.

But do high school social studies teachers favor career education? Ohanneson in a random sample of 900 California high school teachers found, as expected, that vocational/industrial arts teachers gave considerable more support to career education than did academic/general teachers. Teachers who had considerable full-time nonteaching work experiences also expressed significantly greater support than those with little such experience. However, of the academic teacher groups, social studies teachers generally believed somewhat more strongly than the other teacher specialty groups that the schools should engage in career education.[5]

---

[4] Henry D. Olsen, "The Place of Career Education in Elementary Social Studies," *Social Studies Review*, **12**, Spring Issue 1974, p. 34.
[5] Greg Ohanneson, "Finding, Preparing, and Deploying Teachers for Career Education, *Social Studies Review*, **12**, Spring Issue 1974, pp. 19–25.

While the attitudes of social studies teachers are somewhat encouraging to career education, some researchers have reported that high school teachers may be less amendable to curriculum change efforts than elementary teachers. High school teachers relate to their fields more than to an overall school philosphy or purpose. In addition, high school teachers cooperate less as a staff and are less dependent on their principals. Often they use their topic specialization to strengthen their resistance to change.[6]

It is therefore little wonder that many career education enthusiasts tried to get their program into the elementary school. But it was not just the perceived resistance of academic high school teachers that inspired this thrust. Research has indicated that even young primary students have values about the desirability of certain jobs and that work study skills and habits are usually pretty well established by the end of the elementary school experience. In addition, attitudes toward authority, being open to new ideas, a good self-concept, and the ability to work together in groups are developed in the early years and have important consequences in both one's work career as well as in personal life.

Teachers use all different types of methods for career education—simulation games on careers, role-playing job interviews, field experiences to observe workers at their jobs or reading biographies on the importance of work in the lives of famous people. But certain types of activities are usually more likely at certain grade levels. The following section concentrates more specifically on career education activities in the narrow sense and not upon developing good self concepts or other broad goals which are part of the teachers' goals for students regardless of subject area.

Career Education: The Primary Level

At the primary level, awareness of various workers can be initiated by having students report and investigate more thoroughly the jobs of their parents, school employees, and community workers. However, just concentrating upon a few stereotyped community workers such as the police officer or the firefighter may not be as desirable as a more in-depth treatment of the wide variety of occupations in the various job clusters. Thus, students in a working class community should be introduced to jobs that their parents or relatives do not hold such as an optometrist or a marine biologist while many affluent suburbia classrooms might benefit from a study of certain blue-collar occupations such as truck drivers or construction workers. In addition, girls and minority students should see themselves in responsible and nontraditional roles. For example, materials might portray a doctor as a Puerto Rican man living in New York or a woman as an airplane traffic control officer, business executive, or crane operator.

Because many elementary teachers (and teachers in general) often lack a detailed knowledge of various occupations, sets of sound filmstrips for the primary grades on such occupations as doctor, jet pilot, and architect as well as some less well-known occupations such as toymaker, quiltmaker, photographer, and artist have been popular. Some of the

---

[6] Dale Mann, "The Politics of Training Teachers in Schools." *Teachers College Record*, **77**, February 1976, pp. 323-338; Michael Fullan and Alan Pomfret, *Review of Research on Curriculum Implementation*, Ontario, The Ontario Institute for Studies in Education, 1975; Richard E. Gross, "The Social Studies Teacher: Agent of Change?," *The Social Studies*, **67**, July-August 1976, pp. 147-151.

media concentrates on products such as cotton and how we use it or digging coal to make electricity for us. Then, in describing the process of producing power or building a road, a wide variety of occupations are shown. Some of these filmstrips or case study booklets do give an accurate portrayal of the job and the effect the job has on a person's life style. Often highly interesting occupations such as a pet shop owner or park ranger have been used as subjects of the case studies.

Thus, primary students can be introduced to the diversity of jobs within *all* 15 of the job clusters. From each of the occupations, they can gain some insight on the qualities and skills necessary to be successful at the job. In addition, many primary teachers have called in community resource people who tell about their jobs and who often bring their tools with them. Children then have followed up with murals or booklets on the various "Workers That They Know." Hopefully, students will also gain a respect for all workers, and diminish their stereotypes about jobs. In addition, students may take field trips to see various types of workers such as sales clerks.

Intermediate Grades — Middle School/Junior High

Career awareness and exploration can take many different forms at the intermediate and middle grades. Above the primary level, more filmstrip series and related materials concentrate on how jobs are interdependent upon each other. Thus, a filmstrip or paperback entitled *Going to the Hospital* shows the anesthetist, X-ray technician, the nurse's aid, the orderly, and the dietitian as well as the more familiar doctor and nurse as all part of the health team. Or the filmstrip or paperback may show the wide range of skills and occupations required to produce a popular TV program or a product. In addition, more of the materials tend to show more explicitly the various levels of training required for different types of careers and point out more clearly the economic benefits as well as the disadvantages associated with different jobs.

Although some primary teachers do visit sites such as the supermarket or the bakery to show their students the jobs of workers, middle grade and junior high school teachers are more likely to use field experiences where students can actually see workers on their job site. The division of labor as well as jobs of workers can be illustrated by a visit to a clothing factory. However, teachers should be careful that the factory or office visited is not too complex or abstract for their students. Typically, a visit to a computer center is not as useful as a factory that may make a single product such as soft drinks or bicycles.

Some teachers have followed up on site trips by having their own students make or sell some product of their own — school T shirts, aprons, cookies, holiday gifts, and the like. In this way, students actually act out the various roles involved in making and selling a product or service. Others have set up career stations where students do a sample of tasks related to a given occupation.

As students study other nations or an earlier period of American history, they may also focus on the jobs found at that time period or in a different culture. Students then can make a comparison and note why changes probably have occured in the course of time or why different cultures might have different kinds of workers or a higher percentage of farm families. To deal with the present, students can collect pictures from various magazines and categorize them into the 15 main job clusters.

The affective domain should not be neglected. Through a variety of value exercises on what they like to do and their hobbies, pupils can try to see the relationship of their individual interests, abilities, and values to possible choices of careers. However, at this stage, pupils should not be pressed to make "a final career choice" but should be encouraged to be tentative about career goals and be aware that each person has the potential for success and satisfaction in a number of occupations.

Career Education in the High School

Usually high school students become more interested in possible careers although most remain very fuzzy about what they want to do in the future. For this reason, a few schools have found that setting up a separate elective course entitled something like "Goals and Career Planning" is well received by the students. Often these courses focus first on the interests and values of the students, use of the career library, and then an eventual in-depth exploration of one preferred career choice. If possible, the student also visits and interviews a worker of his/her preferred career choice and if at all possible, follows the worker around for a full day—called shadowing. In a few cases, actual experience in working with this person has been provided as students are released from school or spend their vacation time working in a hospital, laboratory, or a beauty salon. Sometimes stepping stones such as volunteer or community work are used to give students a taste of a job experience and some schools offer credit for such endeavors. Mock interviews have also been

used to acquaint students with tips on how to acquire a job.

More common than a separate course on the high school level has been the setting up or expanding a library or center as a career library. More high schools now have more career educational resources describing the thousands of possible careers and the training and skills required for them. The catalogues of colleges and universities, information on trade schools and apprentice programs are also usually found in the career library as well as general information on occupational trends. In some schools, in either the English or social studies classes, a certain minimum amount of time is now directed toward career awareness and students are required to use the career center.

In addition, as part of the general high school reform movement, more students are actually interested in work experiences outside of the classroom. Some high schools have set up programs to allow a limited number of students to be employed and, again, to earn a certain amount of unit credit for their work experience. However, some teachers are concerned that students might get exploited in their job experiences and have not encouraged students to sign up for work experience programs. In addition, proper supervision off-campus for work experience programs is an unresolved problem in many schools.

Many schools have designated a person as career education director or a similar title. In some cases, a placement office or jobs, especially for part-time jobs, is part of career education. In addition, the career education director has usually tried to encourage every teacher in the school to make students aware of possible careers as well as how each subject is relevant. Thus, an infusion approach to include career education in existing courses appears to be more widely practiced on the secondary level than any other method.

In response to these concerns, some social studies teachers have set up interesting career education projects. A social studies teacher may emphasize the various jobs in the category of public service — law, government, social service, education, sewage disposal, and the like. Or all the possible jobs that are directly or indirectly related to the various social sciences can be examined by the students. Some economics teachers now include more career education by presenting more material on the world of work and knowledge of the American socioeconomic system. In addition, any social studies program that emphasizes taking account of one's values in decision making and allowing students the opportunity to practice these skills is probably making a contribution to career education.

Career education is a relatively new face on the educational scene. It holds great potential for uniting the schools, the community, the government, and business. It could have great impact or it may float away as another fad in education. Already, some social studies programs produced by commercial publishers are advertising that their programs include career education.[7]

However, it would probably require extensive retraining of teachers and changes in the organizational structure of the high school to really put career education into the curriculum. In addition, not all the materials on career education are judged to be of high quality although those produced recently seem to have improved. Therefore, it remains to be seen what will happen to career education and its effect on social studies programs.

---

[7] See especially any projects that have an economic education component such as Lawrence Senesh's *Our Working World*, published by Science Research Associates, Inc., Chicago, Ill., 1973-1974.

Bibliography

Books and Articles for Teachers

Berg, Ivan. *Education and Jobs: The Great Training Robbery.* New York: Praeger, 1970.

Center for Vocational and Technical Education. *A Comprehensive Career Education Model.* Columbus, Ohio: The Ohio State University, 1971.

Frank, Alan R. et al., "Developing a Work Skills Inventory." *Teaching Exceptional Children,* **3,** Winter 1971, pp. 82-86.

Ganitt, Walter V. "Occupational Preparation in the Elementary School." *Educational Leadership,* **28,** January 1971, pp. 359-363.

Loyt, Kenneth B. *Career Education and the Elementary Teacher.* Salt Lake City, Utah: Olympus Publishing Co., 1973.

McMurrin, Sterling M., editor. *Functional Education for Disadvantaged Youth.* New York: Committee for Economic Development, 1971.

Marland, Jr., Sidney P. *Career Education.* New York: McGraw-Hill Book Co., 1974.

NEA Task Force on Vocational Education. *Vocational Education and the Profession in the 70's and Beyond.* Washington, D.C.: National Education Association, 1971.

Norwich, Anthony L. "A Career Development Program in the Chicago Public Schools." *Elementary School Journal,* **71,** April 1971, pp. 391-399.

Vocational Education: Innovations Revolutionize Career Training. Washington, D.C.: National School Public Relations Associates, 1971.

Bibliographies, Program Materials

Write to your own State Department of Education or other states to find what is being done.

Marland, Jr., Sidney P. "Foreword," *Career Education An Eric Bibliography.* New York: Macmillan Information, 1973.

See also full issues in the following: *Social Education,* **37,** October 1973 and *Social Education,* **39,** May 1975.

How can multicultural education move beyond just eating "different" foods?

CHAPTER 19

Multicultural/ Multiethnic Education

Rationale

Historically, and especially in urban areas after the Civil War, the public schools of America were given the task of turning millions of immigrant children into Americans. This included teaching them the English language as well as familiarity with the laws and customs of the larger, dominant white society. Schools almost always encouraged, if not insisted, that the children drop their "foreign" ways such as language, dress, and customs and that they should become assimilated into the American culture as rapidly as possible. Public school educators viewed the results as one of their great accomplishments.

How much assimilation really took place? Social scientists disagree. The melting pot concept was a myth for Afro-Americans, Native American Indians, Oriental-Americans, and some Spanish-speaking groups.[1] However, most experts believe that the white immigrant groups, after struggles against discrimination and prejudice, did achieve political and economic equality by the post World War II period. But many of the immigrant groups—now called ethnic groups (a human collective based on the assump-

tion of a common origin, religion, or race) continued to exist with some of their members gaining their sense of identity from their ethnic group membership. Havighurst estimated that 15 percent of all young people can be readily identified as ethnic by race or by foreign parentage with 85 percent remaining being native-born Caucasians. About half a million of the native-born Caucasian youth are somewhat closely identified with one or another European ethnic group through their grandparents. These young people have the dual task of developing a positive identification with their own families as well as understanding the dominant majority culture.[2]

All students, regardless of their status, should understand ethnic groups in the United States since ethnicity is a fact of life in our society. The schools

---

[1] Barbara A. Sizemore, "Shattering the Melting Pot Myth" in James A. Banks, editor, *Teaching Ethnic Studies*, Washington, D.C., National Council for the Social Studies, 43rd Yearbook, 1973, pp. 73-101.
[2] Robert J. Havighurst and Philip H. Dreyer, editors, *Youth*, The 74th Yearbook of the National Society for the Study of Education, Part 1, Chicago, Ill., University of Chicago Press, 1973, p. 273.

have the obligation to promote understanding and respect for our ethnic diversity. This is not a new task for the schools. Some teachers and community members for generations have earnestly tried to eliminate personal prejudices and to improve human relations within the classroom. Usually, the focus was on improving the acceptance of black Americans, but in a period where religious differences were more pronounced, it also included the idea of acceptance of different religious groups, such as Jews. Teachers of this bent often also supported international understanding of different peoples throughout the world. However, probably most of the teachers who favored promoting understanding and acceptance also supported the concept of the melting pot.

It was the Civil Rights Movement of Afro-Americans that came to a head in the 1960s that really brought the issue of ethnic studies into focus.[3] Black Americans demanded that the schools treat their children with respect, give their children a better quality education, and that the curriculum show the important role and contributions that Afro-Americans have made in the American society.

But some black ethnic programs also had other goals. These programs wanted to develop black leadership and black pride. They felt that black students needed to develop a strong in-group commitment to their own group to fight against the more powerful "oppressive"

dominant society. A strong ethnic identity was felt necessary if black children were to function politically and it was often held that only black teachers were capable of doing this important job.

Soon other ethnic groups—Spanish-speaking, Native American Indians, Polish Americans, and others as well as minority groups such as women—were also demanding that their children receive a better education and that their own group's visibility and culture be supported and respected in the school. A "new pluralism" was advocated. Although ideological differences existed among the various groups, most wanted their children to see themselves as capable individuals who could hold responsible adult roles.

School board meetings often became stormy sessions as different ethnic groups demanded that more minority personnel be hired, that more community control be given to the local neighborhood parents, and that their ethnic group have more visibility in both textbooks and in the whole curriculum. In response to these demands, along with other changes, many school districts initiated narrow program of ethnic studies such as black history courses, Chicano history courses, or made an attempt in the K to 12 curriculum to include more about the contributions and to portray ethnics and women in more positive roles. The areas of social studies, literature, and music were probably most affected by these curriculum changes as authors and editors tapped a broader spectrum of content than they had previously used. Publishers also responded to these demands and their new products and revisions gradually reflected a more multicultural emphasis.

However, not all students were directly exposed to ethnic studies. Initially ethnic studies was felt only appropriate for the particular ethnic group involved.

---

[3] The terms ethnic group and minority group are often used interchangeably. But an ethnic group is not always the same as a minority group. While Afro-Americans, Mexican-Americans, Native American Indians, and others are both members of minority groups (defined as objects of prejudice and discriminated by the dominant society) and ethnic groups, women, gays, physically handicapped people, and others should be considered members of a minority group but not of an ethnic group.

Since ethnic studies had been quickly added to the curriculum, often under pressure, little attention was usually given to scope and sequence. Furthermore, too often ethnic studies consisted of a compilation of discrete isolated facts about heroes and their contributions. Knowing a little about either Crispus Attucks or Paul Revere is not particulary helpful in understanding the concept of revolution. However, study of heroes may be important in certain circumstances. On the whole, most social studies ethnic programs did not organize content around key social science concepts such as culture, scarcity, production, consumption, migration, urbanism, power, and institutions. Instead, they emphasized facts that students were to memorize. In addition, little was done in the area of inquiry and related skills.

Responding to the weaknesses in the various ethnic programs, some educators advocated that a broader view was necessary for ethnic studies.[4] Ethnic studies should be part of the entire curriculum — not just the social studies curriculum — at all grade levels and for all students. NCSS issued guidelines to be used to evaluate programs in multiethnic education or as more commonly known, multicultural education.[5]

Multicultural education, it is felt, should include the many different ethnic groups in the United States and show the diversity within the ethnic group. its present social status, and its whole experience — not just a limited historical ac-

count of its heroes. Therefore, *multicultural* education became the more popular term since ethnic studies now reflected more than one ethnic group's experience.

Multicultural education was loosely defined as including the following: (1) knowledge of cultures and subcultures with an emphasis on American minority and ethnic groups, (2) transformation of personal prejudices so that negative biases are minimized and positive appreciation of all individuals increased, and (3) an emphasis on cultural pluralism instead of the melting pot concept. Bilingual education using the particular language of the community — Spanish, Chinese, or the like — is part of multicultural education. Like multicultural education, it stresses a respect for the culture of the child.

Even though there is broad agreement on what is meant by multicultural education, confusion exists on how to implement a program. Let us look at some of these issues.

The Issue of Assimilation

One important issue in multicultural education that divides both educators and the community is what viewpoint about assimilation is going to be used. At one pole are those who believe that the public schools should teach each ethnic group's students to develop a strong pride and identity in their own culture. Each group's culture should be preserved and respected. The schools should not force students to be ashamed of their culture or to give it up. Instead, the schools should accommodate themselves to the different cultures such as having bilingual programs, if needed, and adjusting teaching styles to the learners' needs.

---

[4] James A. Banks, "Ethnic Studies as a Process of Curriculum Reform," *Social Education,* **40,** February 1976, pp. 76-80. James Banks is one of the best writers on multicultural education and ethnic studies.
[5] National Council for the Social Studies, *Curriculum Guidelines for Multiethnic Education,* Washington, D.C., NCSS, 1976. This task force did not like the term multicultural education because it is believed to be too broad. They prefer the term multiethnic studies.

Logically, this philosophy would also support a separate black studies program or courses for only black students or special courses or a program for Native American Indians or Chicanos. Usually these courses are designed to develop leadership and the commitment to the cause against oppression. Therefore, there is little need for "outsiders." This issue became more important on the secondary and college level but some elementary schools also have put particular ethnic students together for certain time periods with classes taught by teachers and/or community leaders for the purpose of fostering ethnic identity.

At the other pole are those who support the melting pot concept and believe that the public schools should encourage only one common culture for all students. Individuals hold this position for a variety of reasons. Some believe that the present emphasis in the public schools on several different cultures is divisive and harmful to the American society. Other educators state that they are only being frank in demanding conformity to the major cultural values since the schools are essentially middle class with a stress on the use of the English language, mathematical aptitude, reliance on written communication in English, planning, deferred gratification, and a time sense. These educators maintain that if the school is to honestly equip minority and ethnic students to move into the more respectable jobs in the mainstream of society, students, regardless of their background, will have to use the "King's English" and other related skills and attitudes to function in the larger dominant society. Thus, according to this viewpoint, while individuals can retain such ethnic elements as religion, dance, food, music, and the like, students to be successful in the dominant American culture will have to accommodate themselves to the basic values of the culture if they

wish to achieve a middle-class style of life—a goal that most parents want for their children. In other words, usually to gain social mobility requires some degree of assimilation into the dominant culture.

Probably the most accepted philosophy among educators, at least as officially formulated, is a middle-ground position of cultural pluralism that stresses mutual appreciation and understanding of every ethnic group. Thus, cultural pluralism accepts and respects cultural differences. This multicultural philosophy believes that students in school need to study many ethnic cultures including the dominant ethnic culture. Students should be able to function both in their own ethnic community, other ethnic groups, and the larger culture of the society. All ethnic cultures as well as the dominant American culture should be respected. However, the final decision on what style of life to lead should be left to the individual who may choose to reject or to accept his/her particular ethnic culture.

In practice, the middle-ground philosophy of promoting both assimilation and pluralism often is a little fuzzy as contrasted to either the strong ethnic identity approach or the melting pot concept. This philosophy of multicultural education also has some problem areas since it is esentially a compromise doctrine. Is it possible that an ethnic child will receive no pressure from the school to assimilate? Are bilingual programs and units on ethnic studies regarded as second rate?

Typically, this approach to multicultural education emphasizes the positive view of the advantages of maintaining and living in a multicultural society without pointing out some of the real disadvantages. Actually, living in the larger society and in an ethnic community may be painful at times because of value conflicts. For example, on the individual level loyalty to a large family-kinship group cannot be maintained if one accepts an offer of an attractive promotion a thousand miles away. Multicultural education may be a source of tension in a community. However, the emphasis on the strains in living in a multicultural society should not ignore the heavy price individuals pay and have paid when they live in a discriminatory society. But pluralism demands a high level of good will, generosity, and commitment to complexity that may indeed be beyond some individuals' capabilities.

The Place and Personnel of Multicultural Education

Should multicultural education be a separate course or part of the general curriculum? This is more of a problem at the secondary level. Those who favor a separate course usually believe that not enough is being done in the regular curriculum. Band-Aid solutions are applied, according to this view, and students leave schools with little exposure to the various ethnic groups.

On the other hand, many educators believe that too few students, unless it is a required course, which is rare, take multicultural or ethnic studies courses. Therefore, it makes sense to incorporate multicultural education into existing social studies as well as other courses. These educators maintain that curriculum materials such as textbooks have moved a long way toward a multicultural viewpoint. Therefore, in the social studies department, existing courses such as U.S. history, civics, government courses, and sociology are incorporating a multicultural point of view. This presumes that teachers do actually support and want to implement a multicultural perspective. Since there is some evidence that elementary teachers are spending less time on social studies programs, a natural area for multicultural education, what actually is being done in many classrooms may be marginal.

In addition, advocates of multicultural education believe that the concept of multicultural education should permeate the whole school—the extracurricular program, assemblies and plays, as well as the decorations. Thus, according to this viewpoint, a few courses cannot do the job. The whole school environment, including such areas as guidance, should have a multipluralistic emphasis. The area of evaluation/testing should also be examined.

A hard look at the curriculum raises the question of who is to be included as an ethnic group and how much time should be spent on the various ethnic groups in the curriculum. Curriculum planners disagree on whether Native Hawaiians or women or some other group should be given special attention under a multicultural program. They are conscious that in a given year on both the elementary and secondary level, the curriculum normally cannot directly include units on Native Hawaiians, Cuban-Americans, Filipino-Americans, Puerto Rican-Americans, Native American Indians as well as relevant culture studies of foreign immigrants. Because of time pressure, the direct study of these groups ideally should be delegated to different grade or age levels so that each ethnic group can be treated in depth.

Thus, serious problems presently exist on how to achieve a scope and sequence in multicultural education. First, political pressures—especially when competing ethnic groups in the community all want their "share" of time—often make parents angry if their ethnic group is not "covered" in the second grade while their own child is in the second grade. Furthermore, teachers themselves, especially on the secondary level, but even on the elementary level, now feel that they should be able to do their own thing in the classroom and are not quite as conforming to administrative directives on scope and on how much time should be devoted to the Samoans or to the Arabs.

Often a good reason exists why some teachers are not enthusiastic about a multiethnic curriculum. Teachers may have little background on the historical experiences, the present status, or the perspectives of various ethnic groups. Along with these limitations, they may feel uncertain as to which teaching strategies work best in an area that has a heavy emotional context.

Teachers cannot always respect the ethnicity of the child or young adult and ake use of it in a positive way. Ethnic leaders believe that the schools are frequently staffed by teachers and other personnel who are not sensitive to cultural differences in the classroom. Teachers are frequently not personally or professionally ready for multicultural education. Yet often the only in-service training they receive is a quickie rush course that something needs to be done and that the community is angry at them for not doing enough in multicultural education. Most schools have not had a systematic program to help teachers become both supportive and effective in multicultural education.

It is not the cognitive learning here that upsets some teachers. Instructors feel stymied when doing their best if some of their students do not respect cultural differences and resort to stereotyping, scapegoating, and prejudice both in and outside of the classroom. Reflecting ideas of their parents and the community, ethnocentric viewpoints are common and not easily changed. In addition, eth-

nic conflict outside the classroom does not help in acceptance of different cultures inside the classroom. Students, even very young pupils, frequently regard any differences from their own as inferior.

Sometimes teachers get discouraged. Often they are more ready to turn to different and more rewarding areas where success is more likely to be achieved. It is difficult to "plug away" at multicultural education, especially if there is not a supportive climate at the school and in the community for such experiences. In particular, criticism arises when teachers employ the technique of emphasizing "the sins committed by Anglo-Americans," which may anger the Anglo-American community. Thus, multicultural education in many communities has found it both difficult to get a place in the curriculum and the total school environment and to remain there.

Materials and the Criteria Problem

Most experts agree that the typical textbook formerly presented a version of history and our present society in which the role of ethnic groups and women was omitted or distorted in print, as well as in pictures and illustrations. This was also true of the associated media and other materials found in the classroom. Typically, a bland interpretation of American society from the dominant culture was portrayed without emphasis on the seamy sides of our culture. In particular with regard to multicultural education, history often was written in a fashion as to ignore how different groups perceived issues such as how the Indians felt about the Indian wars or how the Spanish-speaking living in the Southwest felt about the result of the Mexican war.

Now, most multicultural experts recommend that students should study history as well as other subjects from the diverse ethnic perspectives and not just the dominant culture's viewpoint.[6] Knowledge distortion has been harmful both to ethnic groups as well as Anglo students. Hopefully, students can also learn to examine issues from an international model to see how Asian nations or South American nations, also view a given issue.

As a result of the much needed reform in this area, many school districts and states are now looking carefully at the ethnic and minority biases of their textbooks, media, materials in the library and the classrooms, their school newspaper, and drama productions. Many schools and states have adopted rules or criteria that should be used in the selection of materials. This usually involves a system of getting more input from the community in making decisions, especially with regard to textbook adoption. Panels of teachers, administrators, and parents are set up to screen materials.

Stormy problems have arisen in this process. In particular, publishers say that this has led to incredible nitpicking by special interest groups that have resulted in fine books being rejected. Obviously, blatant racism or sexism should be eliminated. But should a book be rejected because of a drawing of a rather stout, but attractive black woman? Some felt that this picture was stereotyping black women. Or should books be turned down for failing to depict Asian-Americans or for an imbalance in male/female representation? Of course, the answer to these questions hinges on what criteria are used. Should all illustrations contain approximately 50-50 representation of males and females? If Asian-Americans

represent at the most 1 percent of the American population, what proportion of print and illustrations should be devoted to Asian-Americans? What if historically, the role of certain groups at certain time periods was of a lower status? Should this be portrayed or does this reinforce the low status associated with a given group?

These thorny problems are not easily solved because of the different way people see the issues. Most educators believe that textbooks and associated media have come a long way toward overcoming some of the biases that have marred them. Most materials now try to treat ethnic groups and women sensitively. However, lack of space and concept level reading problems still limit what a single textbook can cover. For example, it is difficult to point out all of the time all the diverse points of view on a given issue. This does mean that a given textbook or related material may seem inadequate according to some people's standards. While no one wants censorship, one impact of the screening processes is that teachers are now more restricted in their choice of materials.

Most of the newer materials have improved; but they are not all uniformly good and should be carefully reviewed. Teachers now must spend more time in reviewing materials, a job that typically is done after school and without compensation. Ideally, released time should be provided to enable teachers to professionally and carefully evaluate materials. Even so, problems may still exist on what criteria should be used in the selection of materials.

Methods and the Future

Because of the relatively recent adoption of multicultural education in the schools,

---

[6] James A. Banks, op. cit., p. 78.

many of the instructional guides have merely stressed filling teachers in on the historical perspective, materials and resources of the various ethnic groups. However, there is still a dearth of materials about specific ethnic groups other than Afro-American, Chicanos, and Native Americans. Much still needs to be done to eliminate curriculum gaps.

While concentrating on content, not enough attention has been paid to teaching methods. Not that multicultural education demands any unique methods. However, the affective domain is of extreme importance in this area and more field tested materials and values strategies are needed by most classroom teachers. In addition, games and role playing, small group discussion, reading books—both fiction and nonfiction—and using community resources are particularly helpful. (See Section III for further details.)

Thus, multicultural education, a means of liberating all students from their narrow perspectives, faces many problems. Not all agree on how much assimilation should be encouraged by the schools or how teachers can be trained for multicultural education. Material selection is still a problem. In addition, for a multicultural program to be effective, the whole educational environment, including the staff, should probably represent the diversity in our society. Many schools, due to a variety of reasons, do not come near this goal.

The real success of multicultural education clearly depends on how thoughtfully these problems are approached, and whether they can be satisfactorily solved. Advances in multicultural education, however, offer much promise for enriching and updating the entire social studies program and for enabling students to attain some of our important goals.

Bibliography

Books

Banks, James A. *Teaching Strategies for Ethnic Studies.* Boston: Allyn & Bacon, 1975.

Banks, James A., editor. *Teaching Ethnic Studies.* Washington, D.C.: National Council for the Social Studies, 43rd Yearbook, 1973.

Ethnic Heritage Center for Teacher Education, American Association of Colleges for Teacher Education. *Multicultural Education and Ethnic Studies in the United States.* Washington, D.C.: American Association of Colleges for Teacher Education, 1976. The best and most recent bibliography on concept materials, classroom materials, curriculum materials, and program materials.

Glazer, Nathan. *Affirmative Discrimination: Ethnic Inequality and Public Policy.* New York: Basic Books, 1975.

Ramirez, Manuel and Alfredo Castaneda. *Cultural Democracy, Bicognitive Development and Education.* New York: Academic Press, 1974.

Social Science Education Consortium. *Ethnic Studies Material Analysis Instrument.* Boulder, Colo.: Social Science Education Consortium, 1974.

Tyack, David. *The One Best System.* Cambridge, Mass.: Harvard University Press, 1974.

Articles

See 12 articles in the issue entitled "Toward Cultural Pluralism." *Educational Leadership,* **32,** December 1974, pp. 163-207. See also whole issue of *Phi Delta Kappan,* **53,** January 1972.

Guidelines

National Council for the Social Studies. *Curriculum Guidelines for Multiethnic education.* Enclosed in *Social Education 40,* October 1976, 48 pages. Can also be purchased directly from the National Council for the Social Studies.

How can pen pals help to support global education?

CHAPTER 20

Global and International Education

Rationale

For decades, the deep concern about war, the need for the preservation of some semblance of peace, and the necessity to develop the means to solve the frequent international crises have motivated some educators to set up programs to increase international understanding. How widespread these programs were implemented depended greatly on the climate of opinion in the community and the commitment of teachers to international education. However, confusion about the meaning of the term, international education, as well as similar terms have plagued this field. Exactly what goals and objectives are to be achieved by international education have not always and in some cases, are still not clear today. Too frequently, a general vagueness about doing something "good" about international education has been the order of the day.

A brief review may be helpful to show some of the changes in emphases in international education as well as to show the wide diversity in the meanings of international education. For several decades after World War I, teaching about world affairs or world understanding was

the popular term for educators. The term was pretty general so that a variety of approaches such as sending money to starving children overseas or learning about the League of Nations and international cooperation could be included. However, little was usually provided in terms of a conceptual framework or seldom was there an analysis of the roots and causes of work tensions, or an understanding of the economic realities and the resultant problems of different nations throughout the world. Usually a superficial, and sometimes naive approach to world problems with an optimistic overtone was presented.

In addition, as soon as a "new" or unfamiliar region of the world hit the headlines such as Southeast Asia or India and Pakistan, content about these relatively "new" areas had to be provided to teachers, most who were only familiar with United States, Western Civilization background. This focus on content typically deemphasized the importance of attitudes of students and the need for social participation of students in international projects. Only a few projects such as the National Council for the

Social Studies' Glens Fall Project actually systematically tried both to increase understanding of other people as well as moving into the area of attitudes such as attempting to increase respect for others and developing a sense of responsibility toward the whole world.[1]

In the 1960s, international education became the popular term, replacing world understanding, although it also had different meanings for different people. For some, especially on the college level, international education meant sending American college students abroad to study and to have foreign students study in the United States. Others, in light of the rapid extension of communication and the growing exchange of ideas, science, and technology, focused on the need for young people to learn foreign languages and to become familiar with a different cultural group(s). Still others, often social studies teachers, were shocked at the general low level of student awareness of the so-called "shrinking globe" and wanted to fill in this void.

Some social studies educators believe that international education should try to educate students for *world* citizenship.[2] Generally speaking, those interested in promoting international or world citizenship are in favor of moving away from a national, parochial, narrow outlook of the nation-state. For example, Jack Nelson believes nationalistic education to be dysfunctional.[3] A few also became intersted in promoting world law and building new world institutions.[4]

World citizenship goals immediately raise the issue of the relationship between nationalistic and international education. Generally speaking, nationalistic education, regardless of the country in which it is practiced, involves efforts at producing "good citizens" who will develop positive feelings of loyalty and commitment to their nation, and learn the appropriate behavior and competencies necessary to operate as citizens in that nation. In addition, in many nations at different time periods, nationalistic education has also encouraged negative feelings toward other people in other countries. Frequently nationalistic education has taught the concept of superiority of their own people and the inferiority of other peoples in other nations. This type of nationalistic education, of course, is inimical to the spirit of international education.

But is all nationalistic education counter to international education? Here a difference of opinion exists. Many educators believe that the task of nationalistic education is a legitimate part of their responsibility since each country insists on it. But some believe that, especially as students become older and more mature, critical analysis by students of their own nation's as well as world problems can be encouraged. These educators think that they can promote national as well as international education. Often international education is viewed as an extention of the mutual respect for human beings that extends from the local, state, national, and to the international sphere.

Sometimes the rationale is given that American citizens today must be familiar with the international scene if they are to

[1] Harold M. Long and Robert N. King, *Improving the Teaching of World Affairs: The Glens Falls Story,* Washington, D.C., National Council for the Social Studies, 1964.
[2] Charlotte J. Anderson and Lee F. Anderson, "Global Education in Elementary Schools: An Overview," *Social Education,* **41,** January 1977, pp. 34-37.
[3] Jack Nelson, "Nationalistic vs. Global Education: An Examination of National Bias in the Schools and Its Implications for a Global Society," *Theory and Research in Social Education,* **IV,** August 1976, p. 47.
[4] Betty Reardon and Saul H. Mendlovitz, "World Law and Models of World Order: James Becker and Howard Mehlinger, editors, *International Dimensions in the Social Studies.* Washington, D.C.: National Council for the Social Studies, 38th Yearbook, 1968, pp. 160-170.

function in a world where domestic and international problems are now so often interrelated. These educators stress that goals of world citizenship do not compete with students' loyalty to their nation. They believe that the schools can foster nationalistic education without encouraging negative feelings toward people in other nations. Many of these educators recognize international education as a gradual process since the major values of our society or any other society do not change rapidly. In addition, some educators think that it is essential that students learn to function and to participate in their own national system so that they can potentially change the system to reflect the global realities.

Others believe that international education should be the highest priority and that the schools should inspire a sense of international concern over nationalistic feelings. On the school level in the community, due to political pressures, this issue of what is the highest priority—international or nationalistic education—is not always clearly brought out to the public. Instead, the pragmatic aspects of the need for international education in an increasingly interdependent world are stressed. Usually, this viewpoint about the importance of international education assumes that the schools have some capacity to change society, instead of merely being reflective of current ideas and values. Indeed, some believe that a drastic system change is necessary for world peace and that the present practices of gradualism in international education only serve to perpetuate the problem.[5] Those advancing this position are very much aware of the shortcomings that exist in present day international education.

However, terminology again changed. In the 1970s, global education became the popular term, replacing to some extent the term, international education. It was probably the energy crises as well as concern about the dimensions of human hunger and population that motivated the use of this term. There was a shift from advocating courses with a few weeks on the Middle East or Africa, the United Nations or communism, to a concern of the problems of the developing nations throughout the world and the gap between the rich and poor nations. Here, the global perspective stresses the increasing interdependence of nations, global hunger and poverty, population problems, worldwide pollution, nuclear warfare, and what can be done about these problems. Global education embraced all of the following: "war prevention, social justice, ecological balance, world economic welfare, alternative futures, conflict management, social change, transnational institutions, global political development, and the need for international machinery to tackle these problems effectively."[6]

More generally, global education tries to show the similarities between peoples rather than stressing their differences. It recognizes the common humanity which underlies all cultural differences. It also stresses the necessity to think about loyalty to the whole planet and not just one's own nation as the center of the world. In addition, the emphasis is on the system as a whole—the spaceship earth—or looking at the world from the moral unity of the human race, a natural law viewpoint. The "spaceship earth" idea also implies that we are affected by actions of other nations.

On the elementary level, the term "worldmindedness" has also been popu-

[5] Saul H. Mendlovitz, "The Case for Drastic System Change in the Global Political Community," *Social Education*, **37,** November 1973, pp. 615–617.
[6] James Becker, "Perspective on Global Education," *Social Education*, **38,** November-December 1974, p. 681.

lar. As defined by King, worldmindedness encompasses a humanistic framework for the social sciences. The emphasis is that this nation is a multicultural society as well as trying to allow elementary students to achieve a world perspective through music and art. According to King, the error of too many schools has not been that Euro-American cultural information is not good or worthwhile but too often this has been the only point of view.[7]

Thus, as this brief review has indicated, a confusion in terms, objectives, and practices has existed in international or global education. It has not always been clear what is meant by these terms and the potentially conflicting relationship between nationalistic and global education has not been resolved. In some cases, this fuzziness has probably been a deliberate policy so that the local community would not feel that international education was being promoted at the expense of nationalistic education. However, too frequently many programs in global and international education are not well thought out and depend on occasional efforts such as a UNICEF Halloween Trick or Treat Campaign or one teacher's efforts to help the suffering victims of an earthquake.

The Place of Global or International Education

Global or international education, like many other current issues is not just limited to the social studies. Indeed, music,

the arts, literature and folk tales throughout the world can give enrichment to the lives of many people. In addition, foreign language instruction usually has some objectives in understanding the culture of the language that is being taught. Science is also an international area.

However, the social studies are seen as an important vehicle for global or international education. But the extent of implementation of global or international education in the curriculum of schools throughout the nations is unknown. Little exists in the way of survey data on the practices of global education.

Informed opinion agrees that in many schools little appears to be done in global or international education. Surveys of college students and adults on international understanding and an international perspective have not been very optimistic. Indeed, many in the adult population hold very highly stereotyped views about other peoples and other nations.

Concern also has been expressed that the present emphasis on minority/ethnic studies, especially on the elementary level, may also limit global or international education. It is true that respect for the dignity of all people, a goal of international education, does start at home and multicultural education can be a good steppingstone toward international understanding. Many ethnic studies programs do not take this final step but concentrate solely on the United States. However, some ethnic studies programs do focus on the "root" culture of the different ethnic groups so that some attention is devoted to non-United States nations.

But there are strong feelings that more on global and international education should be infused into the primary and intermediate levels, areas in which traditionally international education pro-

---

[7] Edith W. King, *The World: Context for Teaching in the Elementary School*, Dubuque, Iowa, William C. Brown Co., 1971, p. *ix*.

grams have been pretty much hit and miss and not systematically thought out. This viewpoint is bolstered by research that indicates that by the intermediate grades children have developed a sense of national identity, and a belief systen about their own and other nations.

Of course, part of the problem is what is meant by global or international education. Is the world history course at the secondary level or the unit on Bali for the primary grades to be considered part of global or international education? The answer to this question depends partly on the definition of global or international education. The content area of global education — war prevention, conflict management, social understanding, and the like — covers a very broad area. Goal objectives usually have not been carefully spelled out.

Let us examine some statements of goals of global and international education.

In *Intercom*, the authors (King, Branson, Condon) state the following:

"Global perspectives are ways of looking at the world and our relationship to it. Intrinsic to such perspectives are: (1) an understanding of the earth and its inhabitants as parts of an interrelated network; (2) an awareness that there are alternatives facing individuals, nations, and the human species, and that choices made will shape our future world; and (3) an ability to recognize that others may have different perceptions and may prefer different choices."[8]

Now note the goals listed in the National Council for the Social Studies booklet on international education.

1. Developing an appreciation of universal values
2. Contributing to national development and power

3. Building international understanding and cooperation
4. Working for world peace
5. Preparing for world peace[9]

Note that the NCSS's booklet does not envision a conflict between contributing to national development and power and working toward world peace and international understanding.

The Kettering Foundation's position is that the goals of international education should include acquiring sensitivity and understanding of other people's culture and values, improving the data base to make intelligent decisions, and learning the nature and importance of history in shaping contemporary societies.[10] It is interesting that here, in this set of goals, history has a role.

Using any of the goals as criteria, it is evident that much of what is taught in social studies programs does not meet most of the criteria. For this reason, those concerned about promoting global or international education have tried and are trying to internationalize the current curriculum in existing world history courses, U.S. history courses, and civics and government courses on the secondary level as well as all courses on the elementary level. In general, an inquiry approach with its emphasis on skills is being encouraged as well as a more comparative approach, such as looking at the several areas throughout the world where the agricultural revolution took place in-

---

[8] David C. King, Margaret S. Branson, and Larry E. Condon, "Education for a World in Change," *Intercom*, **84/85,** November 1976, p. 4. This whole issue is valuable, especially the sample lessons for global education from grades K-12.
[9] Richard C. Remy et al., *International Learning and International Education in a Global Age*, Washington, D.C., The National Council for the Social Studies Bulletin 47, 1975, p. 72.
[10] Report by William Shaw, Charles F. Kettering Foundation, and the Gottlieb Duttweiler Institute of Zurich, Switzerland, *Global Education Helping Secondary Students Understand International Issues*, Charles F. Kettering Foundation, 1974.

stead of just concentrating on a Western Civilization approach.

On the positive side, despite the slowness in implementing any curriculum change, there has been an increase of materials in social studies education on the topics of war/peace, conflict and conflict resolution, the realities of power and its consequences, future studies, the value questions in international problems, and the systems approach of political science. All of these content trends, mostly on the secondary level, reflect a more hard-nose approach to global or international education as well as offering a conceptional framework for the analysis of problems. The anthropology projects have also tried to increase cultural understanding. On the elementary levels, more teachers are introducing foods, toys, and games from other cultures.

Further reflecting this trend has been the increase in the number of simulated games and media that deal with international problems. Especially at the junior and senior high school level, many games are on the market that actively involve students in a conflict or international crisis. These games also have moved into the affective domain as students are placed in roles such as being the underdog or disadvantaged. Mock U.S. conventions as well as international simulations also have become more popular.

Thus, global or international education is striving for a more prominent role in the social studies curriculum. Global or international education is seen as more than just understanding and knowledge but also as a process in which skills are necessary to interpret the media and to function in an intelligent manner about international questions. The affective domain as well as social participation are seen as important in gaining a global perspective.

Methods of Global or International Education

Just as in other areas of the social studies curriculum, no one method is unique to teaching global or international education. However, special attention has been given to the case study in promoting global or international education. A case study usually focuses on a specific person or issue such as a family in a developing nation that must move to the city because they cannot make a living farming. The advantage of a case study is that students often can identify with other human beings with problems. However, teachers must help students to check how representative are the case studies. In other words, how many people in a given country such as Brazil are moving to urban areas? Unless this is done, frequently students are willing to overgeneralize from a single case or lose the major concept that the case study was to illustrate. This is always a problem of inductive materials. Yet despite its disadvantages, the case study can be effectively used to promote global understanding.[11]

Another promising method has been the resource visitor who has lived in another country. Often foreign students attending institutions of higher education in the community are effective in capturing the attention of students and are knowledgeable in explaining their own nation to American students. However, students should realize that foreign students studying in the United States are often a selective group and may not be representative of the nation. Exchange

---

[11] David C. King, "The Pros and Cons of Using Case Studies," *Social Education,* **38,** November-December 1974, pp. 657–658.

students on the high school level from different countries also can serve as valuable resource people on both the elementary and secondary level. People who have lived for several years in a foreign country as well as possible speakers from embassies and trade organizations often can be effective, especially if they bring slides or media with them. Private organizations such as the World Affairs Council with its many branches throughout the United States also can be used to secure speakers.

In addition to these resource persons, "pen pals" also have been popular, especially at the elementary level. Here the objectives are often to promote friendliness toward others as well as an increased understanding of how a different group of students live. Students can learn firsthand information about other students of their own age level. Teachers, of course, must make sure that students know the mechanics of letter writing and put the proper postage on their letters.

Here are some sources for pen pal names: People to People, P. O. Box 1201, Kansas City, Mo. 64141; World Pen Pals, University of Minnesota, Minneapolis, Minn., 55404; Letters Abroad, Inc., 18 East 60th St., New York, New York 10022; and Youth Pen Pal Exchange, Box 6992, Washington, D.C. 20020. Some of these organizations have a small fee attached to each name acquired.

Following more in depth with pen pals, some classes have made arrangements to exchange ideas with another class in a foreign country. Often tapes, booklets, pictures, photographs of the children, class, school, and community are sent to the exchange classroom. Students often describe how their community makes a living as well as what games, sports, and holidays they like. These exchanges have often been very successful because they are on the students' own

level of understanding and can provide insight on their own lives as well as how other people live.

While pen pals and class exchanges have been popular for many years, a decline in activities involving students in learning about the United Nations and its specialized agencies has probably occurred. This unpopularity is related to the present evaluation of many Americans about the usefulness and lack of importance of the United Nations. Additionally, this decline may reflect the new social studies' emphasis on concepts and skills instead of just memorization of facts about the United Nations or any other topic.

Instead, a comparative approach is more widely used, especially in such areas as family studies and world religions. Skills needed in the analysis and interpretation of media are now being given a little more attention than mere memorization of facts. The movement toward inquiry learning has probably helped in making teachers more aware of the importance of skills rather than content per se.

Thus, a wide variety of approaches—both new and old—continue to be used in global or international education. Many of these approaches are moving into the area of values and social participation. In a few schools, for example, analysis of such issues as world hunger have brought about social action commitments on the part of some students to give the money "saved" from fasting to the poor of the world or to ride a bike instead of using a car. These emphases do show some of the changed directions of global or international education.

Two issues—teacher training and text materials—still remain of importance. Many experts have stressed the need for teachers at all grade levels to have experiences that promote international or global understanding. Frequently, travel is cited as a promising practice. However, we know that too frequently, unless the travel experience is properly planned, travel can reinforce previous stereotypes. Therefore, a need exists for more travel and exchange programs for both teachers and students to gain insight on how different people in different cultures live. In addition, most curriculum materials including textbooks tend to support a nationalisic viewpoint. While improvement by international scholars and educational writers have been accomplished, attention should be taken that curriculum materials do not foster negative feelings toward other peoples and nations. Promising has been the work in the European Common Market where current event newspapers are being produced for students in various countries. UNESCO publications also exist to help teachers.

But it is not just printed materials that need to be improved. Global education experts have pointed out the tremendous influence of television with its emphases on hostility, explosive events, and catastrophes on the international scene. The heavy influence of television has made more teachers aware of the deficiencies of just trying to be a dispenser of the latest facts. Instead, Remy and his coauthors recommend that young people need the following skills:

1. "Understand the use, limitations and liabilities of the whole range of media."
2. " 'Read' public statements of governments, official denials, announcements from official sources and public relations messages.

3. "Detect typical biases in the media."
4. "Recognize the cultural contact which helps explain human behavior."
5. "Piece together fragmentary information from different sources in order to arrive at a plausible explanation of an international affairs issue or event."
6. "Perceive the process of news gathering and distribution, including the way in which certain biases are built into the process."[12]

Thus, more has to be done on media analysis with special attention to television and learning to use a wide variety of sources of information. This means that the weekly commercial school newspapers, which many teachers have depended on for giving students a world understanding, must be supplemented by other sources. This underscores the importance of checking where students are at the present time in dealing with sources.

Through the years, global or international education has gained a little more support and commitment from more teachers. No single one approach is probably desirable as long as students become aware of the different ways of viewing the world and have the skills to select, and to evaluate events. In addition, students must be informed and able to participate in their own society as well as continuing to be interested in international problems and issues after they leave school. Indeed, this is a large job for the schools and it is uncertain how fast the schools can move.

---

[12] Richard C. Remy, op. cit., p. 75.

Bibliography

Organizations

The African-American Institute, School Services Division, 833 United Nations Plaza, New York, N.Y. 10017

American Freedom from Hunger Foundation, 1100 17th St., N.W., Suite 701, Washington, D.C. 20036

Center for Global Perspectives, 218 E. 18th St., New York, N.Y. 10003

Foreign Policy Association, 345 E. 46th St., New York, N.Y. 10017

Institute for World Order, 1140 Avenue of the Americas, New York, N.Y. 10036

Overseas Development Council, 1717 Massachusetts Ave., N.W., Suite 501, Washington, D.C. 20036

U. S. Agency for International Development, Office of Public Affairs, Department of State, Washington, D.C. 20523

U. S. Committee for UNICEF, 331 E. 38th St., New York, N.Y. 10016

World Bank Group, 1818 H. St., N.W., Washington, D.C. 20433

World Law Fund, 11 West 42nd St., New York, N.Y. 10036

Journals, Magazines, Newsletters

Development Forum. Center for Economic and Social Information, United Nations, Palais des Nations, CH-1211 Geneva 10, Switzerland.

Futures. World Future Society, P. O. Box 19285, 20th St. Station, Washington, D.C. 20036

Headline Series. Foreign Policy Association, 345 E. 46th St., New York, N.Y. 10003.

Intercom. Center for Global Perspectives, 218 E. 18th St., New York, N.Y. 10003.

Progress Report. Institute for World Order, 11 W. 42nd St., New York, N.Y. 10036.

The January 1977 issue of *Social Education,* **41** (#1) is mainly devoted to global education.

Books/Pamphlets (also see footnotes)

Becker, James. *Education for a Global Society,* Fastback #28. Bloomington, Ind.: Phi Delta Kappa Education Foundation, 1973.

Henderson, George, editor. *ASCD Yearbook Education for Peace Focus on Mankind.* Washington, D.C.: Association for Supervision and Curriculum Development, 1973.

Juncker, Sigrid and Jo Ann Larson, editors. *Civic Literacy for Global Interdependence New Challenge to State Leadership in Education.* Washington, D.C.: Council of the Chief State School Officers, 1976.

King, David C. *International Education for Spaceship Earth,* 2nd edition. New York: Foreign Policy Association, 1971.

Millar, Jayne C. *Focusing on Global Poverty and Development: A Resource Book for Educators.* Washington, D.C.: Overseas Development Council, 1974.

Why are mock trials often effective in law-related education?

CHAPTER 21

Law-Related Education

Rationale

The growth of law-related education in the K to 12 curriculum, which was only indirectly found in most schools 10 years ago, has been due to a variety of factors. First, there has been a growing awareness of how often and how frequently law permeates our daily lives. From the cradle with its required birth certificate to the grave where the law determines how an individual's estate is to be distributed, ordinary citizens come in contact with a vast array of laws necessary in a complex society. These laws may range from a simple annual payment for a car license to filing the complex income tax forms of the Internal Revenue Service. As individuals purchase a candy bar or a house, buy phone service and medical treatment, they find that laws also govern buyer/seller relationships. Then in their personal lives, as Americans marry or divorce, quarrel with their landlord/lady or their neighbors, send their children to schools required under compulsory education laws, or speed down the highway, individuals constantly come into contact with the law. Some of these encounters are pleasant as when the Internal Revenue Service sends us a refund check. Other incidents dealing with law are not as pleasant. However, ignorance of the law does not usually excuse us from our responsibilities.

In the larger political issues of the day, people are also affected by laws. To solve almost every single political problem—local, national, and international—requires the framing of new or the revision of existing laws and regulations. Problems from pollution to the maintenance of the peace are subject to law as communities, states, nations, and international bodies try to find a fair and equitable way of solving problems. In some instances, laws must be changed since laws may reflect the changing times. In these cases, the law is a dead weight that results in a lessening of liberty and justice for all.

Along with awareness of the pervasion of law in our lives, a second influence for law-related studies has been the growing dissatisfaction by students and experts about the existing civics and government courses given at the junior and senior high school level. For example, a 1973 survey indicated that half or more of the seniors had the following complaints about their senior high school civics and government courses: (1) not enough time was spent on controversial events such as race relations, which were important in their lives; (2) they were not given a realistic picture of how American politics worked and how to participate in politics; and (3) much of what was taught was not new. Furthermore, only 41 percent said that the course stimulated their interest in public affairs and politics.[1]

Indeed, too frequently, the typical civics and government courses have tended to emphasize mainly the structure of the government—there are three main branches to the federal government, senators are elected for a six year term of office, and that the president has certain powers as outlined in the Constitution. In addition, often only an idealistic version of the American government and the legal system is presented. Yet students are often aware that the reality is something different from the ideal.

Even today, in many civics and government courses, noncontroversial safe topics such as the formation of the Constitution are stressed with little analysis of "hot" political issues, especially those within the high school itself or the local community. Typically, a more passive view of citizenship is still being taught with few provisions in the curriculum for teaching students the skills for active participation in the political arena. In addition, little attention is usually given to the rights and redresses individuals have as a citizen or a consumer—what to do when arrested or when a victim of a fraud.

Third, the movement of the new social studies in the 1960s also emphasized a more important role for thinking or inquiry in social studies education. This view, although not new, held that controversial issues were not to be ignored but ought to be viewed as a stepping-stone for critical thinking. Values educa-

tion in the 1970s also gave a more prominent role for students to consider their own value positions and those with different values when dealing with controversial issues.

Thus, while many experts felt that the old traditional conceptions of citizenship with a passive orientation were not working, this message was not always received by the teachers or the community. While some citizens were concerned that many more adults in the nation were becoming increasingly alienated from their political institutions, numerous government teachers have continued to teach their courses pretty much in the traditional way. However, some teachers looking for more promising approaches to student civic learning have found law-related education suitable.

In addition to these reasons, research has indicated that the elementary years are most important in the formation of political attitudes. In spite of this we seem to be moving civics out of the eighth- and ninth-grade level, thus losing the possible impact of a capstone course. Additionally, many low-income elementary school children as well as middle-class children do not have high efficacy feelings. But while many elementary students have low efficacy concepts, research also indicates that elementary children have the capacity to handle concepts such as law, justice, and the community and could be encouraged to think about possible solutions to problems.

Finally, an important role has been played by the law profession itself in support of law-related education in the elementary and secondary schools. Many lawyers want students to conceive of law as an evolving process that offers promise in trying to solve problems in a fair and equitable manner. In some cases, lawyers are also concerned about the "negative" image that some of the public holds for their profession. Therefore, in many

---

[1] M. Kent Jenning, "Political Trends and the Undergraduate Classroom," reported in *DEA News*, Fall 1974, pp. 3, 7, published by the American Political Science Association.

states and in many projects, lawyers have supported law-related education—financially, in the legislative bodies, and giving their own personal time as resource people in the schools.

All of these factors have contributed to the development and implementation of law-related education. However, this does not mean that the definition of law-related education is precisely clear. Different law-related education projects have emphasized different things. While none of the law-related education projects aim at producing junior lawyers with the technical knowledge that law schools give to their students, some projects, using the "Street Law Model" stress more practical concerns such as juvenile justice, consumer law, housing law, and criminal justice (see Houghton Mifflin's *Justice in America* series). Usually in these programs an objective is to make students more aware of their own rights. On the other end of the spectrum are the concept oriented programs stressing authority, justice, responsibility, freedom, and property (the Law in Free Society project).[2]

However, with the exception of social participation and social action, almost all projects in law-related education would probably agree with Gerlach and Lamprecht's objectives for law-related education:

1. To promote student understanding of society and its system of laws by showing students how they may effectively function within the law.
2. To clarify student attitudes, values, and perceptions regarding the law and our legal system.
3. To develop critical thinking abilities and problem-solving skills in students.[3]

---

[2] Isidore Starr, "Law Studies Projects—Alternative Models," *Social Studies Review,* **14,** Fall 1974, #1, pp. 12-14, 48.
[3] Ronald A. Gerlach and Lynne W. Lamprecht, *Teaching About the Law,* Cincinnati, Ohio, The W. H. Anderson Co., 1975.

But a major question remains: How is law-related education to be incorporated into the curriculum?

The Place of Law-Related Education

Again, while citizenship, multicultural education, and fair play are the responsibilities of the whole school, the social studies is seen as an area of particular importance in law-related education. On the secondary level, the social studies department must decide whether law-related education should be taught as a separate course or whether it should be incorporated into the existing courses. A few school systems has initiated a semester or minicourse in law-related education. In some cases, where it is a required course for all students, content from drug education, family life, and health and driver education may be included in this course. Where it is an elective course, it is more likely to have a social studies perspective.

However, most schools that have moved into law-related education have tried to incorporate it into existing units or eliminating some units and replacing it with law-related education. This practice is most noticeable on the elementary level as well as in civics and government courses. Many junior high schools also have short miniunits, often of one or two weeks duration, on such topics as search and seizure, arrest, and the juvenile court system.

Methods in Law-Related Education

While law-related education uses all the methods of teaching such as employing media and values exercises, the following three strategies have been stressed in law-related education: (1) the case study approach, (2) using community resources such as courts and attorneys, and (3) simulation, role-playing and gaming. Let us look briefly into these methods that have been used from kindergarten to the twelfth grade in law-related education.

The Case Study Approach in Law-Related Education

A case study may be defined as a collection of data about a *single* individual or a single social unit such as a business or a labor union. While some cases, and especially on the senior high school level, are actually based on true historical cases, often designers of law-related education use fictional or more simplified versions of actual cases. In addition, a case study need not always involve individuals in contact with the legal system. For example, a case study could be about a teenage babysitter who overuses his/her authority or be about Little Red Hen to offer primary students insights on what is "fair." Incidents from Golding's *Lord of the Flies* or *Aesop's Fables* can also be used as case studies. Thus, the definition of what constitutes a case study is very loose.

By its nature, the case study approach is inductive in nature since it focuses on a single individual, event, or issue. Often case studies appeal to human interest since they show individuals caught between conflicting demands or facing a real crisis such as a possible prison sentence. Frequently, case studies are openended and have a detectivelike quality that is appealing to students: How is the case going to end? Therefore, case

studies can be motivating to many students. But ideally the case study should lead students to make valid generalizations. Case studies should illustrate some concept such as the right to privacy or some principle such as what is a fair procedure. Unless they do so, the case study approach may not be very fruitful in terms of student learning.

However, the case study approach is not without its disadvantages. Student must obtain the background information and understand the facts of the case. To avoid reading problems, sometimes the teacher reads the case to students. When this is done, it is important that the case study is not too long so that the attention span of students will not wander. In other cases, media such as sound-film-strips are used. Regardless of the method, it is essential that students get the "facts" of the case study if they are to do any analysis of the case study.

In many instances, designers of law-related education materials have been remarkably successful in getting even primary students to think about whether or not a community should have a dog lease law or whether or not a community should sell its zoo and put a shopping center in its place. These experiences are real to most students since they have encountered problems about dogs in their community and know what a shopping center and a zoo is.

In other cases, designing case studies for law-related education is more difficult. Students may not be motivated to learn how a farm laborers' dispute with management could be resolved. Sometimes what were thought to be as high interest cases such as the right of teenagers to have long hair styles is seen as irrelevant by students whose own schools have changed dress and hair rules. Or a former controversial topic such as amnesty for young men who refused to be drafted during the Vietnam war may have passing interest to students now that the United States has a volunteer armed force and students know little about the Vietnam war. Yet if students do not initially become interested in the case study, they often do not generalize about the principles or concepts illustrated in the case. Therefore, it is necessary for teachers to revise, to update, and to be constantly on the lookout for new case studies that have a high interest to most students.

Then, after checking if students are familiar with the facts, the teacher must use effective questioning skills to allow students to make judgments about the case. Sometimes teachers divide the classroom into small groups and write out a few good questions for the small groups to discuss. Regardless of the method used, students should be allowed the opportunity to think about the various alternatives and consequences that are usually present in the case study. Also necessary is the consolidation of concepts and principles. Case studies sometimes encourage students to focus on unimportant details such as where a young person, a runaway, stayed while away from home, instead of thinking about what the meaning of "incorrigible" might be. Additional examples are often effective to clarify concepts and to point out the wide range of settings that the concept may be applied to in the American legel and political system.

Using Community Resources in Law-Related Education

As in other units, law-related education often can be even more effective by using field trips and guest speakers. The first step for teachers at all grade levels is to secure a free copy of the *Directory of Law-Related Education Activities* from the American Bar Association, 1155 East 60th St., Chicago, Ill. 60637. This guide lists information by states on the over 250 projects throughout the United States. In some cases, projects located in your state or local area have established a liason person who can easily secure the services of a lawyer to visit your class or to facilitate arrangements for your class or some students to visit courtrooms.

Of course, law-related education can use field trips or guest speakers from one or all of the following agencies: the local, state, and national justice agencies such as the local police, the state police, and the Federal Bureau of Investigation; the local, state, and federal courts; the offices of the public defender and the public prosecutor; and the various people and facilities connected with corrections such as probation officers, work camps, and detention halls for juveniles. In addition, lawyers from the local bar association, government agencies dealing with consumer and environmental problems, students from the local law schools, and other speakers from other groups may also be used in law-related education.

What steps are necessary to make effective use of community resources? Good planning is always essential but for field trips it is of the utmost importance. Ideally, the teacher should scout out the field trip before any students take the trip. Reconfirming phone calls are often essential to be absolutely certain that something will be going on in the courtroom or that the speaker such as a police officer has not been called out on an emergency. Typically, students do not gain much by listening to the tail end of a technical business case. For this reason, some teachers have found that the Small Claims Court or the Traffic Court to be effective since the cases generally are within the understanding of most students and many cases are tried within an hour.

If at all possible, asking the judge or other officials to set aside some time to talk and to answer students' questions is usually a highly rewarding experience. Other agencies may provide a guide or give an orientation before students tour a facility. Data such as the number of cases heard or referrals in a given year should be secured for students to examine and to analyze.

However, due to school schedules and transportation problems, it is not always possible to have field trips. Now, more schools, especially for older students, are releasing students in small groups to visit such facilities as the Juvenile Probation Department or a correction institution. With or without their teacher, students must be told what they are looking for. Using guidesheets if often effective to make students better observers. Again, after the trip, it is necessary that students debrief their experience so that any misconceptions can be cleared up and the teacher can evaluate the effectiveness of the field experience.

Often it is more convenient to use speakers who can come to the classroom. Again, good planning is essential. After locating a speaker, you should try to have the speaker give a general overview of his/her job in five mniutes and then ask our students to ask questions of the speaker. This avoids the problem of the speaker becoming too technical or speaking on topics that are not of high interest to students. But this technique to be successful does require that the students be prepared with good questions. In an emergency, the teacher should also have a few good questions for the speaker in the case of silence.

In addition, the speaker can sometimes involve students. Judges have presided at mock trials and police officers

have demonstrated how they search an individual. Probation officers and students can role play the procedures used in detention of juveniles or what happens in juvenile court.

An evaluation should always be made as to the usefulness of the speaker. A debriefing, often the next day, can reinforce what has been learned and clarify any questions. Typically, teachers continue to use effective speakers and drop those that have not been as effective. Teachers are pleased to find how cooperative public agencies are about sending a speaker to the classroom. Often these speakers score high on having pleasing personalities. In fact, teachers may have to point out that the speaker may not be representative of the group he/she represents.

Use of field experiences and guest speakers can put meat on dry bones of textbook materials. Speakers reflect the current practices and viewpoints. They can add to increased understanding of our law system. However, to be used effectively requires planning, briefing, and prequeries for the guest, helping students both to observe and to ask good questions, and debriefing and summarizing what has been learned.

Simulation, Role Playing, and Gaming

Presently, the term simulation, role playing, and gaming are used very loosely and sometimes interchangeably. But a simulation provides the students with a model of a situation that has been simplified such as a mock trial. Role playing calls for the participants to put themselves into someone's shoes. Usually, a problem story or dilemma initiates the role playing in which students then act out their roles in an unrehearsed dramatization. Gaming is an activity following a set of rules among opponent players. The objective is usually to win and some strategy is usually necessary to achieve this result.

In general, these three strategies are not used so much for information giving but to allow students to learn about the process in which decisions are made. Thus, in a mock trial students must not only identify the conflict or values and interests in the particular situation but should think about different possible solutions and the probable consequences of the solutions. All three strategies have the potential to encourage thinking with attention to value conflicts.

Most simulations, role playing, and games are highly motivating since they give students the opportunity to participate actively instead of sitting in their seats. But nothing guarantees success in these ventures. Teachers must carefully review what games, role playing, or simulation exercises are best suited for their particular class(es). In addition, with commercially prepared material, teachers must read carefully the teacher's manual so that the rules and procedures are clear. Then, in introducing the strategy, the teacher must give clear instructions and encourage students to participate.

One cannot usually throw primary children or even high school students into such situations and expect them to perform. Warmup exercises often are necessary to make students more open and less fearful of performing. Roles must be explained. For example, a discussion beforehand could center on what possible arguments dog owners might present against a lease law or what workers who sleep during the day feel about barking dogs.

Of course, the teacher's role during the game is that of an observer or mediator. Areas of difficulties should be noted. It is essential to debrief the experience for the ultimate test of a simulation, role playing, and gaming is the degree of learning and insight that students have gained from the experience. If the results appear meager, the teacher must evaluate if the time were well spent. In some cases, students may need to backtrack with more simple exercises and gain more skills before attempting further experiences.

Most teachers who have not used gaming or simulations feel more comfortable if they first go through a mock trial or participate in a game themselves. A great need exists for further in-service training in law-related education, a field in which most elementary and secondary school teachers are unfamiliar.

Bibliography

Resource Materials

For the best listing of curriculum materials, media, and gaming in law-related education see the following: *Bibliography of Law-Related Curriculum Materials: Annotated* published by the American Bar Association, 1155 East 60th St., Chicago, Ill., 60637; *Media: An Annotated Catalog of Law-Related Audio-Visual Materials* and *Gaming: An Annotated Catalogue of Law-Related Games and Simulations* are also available from the American Bar Association at no charge.

Curriculum Materials

Basic Legal Concepts Curriculum. Ginn and Co., 1974.
  Justice and Order Through Law Series by Robert S. Summers, A. Bruce Campbell, and John Bozzone. Five units and a teacher's guide.
  The American Legal System Series, by Robert S. Summers, A. Bruce Campbell, and Gail F. Hubbard. Five units and a teacher's guide.

Bill of Rights Newsletter, Todd Clark, editor. Constitutional Rights Foundation, 6310 San Vicente Blvd., Los Angeles, Cal., 90048. Published quarterly with themes such as Juvenile Justice, Student Protest and the Law, Sex and Equality, and the Power of the Free Press.

Consumer Law Resource Kit, Changing Times Education Service. 1729 H St., N.W., Washington, D.C. 20006, 1971. Four units on Consumer Law, three units on the Marketplace, and five units on Money Management.

Justice in America Series, Robert H. Ratcliffe, editor. Houghton Mifflin Co., One Beacon St., Boston, Mass. 02107, 1974. Six units including a teacher's guide.

Law in a Free Society, Charles Quigley, Director, 606 Wilshire Blvd., Suite 600, Santa Monica, Cal., 90401. On each of eight concepts—authority, justice, privacy, responsibility, participation, diversity, property, and freedom—there is *A Casebook, A Curriculum,* and *Lesson Plans* (three separate volumes for each concept). This K-12 program is also starting to produce curriculum materials for students.

Our Living Bill of Rights Program. Encyclopedia Britannica Educational Corp., 425 N. Michigan Ave., Chicago, Ill. 60611. Four cases.

Oxford Series. Oxford Book Co., 11 Park Place, New York, N.Y. 10007. Four series.

People and the City Program, Larry Cuban, editor. Scott, Foresman and Co., 1900 E. Lake Ave., Glenview, Ill. 60025. Eight booklets.

Public Affairs Pamphlet Series. Public Affairs Pamphlets, 381 Park Ave. South, New York, N.Y. 10016. Sixteen pamphlets.

Sociological Resources for the Social Studies: Delinquents and Criminals: Their Social World by Helen M. Hughes (booklet entitled "Delinquency." Allyn and Bacon, Inc., Rockleight, N.J. 07642.

Teenagers and the Law by John Paul Hanna. Ginn and Co., 191 Spring St., Lexington, Mass. 02173

Trailmarks of Liberty Series. Houghton Mifflin Co., Boston, Mass. 02109. Three books including one for the fourth to fifth grade level.

Unit Books/Public Issues Series. Xerox Education Publications, Columbus, Ohio 43216. Eleven inexpensive pamphlets.

Voices for Justice: Role Playing in Democratic Procedures, Charles N. Quigley and Richard P. Longaker. Ginn & Co., 191 Spring St., Lexington, Mass. 02173.

What is the role of the teacher in drug education?

CHAPTER 22

Drug Education

Rationale

Drugs are defined as substances which, by their chemical nature, influence the structure or function of living tissues. This definition not only includes opiates, *Cannabis sativa*, stimulants, depressants, hallucinogens, but also alcohol, nicotine, and glue sniffing. However, in the mind of the public and most students, alcohol and tobacco are not generally regarded or considered as drugs. In addition, many associate the "drug problem" with only nonmedical purposes. Actually, the extent of legal drug use such as prescription drugs like tranquilizers and the over-the-counter drugs such as sleep inducers is extensive, if not massively overused. According to experts, therefore, drugs are defined as including "hard" illegal drugs, prescription drugs, alcohol, and tobacco.

For decades, many states and local school districts had laws on the books mandating that the schools should teach about the evils of alcohol, tobacco, and narcotics. Since "hard" drug use was generally confined to low-status and minority groups in urban centers, little was usually done about any type of hard drug education in the schools. Instead, drug abuse was generally left to the law enforcement agencies.

However, in the late 1960s, the public became greatly alarmed at the extent of drug use among students. Drug usage dramatically increased in both the youth as well as the adult population. A comparison of data of the years 1969 and 1972 by the National Commission on Marihuana and Drug Abuse showed significant increases among junior and senior high school students in the use of alcohol, tobacco, and marihuana. In 1969, 10 percent of the junior high school students and 15 percent of the senior high school students reported having tried marihuana. In 1972, this had increased to 16 percent on the junior high school level and 40 percent of the senior high school students. In 1972, junior high school students increased the use of inhalants. There were also increases in the use of hallucinogens (up to 6 percent in the junior high and 14 percent in the senior high), stimulants (9 percent of the junior high and 19 percent of the senior high), and depressants (8 percent for the junior high, 16 percent of the senior high school students.[1]

---

[1] Bill C. Wallace, *Education and the Drug Scene*, Lincoln, Neb. Professional Educators Publications, Inc., 1974, pp. 55-58. The original source is *Drug Use in America: Problem in Perspective.* Second Report of the National Commission on Marihuana and Drug Abuse, Washington, D.C., U.S. Government Printing Office, 1973.

Many parents and community leaders wanted to keep "kids off dope" and pressed for drug education as a high priority in the schools. It was the illicit drug usage that caused the most concern. Typically, these adults were not worried by the fact that it was adults over twenty-one who actually accounted for the greatest proportion of use of tobacco and alcohol, prescription and nonprescription drugs. It was the "hard" drugs that the kids were using that worried them.

However, not all parents were united in the crusade for drug education. Some parents advocated a more tolerant or liberal approach to the use of drugs. Other parents gained a little comfort from the fact that most high school students were concentrating on tobacco, alcohol, and marihuana that they planned to continue to use in the future. In contrast, most students do not plan to use opiates, inhalants, hallucinogens, stimulants, or depressants. Large proportions of high school students—well over 80 percent—have never tried these hard drugs. In addition, with the important exception of alcohol, most students have low to moderate use of such drugs, usually confined to weekend parties. Others were not as optimistic. They felt more young people each year were using both drugs and alcohol. In addition, more younger students from the ages of 8 to 14 were becoming involved.

But the widespread use and increased use of illegal drugs meant that it was impossible for law enforcement agencies to control the drug problems. Many citizens believed that the drug problem was a crisis situation. Therefore, many adults with their faith in education, demanded drug education programs for the schools.

The explosion of drug education programs, of course, was also helped by the Federal Drug Education Act of 1970.

Under this act, every state department of education received funds to develop curriculum materials and guides, to provide consultants and information, to offer training and money for curriculum materials and media. A 1973 poll by *Nation's Schools* reported that 83 percent of the schools had ongoing drug education programs.[2] Indeed, this was a dramatic increase within a relatively short time period.

Drug Education Programs

What forms did the mushrooming drug education programs typically take? Usually little attention was given to spelling out the goals and objectives of the program other than the understanding that the priority was to prevent drug use by youth or for those already using drugs, to reduce or to eliminate completely drug usage. The focus was generally on only hard illegal drugs.

Initially, the most common approach of drug education was "to scare the hell out of the students." Since at this time most teachers had a limited background on drugs, frequently the schools turned to community representatives. Often a program was arranged featuring a local physician, a law enforcement officer, and sometimes a former addict. Typically, the physician and the law enforcement officer tended to exaggerate the degree that drugs promote bodily damage and to cite individual cases in which students were ruined by drugs.

In some cases, the students in the audience probably had a better understanding of drug effects than their men-

---

[2] "Drug Education Poll," *Nation's Schools,* **92** August 1973, p. 33.

tors. Many students in such programs, particularly those who had used marihuana or knew of other students who had used it, were very skeptical of the speakers since their own friends or they themselves did not seem to be suffering the horrible effects as described by the speakers. Conflicting research reports, for example, on the danger of marihuana as a entryway for hard drug usage, further confounded instruction. A credibility gap therefore developed and students often dismissed the total drug program as being worthless. The credibility problem still exists today since even among experts a controversy exists on what effects different drugs have on different individuals and especially what are the long-range effects.

In addition, most early efforts on drug education hit hard on moral indoctrination as the main technique. Students were preached to about the personal degradation of drug effects and the grave consequences of using drugs. While not ignoring the havoc drugs can have on individuals and the community, many times poor, emotional content was used in courses. Students who were caught using drugs were chastised as common criminals.

As funds became available for in-service education, the question arose of who should teach drug education. The elementary level with home room or even team teachers was not as much of a problem as the departmentalized junior and senior high school. Where drug education was implemented on the elementary level, it typically was integrated into existing health or social studies units. At the primary level, the focus was on protecting health, the importance of sound nutrition, and the role of medical personnel in keeping individuals healthy. The middle grades emphasized the idea that every substance taken into the body by any means—eating, injection, smoking, and sniffing—enters into the functioning of the body and affects its conditions. Therefore, drugs in any form should not be taken except when prescribed by a physician.

Since research has indicated that it was usually at the junior and senior high school level that students begin to use drugs, the focus of most drug education programs was at the junior and senior high school levels. Here, different schools made different decisions on who was to be responsible for drug education. In some schools, science teachers focused on the chemical reactions of drugs while physical education teachers discussed leisure and social studies teachers emphasized the broader social implications of drugs in society. In other cases, the guidance department took the major responsiblity of teaching and setting up programs.

In the typical situation, schools allocated drug education to a specific subject area which was a required course for all students. Thus, a drug education unit of a certain duration such as three weeks might be taught in all ninth grade civics or physical education classes. In some schools, however, a separate course—one semester or a minicourse—on drug education was combined with other mandated subjects such as venereal or communicable diseases, driver education, and guidance.

After decisions were made on who should teach the course, teachers and counselors became more familiar with knowledge on the effects of drugs. Therefore, most courses became more scientifically oriented with special emphasis on the chemical basis of drugs and their effects on the mind and body. The result has been that many young people learned a great deal about drugs, their usage, and their effects from these courses. Cynics said that the courses taught kids to be better consumers of different drugs. Critics also felt that the emphasis should be changed from drugs to the user and society. This holds important implications for the social education programs.

The rationale for the fact emphasis on drugs assumes that if students are given the facts, they will immediately stop using drugs or not use them at all. This assumption, of course, ignores the allure of drugs and the reasons why students as well as adults take drugs—for pleasure, for insight, for escape, for curiosity, and other reasons. This approach also passed over the research data that drug use in young people can be predicted with high accuracy by examining certain characteristics of students' families such as class, religion, drinking habits, medical practices, and attitudes toward authority. The fact approach also neglects the broader problem of why our culture is permeated by drug use and how social problems such as racism, unemployment, alienation and the like also set the stage for drug usage.

Thus, drug education is a pecularily sensitive area, for many an area of ambiguity of what is best for both the individual and society. Drug education involves the norms of the peer group, the national youth culture, as well as family and community values. In addition, students often cannot be as detached as they consider drugs since they are or know students or family members who are using drugs.

It is little wonder, in light of these various difficulties, that most drug education programs were not successful, at least if the criteria of reduction of drugs is used. In addition, critics of drug education programs are outraged that much of the information is grossly inaccurate or incomplete. This has definitely been proven with the media on drug education. The National Coordinating Council on Drug Education (NCCDE) in the 1973 review of 220 audiovisuals found that about 80 percent contained factual errors as well as other problems such as artificiality and scare tactics. Only a small percentage—31—were recommended.[3] The significance of the inaccurate media cannot be ignored since many drug education programs depend heavily on media.

In general, most media on drug education as well as printed publications had the following errors or misleading information.

1. Stating that a particular drug *always* or *never* causes a specific reaction. Most films ignore the fact that the effects of a drug vary with dosage, method of administration, frequency of use, mind set, the environmental setting, and individual body chemistry.

2. Media tend to blame drugs for all problems instead of pointing out the influence of nondrug factors. An example of this error is stating that heroin causes crime, hepatitis, and malnutrition. The role of heroin is more indirect as addicts resort to stealing to get cash, dirty needles transmit disease, and malnutrition is more likely to result when an individual is not eating properly because of money to maintain his/her drug habit.

3. Most media support or favor only one particular rehabilitation model or proposed law to solve the problem. Yet a need exists to stress a multisolution to treatment as well as institutional and social reform to solve the complex problem of drugs in our society.

4. Media on drugs stress that only illegal drugs are harmful.

---

[3] National Coordinating Council on Drug Education, *Drug Abuse Films*, Washington, D.C., The Council, 1973.

In addition, some media are filled with inaccurate information about specific drugs. Furthermore, few distinctions are made about drug users—the experimental user, the periodic or recreational user, the compulsive user, and the ritualistic (seeking spiritual or religious experience) user. Some media also imply that only young people and that only certain minority/ethnic groups use drugs. Furthermore, media tend to deemphasize that many young people suffer identity confusion and have other problems that might explain why they use drugs.

Others point to additional shortcomings in many drug education programs besides the inaccurate and biased media and materials. First, many feel that current efforts are often uncoordinated at the different grade levels, with the different subject areas, and with what the community is doing. Others believe that many drug education programs may actually increase the curiosity of those who are willing to experiment. In addition, some feel that as illegal drugs are discussed objectively time and time again, they become more familiar and acceptable to young people. Others have pointed out when speakers are allowed on campus who advocate more liberal drug laws, they tend to communicate better than their young audience than the scientific-oriented teachers.

Still others feel that any course labeled "drug education" has two strikes against it as shown previously with most alcohol and tobacco education courses. Drug education, according to this viewpoint, is better incorporated into social studies units such as crime, peer groups, value conflicts, alternative life-styles, and the like than directing attacking the drug probem per se. In fact, cynics, looking at many drug education programs, state that the drug education programs may do more damage than the drugs.

Promising Practices in Drug Education

The climate of opinion about drug education has changed since the 1960s although the drug problem certainly has not been solved. In 1972, The President's Commission on Marihuana and Drug Abuse recommended that the use of marihuana be decriminalized but heavy penalties be retained for cultivating, trafficking, and possessing it. By 1975, six states like California had eased pot or marihuana laws. In other states and communities, enforcement against the use of marihuana became more lax.

Under President Ford's administration, the federal government followed a policy with a focus on drugs that are the greatest risk to users. According to federal priorities, the following were judged to be of most risk to individuals: (1) heroin, amphetamines, and mixed barbiturates, (2) cocaine, hallucinogens, and inhalants, and in the last category marihuana was considered the least serious of the illicit drugs. However, this more relaxed view on marihuana was not uniform. New York passed a law that possession of one fourth to one ounce of marihuana for first-time offenders is a felony with a maximum prison sentence of 7 years and second time offenders face a maximum 15-year sentence.

Many schools' drug education programs became more relaxed and, in some cases, faded away. Some schools continued their drug education programs but at lunch hour, students openly violated the principles of the course. Other schools continued to be strict about the possession of drugs on the school premises while others only punished students if they tried to sell drugs on campus. The whole area of administrators/teachers' rights to search and to seize drugs on campus became legally confused.

But not everyone agreed on becoming more lax since the drug problem was serious and growing. Marihuana use was increasing and more younger students were trying drugs. The National Institute on Drug Abuse estimated that 6 percent of the high school age group uses marihuana daily and a like percentage drink hard liquor daily.

Educators reevaluated drug education programs, most of which had been imposed on them by administrators or the community. Several value education approaches were deemed to be especially helpful for drug education. Sidney Simon and his colleagues' value clarification approach became more popular. This particular value education approach aims to help students become more aware of and to identify their own values and those of others. Students are also encouraged to recognize their own values and the interrelationships among values, to uncover and resolve personal value conflicts, to share values with others, and to act according to their own value choices.[4] This approach uses both rational thinking and emotional awareness in the examination of values.

The value analysis approach was also recommended for drug education. This approach, advocated for years by many experts in the social studies, probes the pros and cons of drug usage. It uses many diverse viewpoints such as conflicting text materials. The purpose of this approach, which is fundamentally a rational-analytical approach, is to force students to give reasons and evidence for their positions.

Still others, although fewer in number, favored a social action approach in values education. This approach emphasizes teaching skills needed for students to become active participants in society. For example, an examination of the drug industry has been used in some classrooms. Students have examined drug advertising and promotion, the pushing of drugs by the medical profession on depressed women and the elderly, and the issue of profits of the drug industry. Some classes have distributed their findings to the community. In certain instances, there has also been a study of the underworld factors behind the pushing of drugs. In a similar manner, the alcohol and tobacco industries also have been used as topics of study by students.

All of these values approaches have been aided by both an increase in quality and quantity of textbooks and related media. Materials are now more open ended as well as being more accurate. Scare techniques are declining and more emphasis is being placed on being objective and seeing the relationship of the drug problem to social problems in the larger society. However, close scrutiny in examination of materials is still the order of the day.

Along with using value approaches, some advocate that the schools work more closely with the community on drug education. This might include setting up a committee representing students, parents, teachers, administrators, and law-enforcement agencies. From these discussions, priorities should be formulated. This could include setting up a drug crisis line and analysis center, if it does not already exist, or designing more appropriate drug educational programs for both parents and students.

Guidance counselors also recommend the value of working with small groups. This approach assumes that young people who are both given the opportunity to learn accurate information about drugs and who can discuss this information with their peers in small groups led by skilled discussion leaders

---

[4] Sidney Simon et al., *Values Clarifications: A Handbook of Practical Strategies for Teachers and Students*, New York, Hart Publishing Co., 1972.

are less likely to be involved in drugs. Where this approach has beem implemented, favorable results have been noted.

As with small groups, the importance of the instructor cannot be stressed enough. Wallace has argued that it is necessary for every teacher to combat drug abuse by setting up an educational atmosphere conductive to learning, meeting the needs of students, and bringing humanness into the classroom. This approach also requires teacher skills in recognizing personality characteristics of potential users, and the need for effective communication with students. Wallace feels that every classroom teacher is the key to an effective program of drug education.[5] Teachers do not need in-service education courses on the specific reactions or effects of drugs as much as developing general methods of being effective teachers.

In light of the importance of teachers and the whole staff in the school, many advocate that teachers and staff get together to discuss where they presently stand in their drug education programs. Have the plans formulated five years ago lost relevancy? What policy do elementary teachers believe should be used to curb overactive students? Are drugs or medications the answer? What policy should be used in the junior and senior high schools for students using drugs on campus? Off-campus? What kind of drug education program, centered at what department or departments, is indicated? In many cases, a clarification about these policies is needed.

Within a relatively short time, drug education expanded quickly into the schools. However, drug education programs were generally imposed on teachers in a crisis climate and the effectiveness of the drug education program is questionable. The future of drug education programs in the schools in uncertain. Will they gradually be deemphasized? Or will they take a new format with more consideration given to a values education approach? The future of drug education is unknown but drug education offers the schools an enormous challenge in an era in which drug use is increasing. Social studies teachers need to think if drug education should be incorporated into their own program and in what manner.

---

[5] Bill C. Wallace, *Education and the Drug Scene*, Lincoln, Nebraska, Professional Educators Publications, Inc., 1974, pp. 99-105.

Bibliography

Curriculum Guides
Write to state Boards of Education in the various states.

Media Reviews
Write to National Coordination Council on Drug Education, 1211 Connecticut Avenue, N.W., Washington, D.C. 20036 for *Drug Abuse Films* available for $5. Also see Lawrence R. Hepburn and Mary A. Hepburn, "Pushing Drug Education in the Social Studies: A Rationale for Materials Selection and Reviews of Recommended Media," *Social Education,* **38,** March 1974, pp. 303-314.

Organizations
National Coordinating Council on Drug Education, 1211 Connecticut Ave., N.W., Washington, D.C. 20036.

Student Association for the Study of Hallucinogens, 638 Pleasant, Beloit, Wisc., 53511.

National Council on Alcoholism, 2 Park Ave., New York, N.Y. 10016

Alcoholics Anonymous, 2660 Woodley Rd., N.W., Washington, D.C. 20008

Books
Blum, Richard H. et al. *Drugs I: Society and Drugs, Social and Cultural Observations. Drugs II: Students and Drugs. College and High Schools Observations.* San Francisco: Jossey-Bass, 1969.

Blum, Richard H. et al. *Horatio Alger's Children.* San Francisco: Jossey-Bass, 1972.

Brecher, Edward M. et al. *Licit and Illicit Drugs.* Mount Vernon, N.Y. Consumers Union, 1972.

Cornacchia, Harold J. et al. *Drugs in the Classroom, A Conceptional Model for Schools Programs.* St. Louis, Mo.: C. V. Mosby Co., 1973.

Drug Use in America: Problem in Perspective. Second Report of the National Commission on Marihuana and Drug Abuse. Washington, D.C.: U.S. Government Printing Office, 1973.

Hozinsky, Murray. *Student Drug Abuse: A Rational Approach for Schools.* Denver, Colo.: Love Publishing, 1970.

Marihuana and Health. Second Annual Report to Congress from the Secretary of Health, Education, and Welfare. Washington, D.C.: U.S. Government Printing Office, 1972.

Marin, Peter and Allan Y. Cohen. *Understanding Drug Use: An Adult's Guide to Drugs and the Young.* New York: Harper & Row, 1971.

Ray, Oakley S. *Drugs, Society and Human Behavior.* St. Louis, Mo.: C. V. Mosby Co., 1972.

Witters, Weldon L. and Patricia Jones-Witters. *Drugs & Sex.* New York: Macmillan Publishing Co., 1975.

Does the school r.eed to teach about the family?

CHAPTER 23

Family Education

Rationale

Across human societies the single basic and absolutely necessary institution is the family. Regardless of the number and sex of family members, their rules, functions and relationships to each other, the societal framework of every culture includes (begins with) some kind of family unit.

This is, in fact, perhaps the only social experience common to all humans. Each of us and each of our students has lived in some kind of familial unit and will in the course of our lifetime devote a great portion of our energies and resources to concerns of a family nature.

Despite this inescapable fact, the status of the family, as a focus of study in the formal curriculum, is quite a different matter. Frequently ignored altogether, occasionally shunted from one department to another, and usually offered only as an "elective," the family as a unit of study is the stepchild of the curriculum.

In this chapter we will review briefly some of the factors producing this situation. We will also examine the current and most frequent modes of curricular treatment of the family and survey a few of the issues, problems and dilemmas attending this field of inquiry.

Why, if everyone of us has had some direct experience and knowledge of a family, should the already overcrowded school curriculum be expected to assume yet another responsibility in this regard?

The "knowledge" we derive from our personal family experience is burdened and shaped by insurmountable subjectivity and emotion and is not always a reliable guide to truth or to action. The knowledge made available by social scientists can counterbalance this bias by disclosing facts of which we are ignorant and open our eyes to situations and alternatives heretofore unrecognized by us.

Even the mention that we are living in a time of dramatic social change is to belabor the obvious. The entire societal framework is sustaining drastic shifts and changes and without doubt the greatest stress falls on the traditional family unit.

A Bureau of the Census report reviewing the period 1970–1976 confirms several trends in today's society: an increase in the number of persons sharing living quarters with an unrelated person, increased divorces among young adults, more families headed by women with no husband present, and more children living with only one parent. The report notes that "later marriage (has) gained general acceptance. . . . (and) that a higher proportion of adults may never marry during their lifetime than in the recent past."[1]

It is certain that each of us, teachers and students alike, will wrestle at some time in our lives with such questions as:

"What are the goals, functions, responsibilities, and roles of family members?"

"What are the actual obligations of family members to each other and under what conditions should be the duration of contract for these obligations."

"What collectivity of individuals constitutes a family and should thus be recognized as a social, economic and legal unit?"

Current Curricular Practices

Let us first survey current curricular practice with respect to the family. Where in a student's K to 12 course of study does he or she have occasion to consider the family and what is the nature of this learning?

In the elementary school, study of the family and family life comprises a fairly standard social studies emphasis in the primary grades. The course on "Families" in *Our Working World,* by Lawrence Senesh (Science Research Associates) moves from a view of families here and around the world to the consideration of "What makes me like I am?" and the effect of family life on personal development. Changes in family structure are considered, and a rather heavy emphasis is given to the family as an economic

unit. The course concludes with an excellent lesson series on family decision making and future planning.

Several notable efforts have been made in recent years to treat the family with an interdisciplinary perspective. Among these is *Man: A Course of Study* (MACOS), a curriculum for the upper grades drawing largely from anthropology but using comparative study methods typical of the behavioral sciences and drawing heavily on psychological and sociological insights.

Another outstanding example of interdisciplinary treatment of the family is the *Family of Man* curriculum for grades K to 5 developed under the leadership of Professor Edith West and edited by Charles Mitsakos. The project includes eight family studies: Hopi Indian family, Japanese family, family of early New England, Ashanti family of Ghana, kibbutz family in Israel, Soviet family in Moscow, Quechau family in Peru and the Algonquin Indian family. The program is developed by assuming the primary importance of presenting to students at an early age information about many cultures.

The *Human Sciences Program* (HSP), developed for use in the middle school, provides students an opportunity to trace their own family heritage through their research on one ancestor.[2] This research was to include interviews and/or correspondence with living family members, use of family documents (a family bible; birth, death or wedding certificates; property deeds; letters) and photograph albums.

---

[1] Bureau of the Census, "Marital Status and Living Arrangements: March, 1976" (series P-20, No. 306), Superintendent of Documents, U.S. Government Printing Office, Washington, D.C.
[2] Human Sciences Program, Level I Module, *Learning* (Experimental Edition), Boulder, Colo., Biological Sciences Curriculum Study, 1974.

The HSP module, *Reproduction*,[3] included important emphasis on the family. A noteworthy sample activity was that titled, "What is a Family?" The activity asks students to use a set of "What Makes a Family?" cards. Each card describes a group of people living together. Students are to read each card and discuss which groups of people they would consider to be families. They are encouraged to show the cards to people of different ages to see if their perceptions differ.

In the module, *Rules*,[4] the HSP curriculum encourages students to develop, by means of survey and interview, a profile of their own community's "typical" family unit and of the predominant views held in the community toward family-related issues.

Exploring Human Nature is a high school course intended to blend a cross-cultural and psychological view of what it is to be human. Unit 2 deals with the family in its social context. The curriculum is rich with cross-cultural comparisons. It supports the conclusion that humanness may be attained by means of widely varying experiences, and that the family structure and behavior peculiar to one culture have emerged in order to satisfy the social and personal needs unique to that culture.

The social studies course offerings in many high schools provide opportunity for a student to elect a course in sociology and/or psychology. Typically each of these courses may include a two or three week unit on the family.

The sociology course usually exposes the student to demographic factors describing the family and relates these factors to social class membership and/or to apparent shifts and changes within the

social framework. Current data describing marriage, divorce and family size are considered. The student also becomes familiar with the sociologist's perspective by learning to use the powerful concepts of *role* and *norm.* Frequently, the family unit in a sociology course includes some comparative material between cultures and/or subcultures, such as the family in Red China and in the United States or the urban family compared with the rural family. Notable and very usable example of instructional materials in sociology are those developed by the Sociological Resources for the Social Studies (cited in this chapter's bibliography). This project was sponsored by the American Sociological Association and funded by the National Science Foundation.

A high school psychology course will commonly treat the emotional and affiliative aspects of the family and view the family as a significant aspect of support in the developmental stages of infancy, childhood and adolescence. The family experience may be studied as an important source of a child's self-concept and self-esteem. Many psychology texts encourage the student to take a forward look toward his/her adult responsibilities as a spouse and parent.

The family is often a topic of consideration in home economics courses that range in focus from home management and enhancement to varying nutritional requirements for children and adult family members. Family economics and budgeting are usually studied in a course such as this. A frequently offered class is "Family Life." This course of study may touch on many of the topics already mentioned, but a major amount of time is devoted to courtship and marriage and to sex education.

Sex education courses, per se, are available (and, in some cases, mandated) in many high schools. Whether sponsored by the physical education depart-

---

[3] Human Sciences Program (ibid.), Level II Module, *Reproduction* (Experimental Edition), 1975.
[4] Human Sciences Program (ibid.), Level II Module, *Rules* (Experimental Edition), 1974.

ment, the health education faculty, the home economics teachers or in social studies, it is certain that the decision to offer the course at all is not easily taken. While many educators and parents alike view such a course as increasingly important, a clear and easy consensus on the specific nature of the course has been all but impossible in our pluralistic communities. At issue are the specificity of course content as well as the value and norms concerning sexuality and sexual behavior implicit in the course materials and presentation.

Issues and Dilemmas

What are the issues, problems, and dilemmas surrounding the place of the family in the curriculum? Two are paramount. First, is instruction in this area the clear and legitimate responsiblity of the school? Second, what precisely should be taught and how should it be presented? The two questions are virtually inseparable.

Many parents view what is taught their children about family life as an unwarranted invasion of instructional territory for which they alone are responsible. The family is, after all, our most sacrosanct institution; for a school course to suggest the viability of alternative family structures or the possible feasibility of divorce or to provide information about sexuality and procreation deeply offends the conscience and the prerogatives of some parents.

A Congressional protagonist of this perspective used some of the curricula reviewd in this chapter as ground for his arguments in the "Great Congressional Curriculum Debate of 1976":[5]

[5] For review and discussion of this Debate, see Karen B. Wiley, "NSF Science Education Controversy: The Issues," *Social Science Education Consortium Newsletter*, Number 26, July 1976.

"Like MACOS, the "Human Sciences Program" is a sophisticated and lethal assault on Judaic-Christian family values, privacy of students and their families, and the mental health and development of young adolescents. . . .

"Many dangerous behavioral techniques, such as role playing and open discussion of feelings, are used to mold the children's minds in complete disregard of their rights to privacy. . . .

"Instead of learning through normal methods of reading and teacher lectures, 11-, 12-, and 13-year-olds enrolled in the "Human Sciences Program" become little investigators and opinion pollsters collecting all manner of data on their families and friends concerning social, moral, religious, economic, and political activities and beliefs." (Conlan, Congressional Record, March 25, 1976, p. H2391)

On the other hand, a growing majority of parents, it seems, are concluding that some kind of formalized learning in this area is not only desirable but essential. By offering many of the family focused courses on an elective basis, schools have attempted to be responsive to both groups of parents.

It is easy enough to say that the social needs are now such that the school must make available some education for family living albeit at the student's option. To weigh the problem of *what* this education should include is to plunge into murky depths.

The most basic, almost insurmountable, difficulty is the problem of definition. When we speak of "the family" are we referring to the model middle-class (probably white) nuclear family with its members playing out their traditional roles? If the answer is "yes," what does this say to the millions of students who live in very different family circumstances and to ethnic, racial and social class groups whose mode of family living may be other than this middle-class model?

The presentation of almost any material about family life might be, and frequently is, interpreted as giving at least implicit support to certain norms and life-styles and perforce stigmatizing any variation from these. Until recently, material depicting family activities showed only white families with the father and mother (both present) cast into traditional roles of breadwinner and homemaker. Minority groups, racial and ethnic, and women's groups have sought a more balanced, less stereotypic representation.

We have within our communities an increasing number of familial-type arrangements, people sharing a residence and a sense of "home" as well as the day-to-day concerns and intimacies (sexual or not) of home maintenance.[6] Such groups, not necessarily linked by law or lineage, as single parents, common-law couples, communal groups, homosexual couples, view themselves as families and are, in turn, more commonly recognized as family groups. However, any "atypical" group (again, departing from the middle-class nuclear family norm) residing together continues to risk social stigma, a stigma formalized in the form of tax laws, zoning regulations, insurance provisions, rental agreements, and so forth.

Keeping all of this in mind, the sweeping cross currents of conservatism

and liberalism that wash continually across the curriculum, the emergence and openness of alternative life-styles and the understandable and too-long-delayed demands of minority, ethnic, and womens' groups, how is the school to resolve even this single issue of defining a family group? How, indeed, can we settle on a definition that satifies all interested parties and gives students a realistic and reliable sense of the society in which they are about to assume full status? To "simplify" the task by limiting the study only to nuclear families seems to fall far short of honestly confronting the issues involved. Nor can such a limited focus serve to "protect" students from knowledge of other arrangements, but can only insure that their awareness of these will come about in informal, and not always reliable, ways.

Important Omissions

This summary view of the current status of family education in the American public school curriculum cannot be complete without at least a cursory exploration of what is *not* being taught. By and large it is fair to say that the curriculum (particularly at the secondary level) pays little attention at all to human relationships. Furthermore, the giant portion of this already small piece is devoted to a study of and preparation for secondary relationships: citizenship, consumer roles, employer-employee relationships, and so forth. We seem, by practice and probably policy, to eschew giving serious and consistent attention to primary relationships.

The role of family member is among the most significant interactive roles available to a human being. It affords probably the richest opportunity for the expression and experience of one's own humanness. Training for intimacy and

---

[6] Helpful elaborative material deliberating appropriate curricular treatment of alternative life styles and living cluster may be found in John F. Cuber, Martha Tyler John, and Kenrick S. Thompson, "Should Traditional Sex Modes and Values Be Changed?," Chapter 3 in *Controversial Issues in the Social Studies: A Contemporary Perspective*, Raymond H. Muessig, editor, 45th Yearbook of the National Council for the Social Studies, Washington, D.C., 1975.

for parenting is not seen as the clear responsibility of the school; nor does our society clearly assign this domain to any institution other than the family itself. In our pluralistic society, families vary greatly in their willingness and ability to assume this training task. The result is that for many, if not most of us, the basic human task of learning to live in a loving, intimate relationship with others is left to chance.

We have, of course, in the social technology of our culture a sophisticated knowledge about such relations and about the personal skills required for their nurture and maintenance. Almost none of this, however, finds its way to the adolescent student by route of the formal school curriculum. It is ironic, is it not, that the same student has ample opportunity at school to learn other skills; he or she may learn to type, to drive a car, to play golf, to balance an equation, but if this student is not already skillful in relating to his or her fellow human beings, he/she will not learn this most vital art in school, except in a peripheral and random way.

Even if the social mandate were to change and delegate a clear share in responsibility for these matters to the school, monumental preparation and changes would be required. Foremost among these would be the careful training of teachers in content and method of great contrast to their current training. The thoughtful development of a long-term curriculum and of appropriate instructional materials is also a necessary prerequisite. But behind all of this looms the awesome but essential first step: that the multitude of diverse social groups comprising the school's clients, patrons, and practitioners come to a clear agreement that preparation for adult roles of partnering and parenting is tragically inadequate in our society and that the school should take remedial steps. The realistic anticipation of such a change occurring is far from hopeful.

Bibliography

Bureau of the Census, "Marital Status and Living Arrangement: March, 1976" (series P-20, No. 306). Washington, D.C.: Superintendent of Documents, U.S. Government Printing Office.

Exploring Human Nature. Experimental Edition. Grade Level 10-12. Funding Source: National Science Foundation. Project Director: Anita Gil, Social Studies Program, Education Development Center, 15 Mifflin Place, Cambridge, Mass.

Family of Man Curriculum. Newton, Mass.: Selective Educational Equipment, Inc. 1973.

Human Sciences Program. Biological Sciences Curriculum Study. Boulder, Colo.: Experimental Editions, 1974.

Senesh, Lawrence. *Our Working World.* Chicago: Science Research Associates, 1973.

Social Education (special issue on the American Family) Oct. 1977.

Sociological Resources for the Social Studies. Boston: Allyn & Bacon, Inc.

Episodes in Social Inquiry Series. (Each Episode consists of a Student Manual, Instructor's Guide, and Printed Blackline materials for student handouts.)

Divorce in the United States. (Involves students in the analysis of marriage case histories to determine the social facts about divorce and the effect it has upon society.)

Family Form and Social Setting, 1971. (Looks at the structure and functions of the family in ancient Hebrew society, on a kibbutz, and in the students' own families.)

Family Size and Society, 1972. (Allows students to explore the social determination of family size, the effect of average family size on population change, and the social implications of rapid population growth.)

Readings in Sociology Series:

Life in Families, 1970, compiled and edited by Helen MacGill Hughes. Readings chosen as interesting representations of the family and family life as seen by the sociologist.

Wiley, Karen B., "NSF Science Education Controversy: The Issues, *Social Science Education Consertium Newsletter* Number 26, July, 1976.

Chapter Opening Photo Credits

Author Index

Note: Authors listed in chapter bibliographies are not included in this index.

Subject Index

National Coordinating Council on Drug Education, 366

National Council for Social Studies (NCSS), 7
   Curriculum Guidelines for Multiethnic Education, 224, 334, 341
   Glens Fall Project, 344
   International Learning and International Education in a Global Age, 346
   statement on consumer education, 315-16

National program, 7, 25

National Science Foundation, 149

Natural science, 75, 80, 81, 93, 143, 158, 159, 168

New social studies, 4, 5, 6, 15, 157

Newspapers, 197-99, 256, 258, 263. *See also* Current events

Objectives, 253. *See also* Aims

Observation, 258-59, 269

Office of Economic Education, University of Hawaii, 134

Ohio University Manpower and Economic Education project, 132-33

Open classrooms, *see* Individualization

Opinion pools, *see* Questionnaires

Organizing program, 33-59
   back to basics, 41-42
   behavioral objectives, 42-43
   community involvement, 34-35
   components, 33-34
   current affairs, 35-36
   empathy, 37
   group responsibility, 37
   integration of subjects, 38-39
   knowledge growth, 37
   lesson planning, 56-59
   long range-unit planning, 48-55
   resources, 55
   skills, 38
   task variety, 38
   teaching group skills, 47
   teacher-student planning, 43-45
   time management, 40-41

Our Working World, 5, 21, 125, 132, 158, 187, 374

Ourdoor education, 305

Parents, 7

Patriotism, 161

Patterns in Human History, see Anthropological Curriculum Study Project

Pen pals, 349

People in Action, 188-89

Personalism, 146n

Phenomenology, 146n

Pictographs, 278, 281

Planning, 249, 260-61. *See also* Lesson planning

Policy disciplines (sciences), 115-138, 141
   and social studies, 138

Political attitudes, 354

Political behavior, 124

Political community, 116

Political science, 116-124
   approaches to teaching, 117
   behaviorist school, 117
   descriptive-structural approach, 117-118
   legal-institutional approach, 117-118
   nature, 116
   philosophical-normative approach, 117-118
   prescriptive-proscriptive approach, 82-83
   in social studies, 123
   subdivisions, 116-117

Political scientist, 87

Political socialization, 124

Power, *see* Core concepts

Presidential election lessons, 248-49, 290-93

Primary grades, 5, 279-80

Primary sources, 96, 257-58

Primatology, 160

Problem inquiry model

Problems of Democracy, 157, 157n

Problem solving, 22-23, 237-40, 242. *See also* Inquiry

Process, social science as, 79

Product, social science as, 79

Project Social Studies of University of Minnesota, 124

Psychiatry, 141, 145

Psychoanalysis, 145-46

Psychobiology, 141

Psychohistory, 141

Psychologist, 86-87
   social, 148

Psychology, 91, 141-149
   abnormal, 142
   comparative, 143-44
   definition, 142
   developmental, 144, 146
   educational, 145
   existential, 146
   faculty, 145
   general, 144
   gestalt, 145
   high school, 149
   organizational, 145
   schools of, Associationism, 145
      Behaviorism, 145
      Gestalist/Gestaltist, 146
      Humanistic, 146
      Structuralistic, 146
   social, 145
   structure, 147

subdivisions, 143
Third Force, 145n, 146
Psychology and core concepts, 148
Psychology and elementary and secondary
curriculum
Psychometry, 145
Pupil attitudes, 13
Purposes, *see* Aims

Questions, 104
analytical, 95, 147
social science, 78, 115
Questionnaires, 107, 259, 265, 271
Question-asking, 96, 121
in political science, 121
Questioning, 225-27, 247-48, 252-53, 261-62, 293-95

Rationales, 8-9
Reading, 209-210, 265-266
Realia, *see* Artifacts
Recent trends, 7-8, 15-19. *See also* Inquiry; New
social studies
Research, 249, 269, 289-90
psychological, 148
Research methodology, 120-21
case studies, 121
experiment, controlled, 121
field studies, 120
interview, 120
observation, 121, 156
questionnaire, 155
Resource (and resource allocation), *see* Core concepts
Resources for planning, 55-57
Resource visitor, 348-49
Retrieval charts, 271
Ricardo, David, 126
Role playing, 230, 259, 265-66, 358-59

Sampling technique, 263-65, 284-85
San José State University, Economics in Society
project, 134
School designs, 16-17
School organization, 16-17
Science, 79
Scientific method, 85, 240-42. *See also* Inquiry
Secondary school, *see* High school
Secondary sources, 257-60, 265-66
Self-evaluation, 67
Senesh, Lawrence, 125
Sex education, 375-76
Significant others, 153
Simulated games, 230-31, 348, 358-59
Skills, 5, 9, 37, 279-80
group, 47. *See also* Small group techniques

see also specific skills such as Group work; Reading;
etc.
Skinner box, 146
Small group techniques, 232-33
Smith, Adam, 126
Social action approach, *see* Action learning
Social change, *see* Core concepts
Social Darwinism/Darwinist, 153
Social education, 1-13
Social responsibility, 7
Social science 8, 19-21, 77, 89-90, 94, 202
characteristics, 79
definitions, 75-77
humanistic aspects, 75-77
scope, 77, 84
and social studies, 167-68
compared, 76, 88
structure, 81-82
values, 76
Social Science Education Consortium, 15, 127, 163
Social Science Laboratory Units, 4, 252-53
Social science projects, 4, 16, 252-53
The Social Sciences: Concepts and Values, The, 179-80,
208
Social studies, 77, 98, 157
elementary school, 171-200
media, 195-200. *See also* Elementary school
other materials, 187-190
textbooks, 176-187
trade books, 191-195
trends, 169-177
middle/junior high, 203-211
middle school, differences, 203-204
organizational patterns, 205
textbooks, 207-211. *See also* Junior high; Middle
grades, *and* Primary grades
Social studies curriculum, *see* Curriculum
Social studies projects, *see* Social science projects
Social Studies in Secondary Education (1916), 98n, 123
Social systems, 25-27
Socio-civic instruction, 123
Socio-drama, *see* Role playing
Sociological Resources for Social Studies, 158, 375-76
Sociology, 92, 150-158
concepts, 153
curriculum, elementary and secondary, 157-158,
375-76
nature, 149-150
structure, 153-54
subdivisions, 151-52
Source method, 256-58
Structure (of disciplines), 102-3, 118, 127, 153-54, 157,
167-68
Student-teacher planning, 43-45

Summative evaluation, 62
Surveys, 86, 87, 104, 129, 148, 153. *See also* Questionnaires
Syracuse University Social Studies Curriculum Center, 127
System, 88, 118-19
  social science as study of, 75, 76
  societal (social), 75, 76, 153
Systems model of instruction, 25-31
System of values, *see* values systems

Taba Social Studies Program, 4, 157, 167, 177-178, 252
Tables and charts, 271-275
Taxonomy of Educational Objectives, 64
Teacher education, *see* Teacher training
Teacher qualities, 11, 12, 27
Teacher-student planning, 43-46
Teacher training, 6, 18, 349-50, 377-78
Teaching techniques, 258-261
Team teaching, 17
Techniques, *see* Teaching techniques
Technology (and industrialism), *see* Core concepts
Television, 12, 18, 196-97, 279-80
Tests, 46-49. *See also* Evaluation in social studies
Thinking, *see* Critical thinking; Problem-solving
Time management, 40-41
Tinker versus Des Moines (1969), 124
Tobacco, *see* Drug education
Topics, *see* Unit planning
True-false questions, 68

Unit planning, 5, 21, 22, 47-55, 297
University of California Asian Studies Project, 99
  World Studies Program, 167
University of Chicago History-Social Science project, 99
University of Chicago Anthropology, Curriculum Study Project, 167
  Patterns in Human History, 167
University of Chicago Industrial Relations Center Economics Education project, 134
University of Georgia Anthropology, Curriculum Project, 89, 167
University of Hawaii Office of Economic Education, 134
University of Michigan, 158
University of Minnesota, Project Social Studies, 158, 167
Utah State University Social Studies Project on Public Issues, 158

Value, 80, 84, 85, 153, 166
Values clarification, 24, 213, 368
Value-free, 115

Values education, 8, 9, 12, 213-18, 243, 298-99
  action learning, 213-14
  analysis approach, 216
  inculcation, 216
  Kohlberg's moral development, 214-16
  Simon's values clarification, 213, 368
Values systems, 85, 166
Von Ranke, 93
Vocational education, *see* Career education

Walden Two (B. F. Skinner), 146
Windows on Our World, 180-81
World affairs, 343-44. *See also* Global and international education
World citizenship, 344. *See also* Global and international education
World Law, 343
Worldmindedness, 345-46
World understanding, 343